Beyond Control

Status Offenders in
the Juvenile Court

Edited by
Lee E. Teitelbaum
Professor of Law
University of New Mexico

Aidan R. Gough
Professor of Law
University of Santa Clara

345.73
B 573

Ballinger Publishing Company • **Cambridge, Massachusetts**
A Subsidiary of J.B. Lippincott Company

This book is printed on recycled paper.

International Standard Book Number: 0−88410−202−5

Library of Congress Catalog Card Number: 76−30285

Printed in the United States of America

Library of Congress Cataloging in Publication Data

Main entry under title:

Beyond control.

    Bibliography:
    1. Status offenders—Legal status, laws, etc.—United States—
Addresses, essays, lectures. 2. Juvenile courts—United States—
Addresses, essays, lectures. 3. Status offenders—Legal status, laws,
etc.—Europe—Addresses, essays, lectures.
I. Teitelbaum, Lee E. II. Gough, Aidan.
KF9712.A75B4   345'.73'08   76−30285
ISBN 0−88410−202−5

Dedication

For Pat, Mike, Tom, Herta, and Peter

Contents

List of Tables

Acknowledgments

Separated by geography and needing to tap many founts in the preparation of this work and our respective *Standards* volumes which preceded it, the editors have separate sets of thanks to render, which we wish to do individually but conjointly. We are deeply grateful to all those who helped us, as we trust they know; their knowledge notwithstanding, our gratitude bears reiteration here. The opinions herein are of course ours and our authors'; expression of our thanks to others does not necessarily import their concurrence with these views.

At the outset, some common thanks are due. This book of readings and preparation of the essays it incorporates were sponsored and supported by the Juvenile Justice Standards Project of the Institute of Judicial Administration and the American Bar Association. The Project is supported by grants from the National Institute of Law Enforcement and Criminal Justice, the American Bar Endowment, The Andrew W. Mellon Foundation, The Vincent Astor Foundation, and The Herman Goldman Foundation. In addition, this project was envisioned and commissioned by the late J. Lawrence Schultz, Esq., first director of the Juvenile Justice Standards Project. We hope that its completion will be a fitting remembrance.

We also owe a common and longstanding debt to Professor Margaret K. Rosenheim, Helen Ross Professor of Social Service Administration at the University of Chicago, who has throughout our work given us models to emulate, counsels to follow, and abiding friendship which has sustained our efforts.

Those thanks, too, to our mates and our offspring. Rather than expend hours and words at the auctorial futility of trying to find yet another way to express our appreciation to our families for their putting up with no little tribulation and much inconvenience, and the fact that we are awfully grateful indeed, we will leave it at that: Had we not had them and their assistance and support, this book would still be a gleam in the editorial eye.

* * * * * * * * * * * * * * * * * * * *

I would like to thank, however inadequately, Mss. Janet McLaughlin McKay, Maria R. Geer, and Elizabeth Davenport, my research assistants and best critics, who dealt with good will and great skill with both substantive and technical problems in the preparation of this volume. Ms. Adele Hunter and Ms. Josephine Chen likewise deserve more than this expression of appreciation for typing, checking, and redoing endlessly the various drafts through which these essays have gone, always with intelligence and good humor. Mss. Janet Cox, Carol Kennedy, and Elizabeth Smith have also helped, at odd and often inconvenient times, with preparation of parts of this manuscript, and I am most grateful to them as well. Finally, a special debt to Dean Frederick M. Hart of the University of New Mexico Law School must be acknowledged. He made the Law School's considerable technical facilities available, without which this project would have been vastly more difficult.

L.E.T.

University of New Mexico
Albuquerque, New Mexico

* * * * * * * * * * * * * * * * * * * *

A good many people have given me a great deal of help on this work and on the *Standards* volume with which it deals, without which neither could have been completed.

As this project began, Penelope Jane Tomlinson and His Worship Professor Terence Morris of the Sociology Department, The London School of Economics and Political Science, University of London, went far out of their way to give their ideas, their time, their stimulation and, most importantly, their affection.

Throughout it, James B. Murray, Chief of Police and Public Safety Manager of the City of Milpitas, California, Lecturer in Administration of Justice at San Jose State University, has provided sound argument, a devil's advocacy, editorial oversight, the use of his typewriters and copying equipment when mine wouldn't work at 0400 hours, immeasurable litres of coffee, and the long-suffering support of his entire department. To him and to them, I owe a vast debt; forty-five or so being too many to name, I must aggregate them, but that diminishes neither their contributions nor my appreciation.

Jerome A. Lackner, M.D., J.D., Director of Health of the State of California, Lecturer in Law and Medicine at the University of Santa Clara, and The Honorable William S. White, Presiding Judge of the Juvenile Court of Chicago, Illinois, have given enormous help since long before this work was undertaken. Anthony

E. Atwell, M.D., director of the Child Custody Clinic and Clinical Assistant Professor of Psychiatry at Stanford Medical School, has patiently given me entry to provinces to which I previously had small passport and no visa. Joseph E. Giansiracusa, M.D., F.A.C.P.; David H. Eby, Jr., M.D.; Stephen C. Telatnik, M.D.; and Michael F. Martin, M.D., have together with their office staff provided creative help, supportive care, stern lectures, the counsels of friendship, and excellent remedies of varying proofs as occasions required.

Dean George J. Alexander of the University of Santa Clara School of Law has read, listened to, discussed, solaced, and otherwise put up with my labors to a degree that should not be asked even of a dean. Since my appreciation and affection cannot be boxed into short compass, it suffices to say that he has given the notion of "amicus curiae" new dimensions.

Kristine Mackin McCarthy of the California Bar and Coeta J. Chambers, Patricia P. White, Mary L. Pilibos, Susan C. Hultberg, and Kathleen T. Thompson, R.N., of the Santa Clara School of Law have served as research assistants, and have given unstinting legal aid and emotional bolster to an increasingly grumpy and intellectually dessicate employer. They have contributed a very great deal indeed, and the expression of that debt in no way requites it.

Juene Witt, Katherine Petty, Christine Tondreau, Margaret Parkin, Salvadore Cordaro, Eva M. Elzingre, and Jeannette Bullock have ably handled various parts of the typing, somehow managing to reduce manuscripts rivaling Linear B to a state of some comprehensibility. My thanks to them are inadequate recompense.

Finally, Reserve Police Officer Shawn Aileen Murray of the Milpitas, California, Department of Public Safety, my partner in crime (or perhaps one should say for these purposes my *particeps non criminis*), has throughout all this given diligent, tart, and perceptive comment, willing and acerbic moral support at exceedingly odd hours, well-reasoned ideas and critically needed assistance in helping me to organize and survive a seemingly boundless cascade of paper. She has an especial place in respect of this volume and the *Standards* themselves, and I trust that despite her well-honed and healthy skepticism, she will never doubt that her peculiar adjuvance was absolutely essential to my getting anything done, and that I cherish both the help and its giver.

A.R.G.

University of Santa Clara
Santa Clara, California

Introduction

Although proceedings involving children who are beyond parental control, have run away, are truants from school, or otherwise have committed acts wrongful only for children make up a very substantial part of the business of our juvenile courts, there is a devastating lack of information about them. No single work has previously addressed the nature, extent, and effectiveness of juvenile court treatment of these cases.

This book of readings attempts to fill some of the gaps in available knowledge by exploring the theories that lie behind the status offense or non-criminal-misbehavior jurisdiction over children, presenting current empirical data concerning the operation of courts and other agencies in these matters, and considering a variety of suggestions for change in the treatment of young people classed as "Persons in Need of Supervision" (PINS).

This collection of readings can, with some arbitrariness, be divided into three parts. The first focuses on the theory and practice of "beyond control" jurisdiction, and is introduced by an essay by Professor Teitelbaum and Ms. Leslie Harris of the Public Defender Service of the District of Columbia which traces shifts in attitudes and strategies with respect to the family and particularly those concerning the parent-child relationship. The next paper, by R. Hale Andrews, Jr. and Andrew H. Cohn of the Massachusetts Bar, presents perhaps the most comprehensive available empirical study of PINS law in any jurisdiction. Their investigation, while confined to New York State, examines the operation of Family Courts both within and outside of the city of New York. By way of comparison, Fré Le Poole of the New York Bar offers the first real glimpse of how such matters are handled in Europe in her analysis of practices in West Germany, France, Sweden, the United Kingdom, and particularly, the Netherlands.

The next set of essays deal with particular problems presented by PINS jurisdiction. The first, by Professor Anne Rankin Mahoney of the University of Denver, discusses from a sociological perspective the significance of using juvenile court procedures to regulate parent-child relationships. Professor Mahoney presents data to suggest that ultimately such intervention, however well-intentioned, may have serious and undesired long-range effects on the careers of child and family. Alan Sussman of the New York Bar reviews the problems of sexual discrimination commonly associated with PINS practices. Professor Al Katz of the State University of New York at Buffalo Faculty of Law and Professor Teitelbaum then examine the relationship of PINS legislation to the rule of law and the doctrine of statutory vagueness, concluding that reliance on the rule of law in this area produces a set of fundamental and insoluble paradoxes.

The last group of papers address proposals for maintenance, modification, and elimination of PINS jurisdiction. The Honorable Lindsay Arthur, Presiding Judge of the Juvenile Court of Minneapolis, argues for the retention of the juvenile court's power to intervene in cases of non-criminal misbehavior. Professor Floyd Feeney of the Center for Administration of Criminal Justice, University of California at Davis, discusses the Sacramento County Project and suggests a family-centered no-fault approach to the handling of such cases. To conclude the work, Professor Gough examines the factors that argue for change of the present practices and discusses the provisions of the proposed American Bar Association—Institute of Judicial Administration *Standards Relating to Non-Criminal Misbehavior.*

We believe that the questions presented by the juvenile court's status offense jurisdiction are enormously important, and we hope that this work will contribute to their resolution and to the development of an appropriate jurisprudence of intervention in matters of family conflict. This effort has been greatly rewarding for us; if our readers find something of the same value, we will have done what we set out to do.

 *Chapter 1*

Some Historical Perspectives on Governmental Regulation of Children and Parents*

Lee E. Teitelbaum
Leslie J. Harris

INTRODUCTION

The question of what ought be done about children who disobey their parents presents fundamental issues of the proper relationship between parents and child and the proper role of the state in defining and dealing with apparent rupture of that relationship. The salience of these issues is revealed by the variety of recent suggestions to modify or eliminate official intervention in such cases and, for that matter, by this book of readings addressed to empirical and theoretical problems involved in state regulation of parent-child relationships.

It would be of great value to have an integrated history of governmental regulation of the family which treated the conditions affecting a society's view of how kinship groups should be ordered, the functions they are expected to discharge, and the appropriate strategies for promoting these attitudes. This essay has two more modest goals. The first is to suggest that views of the family and its regulation have been no more constant over time than views of other economic, social, political and legal matters. Correlatively, we hope to show that views of the family are intimately and reciprocally related to prevailing economic, social, political and legal propositions; that is, that what people expect and demand from families is part of what they expect and demand from society as a whole. The second goal is to sketch, and only that, some of these propositions in connection with former and current views of the American family. This sketch reveals considerable ambivalence in modern child-saving laws, particularly

*Both authors wish to express appreciation to Professor Pamela B. Minzner of the University of New Mexico School of Law for her helpful comments on this manuscript. She has, of course, no responsibility for any errors the reader may discern.

those dealing with youthful disobedience, which results from an effort at the turn of this century to incorporate views of the family appropriate to Puritan society into the radically different context of progressive America.

The discussion will focus principally on expressed beliefs and policies regarding social and family functions and what they seem to have implied for regulation of parent-child relationships. This approach largely but not entirely implies abandonment of empirical considerations. Although, for example, we know that there were small family groups in the Middle Ages, our concern will be with formal conceptions of the family which, generally speaking, were directed either to large family groups or to single representatives of kinship groups. This emphasis is justified not only by the brief compass of an essay but also by the general aim of the discussion, which is to set out beliefs that, accurate or not, seem to have affected legal regulation of the family. For this purpose, it does not matter whether, as was sometimes claimed, maternal employment led to increased infant mortality; that it was believed is sufficient to explain why persons holding that view mistrusted families with working mothers.

Moreover, unlike a definite history of parent-child relations, the present essay deals only with the modern family, which appears during the fifteenth and sixteenth centuries together with the rise of a money economy, humanism, and Protestantism. The Roman family, which accorded a father life and death power over his sons and in Maine's phrase "constitutes one of the strangest problems in legal history" [1], must be excluded, as is the Anglo-Saxon family in which, it seems, the father could sell into slavery a child younger than seven and perhaps could lawfully kill a child "who had not yet tasted food" [2]. Even the medieval family will largely be ignored despite the still-current importance of doctrines developed during that period, particularly in relation to transmission of wealth from parent to child. The first part of this discussion deals with the rise of the modern view of the family and the relationship of Protestant and Puritan views with respect to family roles to broader social, economic, political and religious propositions. The second part addresses the development of notions concerning the regulation of the family under the social and intellectual conditions of eighteenth and nineteenth century America, and the third part deals with views of children and parents associated with the progressive and child-saving era after the Civil War. The conclusion looks briefly to certain elements of continuity and change in American views of the family and suggests that current laws concerning disobedience suffer from a resort to tradition that may have been misplaced even a century ago.

THE RISE OF THE MODERN FAMILY

The "modern" view of the family, to which we have limited our attention, is one which emphasizes an inward-looking conjugal unit and parent-child relationships rather than large groups (clans) or linear (generational) relationships. There is, concededly, a degree of arbitrariness both in placing the rise of this view of the family in the fifteenth and sixteenth centuries and in considering families of that period modern. Families of the sort we call modern doubtless existed during the Middle Ages, particularly among the burgess and villein classes. Aristocratic families also seem to have shared the authoritarian organization associated with the "modern" Puritan theory, a matter occasioning little surprise in view of their common religious base, the Fifth Commandment [3], and of the position of younger children who neither inherited nor were expected to work, leaving them dependent on parents and family for lifelong provision[4]. On the other hand, families during the fifteenth—or for that matter the seventeenth—centuries differed in size and organization from the current mode. Not only were there more children, but the idea of family for legal, social and religious purposes included certain unrelated members such as apprentices and sometimes servants living in the home [5]. The household was more "extended" than the nuclear unit which is said to characterize post-industrial society.

Nevertheless, associating the "modern" family with this period is justifiable. It is generally agreed that a gradual shift from kinship or lineage to the inward-looking conjugal unit did occur, although the beginning of this process has been located at various points [6]. We follow Aries in settling on the fifteenth and sixteenth centuries, without much concern for greater precision [7]. This transition involved displacement of feudal views, which typically made little place either for the family as a small group or for parent-child relations. Medieval law and custom depended on principles of status and, within that, of hierarchy and representation which were expressed in a linear view of the family [8]. Rules of inheritance, for example, were devised to assure that lands held in military tenure remained with a single person whose duties could easily be identified and enforced. Ultimately, the interest in facilitating rendition of assistance from vassal to lord resulted in the institution of primogeniture, limiting inheritance of certain lands to the eldest surviving son [9]. Other children, however important their relationships within the family might have been, went largely without formal provision or recognition [10].

Moreover, when childhood was recognized—usually in the event of a father's death or capture abroad—the medieval eye remained on fulfillment of feudal duties. Infancy was important principally as it negated temporarily the assumption of responsibilities, and what we would now call ages of majority were set according to the adult activity which the heir would assume [11]. Notions of wardship over the child were similarly tied to adult interests. Custody of infant heirs to a military tenure devolved upon the lord, both to protect the child against designing relatives and to assure the male child's proper education. Initially, the lord had control of the marriage of male and female wards as well; the importance of the marriage right as to female heirs lies in the rule that her husband assumed control over her estate and responsibility for its associated duties. These were, it should further be emphasized, rules for heirs who would assume specific obligations under the feudal system. Guardianship over children who were not heirs was little regulated by medieval law, since it had no importance to adult affairs [12].

Significantly, the network of feudal incidents diminished when personal service and its corollary, land tenure, were not important. A case in point is that of the merchants, artisans, and other town dwellers of the enfranchised boroughs for whom restrictions such as impartibility of inheritances were inapplicable. As Goebel observes, "Family organization is on a much different footing in a burgher's house than among the gentry. From the nature of city enterprise, movable values at an early date are of relatively greater significance than elsewhere. The liberty of dealing freely with real property makes it easier to look out for all children. The cohesiveness of family group is not distrubed by alien wardships [that is, wardship of heirs in the lord] and dictation over marriages" [13]. It is in the towns that the family can be formally viewed as a group, and it is with their rise that more modern views of the family come to official recognition.

It is, therefore, usual to identify the rise of the modern family with the decline of feudal society. A variety of political, social and religious developments contributed to this transition. Decimation of the population by the plague of 1348–1350 transformed a society in which owners had ample labor and villeins little security or reward to one in which labor was scarce and could become dear. One result was the widespread introduction of wage-labor in place of labor tied to tenure on land [14]; another was the growth of sheepherding on land that could not be farmed for lack of labor, from which developed during the fourteenth and fifteenth centuries that quintessential expression of English capitalism, the wool industry. The plague thus provided strong impetus toward an economy less closely tied to personal service and land ownership and increased vastly the number and power of families for which the linear relationships of feudalism were relatively unimportant. By the sixteenth century a nation of shopkeepers was emerging.

Governmental response to the conditions brought by the plague, perhaps intended to support the vassal relationship, in the long run weakened it. During the plague years themselves, the villeins—hard pressed by rising prices and appreciative of new opportunities for improvement—either left the land or demanded a higher return for their labor. Royal authority entered the breach through statutes intended to regulate the labor force by, among other things, fixing wage scales and prohibiting movement from the land [15]. While it seems that these regulations were not highly effective [16], the direct participation of royal (central) authority was important in the continuing struggle to reduce manorial authority. Indeed, by the end of the sixteenth century, the English monarchy had succeeded in destroying all but the vestiges of feudal political structure [17]. In consequence, the mediation of lord between vassal and king was replaced by direct submission of all subjects to monarchical authority. Feudal political principles, like feudal economics, were largely moribund by the sixteenth century.

Another major element in the disintegration of the medieval system was the rise of Protestantism, which affected religious authority in much the same way that economic and political changes affected secular relations. As the latter permanently weakened the mediation of lord between vassal and royal authority, Protestant attack centered on the necessity of priestly participation in the enterprise of salvation. In place of the church, Protestants substituted a direct relationship between man and God. Salvation became the product of divine election and was reserved to a few; it could not be earned by good works, confession or obedience to Church discipline.

Protestantism swept through England during the sixteenth and seventeenth centuries, principally among the rising class of merchants, artisans, and professional men who had largely been excluded from attention and reward by medieval and Catholic institutions [18]. The individual success of burghers had been constrained by the guild system, which regulated what could be charged, and by the Catholic condemnation of lending money at interest in any form [19]. Indeed, Catholic doctrine generally disfavored accumulation of wealth in money while praising mendicancy as an exercise in Christian humility [20]. No wonder, then, the appeal of Heinrich Bullinger's sixteenth century *Decades* condemning idleness and praising industriousness, or Joseph Hall's assurance that "Ye may be at once rich and holy" [21]. As long as economic matters were undertaken with pure motives, to help the community and to glorify God, they were not only legitimate but praiseworthy in the Protestant view. It was now the idle—monks, as well as beggars and vagabonds—upon whom divine wrath, properly understood, fell.

The Puritan Family and Its Functions

The emergent middle class, Protestant society was not, however, a comfortable one, particularly for its Puritan members. However much they welcomed increased freedom in economic activities and their greater social and political importance, Protestant and Puritan perceptions of society were not complacent. The weakening of traditional forms of authority, while necessary to their ascendency, may also have led to fear for the collapse of authority generally among those strata of society—the poor and the peasantry—who most required external control. Beggars, vagabonds, and the like comprised the "many-headed monster"—the mob—in whose rootlessness and uprisings industrious burgesses and landed gentry alike saw the threat of sporadic crime and wholesale revolution. For Puritans, the concern for social order was peculiarly acute; they saw themselves immersed in an age of chaos and crime, against which both individual and collective conscience were required to maintain a close and perpetual guard [12].

This Puritan rage for control was, however, only more acute than that of their contemporaries in England; it did not in its authoritarian implications substantially diverge from general opinion during the age of absolutism which succeeded feudalism. Indeed, the dominant theme of seventeenth century thought was the need for stringent social control lest the natural inclinations of men destroy society. Hobbes' Leviathan is the most authoritarian of states: entire submission of subject to sovereign is required to prevent the "warre of every one against every one" which results when men live in a state of nature. Absent a "common power to keep [all men] in awe," there is "no place for Industry . . . and consequently no Culture of the Earth, no Navigation, nor use of the commodities that may be imported by Sea . . . no Knowledge of the face of the Earth; no Account of Time; no Arts; no Letters; no Society, and which is worst of all, continuall feare, and danger of violent death . . ." [23]. In short, because of the fundamentally selfish nature of men, civil authority of the strongest kind is necessary to guarantee civilization.

The political and theological mode of Protestant and Puritan thought was not less authoritarian and absolutist. The Christian corollary of Hobbes' state of nature is found in the doctrine of original sin which, for Calvinists, was only removed by regeneration for an elect few—and even they required collective and continual "stirring up . . . to greater godliness" [24]. Moreover, the Calvinist God, like temporal Kings, lays down His wishes in the form of laws which, as a Covenant between God and man, require strict observance. The Congregations themselves undertook supervision of the Covenant for their members, but for the mass of unregenerate society, civil authority embodying the Covenant was necessary to assure its enforcement. "[T]ake sovereignty from the face of the earth," said the Puritan Robert Bolton, in Hobbist fashion, "and you turn it into a cockpit. Men would become cut-throats and cannibals. . . . Murder, adulteries, incests, rapes, robberies, perjuries, witchcrafts, blasphemies, all kinds of villainies, outrages and savage cruelty would overflow all countries" [25].

The embracing notion of Puritan thought was, accordingly, one of discipline in all respects [26]. Religious discipline involved attendance at church and sincere reflection upon moral lessons and the meaning of the Covenant. Labor discipline was not less important. Nothing is more characteristic of Protestant thought than its insistence upon the duty—not merely the dignity—of work [27]. The appeal of this doctrine to small employers and artisans, for whom thriftiness and hard work were daily requirements, was plain. They readily viewed with odium beggars and for that matter monks and gentry who did not labor. Labor discipline was also related to the requirements of social discipline in general; if only men were industrious, it was thought, stealing and other crime would disappear [28]. The idle, often enough, were equated with the unregenerate [29], but there was hope that through acceptance of discipline in some sense, the ungodly could be brought to right behavior and compliance with the Covenant.

The basic agent of this pervasive social control was neither manor nor parish but household, the "first combination" of mankind. Authority wrested from the Church and from the vassalage relationship was not lost, but relocated in the household and particularly its head. The husband-father now mediated between his dependents and God on the one hand, civil government on the other. The family became both model and guarantor of the general society:

> In the society [which the preachers] were helping to shape, the family household, with its extensions in farmstead and shop, and in its relation to religious life, was assuming an importance that it had not had in feudal, monastic, or courtly society. The preachers described it again and again as a little church, a little state . . . [30].

Raleigh expressed the view that the first governors were fathers of families, comparing the king to the "master of the household" [31], and Cotton Mather wrote that "families are the Nurseries of all Societies; and the First Combinations of mankind. Well-ordered Families naturally produce Good Order in other Societies" [32]. The family's role as guarantor of religious and secular morality is reflected in Wadsworth's *Well-Ordered Family*, a basic Puritan text:

> Without *Family care* the labour of Magistrates and Ministers for Reformation and Propagating Religion, is likely to be in great measure unsuccessful. It's much to be fear'd, Young Persons wont much mind what's said by Ministers in Publick, if they are not Instructed at home: nor will they much regard good Laws made by Civil Authority, if they are not well counsel'd and govern'd at home [33].

Puritans saw in children the evil nature of man generally: original sin prior to regeneration. The godly father was charged with responsibility for repressing the wickedness of his children, and was supported in this enterprise by a claim to absolute obedience of the kind associated with sovereignty in the greater society. "God chargeth the master of the family with all in the family," a Puritan text observed. "Hence . . . it belongs to all governors [fathers] to see that their children, servants and inferiors whatsoever keep the Lord's day" [34]. The *Homily Against Idleness* made the same point with regard to inculcation of and insistence upon the duty of labor [35]. Children must be trained to work in order that they may sustain themselves and relieve the want of others, and the radical wing of Puritanism went so far as to argue that a father must refuse to maintain at home a daughter capable of earning her own living [36].

Affection was a poor second to control in the relations of parents to their young. The theory of child-rearing expressed by John Robinson in *Of Children and Their Education* was widely shared by strict Puritans, including those who settled America:

For the beating, and keeping down of this stubbornness parents must provide carefully for two things: first that children's wills and wilfulness be restrained and repressed, and that, in time; lest sooner than they imagine, the tender sprigs grow to that stiffness, that they will rather break than bow. Children should not know, if it could be kept from them, that they have a will in their own, but in their parent's keeping: neither should those words be heard from them, save by way of consent, 'I will' or 'I will not' [37].

Sovereigns of family government were enjoined always to remember that the young child "which lieth in the cradle . . . is altogether inclined to evil. . . . Therefore parents must be wary and circumspect, that they never smile or laugh at any words or deeds of their children done lewdly . . . " [38]. If the child ended up among the elect, then his right conduct could be expected, but hypocrites—the unregenerate who nevertheless acted as if he were saved—had uses as well, for at least they kept the Covenant. "Lewd sons and servants," therefore, must be brought to "submit themselves both to the public worship of the Sabbath and private duties in the family." If Godliness could not be produced, a reasonable counterfeit would serve instead [39].

The Puritan Family in the Colonies

If any one thing emerges from the foregoing, it is that Protestant and particularly Puritan views of religion, economy and government were integrally and reciprocally related to their views of the family. Each took discipline as its principal function, and each was concerned with all aspects of discipline. In the view of strict Puritans, however, neither English society nor English religious institutions adequately embodied the discipline of the Covenant. It was not that their notions had entirely failed of acceptance; Puritanism was, after all, a variation of the dominant Protestant and humanist world view [40]. An Elizabethan statute was directly addressed to maintenance of religious discipline, penalizing by fine any head of household who failed to see that his children and apprentices attended church [41]. The poor laws, which withheld aid from the voluntarily idle, generally reflected Puritan doctrines of the duty of labor, and the authoritarian social and political views held by strict Puritans found some legislative and administrative expression [42].

Half a loaf was not, however, sufficient to sustain a people hungry for the *Civitate Dei*. In the religious sphere, the Puritans observed with horror the ascendency of Arminianism—the belief that men of their own will could achieve salvation—and with displeasure that of presbyterianism with its low standards for membership in the church and its lay hierarchy. In society and government they saw pervasive corruption, overreaching, and wrongdoing. Particularly obnoxious were the ecclesiastical courts, which they considered both corrupt and wrongheaded. The Puritans were caught in a dilemma from which no escape was possible at home. To enforce discipline, state power was required, particularly that available through the church courts; however, the church courts were governed by a hierarchy opposed to Puritan views and to strengthen their hand was unthinkable [43].

Often reluctantly, therefore, Puritans thought of removal from England as the only avenue for establishment of the kind of government required by the Covenant. Many of the Puritans who emigrated to America did so only as a last resort, and without the Separatists' desire to dissociate themselves formally from the Anglican church. What they did believe was that existing circumstances greatly compromised their relationship and that of their families with God. John Winthrop, who was not himself a Separatist, felt immigration necessary because, as things were in early seventeenth century England, "The fountains of learninge and religion are so corrupted that most Children even the best wittes and of fayrest hopes, are perverted corrupted and utterly overthrowne by the evill examples and licentious government of those seminaryes" [44]. Similar perceptions accounted for much of the great movement from England to the colonies, including Massachusetts, in the years between 1630 and 1640, during which the latter was firmly established, substantially enlarged, and provided with a definite social and political shape.

It is fair to view the New England experiment as one in right life and government; the colonists, like Bunyan's Pilgrim, sought a heavenly city which could not be found in the complacent society of contemporary England [45]. The difficulties of the experiment cannot be overstated, however. Its population could not be limited to the elect, who were never great in number; therefore, the unregenerate must be controlled in an environment that was hostile to survival itself. And if, as Michael Walzer has said, the essential Puritan experience was anxiety [46], the wilderness of New England was calculated to sharpen the fear of chaos which accompanied even a lake county Puritan. Thus, the circumstances of colonization tended to encourage insistence upon social control even beyond what the motive for emigration would have suggested.

The nature of the Puritan enterprise and the social strategies employed to enforce discipline are clearly revealed in colonial laws regarding the family. We have already seen that, in Puritan and Protestant thought generally, the household was accorded central importance as an agent of social and economic control. The Puritans of Massachusetts insisted most strictly upon this same view, and enacted a remarkable body of laws to enforce it. Among the earliest ordinances is the following:

If any Childe or Children above sixteene years old and of sufficient understanding, shall Curse or smite their natural father or mother, hee or they shall bee put to death; unless it can bee sufficiently testified that the parents have beene very unchristianly negligent in the education of such children, or so provoke them by extreme, and cruel, correction that they have beene forced thereunto to preserve themselves from death, maiming. Exod. 21:17. Lev. 20:9. Exod. 21:15 [47].

Likewise, the laws went on to provide, as Deuteronomy does, that:

> If any man have a stubborn or rebellious sonne of sufficient yeares and understanding, viz. Sixteene yeares of age, which will not obey the voice of his father or the voice of his mother, and that when they have chastened he will not harken unto them; then may his father and mother, being his naturall parents, lay hold on him and bring him to the Magistrates assembled in Courte and testifie unto them, that theire sonne is stubborn and rebellious and will not obey their voice and Chastisement, but lives in sundry notorious Crimes, such a sonne shall bee put to death. Deut. 21:20—21 [48].

These laws are principally important symbolically, for what they reveal about Puritan principles of family governance, since records do not reveal that any child was executed under their authority [49]. Their enactment, however, reflects more than simple Biblical literalism, for not every Biblical command became statute and not every Biblical penalty was imposed when the substance of an injunction was adopted in the civil law. What they reveal most strongly is fear for the dissolution of the institution upon which all relied for the strength of civil and religious society and for whose preservation many originally left England. In great part, economic conditions—and not merely chronic anxiety—accounted for this perception. Labor in the colonies, even more so than in England, was a family enterprise (always remembering that "family" included servants and apprentices). Farms and small business predominated, for which patriarchal family organization was peculiarly well-suited [50]. By 1662, for example, each householder in Andover, Massachusetts, owned at least 100 and as much as 600 acres of farming land [51]. Family farms of this size obviously required all the labor that could be had from its members, which meant that sons were expected to assist on the farm virtually through adulthood. Various strategies were employed to maintain the dependence of children on parents for longer periods than is now common. Greven summarizes these techniques in the following way:

> The family . . . was held together not only by settling sons upon family land in Andover, but also by refusing to relinquish control of the land until long after the second generation had established a nominal independence following their marriages and the establishment of separate households. In a majority of cases, the dependence of the second-generation sons continued until the deaths of their fathers [52].

In England, these devices would likely have been by themselves sufficient to maintain the unity of the family; land and other sources of wealth was scarce and movement by children was artificially limited by these conditions. In the colonies, however, abundance of land and scarcity of labor combined to reduce the economic dependence of sons on their parents [53]. It is significant in this connection that the laws just quoted are not addressed to the socialization of young children, but to those of the age of sixteen—physically and almost emotionally mature—who present an active threat of family disruption. Social control was required to carry a burden at least partially borne by practical economics in Europe.

It was consistent with the Puritan theory of child-rearing that this dissolution perception was attributed largely to failure of discipline and education on the part of parents and masters. Signs of this apprehension are found in the Massachusetts laws of 1648, which established a mechanism for surveillance of families:

Forasmuch as the good education of children is of Singular behoof and benefit to any commonwealth, and whereas many parents and masters are too indulgent and negligent of their duty in that kind: It is therefore ordered that the select men of every town, in the several precincts and quarters where they dwell, shall have a vigilant eye over their brethren and neighbors to see, first, that none of them shall suffer so much barbarism in any of their families as not to endeavor to teach by themselves, or others, their children and apprentices so much learning as may enable them perfectly to read the English tongue and knowledge of the capital laws, upon penalty of twenty shillings for each neglect therein [54].

This law was not primarily symbolic in nature. The Puritans too, as we have seen, had a highly instrumental view of the family; it was institutionally relied upon for socialization and control purposes. And, it appears, the governors were ready to enforce these laws. A number of successful prosecutions of persons unable or unwilling to make a "little church" and "little commonwealth" of their households are found in colonial records [55]. As the colony grew, however, surveillance by select men became more difficult and concern grew as well. These circumstances led to the establishment, between 1675 and 1679, of the "tithingmen," perhaps the ultimate expression of both the institutional significance of the family and societal concern with its effectiveness. This scheme required the select men of every town to "choose some sober and discreet persons to be Authorized from the County Court, each of whom shall take the Charge of *Ten* or *Twelve Families* of his Neighbourhood, and shall diligently inspect them, and present the names of such persons so transgressing to the Magistrate, Commissioner, or Selectmen of the Town, who shall return the same to be proceeded with by the next County Court, as the law directs" [56]. Initially empowered to investigate drunkenness, the tithingmen were soon ordered—like constables in England under Coke's instruction—to attend to disorders of every kind in the families for which they were responsible [57].

The poor laws, adapted from Elizabethan models and widely adopted in the colonies, served much the same purpose. In the Puritan mind, idle people were not only people who violated the duty of labor but were presumptively wicked in other respects as well. It was, therefore, routinely assumed that the poor were unable to rear children in the various aspects of discipline and provision for removal of children from their custody was routinely made.

What, then, could be done with children whose parents failed to inculcate Puritan discipline? Under the poor laws and the special ordinances referred to previously, the ultimate sanction was placement of the child in another family, ordinarily through the agency of involuntary apprenticeship. The poor laws had always provided for the "binding out" of the children of the poor to respectable families, so that they might work and learn the other aspects of social living. The Massachusetts laws dealing with neglect of parents to educate their children contemplated the same result; the statute authorizing surveillance by select men concludes by providing:

> And if any of the selectmen, after admonition by them given to such masters of families, shall find them still negligent of their duty in the particulars aforementioned, whereby children become rude, stubborn and unruly, the said selectmen . . . shall take such children or apprentices from them and place them with some masters for years (boys till they come to twenty-one, and girls eighteen years of age complete) which will more strictly look unto, and force them to submit unto government according to the rules of this order, if by fair means and firmer instructions they will not be drawn unto it [58].

In this strategy the connection between youthful disobedience and parental failure is explicit. When Sarah Gibbs behaved "very sinfully and disorderly," she was put to service in another home, because of both her wrong and the wrong of her natural family [59].

Regulation of the little commonwealth was, thus, not only part but image of regulation in the general society. Roles within both groups were rigidly defined and explicitly patriarchal. We have already seen much about the expectations held of children and, by analogy, servants, who were held by custom, law, and the Fifth Commandment to a duty of submission. Although the wife was by no means a servant of her husband, her place was also defined closely and "joyful submission" to it was expected:

> In seventeenth-century New England no respectable person questioned that woman's place was in the home. By the laws of Massachusetts as by those of England a married woman could hold no property of her own. When she became a wife, she gave up everything to her husband and devoted herself exclusively to managing his household. Henceforth her duty was to 'keep at home, educating of her children, keeping and improving what is got by the industry of the man' [60].

This style of family organization was supported by the community and by other branches of the family, providing greater interpenetration of household with community than is now the case.

It is true that child-rearing was accorded great importance in this scheme. The father was expected to mediate between household members and society at large by providing children and servants with regard for moral rule, obedience to authority in general, and a "calling." At the same time, the place of children seems not be so much age-as generation-specific. The reasons for and techniques of controlling young persons were not clearly distinct from those for dealing with adults. Puritan sermons, whose importance was great in a society substantially based on Biblical precept, rarely differentiated between infants, youths, or for that matter adult children [61]; the duty of obedience imposed by Massachusetts law was likewise specially applicable to older children. Even the wickedness imputed to infants was nothing special to the young; it afflicted unregenerate adults in the same way and called for the same remedy: surveillance, strict control, and punishment. It has been suggested that adolescence—in the sense of a state of transition—rarely appeared as a private issue in seventeenth century New England. Each generation was expected naturally to assume the place of its predecessor at the appointed time, without turmoil or change [62]. The role assigned to the Puritan family was to facilitate this transition, and was as fundamentally conservative as Puritan society itself.

The strategies to be followed by society in dealing with families flow from the expectations society holds for them. The scarcity of such strategies for households in medieval society bespeaks the minor expectations held by that society for families; the introduction of regulations and mechanisms for dealing with families in seventeenth century England and New England shows the contrary to be true. On the one hand, these strategies were designed to retard family dissolution through the departure and consequent failure of children to discharge responsibilities necessary for economic and social stability. At the same time, Puritans were prepared to intervene in cases of family failure; that is, of failure by parents properly to rear their children, evidenced either by neglect in some regard (including pauperism) or by youthful misbehavior. Even when intervention was required, however, the Puritans continued to rely on the family as a mediating institution. Occasionally, relief was given directly to families in need [63]; more commonly and particularly in extreme cases, children were removed from the unsuccessful natural family and placed with another. Having rediscovered the conjugal family, Puritans elevated its importance to the point that, in order to preserve its benefits as a social institution, provision for disruption of particular (inadequate) families was thought necessary.

It is evident that New England views of family structure and function resemble current views in many ways. It is likewise plain that official intervention when family structure and function failed was approved and in some cases carried out by colonial governments. These resemblances should not, however, lead to the conclusion that present views of the parent-child relationship and strategies for its regulation are substantially the same as those of the Puritans. Significant changes in societal views concerning the general capacity of families to rear children and in the kinds of strategies required in the event of failure occurred in the eighteenth and nineteenth centuries, which the following sections will survey.

VIEWS OF THE FAMILY IN THE EIGHTEENTH AND NINETEENTH CENTURIES

Perhaps the most important changes affecting societal views of the family are associated with changes in general philosophy. We have already noted the patriarchal and conservative nature of Puritan theories of family and society. Heavy reliance was placed on a set of essentially pessimistic assumptions about the human condition. Among the most important of these was the innate wickedness of man, which assured that there would always be sin and negated any general theory of progress on earth. The function of civil government was to repress, as far as possible, that evil; its entire removal was never thought possible. Since the rules by which civil government operated were ordained by God and required by the Covenant, society was served by acceptance of their authority and obedience to their commands.

Even during this period, however, the roots of a radically different view of man's nature and of society appeared. Newton's rationalism and Leibniz' theory of the creative advance of nature reveal the beginnings of doctrines of reason and progress which, under the banner of the Enlightenment, reached full development over the next two centuries. Newton's notion of the world-machine would ultimately replace the personal God of Puritan belief with a clockwinder or mechanistic God Who creates natural laws for the universe which operate without further divine intervention [64]. Associated with this shift was one in intellectual habits: from reliance on faith, magic, and miracles to reliance on human reason, which could discover and even use the laws of nature. There was both modesty and ambition in the rationalistic mode. As Pope's familiar couplet emphasizes, it moved men away from the contemplation of God, Who was unknowable through reason: "Know then thyself! Presume not God to scan! The proper study of mankind is man" [65]. At the same time, rationalism suggested that man and his condition were knowable and capable of improvement by men. This last notion, the potential for progress in this world, implied rejection of the religious doctrine of original sin and of its Hobbesian analog. Enlightenment theory assumed instead that man in his natural state is good, and that the evil that existed (which was as perceptible to rationalists as to Protestant divines) results from his "environment": those religious and social institutions that have obscured the true relation of man to man. Wickedness is, therefore, the result of what man has made of man; the optimism of the Enlightenment lies in the belief that it may also be eliminated through human efforts. "Rid man's mind of a few ancient errors, purge his beliefs of the artificial complications of metaphysical 'systems' and theological dogmas, restore to his social relations something like the simplicity of the state of nature, and his natural excellence would, it was assumed, be realized, and mankind would live happily ever after" [66].

The implications of the Enlightenment world view and of environmentalism in particular for the family are by no means remote. Just as views of the child in Puritan thought faithfully reflected notions of the inherent evil of mankind generally, so for the eighteenth and nineteenth centuries the child represented man in his natural state of innocence. When children went wrong, the causes of corruption were sought in the conditions in which they were raised and, since the family was the immediate environment for most children, attention was early directed to the adequacy of that institution. Education and training of the young were as important in the Enlightenment as before because existing social conditions had not yet been purified. The child thus could not grow naturally and maintain his innocence; he must be instructed in such a way that he can resist evil influences and learn to contribute to society. As Robert Owen, a fair representative of Enlightenment thought, saw it:

[P]lans must be devised to train children from their earliest infancy in good habits of every description (which will of course prevent them from acquiring those of falsehood and deception). They must afterwards be rationally educated, and their labour usefully directed. Such habits and education will impress them with an active and ardent desire to promote the happiness of every individual [67].

The requirement that children, to become enlightened, be reared in an enlightened manner obviously invites doubt concerning the general capacity of parents to discharge that function. While this issue was not always fairly confronted, there was increasing reason to believe that many families were incapable of rearing their children adequately. By the 1820s, environmentalism had produced studies of large numbers of convicted criminals designed to identify the roots of crime. These roots, predictably, always seemed to lead back to a failure in parental supervision [68]. Indeed, there seems to have existed during the middle part of the nineteenth century a widely-held perception that parental authority had weakened and, correlatively, that children were improperly raised. Demos and Demos observe that "In describing the average home, the writers of child-rearing books repeatedly use words like 'disorder,' 'disobedience,' 'licentiousness,' and above all 'indulgence' (i.e., of the children)" [69]. The view that American families were "child-centered"—shared by Tocqueville and other foreign observers [70] and, perhaps, borrowed from them—was thought to explain the perceived wane of parental authority [71].

Location of the causes of crime in unsatisfactory home situations was both congenial to eighteenth and nineteenth century views of social dynamics and confirmed by a set of experiences which might independently have suggested weakness in the family as an institution. Among these were the increased opportunities for children to leave their parents. As we have seen, efforts were made, by the New England colonies in particular, to prevent or at least impede the threatened dissolution of families. Their success was, however, limited. "By the middle of the eighteenth century," Bailyn observes, "the classic lineaments of the American family as modern sociologists describe them—the 'isolation of the conjugal unit,' the 'maximum of dispersion of the lines of descent,' partible inheritances, and multilineal growth—had appeared" [72]. This development profoundly weakened the reliance that could be placed on the family as a social institution. Authority could not easily be maintained when older children could and did remove themselves from the surveillance of the father and, as the settlement of younger generations moved toward the frontier, the close interpenetration of family and community disappeared [73].

A second impetus to loss of confidence in the capacity of families to accomplish their public purposes was the vast European immigration that began in the early eighteenth century. The homogeneity of colonial society doubtless contributed greatly to belief in the capacity of its members to fulfill social functions. However, beginning in the first quarter of the eighteenth century, this homogeneity dissolved in the waves of German and Scotch-Irish who settled the mid-Atlantic region [74]. Many of these immigrants were not only different but poor, lured into indentured service by false promises of wealth and success. The concern raised by this pattern of immigration reached considerable intensity by the middle of the eighteenth century. Benjamin Franklin expressed in 1753 his belief that "the German arrivals were 'the most stupid of their nation,' and would not take instruction from clergy or society" [75]. That this apprehension was as much class-based as nativistic is suggested by the similar observations of earlier German immigrants, such as the Reverend Henry Melchior Muhlenberg, who worried that "So many rotten people are coming . . . and acting so wickedly that the name [of Palatine] has begun to stink" [76]. Moreover, what little English immigration occurred during the generally prosperous Walpole government era gave little reason for enthusiasm; arrivals tended to be either paupers or transported convicts [77].

Liberty from England did not stem the tide of immigration and, during the early 1800s as during the previous century, large numbers of foreigners arrived in the States. Many of these, like their predecessors, came virtually penniless and uneducated, thereby contributing substantially to the pauper and criminal populations. The relationship of immigration to social and family disorganization was widely accepted, as the First Annual Report of the New York Children's Aid Society reveals:

The poor immigrants could not afford to go West, or with the natural caution of ignorance, they dreaded to go. Our poorest streets began to be filled up with a thriftless, beggared, dissolute population. As is always the case in such circumstances, vice and laziness stimulated each other. The poor and idle of a street grew worse for having poor and idle neighbors . . .

Crime among boys and girls has become organized, as it never was, previously. The Police state that picking pockets is now a profession among a certain class of boys . . .

Of the young girls in the city, driven to dishonest means of living, it is most sad to speak. Privation, crime, and old debasement in the pure an [sic] sunny years of childhood [78].

The difficulty lay, it should be emphasized, not merely with the poverty of the newcomers, although this too created a strain on scarce resources. Much concern arose from the different values and goals immigrant families brought with them, together with the peculiar difficulty of adjusting from the (presumably authoritarian) societies from which they came to the "open" society of America. Not understanding the society into which they moved, immigrant families were not well constituted to provide the environment in which their children could learn to become free but not licentious citizens [79].

A third source of declining confidence in the family, especially acute for the immigrant class but not limited to it, lay in the changing structure of family life occasioned by changes in the means of economic production. The Puritan notion assigned working roles to males, homemaking and home educational functions largely to females. Children worked, true enough, but ordinarily within the family; thus labor was or at least could be considered a part of education generally. Even when children were apprenticed out, it was expected legally as well as socially that they would get more than livelihood from their relationships with their masters [80]. Public authorities undertook the responsibility for supervising the families created by binding out or apprenticeship and were authorized to remove children when expectations concerning the moral and practical education of apprentices went unmet.

The shift from home to factory economy adversely affected both the family's function as an economic unit and the familial character of apprenticeship. Early American factories were largely filled with women and children, the former comprising by some estimates between two-thirds and three-fourths of factory labor during the first half of the nineteenth century [81]. Initially, this practice was well regarded as a means of freeing young women from poverty and idleness. What might be beneficial for single young American girls was, however, less desirable for immigrant married women; moreover, the model factories of Waltham gave way, over the course of the nineteenth century, to urban factories with ugly working conditions. Finally, women were placed in competition with men for jobs during hard times, which permanently affected the colonial understanding of their relationship. As Calhoun observes:

Long hours of factory labor abolished family life. Insufficient wages forced parents to set children prematurely to work . . . [W]ith the passing of

home industry woman had to go out into public work or remain a dangerous parasite. The man might go to work without upsetting the home center, though his constant absence could not but weaken old ties; likewise
the children; but when woman ceased to be 'housekeeper' the reality of
the home came into question [82].

Although attempts were made by enlightened factory managers to maintain a
partriarchal view of their employees [83], particularly the children, success in
that respect was uncommon. The result of industrialism was measured in terms
of inability of families to rear and supervise their children, who were left either
to roam the streets or to be put to work in jobs which could not reasonably be
viewed as educational. Nor were surrogate families easily available as placements
for children whose parents were too poor or too occupied to care for them properly. Indenture and binding out remained, it is true, common through the eighteenth and much of the nineteenth century, but as employment moved to the
factory, the effect of indenture was to place the children in settings which were
neither educational nor, indeed, safe. Thus, confidence in the family's capacity
to shape the environment of children was fatally impaired from yet another
direction.

The result of developments in the eighteenth and nineteenth centuries was
continued emphasis on the importance of child-rearing combined with growing
concern for the capacity of families to discharge that function properly. It is
not, therefore, surprising to see interest in the development of strategies for
dealing with wayward or neglected children that relied on non-family institutions. Enlightenment theory aided in that enterprise by encouraging the intervention of the educated to manipulate the environment in such a way that progress
could be achieved. Social engineering, in short, was a mode sensible under, and
perhaps only under, nineteenth century thought.

As one would expect, the development of institutional responses to perceived
family breakdown—whether found in the behavior of children or of parents—was
initially slow and scattered. During the 1800s common schools began to be
established to educate poor children whose parents could not afford to send
them to academies and who could not themselves perform that function [84].
In Boston, where concern for the capacity of families to educate their children
had long existed, school attendance became compulsory during the first part of
the nineteenth century, and the New York Public School Society asked for similar laws in 1832. That this step would involve substantial intervention in parental
control of their children was frankly conceded and justified in Enlightenment
terms:

Truantship in [Boston] is deemed a criminal offence in children, and those
who cannot be reclaimed, are taken from their parents by the Police, and
placed in an Institution called the 'School of Reformation' corresponding
in many respects with our House of Refuge—from which they are bound

out by the competent authority, without again returning to their parents. . . . Every political compact supposes a surrender of some individual rights for the general good. In a government like ours, 'founded on the principle that the only true sovereignty is the will of the people,' universal education is acknowledged by all, to be, not only of the first importance, but necessary to the permanency of our free institutions. If then persons are found so reckless of the best interests of their children, and so indifferent to the public good, as to withhold them from that instruction, without which they cannot beneficially discharge those civil and political duties which devolve on them in after life, it becomes a serious and important question, whether so much of the natural right of controlling their children may not be alienated, as is necessary to qualify them for usefulness, and render them safe and consistent members of the political body [85].

The willingness of the Public School Society to intervene in the parent-child relationship for educational purposes is, by itself, nothing remarkable; Massachusetts early emphasized education out of the home. The theory used by the Society in support of compulsory school laws is, however, broader than the problems created by truancy. It could and did stand for the proposition that parental control over their children was generally subject to official invasion when the former were guilty of neglect so as to compromise the capacity of infants to become good citizens. It also suggested that official agencies of social control could effectively be used to remedy family failure. Thus, the functions imputed to families—education, socialization, and the like—continue to be emphasized, but the importance of relying on families themselves for those functions is thrown into doubt.

That the implications of this theory went beyond truancy is revealed by the increasing use during the early nineteenth century of official agencies in dealing with reported parental cruelty, gross neglect endangering the health, morals, or welfare of children, and the like. Almshouses were more commonly used for the care of pauper children than had been the case, both because they were less expensive to operate than other means and because private family alternatives such as apprenticeship were no longer viewed as desirable [86]. Houses of refuge were established during the same period for the care of children who had been so poorly raised that they could not be reached by voluntary school programs or even by compulsory education laws [87]. The proposal of the New York Society for the Reformation of Juvenile Delinquents in 1824 for creation of the first house of refuge listed a number of classes of potential clientele: vagrant and homeless youths; young criminals; boys with neglectful parents; and some delinquent girls [88]. The variety of problem children to be reached demonstrates a belief that deviance results from a common cause, improper environment, which may be remedied by a common cure, placement in an environment where good habits can be learned. How far this view had gone, even during the early part of the nineteenth century, is revealed in a Pennsylvania Supreme Court decision in

1839, upholding the commitment of a young girl because of her incorrigibility to the Philadelphia House of Refuge. Both the social policy approved and the legal principle employed became common currency in the American philosophy regarding children:

> The object of the charity [the house of refuge] is reformation, by training its inmates to industry; by imbuing their minds with principles of morality and religion; by furnishing them with means to earn a living; and, above all, by separating them from the corrupting influence of improper associates. To this end, may not the natural parents, when unequal to the task of education, or unworthy of it, be superseded by the *parens patriae*, or common guardian of the community? It is to be remembered that the public has a paramount interest in the virtue and knowledge of its members, and that, of strict right, the business of education belongs to it . . . The infant [in this case] has been snatched from a course which might have ended in confirmed depravity; and, not only is the restraint on her person lawful, but it would be an act of extreme cruelty to release her from it [89].

By the middle of the nineteenth century, therefore, significant changes from colonial views of the family and its relation to society had occurred. Circumstances now suggested grounds for doubt about the capacity of many families to rear children in the way necessary for them to become good citizens. At the same time, social, political and intellectual views had also changed in ways that justified and even required adoption of new strategies for dealing with family breakdown. One of these was the conviction that environment caused wickedness, which in turn provided a manageable theory of societal response. That response lay in manipulation of the environment, generally through placement of the child in an institution where proper attitudes could be instilled and encouraged. Through education, houses of refuge, reformatories, and the like, poor and wayward children could be molded "into the form and character which the peculiar nature of the edifice [of American society] demands, and in due time the youth especially may become intelligent, enterprising and liberal-minded supporters of free institutions" [90].

MODERN VIEWS OF CHILDREN AND PARENTS:
THE COMING OF THE CENTURY OF THE CHILD

It is now a commonplace that, shortly after the Civil War, America entered upon the century of the child [91]. While this notion means different things to different people, it surely indicates a belief that something new had occurred in societal views of the place of the child and how children ought be treated. For some, the significance of this period lay in emancipation of the young both from old constraints and from the industrial bondage associated with child labor; for others, it lay in modifying existing institutions to better deal with the needs of children; for still others, the discovery of adolescence as a distinctive stage in development was the important thing. All agreed, however, that the future of society depended on what was done with its children and that "As befits a civilization with a broadening future, the child is becoming the center of life" [92].

It is certainly the case that, beginning about 1870, America gave special attention to the condition of its children and, ultimately, created for them a social role of a kind not previously recognized. Widespread acceptance of compulsory public education and restriction of child labor removed the young from the labor force while ensuring that they would be occupied in some fashion. Special legal and correctional programs for youths were also established, in the belief that their separation from adults was necessary both to avoid their further corruption and to promote their effective rehabilitation. This increasing specialization and activity by governmental agencies was not, of course, limited to children in need of assistance. A "new" role for society in dealing with children was mirrored in "new" roles for society in dealing with other kinds of problems. Laissez-faire capitalism and individualism, for example, now were perceived as threats to rather than as guarantors of social progress, and help was sought in the only available quarter:

> The actual and potential exploitation of natural and human resources, inherent in unbridled capitalism, stimulated a quest for a counterbalancing power. Progressives hoped that government could provide that power. In promoting anti-trust laws, in seeking legislation for the planned use of natural resources, in providing protection for the consumer from irresponsible producers of meat and drugs, the reformers were demanding that the government act as protector of the individual in an age when the individual acting alone seemed defenseless [93].

The idea of the state as protector of children was an obvious extension of the growing resort to state power for protection of the weak and needy.

The newness of this societal attitude towards children was a favorite theme of those who urged adoption of programs for the young [94]. There was continuity as well as change, however, in the century of the child, and both require consideration in assessing attitudes which still predominate in our thinking about parent-child relations.

Environmentalism and Rational Treatment in Dealing with Children

A central belief of those who undertook child-saving enterprises throughout the nineteenth century was that rational treatment programs could guarantee the proper development of children whose environment impeded that development. Reformatories could "remedy the neglect and vice of parents, the failure of public schools . . . and other moral agencies in the outside world"; skill and perseverence would "develop the bent sapling into the straight tree, and transform the embriotic criminal into the excellent citizen" [95]. Public and progressive education would allow every American child to become "a contributor to the wealth, to the intelligence, and to the power of this great democratic government of ours" [96]. The juvenile court was capable of taking the child who had already committed crimes or seemed likely to do so and placing him on the path that leads to "good, sound, adult citizenship" [97].

These correctional, educational and legal programs clearly reflect environmentalist and rationalist theory which had been influential for a century. Their ultimate triumph in the progressive era is particularly significant since triumph was achieved in the face of serious challenges. One of these challenges came from the social Darwinism current among conservative circles in this same period. Social Darwinism did tend to confirm rationalistic theories of progressive development since it drew from biological evolution a belief in the slow, ineluctable and natural progress of society. On the other hand, it lent itself to a distinctive governmental and social conservatism, particularly with respect to the propriety of intervention affecting the process of social development. If, social Darwinists argued, progress in society as in biology was the result of continuous natural selection of the strongest members of the group and elimination of the weakest, governmental assistance to the weak—the "dependent classes"—must necessarily retard the general improvement of society at large. Herbert Spencer would accordingly have limited the activities of government to administration of justice, national defense, and the enforcement of contracts. There was to be no public education, social welfare legislation, sanitary supervision, or regulation of industry, all of which artificially preserve the poor [98].

Despite the considerable appeal of conservative social Darwinism, the laissez-faire approach it implied never quite captured the day. In part, it offended deeply felt notions of decency; Spencer himself declared in favor of private voluntary charity for the remarkably medieval reason that it elevated the character of the donor and hastened the development of altruism in the population [99]. Professor Charles Henderson of the University of Chicago probably spoke for many in implicitly accepting much of the logic of Darwinism while plainly rejecting its ultimate conclusion:

> Some writers have emphasized the value of city life as an agency of social selection; the strong and capable are given a career while the feeble in vitality and character go to ruin and are weeded out. But this kind of social selection is too costly; its lightning strokes kill many of the finest human beings along with the neglected; and not seldom the nursery of deadly germs, physical and moral, is in the homes and streets of the so-called unfit. Those who fall into the doom clutch at the fair and incompetent and drag them to ruin with themselves [100].

The second challenge to environmentalism and progress through treatment came from the hard side of positive criminology. The positivists held that criminals formed an identifiable class whose criminality lay in inherited biological characteristics which constituted them a morally and physically retarded species, resembling lower primates, savage tribes, and children in their instinctive aggressiveness [101]. Non-criminals, by contrast, represented the progress of society. Criminals of the biological type were incurable as Lombroso and his followers saw it. They were, certainly, part of the developmental process, but their low place in that process was determined by nature rather than by environment. Accordingly, treatment was not possible; elimination from the population through eugenic devices, execution, or perpetual incarceration was the indicated strategy.

Ultimately, the implications of this view were rejected, if the theory was not. In the first place, hard determinism was incompatible with the professional aspirations held by a rising class of correctional and social workers who viewed themselves as doctors rather than as guards. They joined forces with the more optimistic criminal theorists, who held that criminal behavior depended as much on social experiences and economic circumstances as on biological traits or that, even though propensity towards criminality was inheritable at least in part, environmental manipulation and particularly moral education, properly undertaken, could neutralize the effects of heredity. Charles Cooley, for one, suggested that the dichotomy between "nature" and "nurture" was artificial and inaccurate. "One's nature acts selectively upon the environment, assimilating materials proper to itself; while at the same time the environment moulds the nature, and habits are formed which make the individual independent, in some degree, of changes in either." To explain how some persons become criminal, he added a sociological theory resembling what is now called differential association: The "well-nurtured boy emulates his own father and George Washington; but the child of the criminal, for precisely similar reasons, emulates *his* father . . . or some other illustrious rascal. The very faculties that serve to elevate and ennoble a child who lives among good associations may make a criminal of one who lives among bad ones" [102]. The superintendent of the Kentucky Industrial School of Reform, for another, assured his colleagues that:

> While I believe heredity, of both moral and physical traits, to be a fact, I think it is unjustifiably made a bugaboo to discourage efforts at rescue. We know that physical heredity tendencies can be neutralized and often nullified by proper counteracting precautions [103].

In the result, nurture and the utility of therapeutic intervention in the careers of deviants triumphed over old and new enemies: the traditional Christian view, which saw in worldly misery an occasion for edification of the elect but not a matter for improvement; the social Darwinist view, which produced the same result in its laissez-faire approach; and the legitimate child of Darwinism, biological determinism, which likewise denied the utility of intervention for rehabilitative purposes.

Contemporaneous developments in educational planning and theory, particularly the arrival of compulsory education on a national basis and the development of "progressive" systems for educating the young, may be viewed as further evidence of the consolidation of enlightenment doctrines concerning the capacity for improvement of men. Although compulsory education had already been locally enacted in a few areas, the trend greatly gained in strength after the Civil War. The reasons for its spread were much the same at the end of the century as at the beginning: the perceived importance of education for good citizenship and social order. Ignorance was viewed as a contributing cause to both criminality and pauperism and laws requiring education of children were part of the scheme of environmental control by which both could be reduced.

> If it be true that a good common school education is recognized as one of the necessaries for an infant, and essential to the discharge of civil and political duties, or, as generally stated, that a diffusion of knowledge among the people is essential to the preservation of free institutions, these so called compulsory or obligatory laws are founded upon the right and duty of self protection and preservation. They belong to the class of laws which are intended for the suppression of vice. They are intended to reach and bring within the influence of our schools a class who cannot be reached effectually in any other way. . . . The simple question is whether it is better to educate the children for our jails and workhouses or to become useful citizens [104].

The social defense motive for compulsory education laws speaks highly of the confidence of educators in their capacity to mold good citizens. This confidence is also revealed in the highly significant shift in educational theory that occurred during the same period. Both traditional and new educational modes were instrumentally conceived: to prevent crime and to improve the quality of citizenship generally. The traditional approach sought to instill discipline through learning (in the sense of mastery of) given bodies of knowledge. The proponents of progressive education saw in this both bad policy and bad psychology. By molding children in the image of existing society, mastery frustrated any useful notion of progress. "If," as Hofstadter observes of the views of Dewey, "a democratic society is truly to serve all its members, it must devise schools in which, at the germinal point in childhood, these members will be able to cultivate their capacities and, instead of simply reproducing the qualities of the larger society, will learn how to improve them" [105]. Accordingly, new educational theory substituted for the learning of "fixed verities" a scientific and rational view of education as the growth of the learner [106]. The social purposes of new educational theory are, of course, quite as salient as those of the older theory. Every teacher, in Dewey's theory, should be seen as engaged "not simply in the training of individuals, but in the formation of the proper social life" [107], a proposition equally acceptable to traditional views of education. The difference is that while orthodox theory viewed proper social life in terms of acceptance of existing institutions, Dewey sought it in the development of new and better institutions.

The thrust of progressive education was clearly child-centered and to a degree individualistic. The idea of growth has roots in the general notion of perfectibility and its effect is to turn attention, not from the social function of education, but from its value for immediate socialization. It becomes an assertion not of the child's place in society "but rather of his interests against those of [a presumably corrupt] society" [108]. A popular expression of this notion makes plain both the child-centeredness and the individualistic potential of the new education: "Already we Americans have discovered that the old system of education will not [work] . . . We have quit trying to fit the boy to a system. We are now trying to adjust a system to the boy" [109]. The same language could be and was used to describe the claimed goals of the juvenile court movement, the reformatory system, and other child-saving and child-centered programs.

The prevailing spirit in education and social theory could fairly be called romantic in its belief in perfectibility. Seeking that perfection, the child-savers of the late nineteenth century compared current institutions for child care, particularly the family, with what they equally romantically imagined the situation to have been two centuries earlier. Current conditions naturally fared ill in that comparison. Modern minded people saw in colonial experience the "good old days . . . [when] a boy worked for his father until he was twenty-one years of age. . . . They were under the influence of home and home training, until they had passed the period of adolescence and were really young men and young women." This halcyon time had, however, passed away. "The scene has changed from the farm to the village or city. The stimulating outdoor life of the farm, filled with duties and responsibilities, has been replaced by the enervating routine of life in store, office, or factory. Together with this loss has come a still greater loss in the diminution of the length of time that the child is under the restraint and guidance of his parents" [110].

In place of parental supervision the reformers saw neglect; in place of rural purity, the city's immorality; in place of a homogeneous, socially dedicated people the diffusion associated with immigration. Each of these themes had earlier been sounded, some from colonial times, but had in the late nineteenth century the conviction and zeal of novelty. European immigrants were thought, then as before, to present a serious social problem. A leading penologist could, for example, say that Hungarians and Italians brought with them a lessened respect for human life than is found among the northern (Anglo-Saxon) races, a family and racial characteristic which could be mitigated but not removed by their contact with the humanizing influences of American culture. "[I] t is not at all unlikely," he concluded, "that juvenile delinquency of the most serious kind in the United States is in some measure to be set down to the boundless hospitality of her shores" [111]. And Judge Mack, whose humanitarianism shows throughout his writings, observed that "Most of the children who come before the [juvenile] court are, naturally, the children of the poor. In many cases the parents are foreigners, frequently unable to speak English, and without an understanding of American methods and views" [112].

Nineteenth century social concern was not, however, limited to immigrant families but extended to all families living in urban conditions. The strength of environmentalism was clearly reflected in the common assertion that cities produced evil; the word "city" itself "symbolically embodied all the worst features of modern industrial life" [113]. On the one hand, urban conditions were held responsible for the increasing rate of dissolution, through divorce, of the family itself. The authority of the father and hence traditional family roles, it was thought, dwindled as the husband became merely the first among wage-earning equals and receded from the center of the family to its periphery. Migration from farm to factory had removed both kin and community control over family relationships and, in this weakened form, the institution could "no longer resist the temptations of unrestrained individualism" [114]. And, indeed, the divorce rate did rise rapidly, quadrupling during the period between 1860 and 1910 [115]. It is certainly arguable that neither the city nor industrialism produced either the conjugal family or its breakdown in any usual causative sense; it is, however, clear that progressives widely believed that divorce was an effect of urban conditions and yet another indication of the grave social disorder existing in the cities [116].

The increasing participation of women in the labor force, which was thought to contribute to divorce by reducing the father's importance, also added to anxiety concerning the health of urban families in at least two other senses. The fact of female employment itself was significant since, although almost all of the female labor force was unmarried [117], there was considerable feeling that working mothers would not adequately carry out the physical and moral aspects of child-rearing. Professor Henderson asserted in 1908 that "The death rate of infants has hitherto been especially marked in cities owing to the defective supply of milk, and probably to the neglect of infants by mothers who work for a living away from home" [118]. Dr. I. M. Rubinow, head of the United States Bureau of Labor, took much the same position, finding in feminist demands for women's economic independence a grave threat to the lower classes:

> To the working-woman [the demand for economic independence] . . . may mean very long hours, unhygienic work, low wages—many of these things in addition to the required minimum of housework—and it certainly means neglect of children, even more than the neglect of the husband's comfort. . . . None of the members of the southern negro's family are better off

because the woman is economically independent. And above all, the child-mortality is greater. Under the present industrial organization, the proletarian woman has nothing to gain and the proletarian child a great deal to lose, by this sort of economic independence [119].

Dr. Rubinow's association of feminist demands with neglect of family reveals another area of concern for the strength of the natural family. The late 1800s entertained a virulent debate over the nature of the woman's role in society and, therefore, in the family. The dispute was not one between men and women but between a group of radical middle class women (with occasional male support) and another group of more traditionally minded middle class women (with considerable male support). Radical feminists, for their part, attacked centrally the traditional woman's role as helpmeet, homemaker and child-rearer. Charlotte Perkins Gilman described the patriarchal family, upon which American society had relied since colonial times, as "a vehicle of masculine power and pride" without parallel in nature [120]. Nor was idleness, the lot of wealthy women, more desirable; the answer lay in restructuring family and society so as to allow the economic and social independence of women in general [121].

There were, it should be said, many points of agreement between the radical feminists and the middle-class women who opposed them. The latter group, who may for want of a better term be called traditional feminists, shared the former's desire for a public role and, somewhat surprisingly, both agreed on the general moral superiority of women. The differences lay in their conceptions of a proper public role. Radical feminists sought economic independence and access to the social and political activities then reserved to men. The traditional feminists sought public roles closely related to the functions usually served, or thought to be served, by women in society. The issue of economic independence was not particularly salient for them because most had sufficient leisure and wealth to afford public service without salary. Moreover, the public services in which they engaged were in institutions for poor children which could be seen as a variation of the theme of motherhood rather than as a form of competition with men [122]. Mrs. W.P. Lynde, speaking to the National Conference of Charities and Correction in 1879, summarized much of the traditional feminist view in observing that work with children offered the "truest and noblest scope for the public activities of women in time which they can spare from their primary domestic duties" [123]. The theme of the indispensability of a woman's touch in dealing with children was regularly sounded; a reformatory without a woman, it was said, is "like a home without a mother—a place of desolation. In reformatory work woman is the good mother. . . . She is the one to whom all look for comfort and relief" [124].

Because the conservative activists relied heavily on traditional role notions, they were jealously protective of the customary conception of the family and the woman's place in it. Angela Bailey Ormsbee, writing on "Wives and Daughters in the Home," urged women to "so spend our days that we may not lessen the mighty tide of womanly influence, remembering always that however great or renowned we may become as artists, poets, scholars or philanthropists, we decrease the debt America owes to wives and daughters if we belittle in any way the hearthstone, the keystone to our nation's prosperity" [125]. By the same token, the child-savers were bound to see widespread inadequacy in institutions for dealing with children, and most particularly the family, if their public function was to be an important one. Here, too, they succeeded. Miriam Van Waters, a staunch spokesperson for the juvenile court movement and for women's roles in it, actually saw salvation for society in helpful intervention:

> It is significant that it was in America that the first juvenile court arose, for from America about the same time the civilized world received its first warning that all was not well with that ancient institution, the home. The first decade of the juvenile court marks the beginning of the rise of the curve of the broken home, which is still mounting. . . . It would appear almost as if the children's court movement were one of those protective devices by which the human race has so often, with apparent blindness, yet with ultimate wisdom, averted or nullified the consequences of some great doom [126].

Both radical and traditional feminists contributed to public concern over the capacity of families to rear their children. The views expressed by the former seemed to suggest abandonment of maternal functions at a time when the need for parental supervision seemed peculiarly great. Compulsory education, child-labor laws, and the discovery by psychologists of the notion of adolescence combined to provide a prolonged period of infancy which occasionally was described as a "natural right" of childhood. The demands of radical feminists were obviously at cross-purposes with maternal (and therefore parental) discharge of that right, and ultimately indicated the need for other agencies to protect the "rights" of children. Traditional feminists, on the other hand, were predisposed to see widespread familial breakdown, in part because they shared common middle class views and in part because their public roles depended on the existence of family disorder. They were prepared to step into the breach created by urban corruption and family dissolution, and step they did. Women lobbied for adoption of child protective legislation, most notably statutes creating juvenile courts, and served as probation officers, contributed to and assisted in detention facilities for children, and in some cities participated in the selection of judicial and other personnel to administer the schemes they had promoted. Mothers *manquées*, truth be told, thrived on the perceived collapse of natural institutions for child care.

The Place and Rights of Children and the State

The current scheme of regulation of children is largely that created at the end of the nineteenth and the beginning of this century. It assumes much about the place of children in society and much about the role of society with respect to its young.

The reformers of the turn of the century created for children a special place in society which was closely related to their perceptions of social and economic reality. Whereas Puritans tended to applaud precocity since it revealed loss of childhood wickedness [127], late nineteenth century opinion sought to remove children from adult activities and character. The young would neither work nor idle, but engage—for a period far more prolonged than had previously been approved—in education and development under the eye of a wise guardian. Their business was the business of perfection and immortality, for in their progress lay the possibility of general social perfection.

Dissociation of children from adult activities was supported by recognition of a growth process distinguishing them psychologically from adults. Progressive educational theory obviously relied on notions of organic development, and the discovery during the same period of adolescence—a natural time of "storm and stress" during which the youth's "previous selfhood is broken up . . . and a new individual is in the process of being born" [128]—came also to confirm the importance of a proper, sheltering environment for the young. Since the chief characteristic of adolescence is instability and vulnerability to various "temptations," it is not surprising to find that concern for proper environment was particularly acute in urban settings. The city loomed as the "prime source of corrupting influences for the young. Its chaotic social and economic life, its varied population, its frenzied commercial spirit, and its dazzling entertainments were all sharply antagonistic to proper growth towards adulthood" [129]. Insulation from this environment was commonly seen as the principal object of the urban family with a developing child: a view that sharply distinguishes modern from Puritan perceptions. Adolescence implies transition or development towards adulthood quite as much as it does the loss of youthful qualities. The Puritan association of childhood with wickedness led them to emphasize development toward maturity; the duties of children to parents were, in any event, more a function of generation than age, as we have seen. Modern views, however, disvalued the developmental aspect of adolescence and, by insulating older children from the adult environment, sought to maintain youthful innocence at the cost of prolonging infantilization in some degree [130].

The development of this sense of place apart from adults was accompanied by the idea of the child's "right" to his place. When parents neglected their children, they deprived them of the "right to life, liberty and pursuit of happiness" to which children are entitled. The child who had gone wrong, by disobedience to his parents or by criminal misbehavior, was described as one who "has lost or has never known the fundamental rights of childhood to parental shelter, guidance, and control" [131]. Prolonged infancy itself was described as a natural right of which youth could not properly be deprived [132]. The same notion has been reaffirmed by juvenile court judges as recently as 1967 in declaring that the child's "fundamental right" is not to liberty but to custody—that is, to care, control and education [133].

This notion of children's "rights" is, perhaps, an unusual one, since it is one that cannot be exercised or, particularly, waived by its holder. Use of such language reveals a certain delicacy on the part of reformers in describing what they had in mind for children. True enough, there was a duty involved, located with the child's parents, but that duty was clearly a matter of state interest. It would have been more accurate, if less politic, to say that the parent owed to the state a duty of proper child-rearing which, if not discharged, entitled the state to intervene to assure that the child received proper care, whether he liked it or not.

The rhetoric of children's rights served, however, to define in less authoritarian and more palatable terms society's role in dealing with children. It was, simply, to intervene as far as necessary to take those children who seemed likely to go wrong and place them on the road to good citizenship. The child-savers, like their Puritan ancestors, took a simplistic view of child-rearing: one which attributed youthful misbehavior to parental failure and inferred from parental failure the likelihood of future deviance. As Judge Cabot said with respect to juvenile court jurisdiction, "Remember the fathers and mothers have failed, or the child has no business [in the court], and it is when they failed that the state opened this way to receive them, into the court, and said, 'This is the way in which we want you to grow up'" [134]. Neglect, disobedience, and crime were viewed as parts of a single process, moving from parental failure to criminality. Moreover, like causes produced like prescriptions. Since deviance resulted from parental neglect, provision of care was appropriate to both criminal and protocriminal. That neglected and deviant children should be treated alike was expressly urged by most proponents of juvenile court legislation, including Judge Mack, who asked rhetorically:

> Why is it not just and proper to treat these juvenile offenders, as we deal with the neglected children, as a wise and merciful father handles his own child whose errors are not discovered by the authorities. . . . [T]he child who has begun to go wrong, who is incorrigible, who has broken a law or an ordinance, is to be taken in hand by the state . . . because either the unwillingness or inability of the natural parents to guide it toward good citizenship has compelled the intervention of public authorities . . . [135].

As Judge Mack's notion that the state can take a person by the hand suggests, courts, administrative agencies, and volunteers were literally thought to act as surrogate parents. Judges not only represented the authority of fathers but were expected to be fathers to the children who came before them. Judge Stubbs of Indianpolis personified that belief in saying that "[I]f I could get close enough to [the delinquent boy] to put my hand on his head and shoulder, or my arm around him, in nearly every case I could get his confidence" [136]. Maternal roles were likewise directly incorporated into programs for dealing with children; female social workers, probation officers, and volunteers would supply the gentle discipline, care and education lacking from natural mothers. Even the court itself was to act as the family would in dealing with its children; formal procedure was eliminated in favor in informal treatment.

> [T]he proceedings under this [juvenile court] law are in no sense criminal proceedings. . . . They are simply statutory proceedings by which the state in the legitimate exercise of its police power, or, in other words, its right to preserve its own integrity and future existence, reaches out its arm in a kindly way and provides for the protection of its children from parental neglect or from vicious influences and surroundings, either by keeping watch over the child while in its natural home, or, where that seems impracticable, by placing it in an institution designed for the purpose [137].

It is true that the child-savers never admitted that they were weakening the natural family; indeed, juvenile court legislation and authoritative spokesmen alike claimed that intervention was designed to strengthen the family [138]. How seriously this pretension should be taken, having regard both to the nature of the strategy involved and the general view concerning the adequacy of certain kinds of families, is debatable. What is certain is that nineteenth and twentieth century progressives were willing to engage in large-scale societal activity to promote the place of children, and that in doing so they were ready to displace natural parents as the nurturers of the young.

CONCLUSION

The theory of society's relationship to children and parents developed during the last century is both forward and backward looking. There is a romantic if not nostalgic quality in its emphasis on the disappearance of the kind of family associated with the nation's colonial period: one in which the Anglo-Saxon father dispensed moral and vocational education to his children while the mother attended to the care of the very young and to the family's general needs. As that institution dissolved under the press of industrialization, immigration, urbanization, and divorce, a replacement was urgently sought. The state itself, through its judicial and correctional agencies, ultimately assumed that role.

There is, therefore, at least a measure of continuity in American views concerning the family and its children. The form of colonial families remained a model for modern views, and progressives, like Puritans, looked to the family for the rearing of the young. Both saw in good parental influence the improvement of society and in its failure crime and social disorder. Both adopted strategies for dealing with perceived parental failure, whether it appeared through the actions of the parents or the conduct of the young. Moreover, the later reformers borrowed extensively and directly from techniques of colonial regulation. One can, without difficulty, find not only the root but also the trunk of many current laws governing parent-child relations in seventeenth century America. The Massachusetts stubborn child law, upheld against constitutional attack in 1971, is a modest revision of the Massachusetts Bay Colony statute of 1654, passed because even then it appeared "by too much experience that divers children & servants doe behave themselves too disrespectively, disobediently, & disorderly towards their parents, masters, & gouvernors, to the disturbance of families, & discouragement of such parents and gouvernors" [139]. Most if not all modern statutes creating jurisdiction over incorrigible children, whether as delinquents or by some other name, have the same origin. Current neglect statutes can similarly be traced to poor laws and special ordinances requiring colonial parents to maintain and educate their young. Finally, great pains were taken by proponents of juvenile courts, in particular, to rest their intervention upon the established English equity doctrine by which courts acting as *parens patriae* exercised power over children [140].

This appeal to continuity on the part of the nineteenth and twentieth century reformers obviously had a metaphorical quality, particularly with respect to *parens patriae* jurisdiction. Its most significant effect, however, lay in masking grave differences in Puritan and Progressive expectations for families and children. In reality, only the form of the early family could have appealed to modern social architects. Puritan family roles were, after all, defined in view of the authoritarian and anti-democratic theories of sixteenth and seventeenth century society. The unconditional duty of submission owed by children to parents was of a piece with the duty owed by subject to sovereign, and it is not self-evident that one without the other is sensible, at least if one believes that as the sapling is bent, the tree will grow. Surely, the political society which Puritans expected to develop from the authoritarian family would have been abhorrent to progressives who, in their own political program, sought to restore (if it ever existed) popular control over government [141]. How the Fifth Commandment, which to Puritans was not only the source of the child's duty but was taken to be God's repudiation of democracy, could be adapted to Progressive needs was never very clear.

Puritan psychology and moral education would not have been more appealing to this century's reformers. Colonial guides to the parent insisted strictly upon breaking the will of the innately wicked child. Fathers in particular were enjoined to train their children in such a way that they would accept without question both the parent's will and Puritan discipline. Both the technique and the goal were opposed to nineteenth and twentieth century views. Modern educational and reformatory theory rely heavily on pursuasion rather than force and often frankly condemned earlier modes. Horace Bushnell observed,

> [T]here is a kind of virtue, my brethren, which is not in the rod—the virtue, I mean, of a truly good and sanctified life. . . . There are, too, I must

warn you, many who talk much of the rod as the orthodox symbol of parental duty, but who might really as well be heathens as Christians. . . . It is frightful to think how they batter and bruise the delicate, tender souls of their children . . . [142].

Few Puritans would have been moved by the notion of childrens' tender souls, and Bushnell's emphasis on parental love would have been equally unusual. Affection for one's children was little recommended and often disapproved, not only by Puritans but generally prior to the nineteenth century, perhaps because such affection is a luxury when infant mortality rates are high and epidemics common [143]. The concern for infant death expressed by anti-feminists at the turn of this century suggests that the loss of children had come to be viewed as extraordinary; it is probably no coincidence that, during the same period, tender concern for the welfare of children as children became salient.

In substantive matters, the gulf between Puritans and Progressives is equally wide. Moral education in New England implied the inculcation of traditional rules and institutions embodied in the Covenant and in civil sovereignty, an attitude that denied everything the Enlightenment promised by way of social progress. The duty of obedience owed by children was identical with the duty to accept revealed truth, yet revealed truth was a principal source of the corruption which in nineteenth century thought impeded the perfection of society. To mold the institution to the boy, as progressive educators and reformatory workers had it, would approach anarchy in Puritan opinion; to educate children so as to reproduce the qualities of the larger society, as Puritans required, was centrally inconsistent with the progress that nineteenth and twentieth century educators sought to achieve.

Summarily put, Puritan incorrigibility laws were sensible because it was assumed that parents are godly and children wicked; when those propositions are reversed, as nineteenth and twentieth century reformers tended to believe, the laws lose part of their rationale. Colonial laws were, in addition, defensible because there was need to keep children under parental tutelage for moral and general educational purposes; the duty of obedience is, however, less rational when it is assumed that parental tutelage is of such doubtful use that responsibility for education is located in public agencies. Finally, incorrigibility laws may have been economically valuable to enforce children's service to their parents, but not when, as at the turn of this century, the family has ceased to function as a unit of economic production and when labor by children outside of the family is discouraged.

If Puritan ideas of child-rearing were almost entirely unacceptable to those who created the modern scheme of government treatment of children and families, how then to explain the continued appeal of colonial strategies and rhetoric? It may be that, in part, resort to tradition was a useful strategy for minimizing the pervasiveness of intervention that marked nineteenth and twentieth century child-saving programs. An effort to restore lost virtue seems less radical than one to create a new system for dealing with an ancient institution. It may also be that the colonial family, like the modern city, came to serve as a symbol for the general social order. Reference to the Puritan family was ultimately little related to what that family really signified, but rather expressed the reformers' longing for a society without the factories, crime, divorce, and social disorganization they saw about them. That the colonial family was designed to serve social, political and economic goals which differed sharply from the expectations they themselves held for that institution became irrelevant.

Symbolic adoption of Puritan family notions and almost literal reenactment of colonial laws cannot be regarded merely as an historical curiosity. It has had real costs, particularly in obscuring the necessity of developing an approach to dealing with parents and children compatible with current conditions and belief. One manifestation of the resulting discomfort is in the now widely accepted movement to treat incorrigible children differently from those who commit crimes, precisely because the wrongfulness of disobedience and the rightness of parents cannot uniformly be assumed. Indeed, over the past two decades, more than half of the states and most model acts have created new jurisdictional categories, variously denominated "Person in Need of Supervision," "Child in Need of Supervision," or the like to cover cases in which the questioned conduct consists solely in disobedience to parental commands [144]. The theory underlying an early model statute, the Standard Juvenile Court Act, represents the now general view:

[I]t is clear that these children are not so much at war with themselves as with their parents. It is equally valid, legally and behaviorally, to say that their parents (or other custodians) are at war with them. The [Standard Act] properly lays no blame in a situation where a child is 'beyond the control of his parent.' We have all seen situations . . . in which the child beyond control is sound and healthy, and the lack of control is due to attempts at excessive control, to highly disciplinary or authoritarian attitudes in control, or to some ignorance or neurotic need on the part of the parent that a normal child may naturally resist [145].

If it seems that the kind of family here described as unhealthy would have been considered well-ordered in colonial New England, that can only add to the conviction that modern child-saving theory and Puritan views of the family are fundamentally incompatible.

Creation of separate jurisdictional categories for incorrigible children, however, goes only so far in resolving the ambivalence incorporated in early laws. Use of a new category for disobedient children typically involves only a change in the formal label to be applied or in the name of the dispositional facility used. Such statutes do not provide a coherent theory for intervention in parent-child disputes. At the most, they assume that youthful disobedience reveals a problem in the family of sufficient gravity to require official intervention and assistance. Although a finding of pathology is substituted for one of blame, the effect of such a change on young persons may not be appreciably different. In addition, the basis for routinely assuming the existence of such pathology in cases of parent-child disagreement has not yet been specified, perhaps because traditional notions of obedience maintain their influence. Nor have the consequences of intervention been fully considered either in light of current child-rearing expectations or in view of what is now known about the effects of judicial activity on its subjects [146]. Yet, without convincing reason for concluding that incorrigibility reveals some abnormal development, without a theory that satisfactorily defines the kind of socialization expected, and without evaluation of the utility of judicial-correctional intervention in this area, courts are left with only the Fifth Commandment to justify and guide their actions.

NOTES TO CHAPTER 1

1. *H. Maine, Ancient Law* 133 (1884).
2. 2 *F. Pollock* and *F. Maitland, The History of English Law* 436—37 (1968).
3. As Goebel has observed, "The family unit in medieval England possessed a far greater corporate unity in fact than the law was ever disposed to admit." *J. Goebel, Cases and Materials on the Development of Legal Institutions* 487 (3rd ed. 1946). Agricultural domains required cooperative enterprise by the entire family, and the duties of children and wives in general were defined respectively by the Fifth Commandment and the gospel of St. Paul. However, the resulting patriarchal family structure with its mutual dependency went largely ignored by the common law. *See id.* at 487—488.
4. Stone, "Marriage Among the English Nobility," in *The Family: Its Structure and Functions* 153, 154 (R. Coser, ed. 1964).
5. Thus, there might well be a dozen members of a household in sixteenth century Exeter, England, and families in colonial New England likewise tended to considerable size. *C. Hill, Society and Puritanism in Pre-Revolutionary England* 443—44 (1964) (hereafter cited as *Society and Puritanism*); Greven, "Family Structure in Seventeenth-Century Andover, Massachusetts," 23 *William & Mary Quarterly* 234, 236—38 (3rd ser. 1966); Demos, "Notes on Life in Plymouth Colony," 22 *William & Mary Quarterly* 264, 270 (3rd ser. 1965).
6. *E.g.,* M. *Bloch, Feudal Society* 137—142 (tr. L.A. Manyon, 1961); *P. Aries, Centuries of Childhood: A Social History of the Family, passim* (1962). Bloch dates the contraction of the family from the thirteenth century, whereas Aries concludes that the concept of the family was unknown in the middle ages.
7. *P. Aries, Supra* note 6 at 353.
8. A corollary of feudal emphasis on personal service was its concern with the rights and obligations of individuals as representatives of groups rather than on corporate rights or relationships. In the Domesday Book, for example, the basic unit was not the village as a group of residents but the village regarded as a manor belonging to a lord. "In the eyes of the law, the man who 'answers for the

manor' becomes more and more the owner of the manor, and the old village organization slips more into the background." 1 *G.M. Trevelyan, History of England* 172—73 (1953). *See also, Goebel, Supra* note 3 at 488.

9. For a summary of these rules and their relation to the family, *see Goebel, Supra* note 3 at 458—461.

10. *See id.* at 459.

11. A male with military obligations, for example, reached majority at twenty-one, when he was strong enough to bear the armor of a knight, but one with agricultural duties did so at fifteen when he could manage a plough. *Id.* at 460.

12. *See id.* at 461.

13. *Id.* at 487.

14. Initially, wage laborers typically had holdings of their own and were not entirely dependent on wages for a livelihood. Wage labor should be contrasted with serfdom; those who received salaries did so as free and not bound agents of the lords for whom they worked. *See C. Hill, Change and Continuity in Seventeenth Century England* 220 (1974).

15. The first of the series of labor regulations commonly known as "poor laws" appeared in 1349. Ordinance of Laborers, 22 Edw. 3, c. 7 (1349); 1 Stat. Realm 307 (1870). For a history of this statutory scheme, *see Riesenfeld,* "The Formative Era of American Public Assistance Law," 43 *Calif. L. Rev.* 175 (1955).

16. A contemporary observer reports that "The labourers, however, were so arrogant and hostile that they did not heed the king's command, but if anyone wished to hire them, he had to pay them what they wanted, and either lose his fruits and crops or satisfy the arrogant and greedy desire of the labourers as they wished." Obviously, responsibility was shared by the lords and abbotts who paid higher wages and they were fined. Laborers, however, were often imprisoned until they promised to take only the wages set by custom. *Chronicon Henrici Knighton,* J.R. Lumby, ed., Rolls Series, vol. 92, trans. M.M.M., in *The Portable Medieval Reader* 216, 220—21 (J.B. Ross and M.M. McLaughlin eds., 11th ed. 1960).

17. *See H. Belloc, A Shorter History of England* 237 (1934).

18. Ashley well describes the antithetical relationship of towns and commercial activity to the feudal scheme: "The growth of the towns means the appearance of non-feudal and non-agricultural forces in society; the rise of a non-service middle class; the appearance of ideas of contract as opposed to custom, and of payment in money as contrasted with payment in kind or in service. . . ." *Ashley, Economic Organization of England* 25—26, quoted in *Goebel, Supra* note 3 at 330.

19. *See generally, C. Hill, Supra* note 14 at 81 *et seq.*

20. The texts supporting this view included Matt. 19:21 ("If thou wilt be perfect, go and sell that thou hast and give to the poor") and Luke 9:3 ("Take nothing for your journey, neither staves, nor scrip, neither bread, neither money; neither have two coats apiece"). *R.H.C. Davis, A History of Medieval Europe* 356 (1958). There was, however, dispute concerning the activities of the mendicant orders, partially on the basis that they took charity better devoted to the inmates of leper homes, asylums, and other really poor people who, as Pierre

D'Ailly observed in *De Reformatione*, "are truly entitled to beg." *J. Huizinga, The Waning of the Middle Ages* 153 (1954).

21. *C. Hill, supra* note 14 at 95, 97.

22. Walzer, "Puritanism as a Revolutionary Ideology," in *Essays in American Colonial History* 25, 40—46 (P. Goodman, ed.) (2nd ed. 1972).

23. *T. Hobbes, Leviathan* 66, 64—65 (1965). Another classic presentation is found in Sir Robert Filmer's *Patriarchea* (1680), which found the absolute authority of kings to derive lineally from the authority granted by God to Biblical patriarchs and, ultimately, to Adam. *See C. Brinton, Ideas and Men* 285—292 (1950).

24. Two Elizabethan Diaries 69 (M. Knappen, ed. 1933), quoted in Walzer, *supra* note 22 at 42.

25. *R. Bolton, Two Sermons I*, 10 (1635) quoted in *Walzer, supra* note 22 at 41.

26. On the importance of discipline in Puritan thought, *see Society and Puritanism*, particularly c.6, and *Walzer, supra* note 22 at 40—46.

27. The use of the term "calling" by Luther and Protestants generally in referring to worldly and economic activities reveals the explicitly spiritual basis of the duty to work. *See M. Weber, The Protestant Ethic and the Spirit of Capitalism* 79—92 (tr. T. Parsons, 1958).

28. *Society and Puritanism* at 144; *Walzer, supra* note 22 at 41.

29. Thus, one Puritan spokesman wrote that "The poor in all places are for the most part the most void of grace" and another that vagrants "are (for the most part) a cursed generation." *Id.* at 285, 283.

30. W. and M. Haller, "The Puritan Art of Love," 5 *Huntington Library Quarterly* 247, quoted in *Society and Puritanism* at 458.

31. *Society and Puritanism* at 459.

32. *C. Mather, A Family Well-Ordered* 3—4 (1699), quoted in *D. Flaherty, Privacy in Colonial New England* 56 (1972).

33. *B. Wadsworth, Well-Ordered Family* 84 (1719), quoted in *E. Morgan, The Puritan Family* 139 (1966). *See also C. and K. George, The Protestant Mind of the English Reformation* 275 (1961); *E. Morgan, Supra, passim; Society and Puritanism* 443 *et seq.*

34. Dod and Cleaver, *The Ten Commandements* 145, quoted in *Society and Puritanism* at 443.

35. *Sermons or Homilies appointed to be read in Churches* 330 (1802), quoted in *id.* at 129.

36. *Id.* at 130.

37. Robinson, "Of Children and their Education" (1628), in *Child-Rearing Concepts, 1628—1861*, 9, 14 (P. J. Greven, ed. 1973).

38. *R. Cleaver* and *J. Dod, A Godly Form of Household Government*, Sig. P 6 and 7 (1621), quoted in *Walzer, supra* note 22 at 44.

39. *See Society and Puritanism* at 257—58.

40. Flaherty's caution in this regard is well taken.

It is essential not to label as Puritan those statutory enactments of the first settlers that were primarily a reflection of the authoritarianism of seventeenth century governments. According to Perry Miller, if 'we wish to take Puritan culture as a whole, . . . about ninety per cent of the intellectual life, scientific knowledge, morality, manners and customs, notions and prejudices, was that of all Englishmen.' Although the advent of Puritan ideology in England infused a new source of strength into the movement for moral reform, this movement itself was by no means a new phenomenon. Motivated more often by economic and social considerations than by religious impulses, local English authorities had long been implementing the kinds of measures that have been branded as wholly Puritan in derivation when enacted in colonial New England. The values that New Englanders embodied in their criminal laws were a combination of typical authoritarian attitudes and the particular world view of a Puritan. *D. Flaherty, supra* note 32 at 165.

41. 35 Eliz. c. 1. *See Society and Puritanism* at 446−47.

42. A study of the town of Exeter, for example, revealed a comprehensive scheme of regulation of private lives, a pattern said to be typical of sixteenth and seventeenth century England. *W. MacCaffrey, Exeter, 1540−1640: The Growth of an English County Town* (1958). And, in his first directive to high constables, Chief Justice Coke required that "all unlawful games, drunkenness, whoredom, and incontinency in private families . . . be reported, as on their good governance the commonwealth depends." Quoted in *D. Flaherty, Supra* note 32 at 165.

43. *See Society and Puritanism* at 246. The wrong-headedness of the ecclesiastical courts lay in two directions. On the one hand, they were over-lenient in punishing those who committed many crimes within their jurisdiction; thus, a Puritan petition to Parliament in 1584 asked for stronger laws against fornication than "only to stand in a white sheet as the manner is now." *Id.* On the other hand, the courts punished with relative severity behavior—such as working on the many Saints days—which was thought by Puritans not only proper but divinely commanded. *See generally, id.* at 145−218 on the Sabbatarian controversy, of which the latter issue is a part.

44. *E. Morgan, The Puritan Dilemma* 40 (1958).

45. *See Walzer, supra* note 22 at 37.

46. *Id.* at 40−42.

47. *The General Laws and Liberties of the Massachusetts Colony* (1672) in *Juvenile Offenders for a Thousand Years* 318−19 (W. Sanders, ed. 1970) (hereafter cited as *Sanders*). Biblical annotations commonly followed the laws of the 1648 code and the language of the laws often closely tracked the injunctions from which they derived.

Connecticut adopted almost an identical provision in 1650, as had the Massachusetts Bay Colony in 1646. *The Code of 1650, Being a Compilation of the Earliest Laws and Orders of the General Court of Connecticut* 30−32 (1822), in *Sanders* at 318; 3 *Records of the Governor and Company of Massachusetts Bay in New England, 1628−1686* at 101 (N. Shurtleff, ed.), in 1 *Children and Youth in America: A Documentary History* 38 (R. Bremner, ed. 1970) (hereafter cited as *Bremner*).

48. *Id.*

49. 1 *A. Calhoun, A Social History of the American Family* 121 (1917) (hereafter cited as *Calhoun*).

50. *D. Flaherty, supra* note 32 at 56–57.

51. *Greven, supra* note 5 at 235.

52. *Id.* at 245–46.

53. See B. *Bailyn, Education in the Forming of American Society* 23 (1960).

54. *Laws and Liberties of Massachusetts* (1648), in 1 *Bremner* at 40.

55. See E. *Morgan, The Puritan Family* 149–150, 77–78 (1966).

56. *Id.* at 149.

57. *Id.*

58. *Laws and Liberties of Massachusetts* (1648), in 1 *Bremner* at 40–41.

59. *E. Morgan, Supra* note 55 at 78.

60. *Id.* at 42.

61. Kett, "Adolescence and Youth in Nineteenth-Century America," in *The Family in History: Interdisciplinary Essays* 95, 97 (T.K. Rabb and R.I. Rotberg, eds. 1973).

62. *Id.*

63. See W. *Trattner, From Poor Law to Welfare State* 19 (1974).

64. See C. *Brinton, Ideas and Men* 369 *et seq.* (1950).

65. *A. Pope, An Essay on Man*, Epistle II, in *The Selected Poetry of Pope* 123, 133 (M. Price, ed., 1970).

66. *A.O. Lovejoy, The Great Chain of Being* 9 (1960).

67. Quoted in *C. Brinton, Supra* note 64 at 387–88.

68. *D. Rothman, The Discovery of the Asylum* 64–65 (1971).

69. Demos and Demos, "Adolescence in Historical Perspective," 31 *J. Marriage and the Family* 632, 633 (1969).

70. *E.g.*, *A. de Tocqueville, Democracy in America* 192–97 (tr. H. Reeve, 1945).

71. *Demos* and *Demos, supra* note 69 at 633.

72. B. *Bailyn, Education in the Forming of American Society* 24–25 (1960).

73. *Id.* at 25.

74. See generally, *R. Hofstadter, America at 1750: A Social Portrait* 3–32 (1973).

75. *Id.* at 22.

76. *Id.* at 23, n. 6.

77. The strength of feeling about immigration is reflected in the bitterness of editorials as well as letters, as the following item from the Virginia *Gazette* (in 1751) reveals:

> When we see our papers fill'd continually with accounts of the most audacious robberies, the most cruel murders, and infinite other villainies perpetrated by convicts transported from Europe, what melancholy, what terrible reflections it must occasion! What will become of our posterity? These are some of thy favours Britain. Thou art called our Mother Country; but what good mother ever sent thieves and villains to accompany her children; to corrupt some with their infectious vices and murder the rest?

Id. at 48–49.

78. New York Children's Aid Society, *First Annual Report* 3—6 (1854), in 1 *Bremner* at 420—21.

79. "The multitude of emigrants from the old world, interfused among our population, is rapidly changing the identity of American character. These strangers come among us, ignorant of our institutions, and unacquainted with the modes of thought and habits of life peculiar to a free people. . . . Would it be strange if in such circumstances, many should mistake lawless freedom from restraint, for true and rational liberty? Shall these adopted citizens become a part of the body politic, and firm supporters of liberal institutions, or will they prove to our republic what the Goths and Huns were to the Roman Empire? The answer to this question depends in a great degree upon the wisdom and fidelity of our teachers and associated influences." B. Labaree, "The Education Demanded by the Peculiar Character of Our Civil Institutions," in *The Lectures Delivered Before the American Institute of Instruction, 1849*, 33—35 (1850), in 1 *Bremner* at 457—58.

80. 1 *Bremner* at 73; 1 *Calhoun* at 72—74.

81. 2 *Calhoun* at 175.

82. *Id.* at 197.

83. *Id.* at 198.

84. A typical explanation of the common school movement is found in the *First Annual Report of the [Ohio] Superintendent of Common Schools* 16—18 (1838), in 1 *Bremner* at 453:

> Though a great majority of our citizens are enlightened and intelligent, it must be admitted, that quite a number do not regard the education of their children with sufficient interest to induce proper individual action; and unless provision for these, other than parental, be made, they will be even worse situated, in many cases, than the orphan.

See generally, sources reproduced in 1 *Bremner* at 439—477.

85. *Twenty-Seventh Annual Report of the Trustees of the Public School Society of New York* 14—16 (1832), in 1 *Bremner* at 260.

86. *See* H. Folks, *The Care of Destitute, Neglected, and Delinquent Children* 3—11 (Reprinted, 1970).

87. *Id.* at 199 *et seq.*

88. New York Society for the Reformation of Juvenile Delinquents, *Memorial to the Legislature of New York . . . on the subject of erecting a House of Refuge* 22—26 (1824), in 1 *Bremner* at 679—680.

89. *Ex parte* Crouse, 4 Wharton (Pa.) 9 (1838).

90. *Labaree, supra* note 79 in 1 *Bremner* at 458.

91. *E.g.*, 3 *Calhoun* at 131.

92. *Id.*

93. E. Ryerson, "Between Justice and Compassion: The Rise and Fall of the Juvenile Court" 20—21 (Ph.D. dissertation, Yale University, 1970).

94. *See, e.g.*, Van Waters, "The Juvenile Court from the Child's Viewpoint," in *The Child, The Clinic and The Court* 217, 218 (J. Addams, ed. 1925); Mack, "The Juvenile Court," 23 *Harv. L. Rev.* 104 (1909).

95. Caldwell, "The Reform School Problem," *Proceedings of the National Conference on Charities and Correction* 71−76 (1886), quoted in *A. Platt, The Child Savers: The Invention of Delinquency* 52 (1969) (hereafter cited as *Platt*).

96. Glenn, "What Manner of Child Shall This Be?", *National Education Association Proceedings* 176−178 (1900), quoted in *R. Hofstadter, Anti-Intellectualism in American Life* 365 (1963) (hereafter cited as *Anti-Intellectualism*).

97. Mack, "The Chancery Procedure in the Juvenile Court," in *The Child, The Clinic and The Court* 310, 311−12 (J. Addams, ed. 1925).

98. *H. Spencer, Social Statics* 265−354 (1954).

99. *R. Hofstadter, Social Darwinism in American Thought* 41 (2nd ed. 1955).

100. Henderson, "Are Modern Industry and City Life Unfavorable to the Family?", in *Family in America* 93, 98 (1972) (Reprint of *Papers and Proceedings of the American Sociological Society*, 1908) (hereafter cited as *Family in America*).

101. See generally, *Platt* at 18−28.

102. Cooley, " 'Nature v. Nurture' in the Making of Social Careers," *Proceedings of the National Conference of Charities and Correction* 399−405 (1896), quoted in *Platt* at 34−35.

103. Caldwell, "The Duty of the State to Delinquent Children," *Proceedings of the National Conference of Charities and Correction* 404−10 (1898), quoted in *Platt* at 33−34.

104. *U.S. Bureau of Education, Legal Rights of Children* 31 (1880), reprinted in *The Legal Rights of Children* (1974). There were, it should be said, both related and unrelated concerns that also contributed to the growth of compulsory school statutes. Among the former one may include the continued belief that the immigrant classes which filled urban areas could not properly educate their children. Among the latter falls increasing concern over employment, particularly among unions in the more highly industrialized areas. Their interest in restricting child labor, which inflated the supply of cheap workers, was obviously supportive of compulsory school laws. On the unions and child labor, *see L. Friedman, A History of American Law* 491 (1973).

105. *Anti-Intellectualism* at 362−63.

106. The differences between old and new modes was described as follows by Francis Parker in 1878:

> It has been extremely difficult for me and my fellow-teachers to throw off the fetters of old habits of learning and teaching, the ancient deeply-rooted belief that words in themselves have some mysterious power of creating ideas; that memorized rules, definitions, paragraphs, constitute so much real knowledge; . . . that a great mass of disconnected facts is useful learning. . . . These great obstacles are being slowly overcome; teachers are beginning to appreciate the kind of mental food that is indispensable to true mental growth. The senses are trained by proper exercise; original observation and investigation are stimulated. . . . We try also to keep steadily in view the important fact that the mind grows entirely by its own activities; that explanations and lectures not assimilated by pupils are fully as bad as the old text-book methods.

Parker, "Report of the Superintendent," in *Report of the School Committee of the Town of Quincy for 1877–78*, 17–19 (1878), in 2 *Bremner* at 1132.

107. J. *Dewey, My Pedagogic Creed* 9 (1929), quoted in *Anti-Intellectualism* at 367. Dewey summarized as follows the points of contrast between traditional and progressive education:

> To imposition from above is opposed expression and cultivation of individuality; to external discipline is opposed free activity; to learning from texts and teachers, learning through experience; to acquisition of isolated skills and techniques by drill, is opposed acquisition of them as means of attaining ends which make direct vital appeal; to preparation for a more or less remote future is opposed making the most of opportunities of present life; to static aims and materials is opposed acquaintance with a changing world.

J. *Dewey, Experience and Education* 19–20 (1938).

108. *Anti-Intellectualism* at 373.

109. *Glenn, supra* note 96, quoted in *Anti-Intellectualism* at 364.

110. Verplanck, "Shortening the Period of Infancy," 27 *Education Review* 406–09 (April 1904), in 2 *Bremner* at 650–51.

111. *W.D. Morrison, Juvenile Offenders* 22 (1897), quoted in *Platt* at 37.

112. Mack, "The Juvenile Court," 23 *Harv. L. Rev.* 104, 116–17 (1909). The less humanitarian saw another risk in the ceaseless flow from abroad: a tendency to discourage reproduction of the fit and thereby increase the population of unfit citizens. Professor Charles Henderson of the University of Chicago and Dr. Francis A. Walker, who was variously president of Massachusetts Institute of Technology, the American Statistics Association, and the American Economics Association, observed with grave concern the decrease in middle class growth at the end of the century and attributed the decline to "the access of vast hordes of foreign immigrants, bringing with them a standard of living at which our own people revolted." *Henderson, supra* note 100 at 104–05.

113. *Platt* at 40.

114. *W. O'Neill, Divorce in the Progressive Era* 2 (1967).

115. *Id.* at 20.

116. *E.g., Henderson, supra* note 100 at 97–98.

117. *O'Neill, Supra* note 114 at 23.

118. *Henderson, supra* note 100 at 94.

119. *Family in America, Supra* note 100 at 38, 42.

120. Gilman, "How Home Conditions React Upon the Family," in *Family in America, Supra* note 100 at 16, 17.

121. *Id., passim.*

122. *Platt* at 75–100.

123. Mrs. Lynde went on to say:

> [Women] neither have nor desire political influence or place, but are ready to give of their talent and time to work for such benevolent or charitable purposes as may lie within the circle of their lives. These are largely women with no higher duty of domestic life demanding their first thought; widows, unmarried women, or women without children, with ability, and

often money, and a conscientious desire to do something that will fill their own lives.... The benefit of that experience, that can be learned so well nowhere else as in their own homes, beside the cradle of their own children, the state can never buy, but they are willing to give.

Lynde, "Prevention in Some of its Aspects," *Proceedings of the Annual Conference of Charities* 167 (1879), quoted in *Platt* at 80−81.

124. Sickels, "Woman's Influence in Juvenile Reformatories," *Proceedings of the National Conference of Charities and Correction* 164 (1894), quoted in *Platt* at 79.

125. Ormsbee, "Wives and Daughters in the Home," *The National Exposition Souvenir* 111 (1892).

126. *Van Waters, supra* note 94 at 218−19.

127. *Kett, supra* note 61 at 98−99.

128. G.S. Hall, "The Moral and Religious Training of Children," *Princeton Review* 26−48 (January, 1882), quoted in *Demos* and *Demos, supra* note 69 at 635.

129. *Demos* and *Demos, supra* note 69 at 635.

130. Something like this view is still held. The National Council of Juvenile Court Judges in 1967 declared that "Immaturity is the natural and normal condition of childhood. Immaturity is not bad, and it's unreasonable to endeavor to turn children into adults prematurely." 18 *Juvenile Court Judges Journal* 106, 107 (1967).

131. *Van Waters, supra* note 94 at 218.

132. *Verplanck, supra* note 110 at 650.

133. 18 *Juvenile Court Judges Journal* 106, 107 (1967).

134. Cabot, "The Detention of Children as a Part of Treatment," in *The Child, The Clinic and The Court* 246, 249 (J. Addams, ed. 1925).

135. Mack, "The Juvenile Court," 23 *Harv. L. Rev.* 104, 107 (1909).

136. *Children's Courts in the United States* xiii (S. Barrows, ed. 1904).

137. State v. Scholl, 167 Wis. 504, 509, 167 N.W. 830, 831 (1918). *See also,* Commonwealth v. Fisher, 213 Pa. 48, 62 Atl. 198 (1905).

138. "The object of the juvenile court and of the intervention of the state is, of course, in no case to lessen or to weaken the sense of responsibility either of the child or of the parent. On the contrary, the aim is to develop and to enforce it." Mack, "The Juvenile Court," 23 *Harv. L. Rev.* 104, 120 (1909).

139. Mass. Bay Records, Vol. III (1644−1657) 355, Mass. Colonial Laws 27 (1887). *See* Commonwealth v. Brasher, 270 N.E. 2d 389, 391 (Mass. 1971).

140. Originally, this was a relatively modest sort of jurisdiction, principally exercised with regard to lunatics and orphans who had no natural conservator. While Chancery courts generally assumed that they also possessed the power to remove a child from the care of unfit parents, the power was not readily exercised. In the first place, they would ordinarily refuse to remove a child from his father's custody if no independent source of support was available. *Wellesley v. Beaufort*, 2 Russ. Ch. 1, 21, 38 Eng. Rep. 236, 243 (1829). More important, Chancery was reluctant to interfere absent the most grave and special circumstances. The cases in which *parens patriae* jurisdiction was assumed with respect

to children with living parents were almost uniformly marked by aggravated factual patterns together with the threat that, without action, the child would be removed entirely from the court's superintending power. In *Cruise v. Hunter*, referred to in *Powel v. Cleaver*, 2 Bro. C.C. 502, 518, 29 Eng. Rep. 274, 283 (1790), the father was an outlaw who resided abroad; the Chancellor's order went no further than to restrain the father from taking the child to the continent or improperly interfering with his education. In *De Manneville v. De Manneville*, 10 Ves. Jun. 52, 32 Eng. Rep. 762 (1804), it appears that the Lord Chancellor intervened only because there was "a fair suspicion of real danger, that the child might be moved out of this country" by his father who was a French national. And the leading case of *Wellesley v. Beaufort, supra*, is in the same mold. The father had accrued debts in England to the point where he was forced to flee to the continent, where he committed repeated and flagrant adultery. Moreover, when the children visited him, the father sought purposely to teach them every vice found in the streets of Paris. The Court intervened when the father sought to assume their custody permanently and remove them to France for further instruction in applied evil.

141. *Ryerson, supra* note 93 at 20.

142. *H. Bushnell, Christian Nurture* (1847−1861), in *Child-Rearing Concepts, 1628−1861,* 138, 151 (P.J. Greven, ed. 1973).

143. *See E. Shorter, The Making of the Modern Family* 199−204 (1975) for both this theory and a critique of it.

144. For a listing, *see* Appendix A of this volume.

145. Rubin, "Legal Definition of Offenses by Children and Youths," 1960 *U. Ill. L.F.* 512, 514.

146. *See, e.g.,* Mahoney, "PINS and Parents," *supra* Chapter 4; Katz and Teitelbaum, "PINS Jurisdiction, the Vagueness Doctrine, and the Rule of Law," *supra* Chapter 6.

✳ *Chapter 2*

PINS Processing in New York: An Evaluation*

R. Hale Andrews, Jr.
Andrew H. Cohn

INTRODUCTION

Over ten thousand young people are processed each year in New York State Family Courts as "persons in need of supervision" (PINS) because they have committed offenses illegal only for persons under sixteen—staying out late, disobeying parents, running away, skipping school. This court processing can be a major incident in their lives with serious consequences [1]. At the minimum, "court" involves various intake procedures. Over 60 percent of alleged PINS also become respondents to formal court charges ("petitions") [2], while many of the 40 percent who are "adjusted" are referred elsewhere for counseling. Warrants are often issued for petitioned youths, and approximately a third of all respondents are detained prior to adjudication. Nearly half are eventually formally adjudicated PINS. Dispositions assigned them include withdrawal or dismissal, some form of probation, and "placement" in private or public agencies or in state training schools [3].

Laws making it illegal for young people to engage in certain non-criminal activities can be found as early as 1646 and are found in most if not all current juvenile codes [4]. Their importance is considerable: at least one-quarter of all juvenile adjudications nationally are for non-criminal misconduct [5], and it

*The authors wish to thank Family Court Administrative Judge Florence Kelley and Director of Probation John A. Wallace of New York County and Family Court Administrative Judge Robert J. Stolarik and Juvenile Probation Supervisor Michael Frenchak of Rockland County and their staffs for the records that were made available for our inspection and for the kind assistance that was extended to us. In addition, the authors wish to thank the Yale Law School for supporting computer analyses of our data, to thank Professor Joseph Goldstein for his helpful criticism of earlier drafts, and to express gratitude to the Institute of Judicial Administration—American Bar Association, Juvenile Justice Standards Project, and its late director, J. Lawrence Schultz, who sponsored our work.

appears that between 40 and 50 percent of all detained minors are charged with such offenses [6]. Originally, jurisdiction over behavior illegal only for minors was incorporated into existing definitions of delinquency, and that is often still the case. In the early 1960s, however, New York and California rewrote their juvenile laws to separate non-criminal and criminal juvenile offenders through the creation of a new jurisdictional category for the former, which in New York was designated "PINS" [7]. The aim was to augment the benefits the court brought to non-criminal youths, who would be spared the delinquency label and, the legislature hoped, provided new services [8]. The PINS statute, therefore, represented an even purer encapsulation of the juvenile court ideal than the court's delinquency jurisdiction. As one proponent of the statute wrote of PINS soon after its passage: "In this class of cases there is no need for judicial power, as in the case of crimes, in order to protect the community . . . *The goal is only to help the child . . .*" [9].

To achieve this general goal, the statute's framers avoided the delineation of standards as to what behavior was proscribed and simply gave the court jurisdiction over any person less than sixteen years old "who does not attend school in accord with the provisions of part one of article sixty-five of the education law or who is incorrigible, ungovernable, or habitually disobedient and beyond the lawful control of parent or other lawful authority" [10]. The statute as written thus makes whatever the youth has done unlawful as long as the parental command is lawful. Instead of standards, the statute relies almost exclusively on the presumed ability—and good intentions—of judges and probation officers to uncover the nature of a young person's problem and to foresee what court-imposed steps will produce a remedy.

In the fourteen years since its formulation, the New York PINS statute has spawned a host of MINS, CHINS, and other progeny and continues to serve as a model for reform [11]. However, there has been dissatisfaction with the PINS jurisdiction in recent years. A number of reports emanating directly or indirectly from the judiciary, for example, have focused on the problems of deteriorated public facilities for juveniles and upon the court's inability to command access for PINS youths to the selective private placement institutions [12]. Reports have also called attention to the inadequacy of resources in the court itself, especially in New York City [13], though judicial confidence in the court's ultimate capacity to help most PINS seemingly remains high [14].

Civil liberties reformers have criticized other aspects of this jurisdiction. There has been an increasing demand for extension of the constitutional rights recognized for delinquency cases [15] to PINS proceedings. The New York PINS statute has been attacked as unconstitutional, and litigation has occasionally produced results such as the decision in 1973 that PINS and delinquents could no longer be held in the same training schools [16].

In the course of these various criticisms, however, surprisingly little attention has been paid to what decisions the family court actually makes about PINS and how it reaches them. The report that follows presents the authors' findings in these respects. It is based on extensive court observation and data collection in two New York State counties, New York (Manhattan) and Rockland. Manhattan needs no further description. Rockland County is situated immediately to the north of New York City and, in 1970, had a population of less than one-quarter million. Although its population is largely "urban," the county includes no city of size. Its larger communities—New City, Nyack, Spring Valley, and Pearl River—are more towns than cities. Together, Manhattan and Rockland counties provide a portrait both of the state's urban centers and of its fast-growing suburban areas, each of which accounts for approximately one-half of the state's PINS jurisdiction. The two family courts and what happens in them present both contrasts and surprising similarities. They differ in physical facilities, available court resources, and in the types of complaints made against PINS. But underneath, they seem to function very much alike.

In subsequent pages, we examine decisionmakers and their decisions in these two counties. A brief summary of court processing is followed by a discussion of the setting and the principal actors in each county. We then present a statistical evaluation of the decisions made by these actors and analyze the results of court processing. The theories underlying the jurisdiction are examined next, and a new set of assumptions from which to approach PINS is suggested.

Note on Methodology

The manner by which cases were processed in each court was examined through three research techniques: a survey of PINS case histories as reconstructed from court, probation, and law guardian records of selected cases in 1972; extensive observation of the handling of PINS cases by courts and probation departments from June through September, 1973; and interviews with all major decisionmakers: judges, police, members of the respective probation departments, and law guardians.

Case Histories. Unless otherwise noted, all of the PINS statistics in this report are based on an analysis of complete histories of 234 PINS cases all of which began in 1972. A separate sample of thirty-one cases was selected to analyze delinquencies that were eventually treated as PINS cases; these cases are discussed separately in a later section of this report [17].

Each case history was compiled by assembling all available records on each case. These included court records (which noted formal appearances, decisions, and various judicial comments), probation files (which contained extensive personal and family information about each youth, various test results, and probation department recommendations for most decisions from intake to disposition), and law guardian files, which were made available to us in New York (no central files are kept by Rockland law guardians). The last occasionally held personal and family information that was not available from probation files, as well as various notations as to legal strategy. As many as five person-hours were spent gathering information on each case by the authors and four research assistants. Anonymity was preserved by substitution of numbers for names, pursuant to agreements made with the respective courts, probation departments, and law guardians.

Cases from 1972 were selected in order to obtain a sample recent enough to be representative of current practice but old enough so that the cases, in most instances, were no longer pending. By examining cases which began sometime between eighteen and six months prior to the time of data gathering, however, we decreased the available time period during which recidivism might be observed to occur. The data may therefore underestimate the rate of recidivism. The extent of such bias is probably minimized, however, by the fact that, since the average age of a PINS youth is about fourteen and one-half years, there generally remains less than a year after court processing within which a youth might recidivate and still be subject to family court jurisdiction.

The titles and positions of persons referred to in this report are those current in the summer of 1973. While there have been changes in personnel and minor changes in procedures since that time, these do not significantly affect the data and findings reported here.

The New York County cases were chosen by a 10 percent random sample [18]. In order to maintain a proportionate sample of cases throughout the year, every tenth case was chosen from the 1,119 cases listed in the probation intake unit docket book. This furnished 112 cases. Records for seven cases could not be obtained and replacement cases were added on the basis of a random digit choice. Due to time limitations only three replacement cases were chosen, yielding a final sample of 108 cases.

In Rockland County, in the absence of a master docket book containing adjusted and court cases, the total number of 1972 cases in each category was determined through an analysis of records and through interviews with probation department officials who handled intake. For cases going to court it was relatively simple to ascertain the total number from court docket sheets. For adjusted cases, a list of all cases noted in the probation department's ledger book was compiled. Entries were eliminated when it became clear that they represented incidents in which no intake procedure at all was involved, but involved some other departmental function. All 126 cases on this revised list of adjusted cases and on the complete docket of all cases going to court were selected for study. (Because different sampling proportions were used for New York and Rockland counties, findings will be expressed in terms of percentages rather than by absolute numbers.)

Forty-six percent of the sampled intake cases thus derive from New York County and 54 percent from Rockland County, a distribution that approximately reflects the proportions statewide between New York City and the rest of the state. Although no statewide records are compiled for cases coming to *intake* (the population from which we chose our cases), 46 percent of PINS *petitions* came from New York City and 54 percent from outside the city between July 1, 1971 and June 30, 1972, the "judicial year" by which the state court system keeps records [19]. Our study found only a 3 percent divergence in the rate at which cases were referred from intake to court in the two counties, and we are confident that the proportions of New York City and upstate cases coming to intake—as reflected in our sample—are very close to the proportions of New York City and upstate PINS petitions filed.

To the extent this sampling is unrepresentative, however, it probably understates the number of PINS from large central cities, since youths from such places as Buffalo, Rochester, Syracuse, and Albany (which the state court records system classes with upstate PINS cases) are probably more similar to PINS in New York City than to those from the towns and cities of Rockland County. Consequently, our study probably underrepresents the incidence of very poor and minority group youths and the problems that particularly characterize their cases, such as neglect [20].

Observations. The observational phase of this study was carried out by the authors and one research assistant for a period of approximately twelve weeks in the summer of 1973. Repeated observations were made of every stage of probation and court processing of cases, including intake interviews (with and without parents present), conversations between respondents and their attorneys, courtroom activity, discussions in judges' chambers, and probation supervision contacts. Observations were recorded after the event, and were later checked for accuracy in interviews. Observations were also rechecked by further observations and comparison of reactions and impressions [21].

It should be noted that the observations were not designed to catch instances of official misconduct, but to determine the basic pattern of case processing and why particular decisions were made. To the extent the presence of an observer might be thought to bias official behavior, any bias is likely to have been in the direction of greater conformity with formal regulations.

Interviews. Extensive interviewing was also conducted in the summer of 1973 by the authors and one assistant. Notes were taken during each interview and were transcribed as soon as possible thereafter in order to preserve the accuracy of the speaker's remarks. Most judges then sitting in the two counties were interviewed, as were many law guardians, probation officers and supervisors, school officials, police officers, and miscellaneous court personnel. These discussions provided a valuable opportunity to explore in depth the backgrounds and operative assumptions of decisionmakers and to clarify particular procedures. Reactions to hypotheses and impressions of the authors were also obtained. Certain comments are presented anonymously, usually at the request of those interviewed.

PINS PROCESSING UNDER THE STATUTE:
A MODEL

Most PINS cases begin with a phone call to the Family Court. All calls are referred to an "intake unit," maintained by the local probation department, whose mission is "to adjust suitable cases before a petition is filed" by means of informal negotiations between complainant and youth [22]. These negotiations can result in simple discontinuation of the complaint, in some form of voluntary counseling and assistance for the youth, or in a referral to court for a formal "petition."

The filing of a petition brings the appointment of a "law guardian" [23], an attorney who represents the youth at public expense. An indeterminate number of hearings may follow. If the youth refuses to appear, warrants may be issued [24]. The judge may order detention in either closed, "secure" facilities or open, "non-secure" facilities if the youth is thought dangerous or likely to run away [25].

If a case is neither withdrawn by the complainant nor dismissed by the judge, an adjudicatory hearing eventually will follow. The youth either admits that he is "in need of supervision," which "admission" is the equivalent of a guilty plea or, very infrequently, there is a trial of this issue. Successful defenses are rare. The prosecuting attorney need only prove that the youth has been involved in more than a single, isolated incident of truancy, disobedience, or other activity that the judge interprets as demonstrating that the child is "incorrigible" or "ungovernable" [26].

Upon a formal adjudication ("finding") of PINS, the court enters into the dispositional process. The judge customarily orders a probation department "investigation and report" prior to any decision. This examination of the youth's family life and personal background may be augmented by I.Q. tests, other evaluations, and diagnoses furnished by court psychiatrists and psychologists.

After the reports are received, the judge must decide on an "appropriate disposition" [27]. Frequently, he places the youth on probation. In cases thought to be more serious, a probation officer attempts to gain admission for the youth to one of the much desired private agencies or to a state camp or school. These institutions are, however, free to reject any youth and, if such efforts fail, the youth is usually assigned to training school [28]. On some occasions, however, a placement cannot immediately be effected and the youth is temporarily placed in the custody of the Department of Social Services. Such measures, while temporary, may continue for long periods while admission to private and state agencies is again sought.

NEW YORK COUNTY

The Setting

The New York County Family Court sits at the corner of Lexington Avenue and 22nd Street. It is ten stories tall, a light grey, Art Deco, stone building erected in 1939. Sculptured family groups (father, mother, and child, all in loin-cloths, grinding grain, working with a scythe, sawing and planting) surmount the first floor windows, and a legend over the door proclaims: "The Sanctity of the Home * The Integrity of the Family."

Now, in 1973, the building is outdated and overcrowded. The walls are a dirty tan, floors a scruffed tile, furniture old. In the summer it is very, very hot; only the courtrooms, judges' chambers and law guardians' offices are air-conditioned. The waiting facilities are crowded and uncomfortable, wooden benches set in rows, and there are, as a recent report on the court critically noted, no facilities for feeding its clients, many of whom have to wait all day [29].

A PINS case begins its life in court at probation intake on the first floor. It then comes before a judge in one of the two court intake "parts" (one-judge hearing units) on the third floor, and eventually goes to a trial part still higher in the building. The first stop, the Juvenile Intake Unit, is housed in a large, noisy, much-partitioned room.

In their attempts to fulfill the task of adjusting a case, the intake officers rely primarily upon a theoretically voluntary interview [30]. Youths are not informed that they have the option of not participating; one officer who began announcing this right of refusal found that no one would talk to her [31]. Voluntary or not, the process does not seem highly successful in resolving family conflicts; 59 percent of all alleged PINS brought to intake are referred for formal court action. Those children whose cases are adjusted are generally asked to attend some form of counseling institution or youth activity, such as the P.A.L. Outside referrals of this kind occur in 70 percent of adjusted New York cases.

Failing adjustment at this stage, a case is sent to the third floor for commencement of court proceedings. Families arriving there find a room the size of a basketball court, filled with wooden auditorium seats and crowded at all hours by parents, children, witnesses, and an occasional stray dog. The petition is typed in a corner of this area and then taken to one of the two court intake parts where hearings are held to consider the necessity of pre-trial detention, to attempt early resolution of the matter, and eventually to refer the case to a trial part for adjudication.

These two intake courtrooms are the largest in the building, and look the most official. However, the formal atmosphere is undermined by deteriorated conditions; while the judge's bench is elevated, the wood panelling that covers the walls is peeling, and in one courtroom the words "IN GOD WE TRUST" inscribed on the wall behind the judge have been reduced to " N   W TRU T."

All courtrooms are staffed by two uniformed court officers with a holstered pair of handcuffs at the belt. They call the cases, introduce parties, and ensure respect for the judicial process by forcing removal of chewing gum and abandonment of newspapers. Paper work is handled by a court reporter and a court secretary. On occasion, an interpreter is required; perhaps one-quarter of the cases involve at least one person who cannot speak English and a Spanish-speaking interpreter is necessarily on call at all times. The public, however, is excluded [32]. The court proceeds at a brisk pace, with judges never leaving their desks as a stream of twenty-five or thirty cases comes through, accompanied by a shuffle of papers so constant and so unending that it seems the court's raison d'être— especially since action is rarely taken beyond hearing a brief "report" and scheduling another appearance.

A case may remain in one of the intake parts for a greater or lesser time, depending on the judge's hopes for settling the dispute informally. There is often, however, an emotional battle over detention, which youths resist fiercely, and the facilities, which are a major public scandal [33].

Sooner or later, many cases are settled at intake: 88 percent of PINS petitions in New York are eventually withdrawn by the complainants or dismissed by the court, and a good portion of these dispositions occur while the case is still in one of the intake parts. If a case is not so settled, however, it must eventually be assigned to one of six trial parts.

These six units are primarily on the sixth and ninth floors. With one exception they lack even the shabby grandeur of the intake parts. Rather, the courtrooms are small square rooms with four aging metal desks forming a rectangle in the center. In most, the only decoration is a large calendar from the United States Steel Company, held to the wall by yellowing strips of scotch tape.

There is a long period of inaction before any adjudication, punctuated by a series of "report" hearings which are no more than brief updates, after which the case is adjourned for several more weeks. The families experience little beyond waiting at these hearings. Cases are not called in any set order. Instead, all persons with a case on the day's calendar are required to be at the court at 9:30, and youths and their parents must sit on wooden benches in one of the grimy, windowless waiting rooms until chance and the court officer happen to favor their case. Parents, who are required to be at every judicial hearing, often lose a day's work and therefore 20 percent of their weekly income each time they must appear.

Eventually, 23 percent of the petitions filed come to a formal adjudication.* Of these, one in five is contested at a trial, a figure probably higher than elsewhere in the state. A lengthy investigation of the youth's background and, finally, a disposition follow.† None of the dispositional plans regularly invoked can generally be considered successful. If a youth is put on probation, as happens in 5 percent of adjudicated petitions, "It is not uncommon that, months after . . . he will not know his probation officer's name or even recognize him by sight" [34]. While there are some new programs such as Alternatives to Detention and

---

*On the average, adjudications occur sixty-eight days after the first intake unit contact. To reach a post-adjudication disposition takes even longer; unless a case is withdrawn or dismissed, dispositions take an average of 204 days to reach.

†Some cases—8 percent overall, which is one-third of all cases reaching adjudication—are dismissed at this late point.

the Urban League's probation program in New York City, they also have the effect of draining the better probation officers from regular programs [35]. Private agency placement, tried with another 5 percent of petitioned youths, is routinely unavailable to precisely those who need it most: blacks, Puerto Ricans, and children with uncooperative families, low I.Q.'s, emotional problems, low reading levels, or drug involvement [36]. Moreover, the value of agency placement once attained is open to question. The Council of Voluntary Child Care Agencies reported last year that "there is practically no accountability on effectiveness" of such placements [37], and its assistant executive director, Mrs. King, noted that "Children who remain in placement a long time tend to have a poor self-image, to be dependent, hostile, bitter toward their families and society, [and] have higher levels of anxiety about their future in the world" [38].

Youths in New York for whom private agency placements cannot be found (4 percent of petitioned cases in our survey) are often placed instead with the Commissioner of Social Services. They are then detained for several months while fresh attempts at placements with the same agencies are made for them [39]. State camps and secure training schools [40] are the final resort, but are seldom used in New York. Their value is also doubtful. New York State Controller Arthur Levitt recently charged that the Division for Youth's resident rehabilitation programs for PINS and delinquents provided the youths with "spotty education, little or no psychiatric care and, in some instances, inadequate living accommodations" [41].

Whichever of these alternatives is chosen, almost one-quarter of PINS cases end—or rather begin again—back in court. Although many youths have only a few months before they turn sixteen and outgrow family court jurisdiction, 24 percent of the PINS cases adjusted at intake and 20 percent of those who have gone to court return at least once [42].

The Actors

Approximately one thousand youngsters start this process as alleged PINS every year.* The decisions that are made about them, to be explored in depth in a later section, are determined by the interactions of four groups of people: the youths themselves (and to some extent their families), probation officers, law guardians, and judges. This section will describe each group of actors, their beliefs and their behavior, as a means of understanding the decision-making process.

The Kids and Their Families. The young persons accused of being PINS in New York vary in age from seven to nineteen [43], although most are fourteen and fifteen. Over 85 percent are from racial minority groups, while white youths

---

*As set forth in the note on methodology, we counted 1,119 PINS cases coming to intake in 1972.

are so rare as to occasion comment. Only one-fifth of the youths, who are more often girls than boys, come from intact families.* Their backgrounds are very poor—family income averages $5,200 per year to support five and often six people, and 50 percent of the families receive welfare. A third of the respondents have been to court before, nearly 50 percent of these within the last six months (see Table 2–1). Forty-five percent of previous court contacts have occurred within the last six months, 34 percent within the last three.

Although occasional cases are presented by schools or involve arranging the return of out-of-state runaways picked up by the police, over four-fifths of PINS are brought to court in New York by their parents or by relatives who are parental surrogates (herein classed as "parents"). Mothers are by far the most frequent complainants, bringing about three-fourths of parental complaints and just over 60 percent of all complaints. The allegations they register against their progeny range from truancy (the most frequently mentioned problem) through coming home at late hours, to matters such as refusing to bathe regularly, banging a door in response to a parental command, habitual lying, attempting suicide, or having an abortion.† Approximately a quarter of all girls are charged with sexual misbehavior and 31 percent of youths are accused of quasi-criminal activity [44].

While some parents seek no more than a male authority figure who will talk with their child, others seek to "humiliate and punish" their children or to have them removed from the home [45]. Suppressed hostility often breaks out in curses or even blows during the long wait before a case is called.

Probation. The first official to make contact with an alleged PINS is an intake officer. The intake officers, the Court Liaison Officers (CLOs) in each courtroom, and the members of the Investigation and Supervision ("Service") branch on W. 23rd Street are all members of the probation department.‡ Jointly, they have responsibilities for working with juveniles deemed to need their assistance. They also have crucial decision-making functions at intake and advisory functions in the court process.

---

*Sixty percent of the youths live with mothers and fathers, 5 percent with fathers alone, while in 14 percent of cases a youth lives with neither biological parent, most frequently (8 percent) with the maternal grandmother.

In many cases in which the youth lives with his mother, the mother lives with another adult male, either a paramour or new husband, while fathers have girlfriends or a new wife. Occasionally one or more of the youth's grandparents also reside in the household. These youths' households also contain an average of 3.1 siblings.

Thirty percent of the girls live with both parents, in contrast to 12 percent of the boys.

†Additional unique allegations contained in case histories (referred to in the aggregate in this study as "other" allegations for purposes of analysis), included being disruptive in school, selling one's clothing, defecating on the bedroom floor, sleeping all day, refusing to do household chores, being selfish and self-centered, forging notes to school teachers, gang membership, and wanting to get married.

‡Members of this branch conduct court ordered investigations and supervise youths put on probation. It was only peripherally studied by the authors and is not, therefore, separately discussed in the text.

Table 2–1. New York County: Characteristics of PINS Children

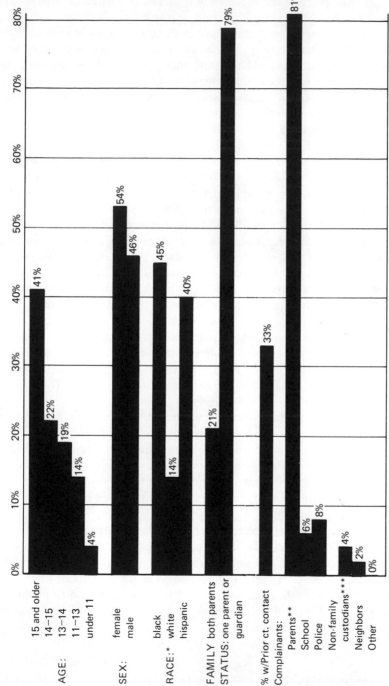

AGE:
15 and older — 41%
14–15 — 22%
13–14 — 19%
11–13 — 14%
under 11 — 4%

SEX:
female — 54%
male — 46%

RACE:*
black — 45%
white — 14%
hispanic — 40%

FAMILY
STATUS: both parents — 21%
one parent or guardian — 79%

% w/Prior ct. contact — 33%

Complainants:
Parents** — 81%
School — 6%
Police — 8%
Non-family custodians*** — 4%
Neighbors — 2%
Other — 0%

*One percent of the sample was Oriental.
**This category includes all relatives.
***Department of Social Services (D.S.S.) and placement institutions.

Though their position seems to imply considerable institutional power, probation officers in New York are generally a discouraged lot. Many are middle-aged and some strongly resent the liberal policies of Director of Probation John A. Wallace [46]. The intake unit lacks any systematic training and, although group meetings are supposed to be routine, they in fact seldom occur [47]. Such factors help explain both the way in which intake officers make critical decisions concerning referral of cases to court and the comparatively minor influence exercised by CLOs in the courtroom.

Intake procedure is haphazard and key decisions are strongly influenced by organizational factors. For example, the person who designates a case as a PINS matter is not an intake officer, but a clerk who, on the basis of a minute's discussion with the complainant, decides whether the complaint is to be categorized as PINS, delinquency, or neglect. Her labeling is seldom questioned—a significant point in light of the extensive overlap this study finds between PINS and youths whose proper legal classification should be as neglected or delinquent [48].

The other major decision at intake—whether to adjust the case—is made by one of the six intake officers [49]. Several factors may then have a role in this decision. The first is ideology. Although some intake officers (especially those most recent to the job) dislike involving any children in the court system, many view court involvement as a positive good. Second, bureaucratic pressure to refer PINS cases to court exists. Once the case is in the court system, intake officers feel definitive action is underway. In contrast, referring the child to another agency for counseling involves the labor of telephoning, the time set aside for another meeting with the parties, and the possibility of a quick return to intake.* Third, parents often exert a great deal of pressure on intake officers to refer a child with whom they are especially angry to court. In many cases, intake officers will feel sympathetic to the "victimized" parents and simply do not want to struggle with a parent, especially since an intake officer cannot prevent anyone who really wishes to from filing a complaint [50]. Some, for instance, customarily interview the accused child while the parent is present, though this inhibits expression of the youth's point of view [51]. This combination of factors sends PINS youth to court far more frequently than is true of other classes of respondents [52].

Once in court, another probation officer plays a role in a youth's case: the Court Liaison Officer. Because of the size and present disorganization of the New York County Court, it is impractical for the probation officer who has investigated or supervised a particular case to be in the courtroom when it goes before the judge. Instead, a CLO is assigned to each courtroom to present probation reports and recommendations and to execute any immediate inquiries or arrangements the judge may order.

In New York, however, much of what CLOs do is simply *pro forma*, with

---

*Thirty-six percent of adjusted youths recidivate.

little real influence on decisions. The law guardians have taken over many of the functions probation used to perform for youths before the court, and are fiercely resented by the latter [53]. Probation often appears fumbling and inadequate. This stems at least in part from such logistical problems as the inability to transport many of the case files across the city each day [54]. In part it also derives from the limited nature of much of what they have to present. Psychological reports, for example, are based on short interviews, usually held after the youth is accused and well aware that he or she is being judged; in addition, they reduce complex circumstances to summary labels such as "adjustment reaction to adolescence" or "passive aggressive personality."

Law Guardians. The objects of probation resentment are a group of eleven or twelve young lawyers from the Juvenile Rights Division of the Legal Aid Society, operating full time in the court under a contract with the city.

The law guardians dominate the court in New York County. This preeminence springs from several sources. The law guardians are enthusiastic and dedicated. They are well supported: they have investigators (ex-policemen) to develop evidence for trial, together with a capable social work staff which can help clients gain access to desired services. They have more time for legal research and, court observers feel, are generally of higher caliber than prosecuting attorneys from the Corporation Counsel's office. But the most important source of this domination lies in the fact that the law guardian is, in most instances, the person whom the youth trusts most and to whom the youth talks most immediately before a court appearance [55].

In part that trust is given because law guardians do what their juvenile clients want. As Kay McDonald, Attorney-in-Charge in New York County, observes: "If you're poor your main problem isn't lack of money, it's all the people who know what's best for you"—a posture law guardians say they try to avoid. Any personal thoughts that do intrude on a PINS case, moreover, are likely to be extremely hostile to the exercise of jurisdiction. McDonald remarks, "This court can do very little to help most PINS kids; the system can't do anything for them that they can't do for themselves" [56]. Another representative view is that "A kid should either be in court as a criminal, or he should be before a social agency" [57]. The law guardians' aggressive representation has made the New York Family Court among the most adversarial family courts in the state if not the nation [58].

The law guardian is usually the first to make contact with a youth and his family after a petition has been filed.* Though different law guardians follow different procedures, most try immediately to arrange a compromise settlement. This may involve an agreement between child and parent as to behavior, arrange-

---

*Each law guardian spends one day a week working in the intake parts, and adds to his or her caseload all the day's new cases.

ments for the young person's attendance at a P.A.L. or drug clinic, or the like. Law guardians also play on parental guilt feelings associated with initiation of legal proceedings against their children. Many of the PINS petitions withdrawn or dismissed in New York owe their outcome to such intervention.

While undertaking this effort with youth and complainant, or in the event of its failure, law guardians fight a continuing battle for legal position in the courtroom. They minimize the seriousness of the offense and the family disturbance in fiercely opposing pre-trial detention and issuance of arrest warrants. Full compliance with statutory requirements is demanded in such matters as the length of time for which a juvenile may be confined before court actions [59]. If the question is whether to put the case down for a hearing in a trial part or to keep it in an intake part, law guardians urge the latter on the grounds that "something may be worked out" to avoid the need for formal court action. Indeed, though the intake parts exist primarily to conduct the equivalent of arraignments for PINS, a law guardian is on occasion successful in keeping a case in intake for months on end, going from one "report" hearing to another [60]. And when a case finally is assigned to one of the six regular trial parts, law guardians maneuver to place the child before the judge thought most likely to react favorably to the youth's case. They agree that securing a sympathetic judge is usually the single most important service they render their clients [61].

Once a case is sent to a trial part, the defense strategy is often one of continued delay, in hopes of exhausting the complainant. When an adjudicatory hearing does finally occur, its timing is more a matter of chance than planning. Here too, law guardians battle hard for their clients. Admissions to the charges are made only with the juvenile's consent [62], and then rarely to all allegations. Instead, the law guardian will agree to admit one of the allegations, usually the least serious, if the court will strike the others, in order to minimize the child's record while bowing to the necessity of a fact-finding of PINS. When the youth does not want an adjudication, the lawyer will force a full-scale trial of the allegations, in which the principal defense weapon is a dogged cross-examination of the complainant, designed to destroy all credibility by revealing the parent as the motivating force in the family controversy. This defense is almost never successful, however,* since the complainant need only prove that there has been more than a "single isolated incident" of disobedience by the youth to meet the statutory test of a "habitual" course of conduct [63].

A law guardian continues to represent his or her client through the dispositional process. As in the attempt to settle cases before trials, the social work staff of the Legal Aid Society is often able to arrange desirable agency placements faster and more effectively than the probation department. If tests are necessary for admission to a program, investigators from the law guardians' office will often go with the young person and his family to ensure their attend-

---

*No instance of a successful defense was observed or recorded in New York County.

ance. But should the judge seek to send the youth to a training school, he is sure to encounter outraged resistance.

Judges. Ultimate decisions are made by a Family Court judge. Of the thirty-nine regular judges of the Family Court for the city, eleven or twelve appear in New York County in the course of a year (eight sit at one time).* With two exceptions, they have a good deal of seniority. Approximately half are women, none is black, and one is of Spanish descent. Two speak Spanish. Judicial attitudes and philosophies vary, of course, but all are persons of integrity and good will, with a genuine concern for the many persons before the court. Some are profoundly involved with the fates of many of the youths they consider. Sadly, however, other judges reflect the impact of years spent in a court with low prestige [64] and few visible results. One or two have alcohol problems, and others have sunk into a general frustration with the poor resources of the court—the unissued warrants, the incompetence and/or inefficiency of the probation department, the lost files, the handwritten records, the inability to get services for the children who need them most [65].

Most judges have a common approach to the PINS cases that come before them, with minor individual emphases. Perhaps encouraged by a statute which makes whatever the youth has done unlawful as long as parental commands are legal [66], judges seem to presume that the child must be the erring party if a family conflict exists. While all judges claim to recognize that some PINS cases involve what one labels "rejecting parents" [67], there is common agreement that "The bulk of the [PINS] cases that come in are problems of the child with no fault of the parent in the child's conduct" [68]. A child is seen to owe obedience to parents under almost all circumstances: "I want you to grow up to be a fine young lady. But you must obey your mother—legally, morally, and in every other way she is your mother, and you must do what she tells you" [69]. Judges also have informal personal standards about juvenile behavior which come into play in making decisions. For example, their feelings run strongly and almost uniformly against any contacts between girls and boys which have sexual overtones, even though such interest is frequently a normal concomitant of adolescent development.

There are great individual differences among the judges, of course. Some are conservative, others less traditional. One refused, for example, to order detention for a youth accused by his parents of smoking marijuana, on the ground

---

*These judges are appointed by the mayor, as are judges for the civil and criminal courts, and they receive $36,500 per year. Many have been politically active: for instance, a former city Commissioner of Labor sits on the New York County Bench, appointed by Mayor Wagner. When appointed, they undergo a one-month training, visiting institutions and sitting with another judge, then a trial period of three years, and then are appointed for ten-year terms. The position is something of a plum. Although it is regarded as the bottom of the judicial ladder, ambitious judges often use, or try to use, the position to run for higher office.

that she could no longer incarcerate people for something she herself had done [70]. Some treat races and sexes alike; others appear to give the occasional white youth better treatment, and there are male judges in the court before whom a truly pretty girl can do no wrong. Nearly all have individual quirks which affect their decisions. One judge thinks truancy is a more serious problem than any other and is accordingly much less inclined than her colleagues to dismiss truancy allegations. Another believes religion will solve whatever problems spur court intervention.

Judges' attitudes towards themselves as decisionmakers are no less certain than their opinions about PINS. Though some admit occasional failures, most judges display great confidence in their abilities to understand and help the youths before them. This is not shaken even by the common perception that "The most troubled, the most disturbed kids that come in are PINS" [71]. "You have to play God—but doesn't every judge when he decides without a jury?" asked one [72]. This confidence manifests itself in quick diagnoses: "She's way too big for her britches, and that's putting it nicely" [73]. Snap solutions follow: "What she needs is a good spanking" [74]. There is almost no expressed doubt that youth's problems can be known, and once known, cured.

It is this set of assumptions which the members of the New York bench bring to PINS cases. As a result, dispositions often turn on superficial factors such as whether the respondent keeps appointments diligently, possesses a high I.Q.,* or behaves as the judge thinks he ought. A smile on the youth's part, whether from nervousness, fear, or any other cause, is commonly taken by the bench as a sign of disrespect and is met with a harsh response. Silence can be a provocative factor as well; the rare child who openly mocks the judge can surely expect an extreme reaction. On the other hand, a respondent who is willing to admit fault no matter where it lies, and promises to do better, is almost assured of lenient treatment.

It is on such grounds that intake, adjudicative, and dispositional decisions are made. As law guardians have aptly noted, it is not legal skill that determines a case. Rather, it is the demeanor of the youth, the scheduling skill of the law guardian, chance, and the judge. The New York County Family Court is a court not of laws, but of personalities.

ROCKLAND COUNTY

The Setting

Rockland County is burgeoning, and new buildings are everywhere. The Family Court is located in one of these: a modern county office building which sits on an island of green in a sea of parking lots.

---

*There is a clear statistical trend in detention for those not detained to have higher I.Q.'s (as measured by Wechsler Intelligence Scale for Children [WISC], results of which are available in a substantial proportion of case records). Similarly, those with findings are over-

The Family Court shows the effect of Rockland's ample resources and presents a striking contrast to that of New York. Visitors to court and probation enter through the marble-slabbed splendor of the building's main lobby, where they are greeted by a "freedom shrine" displaying reproductions of historical documents, such as the Declaration of Independence. The inner sanctum where court clerks and other personnel work is fresh and new; the walls are pastel orange and yellow, and there is wall-to-wall carpeting everywhere. The courtrooms themselves are plush: wood-paneled walls, indirect lighting, and a judge's chair set atop a three-tiered arrangement of platforms. Each of the two Family Court judges has his own courtroom, a personal secretary, and a law clerk as well as private chambers.* The chambers are likewise wood paneled and so newly furnished that brand name tags still dangle from some of the lamps.

Rockland's Family Court, unlike that for New York City, is not overburdened. A population increase of 70 percent in the 1960–70 decade led the state legislature to add a second judge to the Family Court in 1971. Court business is scheduled at specific times, in contrast to the "come and wait" policy in New York, and fewer court hearings are required than in New York. Rockland's proceedings are generally unhurried and have an air of ceremony and decorum.

The first step on the way to the courtroom is at the intake unit operated by the probation department. From a reception area visitors are taken to a room that is a labyrinth of half-wall cubicles which give the appearance of privacy. The intake interview takes place in one such cubicle, first with the adult and then with the youth.

At intake there are certain significant allegations probation officers deem "acceptable" for court. Allegations such as refusal to obey, truancy, disorderly conduct, undesirable boyfriend, promiscuity, late hours, and objectionable companions are usually sufficient to yield a petition and access to court. By contrast, probation officers dislike certain kinds of allegations, such as complaints stemming from fights on school buses. Mention of one of these "disapproved" allegations will ordinarily prevent a case from going to court.

However, little attention is paid to the formal allegations once a youth is on his way through the court process. The attitudes and opinions of the intake officer about a particular youth are more important, since probation officers carry the major burden of court processing.

For 32 percent of Rockland's cases, court processing involves detention.† While the county has its own nonsecure detention facility, the only available

---

whelmingly those with lower I.Q.'s; judges are willing to give a brighter youth a break on the theory that he "might really become something." The more regulating dispositions—suspended judgment, informal supervision, probation, the varying kinds of placement away from home—also go to those with lower I.Q.'s.

*In addition to the two judges and their two law clerks and their two personal secretaries, there are two court officers, two court reporters, one chief clerk, two court clerks, two assistant court clerks, two court assistants, and five court office assistants.

† Only 13 percent of adjusted cases involve detention.

secure facilities are on Long Island. Surprisingly, probation officers prefer to use these distant facilities even though taking a youth there and back involves a round trip of approximately 100 miles. The local nonsecure facility is used only 26 percent of the time, while secure facilities are deemed necessary in 74 percent of detentions.*

Processing of Rockland court cases involves fewer hearings than in New York. A law guardian is assigned at the first hearing and by the second hearing (the first at which the law guardian appears) probation staff and the judge usually seek an admission. Most youths in Rockland admit to all the charges against them. Thus, adjudication as PINS is virtually certain in Rockland. From the moment a petition is filed against a youth there is better than a 67 percent chance that he will be adjudicated a PINS.

After an admission, probation officers work privately in analyzing the disposition, without further court hearings and, in contrast to New York, without any input from the law guardian. Decisions about placement outside the home are made primarily on the basis or probation officers' telephone conversations with agencies. Delays are due chiefly to difficulty in obtaining the psychological tests and psychiatric interviews which are necessary if the youth is to be placed outside his home.† Thus, although there are occasional formal court hearings, most of the actual decision-making on a case is done out of the presence of parent and child, and is largely controlled by the opinions and choices of probation officers.

When probation is ready, it notifies the judge and the law guardian and a hearing is set. Just before the dispositional hearing occurs, the probation officer meets privately in chambers with the judge and law guardian and lays out his or her proposed disposition. This is almost always accepted.

For dispositional purposes, Rockland County has a distinct advantage over New York in its ability to obtain private placements for most of the PINS it seeks to place. Probation officers and judges also acknowledge that they are very reluctant to place Rockland juveniles anywhere that might have many New York City children because they view the latter as too tough for the comparatively tender Rockland youngsters.

Youths who are not placed and whose cases are not withdrawn or dismissed are given some form of probation supervision. Supervision is carried out in three ways: formal probation, suspended judgment, and informal supervision. Formal probation is utilized in 22 percent of the cases going to court. Suspended judg-

---

*The preponderant use of the distant detention center *cannot* be explained solely on the basis of its being a secure facility; two-thirds of detained youths charged with truancy were held in secure facilities as were 100 percent of youths charged with refusal to obey and with vile language. By contrast, all of the detained youths charged with long-term running away were held in nonsecure facilities.

†Obtaining these studies is the responsibility of the probation department. Psychiatric reports are easily obtainable from the psychiatrist employed part time by the court. But for "psychologicals," which include an I.Q. test, probation must wait for psychologists from the schools or from the local state mental hospital to do the testing.

ment, though seldom used in New York, is the most frequent disposition in Rockland County: 32 percent of all cases received this disposition in 1972 [75]. This disposition involves withholding judgment for a period of time in order to see whether, based on the child's post-court conduct, further action is required. It reflects, in a real sense, the essence of the Rockland court ethic. The judge largely submerges his role as a trier of fact and concentrates on dispensing guidance according to what he believes to be youths' "best interests."* The importance of this role is further shown by the use of "informal supervision," which is employed in 6 percent of the cases. Informal supervision allows the court to pass a case to probation as if it had never come to court. Thus, it is a way for judges to dispense with cases they feel should not be in court at all [76] but are reluctant to dismiss because of their belief in the beneficial effects of PINS jurisdiction and of probation department intervention.

Recidivism rates suggest that serious problems are relatively uncommon among Rockland's PINS population. The largest source of subsequent petitions for juveniles stems from the court process itself: 46 percent of all subsequent petitions are either "violation" petitions brought by probation officers against PINS who do not obey the terms of supervision or "modification" petitions brought by agencies seeking to alter the terms of a youth's placement.† Thus Rockland's PINS jurisdiction is an important source of its own further business.

The Actors

The Kids and Their Families. The young people who are brought to Rockland's Family Court are about fourteen and one-half years old on the average, just as are PINS in New York.‡ As in New York, more than one-half (52 percent) of the youths are female, but in Rockland three-fourths are white, 16 percent are black, and 9 percent are Puerto Rican [77].

In contrast to the large number of single-parent households in New York, 56 percent of Rockland cases involve young people who come from homes where both parents are present. Twenty-eight percent live with their mother alone, another 8 percent live with their fathers or another relative, and the rest with other custodians. Rockland PINS are better off economically than their New York counterparts, though they are disadvantaged in comparison to most Rockland youths. Extensive information on family income was not available, but only 8 percent of the youths alleged to be PINS came from families on welfare.

As Table 2–2 reveals, and in contrast to New York, the largest proportion

---

*The judges believe suspended judgment also gives them jurisdiction over parents. One judge, after repeatedly ordering (in conjunction with a suspended judgment) the father of a PINS to go to the Volunteer Counselling Service, declared the father "in violation of a court order" for failure to do so and, after a brief trial, sentenced the father to a weekend in jail.

†Rockland's overall recidivism rate is 29 percent.

‡Only 4 percent are under the age of ten, nearly 70 percent are fourteen years of age or older, and the median age is fourteen years and ten months.

Table 2–2. Rockland County: Characteristics of PINS Children

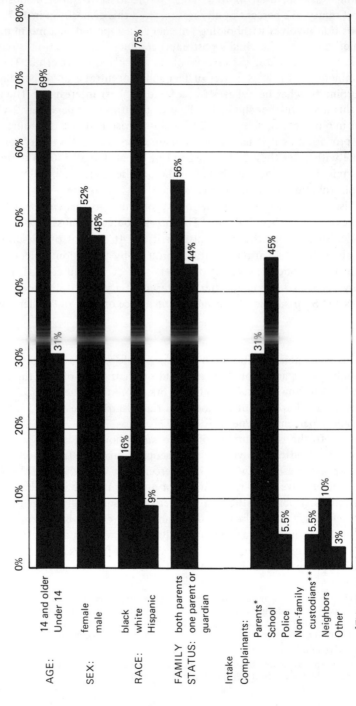

		Percentage
AGE:	14 and older	69%
	Under 14	31%
SEX:	female	52%
	male	48%
RACE:	black	16%
	white	75%
	Hispanic	9%
FAMILY STATUS:	both parents	56%
	one parent or guardian	44%
Intake Complainants:	Parents*	31%
	School	45%
	Police	5.5%
	Non-family custodians**	5.5%
	Neighbors	10%
	Other	3%

*This category includes all relatives.
**D.S.S. and placement institutions.

of complaints in Rockland (45 percent) come from the schools, followed by parents and other relatives. But New York and Rockland are similar in that the predominant allegation is truancy, followed by short-term running away and disobedience [78].

Probation. Rockland's probation department, unlike that in New York, plays a dominant role in the processing of PINS from intake through disposition.* At intake, of course, the opinions of probation about a case determine whether it is sent to court or adjusted and handled informally.† In general probation lends a sympathetic ear to most complainants and sees alleged PINS as difficult youths who require court and probation guidance [79]. This seems especially to be true when the complainants are school officials, who are viewed as fellow workers in institutions beleaguered by troublesome juveniles. And at intake, probation grants schools nearly automatic access to court; 82 percent of school cases are petitioned and sent to court, almost always on charges of truancy.

While parental complainants are not serviced quite as routinely, probation often takes the parents' perspective on intrafamily conflicts. The officer typically agrees with the parent that the child is the problem and, by the end of the interview with the parent, the officer has often filled out a PINS petition. The officer will also assist parents during the interview to formulate allegations "acceptable" for a court petition by probing to identify further charges—whether the youth ever "played hookey," or stayed out after hours when he promised to return, or talked back. Overall, slightly more than one-half of cases with parental complainants are sent to court.

Once a case is in court, probation's dominant role comes from its control over information. Indeed, most of the work on a court case is done by probation staff, who gather school records and psychological tests which are used, together with other information, to write the "social histories" that are to guide judges' decision-making. Unfortunately, probation tends to rely heavily on information given by complainants at the intake interview, and social histories often exclude important information about youths, such as their peer relationships [80]. Moreover, because probation sees itself as very knowledgeable on the subject of PINS youths, it tends to minimize its need for outside information. Officers admit, for example, that they routinely ignore the reports of the court psychiatrist [81].

---

*The juvenile section of the probation department consists of one supervisor and six probation officers.

†Overall, 64 percent of cases are sent to court. If a case is not sent to court the intake officer handles it by a process known as "informal probation." This usually involves a talk with the youth and a warning that if the behavior complained of continues, the officer will bring a formal petition. There is only intermittent monitoring for adjusted cases kept "open" on informal probation. Only the squeaky wheel gets the department's attention. Youths who do not show up for meetings with the probation officers are rarely tracked down. Occasionally counselling for the family is recommended.

Probation officers view the court process as a means to an end: placing a youth back in their guiding hands where they can correct his deficiencies. Any adversary techniques ventured by law guardians are viewed as irrelevant interference with probation's task. Probation staff, accordingly, press law guardians to accept their opinions about what should be done and, since they have control over information-gathering, they usually succeed in this effort. Rockland County probation officers are frequently called by a newly-appointed law guardian seeking information and are ordinarily glad to cooperate with attorneys. They see an attorney's cooperation as an acknowledgement of probation's greater knowledge of what ought to be done with a youth. If, on the other hand, probation officers sense that an attorney is not cooperating with them and is likely to oppose their recommendations to the judge, they will decline to provide information to the attorney [82]. Not only can probation deprive a law guardian of necessary information, it can also increase his workload by not "standing in" for him at routine hearings. If probation and the attorney are on good terms, the probation officer will appear at a hearing for the attorney and telephone him as to what happened.

Ironically, probation concentrates most of its efforts on the court process. Once PINS youths have been placed in probation's care, that care is almost nonexistent. Although caseloads permit probation officers sufficient time for meeting with the youths assigned to them, relatively few such sessions are conducted; work is instead focused largely on court preliminaries in order that still more youths may be brought under probation supervision. But as long as a youth does not bring himself to anyone's further attention and shows up for a limited number of required visits, little is done for or with him.

Law Guardians. Unlike New York City, there are no full-time law guardians attached to the Rockland County Family Court. Rather, as do most counties, Rockland meets the Family Court Act's requirement that counsel be made available in PINS proceedings [83] by maintaining a list of private attorneys who have expressed interest in accepting appointment as law guardians. For new lawyers coming into the county, one way of becoming known in legal circles is to place one's name on this list. Signing up gives a new lawyer a chance to present himself to the Family Court judges—a significant segment of the county's small bench. Actually being chosen to represent a youth, however, may not follow since judges make *ad hoc* appointments rather than rely on a rotation system. While a few lawyers (usually "old hands" known to the judge) appear in a considerable number of PINS cases, for most attorneys service as a law guardian is a rare event.

Because law guardians are private attorneys, inexperienced with the routine functioning of Family Court, they are uniformly dependent on probation to make their tasks manageable. They call the officers to find out the facts about a case, to get family background, and the like. Were probation officers not to supply these facts, law guardians would have to spend a considerable amount of time tracking down things themselves. Because of this dependence on probation officers, law guardians tend to become functionaries of the probation department [84]. In court, they follow probation recommendations rather than "sail into the wind" by denying allegations, demanding to question complainants, or insisting on competent proof of allegations.

The law guardian performs his main role at the formal court hearing where he prepares the audience for the outcome of the pending court "drama." After the conference in chambers at which outcomes are usually decided [85], the law guardian goes into the courtroom to talk to parent and child. He always professes not to know what exactly will happen and explains what he "thinks" the judge "might" do. The law guardian attempts to make the parent and youth satisfied with the result that he knows is about to occur. Then comes the court officer and "all rise" as the judge enters and the reenactment of the decision process is ceremonially staged and the predetermined outcome unfolds.

Judges. The emasculation of the Rockland law guardians begun by probation is completed by the judges, who approve of and support probation's dominant role. The two judges who preside over Rockland's PINS jurisdiction look on the court as a helping agency, not as a trier of fact. Indeed, for Rockland's Family Court judges, the heart of the *parens patriae* doctrine is that juveniles should not be "subjected" to formal legal procedures of the type that confront adults. The judges look upon the adversary process as "rigamarole," and indirectly pressure law guardians to avoid it.

The judges share probation's interest in a perfunctory adjudication process so that the court can extend to a youth the help it has decided he needs. The judges feel they are able to ascertain the "best interests" of youths who come into court even on the basis of brief encounters at hearings, and place great faith in their ability to comprehend quickly a young person's needs. For example, at the first hearing of one case, the judge had the following colloquy with an alleged PINS: "You play any ball at school? (Yessir.) Whataya play? (Basketball.) What position? (Guard.) You a good ball handler? (Yessir.) Can you score? (Uhhuh.) What was your game average? (16 points.) Well, George, I think you'd be better off if you played some more ball. . . ."

The judges' meager supply of information on which to base decisions is not much improved by probation reports. The "social histories" that are given to the judge after adjudication to inform him about proper dispositions begin with a youth's infancy: His mother's account of the difficulty of birth and the age when he first walked. The "social history" then skips immediately to adolescense and the period surrounding the incidents complained of in the PINS petition, omitting all crucial childhood development information. Psychological reports gathered by probation and passed on to the judge are likewise insufficient. They generally rely on short interviews and, as in New York, usually reduce personalities to such labels as "passive-aggressive" [86] or "adjustment reaction to adolescence," without reference to other crucial factors, such as peer relationships. Condensed diagnoses may accurately reflect the fact that many strains in children's relationships with parents and schools stem from problems of growing up, but such assessments provide little useful guidance to the judge.

Rockland's judges therefore fall back on what they call their "common sense" about young people. They have great confidence in the accuracy of their own diagnoses and projected "cures." One judge remarked in a typical case, "She thinks she's a pretty hot number; I'd be worried about leaving my kid with her in a room alone. She needs to get her mind off boys" [87]. On occasion, however, judges will admit in private that they are often not in a position to understand the problems they are called on to solve [88].

The Counties Compared

New York and Rockland counties are thus very different. In resources, the carpets and pastel interiors of Rockland's Family Court are years away from the New York court. Rockland's suburban white adolescents are generally less troubled than New York's minority group youth, though in both counties PINS jurisdiction involves those on the lower rungs of the local socioeconomic ladder. Each county has evolved a distinctive manner of processing cases; New York's probation department is quiescent in the face of law guardian dominance, while the Rockland probation staff largely orchestrates decision-making and dominates law guardian activity.

Yet these differences are dwarfed by a problem common to both counties: unstructured discretion in decision-making, which stems from the absence of useful standards in the PINS statute. This lack of structure to guide discretion has the same effects on decision-making in each county. Since a court by its nature exists to make decisions, the judge, as decisionmaker, is under pressure to decide often very complex parent-child conflicts. In the absence of standards, the pressure to decide has two principal consequences: the judge permits a dominant group of court personnel to exercise influence on decision-making, and the judge falls back upon his personal preferences and idiosyncratic beliefs as a source of standards for decision-making.

Although a different group of personnel is the dominant influence in each county—in New York, the law guardians' in Rockland, the probation department—in both counties the difficulty of deciding the complexities of PINS cases in the absence of standards makes the judge receptive to having this group of personnel exercise disproportionate influence in decision-making.* In so doing, the group's actions reflect its own attitudes about what is "best" for youths and its own internal organizational pressures. Thus, in New York the law guardians have not been discouraged from expanding their role to include placement inves-

---

*To the extent that probation functions as a decisionmaker at intake in adjusting cases or referring them to court, the absence of standards likewise makes it vulnerable to outside influence, particularly from parents.

tigations, "social histories," and other probation tasks; performance of these tasks makes it easier for law guardians to undercut possible objections of probation to case outcomes. In Rockland the judges implicitly collaborate in the probation department's domination of the law guardians, thereby allowing probation to carry out much of PINS decision-making without the challenge of an adversary process.

The other result of the absence of standards is that judges informally crystallize their personal feelings about youths and parent-child relationships to supply standards of their own [89]. However, these informal personal standards often reflect neither legislative intent with respect to PINS matters nor an accurate understanding of the course of adolescent development. Moreover, judges are not supplied with adequate information that might serve as a corrective to their idiosyncratic beliefs. Thus, the frequent judicial bias against signs of any sexual interest and the assumption that the youth is the erring party in a family conflict recurrently play a large role in decision-making. Only a youth's contrition in court and a safely middle class mien serve to lighten the burden of these judicial attitudes.

The consequence of decision-making so largely governed by organizational and personal preferences is, not surprisingly, decisions that appear to deviate greatly from the statutory aim of responding to youths in need of "supervision." These decisions are analyzed more closely in the following section.

SURVEY FINDINGS: A PROFILE OF PINS DECISION-MAKING

In General: Mission Not Accomplished

There are four major decisions in a PINS case: whether a complaint should be referred by intake to court, whether the youth should be detained pending trial, whether a formal adjudication should be made, and, after adjudication, what disposition should be ordered. The preceding sections have discussed some of the general ways in which organizational pressures and idiosyncratic preferences may affect these decisions, as revealed by court observation and interviews. This section of the study presents data which indicate more specifically what factors are and are not empirically significant in making these decisions. The discussion will concentrate first on the relationship between the allegations brought against PINS youths (a factor which one would suppose in the abstract to be among the most important) and the decisions made at each of these points. Thereafter, it will turn to other factors which often actually determine the outcomes of PINS cases.

The principal tool used for this analysis was cross-tabulation, which shows the distribution of cases studied according to two or more variables. Among the variables used were outcomes in each of the four critical decisions just mentioned, the kind of allegations bringing the child to court, the age, sex, race, and prior record of the respondent, the respondent's family's composition and wealth, the existence of facts indicating neglect, the identity of the complainant, and all other circumstances that might hypothetically be associated with the processing of PINS cases. A typical cross-tabulation would show how many complaints against boys were referred to court by intake, how many were adjusted without referral, and the same information about female respondents. Once these distributions are determined through cross-tabulation, they can be analyzed statistically to see whether, among other things, the existence of one variable (for example, the fact that the respondent is a male) predicts or varies with another (e.g., referral to court) [90].

For some purposes, a further device called "multiple regression analysis" was employed. Regression analysis is a technique by which one can determine which of a set of factors (independent variables) that might be associated with some other matter (the dependent variable) actually best predicts the occurrence or direction of the latter [91]. The usefulness of such a device to analyze decision-making in PINS cases is plain. The dependent variables, i.e., the matters to be predicted, are the four critical decisions mentioned above—whether to file a petition, detain the child, adjudicate him a PINS, and choice of disposition. The independent variables (the factors whose relationship to the critical decisions we wish to ascertain) are the other circumstances listed (e.g., identity of complainant, kind of allegation, family income, and the like).

The regression analyses presented here are based on the full sample of 234 cases. Only statistically significant relationships—that is, relationships that are unlikely to occur simply by chance—are reported. All cross-tabulations are likewise based on the full sample and in most instances when statistical relationships are reported, they are statistically significant. A single exception to this rule of reporting only such clear relationships must be noted: cross-tabulations where one of the variables is the allegation against the child involve so many categories (kinds of charges) that the number of cases included in each instance is too small to allow judgments about statistical significance. Nevertheless, the percentages reported are based on consistent trends which provide some substantial support for the conclusions described here.

Referral to Court. Approximately three youths in five (61 percent) are sent by intake to court. A case is even more likely than the norm to be referred for judicial proceedings when the most common PINS allegations—refusing to obey, truanting, staying out overnight, running away—are present [92]. When allegations of sexual activity are present, cases are sent to court at a rate higher than the norm. Allegations of sexual misbehavior, when aggregated, have a referral rate of 65 percent. In contrast, cases involving allegations of criminal activity are referred to court at a rate below the median. Fifty-six percent of cases with criminal allegations are referred to the court.

No consistent logical relationship between allegations and referral to court appears from these data. One cannot predict that a matter will be formally treated because of the severity of the charges placed. Rather, regression analysis indicates that there are six facts which are apt to be of importance in decisions to refer.* A case is likely to be so treated if the youth does not live with both parents,† if he is not charged with harassment, if truancy is alleged, if there is parental neglect, if the youth is older,‡ and if there is no allegation of verbal abuse. Cross-tabulations also reveal that males are more likely than females to be referred to court and that whites are slightly more likely than blacks or Hispanics to receive such referrals.**

Detention. Detention, the second major decision, is authorized by the Family Court Act only in cases where there is reason to believe (1) that the youth is dangerous or (2) that he will run away rather than return to court [93]. Just over a third of all PINS are detained at some point in the processing.††

These youths are curious choices for detention when the allegations against them are considered. Forty-seven percent of all minors alleged to have refused to obey are detained, as are 55 percent of those alleged to have undesirable companions. Neither of these allegations seem, however, to indicate that the youth is dangerous or that he is likely to abscond. On the other hand, an allegation that the youth has run away for a long period, which would seem to involve a higher risk that the respondent will disappear before trial, has only a 25 percent detention rate. Similarly, assault, an allegation that suggests that the child poses a danger to others if not to himself, brings detention for only one respondent in ten. As with the decision to refer for trial, factors other than allegations are crucial to the detention decision. Detention is statistically predictable if the youth's family is on welfare, if "other" allegations are made,‡‡ if there is a short runaway allegation, and if larceny is alleged*** [94].

In addition to deciding whether or not to detain a youth, the judge must, as we have seen, decide whether to order him held in secure or nonsecure facilities. An overwhelming majority of detained PINS (66 percent) are held in the former. Here again, the decision makes little sense if one looks only to the nature of the

---

*These account for 20 percent of the variance.

†Cross-tabulations reveal that 46 percent of such youths are adjusted, only 54 percent referred to court. But only 36 percent of those living with relatives or mothers, 29 percent of those living with foster parents, 25 percent of those living with their fathers, and none of those living with friends or in placement institutions are adjusted.

‡Cross-tabulations reveal that over 50 percent of those under thirteen are adjusted. Around 35 percent of those over thirteen are adjusted, 65 percent being referred to court.

**Sixty-five percent of males are referred to court, and only 57 percent of females. Sixty-six percent of whites, 61 percent of blacks, and 56 percent of Hispanics are referred to court.

††Thirty-five percent. The rate is 25 percent in Rockland, 39 percent in New York.

‡‡See text p. 54 at footnote † *supra*, for a definition of "other" allegations.

***These factors account for approximately 30 percent of the variance.

child's alleged misconduct. One would expect, for example, that children who have run away for long periods would be seen as readier to run away again and therefore in need of closer custody than those with a history of brief absence from home. These expectations, however, are reversed in actuality. Only one out of four youths who leave home for long periods is held in secure detention, while four out of five youths charged with short absences are so placed.*

Adjudication. Adjudication is the next major step in PINS decision-making. Forty-eight percent of all petitions filed reach a finding, almost always upon an admission by the youth.†

Relationships between specific allegations and entrance of a finding seem erratic. Cases where truancy is charged have the highest rate of adjudication, but results for other allegations fluctuate wildly. Short runaways have a finding rate of 46 percent, for example, while an adjudication is entered in only 6 percent of the cases involving long runaways. When sexual allegations are presented, a finding is more likely than when criminal conduct is charged.‡ Indeed, formal adjudication correlates highly with the *absence* of a long runaway allegation, with the *absence* of an allegation of drug possession and with the *absence* of malicious mischief as well as with the *presence* of allegations of truancy.** Cross-tabulations also indicate that children who are adjudicated PINS tend to be somewhat younger than PINS as a whole,†† and that they are more often male than female, more often white than black, and seldom Hispanic‡‡ [95].

---

*On the other hand, the court does respond to criminal allegations in the petition. Where these are present and the youth is detained, 71 percent of youths are held in secure facilities.

†Throughout this and other discussions of findings, it must be remembered that this is an area of vast divergence between the counties: fewer than a quarter of New York petitions reach findings, compared to 67 percent of Rockland petitions. And as mentioned in the discussions of the counties, findings in New York represent chiefly "survival power"—i.e., a case's continuation until all attempts to delay or alleviate the need for a finding have failed. In Rockland, findings are quick and routine.

‡For both types of allegations the totals refer to allegations formally charged in the petition and the intake report and those included elsewhere in the case record. This last factor is used because we found that allegations of both kinds are frequently "hidden"—they are not presented formally, but are discussed by all participants and are a crucial factor in the outcome of the case.

**These factors are revealed as the most important in a regression analysis; they account for 23 percent of the variance.

††Only 37 percent of this group, in contrast to 41 percent of all PINS, are over fifteen. This is perhaps because judges are reluctant to adjudicate a youth who is almost sixteen a PINS.

‡‡Fifty-three percent of petitioned males and only 43 percent of petitioned females receive findings. Racially, whites dominate in that 66 percent of all whites receive findings, 53 percent of blacks receive findings, and only 20 percent of Hispanics do so. This may be in part because Rockland County youths, who receive findings more frequently than New York youths, are almost all white.

Disposition. The last step in the PINS process is disposition. In the jurisdiction as a whole, over 50 percent of cases are withdrawn or dismissed. These outcomes, because they involve no limitation on the child's freedom, we have called "non-regulating dispositions." All other dispositions—suspended judgment, probation, placement in a private agency or DFY camp or school, informal supervision, training school, and placement with the Department of Social Services—involve some restriction of the respondent's liberty and are classed as "regulating dispositions."* Again, dispositional outcomes seem surprising in light of allegations. Late hours, assault, and long runaway are treated very leniently, in contrast to such allegations as truancy and vile language.† Indeed, a contradictory set of factors predicts imposition of a regulating disposition; *absence* of long runaway or criminal allegations, nonmembership in the lowest income groups,‡ a history of truancy, and evidence of parental neglect make that result significantly more likely. These factors account for 51 percent of the variance [96].

These data indicate, then, that variables such as the allegations made, which one would expect to predict whether a case is referred or adjusted, whether the respondent is detained before trial, whether an adjudication is entered, and what disposition will ultimately be made are in fact rarely significant in explaining these critical decisions. This is not to say that no pattern can be discerned. The facts, however, that do predict the direction of intake and court action are perhaps different from what might be expected. In particular, it appears that evidence that respondents charged with being PINS are in fact neglected, the identity of the complainant, and the existence of certain personal characteristics of the respondent are significantly related to the determinations we have considered.

Evidence of Neglect

The New York Family Court Act defines a "neglected child" as a child under eighteen whose parents have either abandoned, abused, or failed to provide necessary care for him or her, and authorizes proceedings to assume wardship over such children [97]. The possible outcomes of a neglect proceeding range from an order requiring the parents to provide better care for the child to removal of the child from his or her family [98].

---

*Seventeen percent receive suspended judgment, 14 percent probation, 8 percent are placed with agencies, 2 percent are placed with DFY facilities, 3 percent receive informal supervision, 2 percent are sent to training schools, and 2 percent are placed with the Department of Social Services, while 1 percent are transferred elsewhere. Another 1 percent are placed with agencies on a nonresident basis, while one case receives a disposition simply classed as "other."

†Seventy-two percent of cases alleging late hours, 71 percent of cases alleging assault, and 100 percent of cases alleging long runaway receive nonregulating dispositions, while only 33 percent of cases alleging vile language and 41 percent of cases involving truancy receive nonregulating dispositions. In general, New York has a high rate of nonregulating dispositions, while suspended judgment and probation predominate in Rockland County.

‡Income data refer primarily to New York County.

Each PINS case we surveyed was examined for evidence of parental neglect. The authors reviewed such evidence after engaging in extensive courtroom observation of neglect cases throughout the summer of 1973. A youth was classified as neglected for purposes of the following analysis only where his or her record contained facts which both fell within the statutory description of neglect and manifested the nature and degree of seriousness on which we had observed courts to base findings of neglect [99]. Typical neglect cases were those involving repeated abuse or parental refusal to provide food and/or shelter.

Thirty-four percent of the youths brought to the intake unit each year alleged to be PINS were found, on this basis, to be neglected. More of these youths are relatively young (under thirteen) than are non-neglected youths. There are approximately equal numbers of boys and girls, but the neglected group has a higher percentage of black youths than of whites or Hispanics.* These neglected youths more often come from broken homes and from families on welfare.† They are usually brought to court by relatives and schools,‡ and the charges against them often derive from the youths' attempts to avoid the abuse and ne-

*Breaking these data down by county, 50 percent of both blacks and whites and 29 percent of Hispanics are neglected in New York; in Rockland, 44 percent of blacks, 34 percent of whites, and only 9 percent of Hispanics are neglected. The following graph reflects the percentage of neglected respondents within the following categories: sex, race, and home composition.

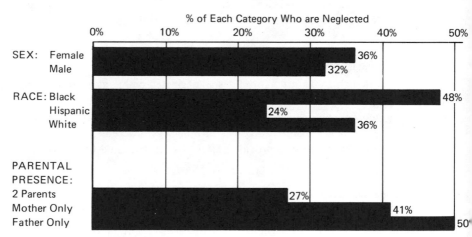

Both Counties: Neglected Youths

†Thirty-three percent of those who are neglected have families on welfare; only 24 percent of those who are not neglected have families on welfare. Income statistics bear out the impression that the neglected are poorer; 54 percent of those neglected have family incomes over $5,000 in contrast to 64 percent of those non-neglected.

‡Forty-two percent are brought by mothers, 5 percent by fathers, 5 percent by other relatives, 38 percent by schools, 5 percent by police, and 5 percent by institutional custodians.

glect they receive at home and to seek the company of friends.* Finally, more of them have had prior court contact than have non-neglected youths.†

These neglected PINS youths, then, form a distinct group: more troubled, more often previously involved with the court, more often black. At each step of processing their neglect seems to encourage the court to give them special attention in the only ways it has at hand: placing more of them under its control and dispensing more of what it considers "help."

At intake, for instance, 75 percent of neglected PINS youths are referred to court, compared to 53 percent of non-neglected PINS youths. Even those neglected youths whose cases are adjusted receive greater attention—some 53 percent of them are sent to other agencies by intake for further assistance, while only 38 percent of non-neglected youths are so consigned.‡

Neglected youths represent 42 percent of all PINS cases that reach the court. These youths are formally charged with avoiding their homes until late hours, associating with companions objectionable to parents, and other allegations which often indicate conflict with parents and other adults. Twenty-eight percent of neglected youths are charged with criminal behavior, while only 20 percent of non-neglected youths are so accused.**

Once before the court, neglected PINS youths are more often detained than non-neglected PINS youths, although they are less frequently placed in secure facilities.†† Later, neglected youths are formally adjudicated PINS more fre-

---

*Although neglected youths constitute only 34 percent of all cases, they represent substantial proportions of the following allegations: keeping late hours and staying out overnight (44 percent and 46 percent respectively), and having an objectionable boyfriend (46 percent). Thus, these youths are charged as PINS for actions that may represent sensible attempts to avoid their harmful homelife and to seek refuge in the company of youths their own age.

†Thirty-nine percent of neglected youths have previous court contacts compared with 23 percent of non-neglected youths.

‡In New York, 75 percent of adjusted youths considered neglected are referred for further counseling elsewhere, in contrast to 69 percent of youths who are not neglected. In Rockland, 33 percent of adjusted youths deemed neglected are referred for further help, while only 11 percent of non-neglected youths are so referred.

**Among cases referred to court, neglected youths accounted for 59 percent of late hours allegations and 64 percent of charges of keeping undesirable companions. Fifty-seven percent of vile language and disorderly conduct charges and 60 percent of allegations of verbal abuse occur in neglect cases.

Drug possession is alleged with 10 percent of neglected youths who are sent to court; the same percentage are charged with larceny; 12 percent are charged with assault. These are the most prevalent criminal allegations; in addition, there are a few cases of malicious mischief and the underage use of alcohol.

††Forty percent of neglected youths are detained, while only 32 percent of non-neglected youths are detained. Curiously, neglected youths have few warrants—a rate of 23 percent, compared to 29 percent with non-neglected youths. This suggests that running away is not a major problem with neglected youths, which is confirmed by the fact that allegations of runaway occur less often in neglect cases than the statistical mean of 42 percent. Thirty-six percent of neglected youths are charged with short runaway, while 38 percent are charged with a long runaway. It is also confirmed by the fact that 42 percent of

quently than their non-neglected peers.* At disposition, the court is more likely to subject a neglected PINS youth to its regulating power: 59 percent of these respondents receive regulating dispositions in contrast to 44 percent of non-neglected youths.† And when highly regulating dispositions (i.e., institutional placements) are considered, all the youths sent to training school were neglected, as were 78 percent of those placed and 50 percent of those sent to Division for Youth camps and to facilities of the Department of Social Services.

Thus, the PINS jurisdiction in practice is systematically extended to encompass cases in which the parents could equally well have been charged with abuse or neglect. Proceeding against the children as PINS, rather than against the parents as neglectful, is open to two objections. First, it is unfair to penalize such youths—whether by training school or merely by the stigma of being processed as a PINS—for a matter in which fault, if it is to be placed [100], should be placed upon the adult. Second, many of the private agencies which provide the best services available to the court will not accept PINS youths but will accept neglected youths. Processing neglected youths as PINS may therefore cut them off from the services which would most appropriately serve their needs [101]. This last consideration takes on special significance when it is appreciated that these youths reappear in court more frequently than respondents who do not appear to be neglected.‡

Identity of Complainants and Court Response

The second major factor associated with decisions in PINS cases is the identity of the complainant. The data support a conclusion suggested by the observation study of New York County and Rockland County described above: that court agencies readily accommodate certain classes of complainants. In particular, when schools, which court personnel perceive as "sister" institutions, are involved, action usually follows. Though parental complaints are treated with more scepticism than those from schools, they usually are taken seriously by the court. Most other complainants get minimal attention.

The Response to Schools: Automatic Aid. Twenty-seven percent of PINS cases are brought to intake by school officials, almost always for truancy.**

---

detained, neglected youths are held because of fear they will abscond, whereas 52 percent of youths who are detained but not neglected are detained for that reason.

With respect to place of detention, 46 percent of neglected, detained youths are sent to secure facilities, in contrast to 88 percent of non-neglected detained youths.

*Fifty-four percent of neglected and 44 percent of non-neglected youths are adjudicated PINS.

†In New York, 25 percent of neglected youths receive a regulating disposition, while in Rockland County 92 percent receive a regulating disposition. In both counties those not neglected receive regulating dispositions at a lower rate.

‡Thirty-four percent of neglected youths recidivate, compared with only 25 percent of non-neglected youths.

**The alleged truants are usually (69 percent) boys, and truancy is the sole allegation in 85 percent of these cases. When it is not, the most frequent accompanying allegations are disorderly conduct and vile language.

Response to these cases is nearly automatic; 84 percent of youths brought to intake by schools are referred to court, in contrast to 52 percent of non-school cases. The routineness of referral suggests virtual abdication in these cases of the intake department's responsibility to attempt adjustment of complaints [102]. Once in court, school cases continue to be processed with particular thoroughness, and formal adjudications are entered almost four times more frequently than is true of non-school cases.* Upon disposition, 82 percent of these cases receive regulating dispositions, usually a form of probation supervision.†

This pattern of response seems regrettable for several reasons. Initially, the behavior occasioning action often seems minor‡ and mishandling of problems by the schools themselves is often cause or catalyst of a youth's problems. As one home-school counselor explained, the schools use the court to "get rid of" youths seen as "peripheral kids" [103] and often do not first explore alternatives within the school system for dealing with the problems such youths manifest. Detention after school and superintendant's hearings may be a sufficient response to some kinds of disciplinary problems. Expanded vocational programs might, for example, help relieve student apathy and truanting since observation of school cases reveals that truanting often results from the child's exclusion—

More than 90 percent of school complaints in the sample occurred in Rockland County, where truancy is less endemic than in New York City and court facilities less burdened. In Rockland any youth with more than fifteen or twenty unexplained absences is routinely referred to court.

In New York, a truancy problem must be considerably more serious before it is brought to court, in many cases involving a year or more of unexplained absences. There are several reasons for this: (1) In the newly decentralized school board structure in New York, many local boards have not continued to hire Attendance Officers, and there is therefore less record-keeping; (2) The school system has more resources for handling would-be truants: "600" schools and special at-home instruction are among the possibilities; (3) The schools, especially in New York County, are put to a stiff test in bringing a PINS case: law guardians often subpoena all attendance records for a youth, demand extensive testimony from school officials, etc. Given this resistance, and the many problems among youths in New York which are more serious than missing a few days of school, it simply is not worth the school's time and effort to bring an offender to court.

It should be noted, however, that parents in New York allege truancy in almost half the cases they bring. This allegation is taken with varying degrees of seriousness by the court, depending on other circumstances.

*This somewhat reflects the predominance of both school cases and findings in Rockland County, but even in New York school cases receive findings at a rate—33 percent—well above the rate for cases initiated by non-school complainants.

†Twenty-five percent are placed on probation outright, 34 percent receive a suspended judgment, and 7 percent are placed under informal supervision. Other dispositions in school cases are as follows: training school, 2 percent; DFY facilities, 5 percent; agency placement, 7 percent; and private, non-residential counseling, 2 percent. The remainder are withdrawn or dismissed.

‡Many of these cases which come from schools do not involve serious problems. However, some 42 percent of school cases involve neglect (though the school does not seem to distinguish the two), and the court, as discussed above, responds strongly to them, with greater rates of referral to court, detention, adjudication, and regulating dispositions. Nonetheless, despite the protestations of court and probation personnel that their extreme response to school cases is justified by this neglect, the majority of school cases at every stage of the processing remain those of non-neglected youths with relatively trivial problems.

because of insufficient programs or because of over-bureaucratized procedures for admission—from much-desired vocational training. In addition, schools might alleviate some truancy-related problems if they better investigated the reasons for a youth's absence; inquiry is limited currently to a letter to the parents followed, after twenty truancies, by a PINS petition.

Schools may also be more capable of useful attention to a youth's needs than the court. School officials are often more familiar with particular children than the court, which relies upon the school for records, tests, background, and family information and therefore operates at one informational remove and necessarily with greater delay.* Furthermore, the remedies available to the court seldom go beyond what the school could achieve without court intervention; usually the court simply orders that a youth be admitted to a vocational program or that he attend school under the threat of probation supervision.

By and large, then, courts do not solve school problems. The high recidivism rate for school cases indicates the doubtful effectiveness of court processing and it is further significant that, in *all* PINS cases initiated by schools where the youth recidivates as a PINS, the subsequent charges are also brought by schools.†

The Response to Parents: Authority Affirmed.   Parents or other relatives are the complainants in the largest group of PINS matters, comprising some 55 percent of all cases at intake [104]. Intake and judicial response to complaints initiated by parents is less automatic than that observed in school cases; only 54 percent are referred to court at intake, 39 percent of parental petitions receive findings, while 33 percent of petitioned cases receive regulating dispositions.‡

This class of cases usually involves conflict between youth and parent over

---

*Although overall processing from intake to disposition is the same for school and non-school cases, the median length of time from intake to a finding in non-school cases is only 42.5 days, whereas in school cases the comparable figure is 79.5 days, nearly twice as long. Dispositions then occur more quickly than in non-school cases, often because they require so little—a simple call to the admissions department of a vocational program, for example.

†A substantial number recidivate on delinquency petitions, and in some of these cases the school is likewise the complainant.

Finally, more than 40 percent of all youths brought on school cases who recidivate do so on violation and modification petitions, compared to 12 percent for non-school cases of recidivism. These petitions represent the court generating its own further business; ineffective probation supervision fails to alter the youth's behavior or the serious problems in the home, the probation officer brings another petition charging violation of the terms of probation, and the whole process begins again. Since most of the youth brought on charges from the schools are fourteen or fifteen, after one or two rounds of court processing they are able to drop out of school to begin work.

‡To some extent, differences from school-initiated petitions in findings and dispositions reflect the fact that more parentally-initiated petitions occurred in New York, with its lower rates of adjudication and regulating dispositions. In both counties, however, parent-initiated petitions received less rigorous handling than did petitions from schools.

such matters as the youth's refusal to obey, his or her choice of friends, sexual activity, verbal behavior, and the like—issues that have become a test of wills between parent and child* in which the question of saving face plays no small part [105]. By the time a parent arrives at intake, he or she is often irate and hostile, a state that is aggravated by the implicit admission of inadequacy associated with seeking help from the court [106]. A flood of claimed wrongs is poured out to the intake officer.† While the officer may attempt to adjust matters, and often has a fairly high success rate with the less insistent,‡ in other cases the officer simply acquiesces in a parent's desire to see the youth in court.**

Once in court, parents often insist on immediate punishment for their children, to which the PINS statute—which makes *whatever* the child has done unlawful as long as the parental order was lawful [107]—interposes no legal barrier. Parental passions—"He is such a liar, his mind is bad and he needs to be put away," said a parent in one case—are on occasion powerful enough to divert judges and other court personnel from questioning whether the youth may have acted justifiably, lawfully, or even more maturely than his parents.

In many cases, the parent's first wish will be to get the youth to court because

*Thus allegations at intake, in cases initiated by parents, include short runaways, 52 percent; refusal to obey, 47 percent; late hours, 37 percent; various forms of unacceptable speech, 21 percent; staying out overnight, 20 percent; undesirable friends, 14 percent; and long runaways, 13 percent. Truancy is alleged in 44 percent. Unique controversies between parent and child, which fit none of our categories, are represented in some 21 percent of the cases.

†Observation in Rockland County indicates that parents bring a "shopping list" of charges to intake. If they feel that the intake officer is not sufficiently persuaded of their desire to have their child brought to court, they often will begin to produce further allegations. Much the same circumstances prevail in New York.

‡Forty-six percent of all cases are adjusted, 54 percent sent to court. Even when the former occurs, adjustment does not mean that youths have escaped all effects of court involvement. There is a time loss and an intrusion into the youth's privacy as the intake process is carried out, and often—74 percent of the time in New York—cases which are adjusted result in the youth's attendance at "voluntary" counseling, frequently under the threat of a return to court. In Rockland the comparable figure is 17 percent, which greatly understates actual "voluntary" referrals because probation records do not record referrals systematically. Moreover, such court involvement, minimal though it may appear in contrast to cases which go on to petitions, can be a significant step in the stigmatizing or labeling process.

**While this is not statistically measurable, observation suggests that this may happen in perhaps one in five cases referred to court. It is reflected in the high percentages of cases with "face-saving" allegation which wind up in court. Where the parent charges the child with various forms of disrespectful speech, 88 percent of the cases are sent to court; allegations of refusal to obey result in the youth going to court 61 percent of the time. Where a parent, usually a mother objects to the daughter's boyfriend, 64 percent of the cases are sent to court, and when the daughter is charged with being promiscuous, fully 80 percent of the cases go to court.

By contrast, where the parent alleges arson, only 50 percent of the cases go to court. And when the parent charges the child with larceny, only 57 percent of cases wind up in court.

he or she has run away or refused to appear, and a warrant will be issued.* As soon as the youth is in court, detention is commonly sought by the parent. Forty-one percent of parent-initiated cases involve detention, in contrast to the 30 percent rate for other petitions. Often, angry parents are able to influence detention decisions by the simple expedient of refusing to take their children home. Despite the official Comments of the 1962 Drafting Committee that the judge should consider filing a neglect petition against parents for such a refusal [108], judges routinely acquiesce in the parents' demand by ordering detention for the respondent.

Though instances of such punitive detention are seldom so labeled in court records, we found that 11 percent of all detention was officially ordered for this reason. Based on observation of detention decisions, we would estimate further that the court allows itself to be used in this way by parents in close to 50 percent of all cases involving detention of children who are brought to court by their parents. Moreover, when such punitive detention occurs, the youth in two out of three cases is placed in a secure facility, a rate of secure detention as high as that when the reason for detention is fear that the child will commit a criminal act.

Thus a determined parent can on occasion effectively bypass the intake process, have a child brought to court, and compel detention of the youth by refusing to take him home. Often that is all that the parent wishes from the court, and most parental petitions are withdrawn or dismissed at this point. It is interesting to note, however, that there is a very low withdrawal rate for certain kinds of allegations that especially involve questions of saving face, as when a girl is charged with some form of sexual activity.†

The Response to Other Complaints. Finally, PINS cases are also occasionally brought by neighbors, police, and various sorts of non-familial custodians. Response to these complainants is minimal.

The Family Court Act provides that any adult may bring a PINS petition [109]. Neighbors are the chief group among persons not related to or institutionally responsible for a youth to take advantage of this provision. These cases amount, however, to only 6 percent (fifteen cases) of the entire sample. Most of them occur in Rockland County and involve white youths. Many of the alle-

---

*Warrants are issued in 38 percent of parent-initiated cases, and in only 14 percent of nonparental petitions.

†For instance, no cases in which an undesirable boyfriend has been alleged are withdrawn, though fully 60 percent are dismissed by the court. Only 24 percent of late hours cases are withdrawn, though 47 percent are dismissed; only 22 percent of the cases with bad companion allegations are withdrawn, though 56 percent are dismissed; none of the verbal abuse cases is withdrawn, though 50 percent are dismissed; only 29 percent of the cases with allegations of overnighting are withdrawn, though 41 percent are dismissed.

Where there are sexual allegations against a girl, whether in the petition or simply known from other sources, only 13 percent of the petitioned cases are withdrawn, while 48 percent of cases involving girls without such allegations are withdrawn.

gations in these cases appear serious; in 93 percent (fourteen cases) criminal allegations (usually assault or malicious mischief) are made against the youth. And, as with cases initiated by parents, the adult complainant is usually very angry and wants to use the court as a way of punishing the youth for acts the adult finds unacceptable.

Yet the response of court and probation personnel to these allegations and to the anger of the complainants is minimal. While probation and court personnel often acknowledge that the youths charged by neighbors have indeed misbehaved or even acted criminally, they are willing in these matters to take a balanced view of the dispute. They seldom fall back on the presumption that in any conflict the youth must be the erring party, which is omnipresent when a parent is the complainant. Moreover, neighbors' charges (unlike those of parents) are evaluated in terms of the stigmatizing effects court processing is likely to have on the youth. Thus, almost 87 percent of these cases are adjusted; of the 13 percent referred to court, none is adjudicated PINS. All neighbor-initiated complaints are therefore withdrawn or dismissed.

Seven percent of PINS cases considered at intake (sixteen cases) are initiated by the police. Just over half of these are referred for court action; only one of these reaches a finding (and receives a suspended judgment); the rest are disposed of without a regulating disposition. With one exception these cases represent actions in which the police have picked up runaways from outside the local jurisdiction, often from outside the state, and brought them to court merely for administrative processing and transfer back home.

Finally, 5 percent of the sample (twelve cases) originate with some kind of non-familial custodian. The results of these cases are so varied that no valid generalities may be offered about them.*

Criminal Allegations and Reduced Delinquencies

Two other groups can be statistically isolated in the cases studied, and the response to them further illustrates the unanticipated paths of court processing.

The first group comprises PINS youths who are accused of activity that would be criminal if committed by an adult.† A second group consists of

---

*Seven of them involve runaways of some sort, three involve truancy, three a refusal to obey, two disorderly conduct, one vile language, one verbal abuse, one larceny, and two "other"allegations. Three-quarters of them go on to court, at which point two of the cases shift complainants or are otherwise recategorized as coming from parents, schools, neighbors, or police; therefore 5 percent of petitions in the sample are categorized as brought by non-related custodians. Once in court, detention occurs in over half of the cases, and findings in 43 percent. Two of the cases are withdrawn, one transferred, one placed with an agency, and three were still pending as of the time our sample was taken.

†This group was derived by aggregating all allegations of actions which, if committed by adults, would be either crimes or violations. While substantial numbers of both boys and girls are involved, the boys tend to be primarily in court for physical violence or crimes against the property or persons of others, while girls are primarily accused of abusing drugs or alcohol.

youths whose court involvement is initiated with a delinquency petition that is reduced to a PINS petition at some point during court processing [110]. Both groups of youths are gently treated by the court.

The first group, those who have allegedly committed criminal acts, represents 31 percent of PINS cases coming to intake. Their acts are, presumably, serious relative to other PINS charges; thus it is not surprising to find that they are detained at a rate slightly higher than that for youths not charged with criminal actions* and are held primarily in secure facilities.† They are also more frequently sought on warrants, which are issued in 39 percent of the criminal cases compared to 23 percent overall. It also appears, however, that they are slightly less likely to be referred to court‡ and, when they are, adjudication is much less likely than in other PINS cases. Only 36 percent of these cases result in findings, whereas the overall PINS adjudication rate is 57 percent. Moreover, and perhaps most surprising, children charged with violating the law receive considerably fewer regulating dispositions than other respondents; specifically, 31 percent receive regulating dispositions in contrast to a rate of 65 percent for such dispositions in cases where criminal allegations are absent [111].

The second group of youths, who initially come to court on delinquency petitions, represent what is in ways a substantial segment of the PINS jurisdiction— 44 percent of PINS cases which receive findings in New York originate as delinquency cases [112]. In order to ascertain how these cases were handled, a limited number were selected for analysis. In Rockland County all such cases in 1972 (nine in all) were examined. In New York County an extensive search of docket books and court files revealed 121 such cases. Every fifth docket entry was selected (yielding twenty-four cases) and four others were chosen randomly. Information was available on twenty-two of these twenty-eight cases. The analysis that follows is based on thirty-one cases; accordingly, the reported percentages only can suggest general trends.

In most respects the youths involved in these cases differ little from PINS,** but they have considerably higher rates of previous court involvement. Over 50 percent of them have prior contact with the court,†† and 39 percent of them have previous court contact on allegations of delinquent activity.‡‡

---

*Forty-two percent of those petitions which allege criminal misbehavior involve detention; cases lacking such criminal allegations have detention rates of only 33 percent.

†Seventy-two percent of those detained are held in secure facilities, 28 percent in nonsecure facilities. Curiously, in only a few cases is the reason for detention listed as possible danger to others. More than 50 percent of the time, the reason for detaining those who are charged with criminal allegations is fear that they will abscond.

‡Fifty-six percent are referred to court in contrast to the norm of 61 percent.

**However, as a group, these reduced delinquency cases overwhelmingly involve male youths (84 percent), in contrast to PINS, who are almost equally divided by sex.

††Their siblings also have higher rates of previous court contact, nearly doubling the PINS rates. Averaging 3.6 siblings, they have an average of 1.1 siblings with court contacts.

‡‡A detailed examination of previous records of such youths was undertaken in New York. It revealed that 59 percent of delinquents reduced to PINS had some form of previous

Police and others (usually witnesses to the allegedly criminal act) are the most common petitioners,* and assault, robbery, possession of a dangerous weapon, and various other allegations involving violent activity are the most common charges against these youths.† This group of respondents appears more cooperative than most PINS, however; only 16 percent of their cases involve warrants, in contrast to a rate of 34 percent in PINS cases, and detention is ordered in only 26 percent of cases,‡ although 35 percent of PINS are detained [113].

Adjudications are made in all of these cases, of course. In some cases, an adjudication of delinquency has been vacated and replaced by a PINS adjudication; in others, the latter is the only finding formally made. These youths seem to demand trials less often than is generally true of delinquency cases but somewhat more often than is true of PINS cases overall.** Especially in New York, the youth's law guardian tries to strike a bargain prior to the adjudicatory proceeding, agreeing to admit all charges in return for the substitution of a PINS petition. In other cases, the reduction comes later, instigated by highly favorable probation reports or by new information presented to the court by the law guardian [114].

Youths whose delinquency charges have been reduced in this way often fare very well at disposition. Almost one-fifth are dismissed outright at this point and, surprisingly, the rate of dismissal is even higher when the youth is charged with assault, burglary, larceny or robbery.†† The majority of youths are placed

---

court involvement: 41 percent of all reduced youths had previously been accused of delinquent acts, and 14 percent of them had been accused of criminal acts on two or more occasions. Moreover, of the 59 percent in New York who had had previous court involvement, more than 60 percent had petitions filed against them—in contrast to a rate of 30 percent in PINS cases. Thus, their previous cases were taken more seriously by the court itself than were those of PINS.

In addition, 10 percent had previous court contacts with PINS allegations; 3 percent had previous court contacts in neglect matters.

*Forty-eight percent of cases had police as complainants, while 39 percent had what we classified as "others."

†Forty-eight percent of cases alleged assault, 32 percent robbery, 19 percent possession of a dangerous weapon, and 32 percent "other" allegations, which include: boys started a brawl by assaulting a policeman who was trying to arrest their friend; youth found without a driver's license, driving a stolen car; a girl stole a check from a woman after forcing her to endorse it; a youth stabbed the complainant twice in the abdomen, causing hospitalization and surgery; a youth forced four eleven-year-olds to strip, then commit fellatio upon him, whereafter he forced the children to jump on broken glass and then he beat them with a leather belt.

‡When detention is ordered, in 50 percent of cases it is because the youth is considered dangerous; in 38 percent of cases because of fear he will abscond, and 13 percent of cases because a parent refuses to take a child home. Detention is overwhelmingly in secure facilities.

**In 13 percent of cases the allegations are denied, prompting a trial. In 60 percent of cases, the allegations are admitted in full; in 27 percent of cases, they are admitted in part.

††Thirty-three percent of those charged with assault are dismissed as are 33 percent of those charged with burglary, 33 percent of those charged with larceny, and 22 percent of those charged with robbery.

on probation.* This pattern of dispositions is remarkable, given the underlying charges and the fact that prior court involvement is more common among youths whose cases are dismissed than among those placed on probation.†

No ready explanation can be given for the minimal court response to these two groups of allegedly criminal youths. Observation suggests that judges and probation officers sympathize with both groups of youths more easily and find them more "normal" than most PINS youths, on the basis of their background factors and demeanor. For example, PINS youths accused of criminal activity more often come from middle class families than youths not charged with criminal allegations. Nearly twice as many youths (43 percent) charged with criminal allegations at intake have families with incomes over $8,000 per year as do youths not accused of criminal activity (23 percent).‡ This comparatively better economic background may generate an empathetic response from court personnel.

Similar background factors appear to soften the court's response to reduced delinquents. They, too, have wealthier families than those of PINS youths overall: 36 percent of them have families with over $8,000 per year income, while only about 30 percent of PINS' families reach this income bracket.** Moreover, only 16 percent of these cases revealed evidence of parental mistreatment, in contrast to a rate of over 40 percent among petitioned PINS youths.

The reasons given for the reductions from delinquent to PINS status clearly reflect the sympathetic response these youths arouse in court and probation personnel. Our survey of court records revealed case after case in which were listed reasons for reduction such as the following: "sympathetic probation report," "good probation report," "child's demeanor—kid's very intelligent." These cases thus represent instances where personal feelings of judges and probation person-

---

*Nineteen percent are dismissed, 52 percent are placed on probation, 15 percent receive suspended judgment, 4 percent are privately placed, and 11 percent receive some other form of disposition. The last were usually transferred to other jurisdictions for final processing. There were also four cases sampled in which disposition had not yet been ordered.

†Most (80 percent) of those dismissed had prior court involvement, while only 25 percent of those placed on probation had such contacts. Of those *without* court involvement previously, only 14 percent are dismissed; 36 percent of those with previous contact are dismissed.

‡This statistic, like all those affecting income, derives primarily from New York County. In Rockland, where there are few income statistics, those with and without criminal allegations at intake have families of approximately equal wealth. In New York, 39 percent of cases where there were criminal allegations at intake had families with incomes over $8,000 while only 13 percent of cases without such criminal allegations had families with incomes over $8,000 per year; 72 percent of cases with criminal intake allegations had incomes over $5,000 per year, compared with 44 percent of cases without criminal allegations. Those cases with criminal allegations at intake, however, also have a high percentage of their number on welfare: 37 percent compared with 24 percent of those cases lacking criminal allegations.

**Rather inexplicably, as with allegedly criminal PINS, a higher percentage of these youths had families on welfare (some 36 percent) than do PINS proper (27 percent).

nel may operate in favor of the youths involved, reversing the usual negative consequences and burdens of court processing. That this reversal should work in favor of a group of youths accused of criminal and often violent acts is ironic.

CONCLUSION

Assumptions Reexamined

In practice, the absence of explicit legal standards and processing guidelines has permitted the Family Court in both New York and Rockland counties to evolve idiosyncratic yet essentially similar modes of decision-making, each heavily influenced by a single group within the court and vulnerable to pressures from adamant and angry parents. An overall statistical examination of these decisions reveals an erratic pattern, reflecting bureaucratic concerns of the dominant processing group (such as whether the complainant represents another institution, like a school) and personal preferences (toward some parents and toward generally more appealing middle class youths).

These findings suggest that current PINS processing in New York State is fundamentally flawed when measured against the goals on which jurisdiction is founded. It remains to consider whether those goals ever can be realized.

Beneath the PINS jurisdiction's goal of "saving" individual youths from "downward careers" lies a series of assumptions. It is assumed that a court can (1) understand accurately a youth's past behavior; (2) predict accurately how a youth will develop in the future without court intervention (and, therefore, whether a youth has an unmet need of supervision), and (3) predict accurately that with court ordered "treatment" a youth's development will follow a different, more "desirable" path than that foreseen in its absence. We submit that courts are unable to do any of these.

Adolescent Behavior: The Limits of Understanding. PINS cases present problems of the maturation of adolescent youths which are far more complicated than those usually considered justiciable. For instance, they typically involve not only the youth but an entire parent-child relationship. This relationship is of greater duration, intimacy, and emotional intensity than most other legally ordered relationships and attains a heightened complexity during the adolescent period as individual youths undergo physical and emotional changes and transfer their dependencies from parents to age-peers. Far more issues on a far greater variety of levels are presented than in relationships between, for example, contracting parties or between tortfeasors and their victims. The issues in a PINS case are, as well, often more difficult to judge than those involving crime or the blatant neglect or abuse which Family Courts frequently face.

The fact that the persons considered are young people makes it especially difficult to deal with such complex problems. Judges share the common propensity to assume that youths are less complicated than they really are and to create a "mythology of childhood" [115] that minimizes the competence and independence achievable by children and youths and maximizes their dependency, incapacity, and need for control and guidance [116]. Such a view further reduces the chance for accurate court understanding and response. And, like all adults, judges are prone to act contradictorily in response to their own ambivalent feelings as to whether youths' needs should predominate over those of adults [117].

The court is further handicapped by inadequate information in trying to cope with the problems presented by a typical PINS case. It often operates under strict time constraints and has limited means of informing itself. For example, as noted in the discussions of the counties, psychological studies and probation investigations rarely provide the court with more than summary labels that fail to capture the complex reality of the underlying problems.

In trying to interpret the past behavior of alleged PINS youths, then, judges are handicapped by the intrinsic complexity of the parent-child problems most cases present, by the implicit assumptions common to most adults that impede accurate perception of young people, and by the related pressures of lack of time and lack of adequate information. It is thus not remarkable that judges generally understand the youths before them only superficially and fall back on personal beliefs about adolescent needs and about how young people should behave. These beliefs (e.g., that sexual interest is "abnormal" among fourteen-year-olds) may be inconsistent with much of current informed thought about adolescent behavior and development.

Anticipating What Will Happen: The Limits of Prediction: Part I. PINS jurisdiction also presumes that the court is capable of predicting what will happen to a youth in the future without court intervention. Yet such prediction is risky business. Take, for example, one of the original justifications for court jurisdiction over non-criminal juvenile offenders: that they were "predelinquent," i.e., likely to become criminal offenders. This notion has been much explored, and neither the predictive nor the preventive abilities ascribed to the jurisdiction by this view bears up under critical scrutiny. Assuming *arguendo* that "predelinquent" means "on the verge of committing a delinquent act,"* there are no empirical data available which establish that "predelinquency" may accurately be predicted by the PINS jurisdiction or by any other means [118]. Extensive studies of high school and college students who repeatedly disobeyed their parents or engaged in other forms of misbehavior during their younger years clearly demonstrate that these individuals seldom become delinquent [119]. Another recent test of the "predelinquency" predictive theory revealed that, when psychiatrists and social workers attempted to predict which adolescents would become delinquents based on background factors similar to those that often

---

*There is no consensus as to what the category "pre-delinquent" means. Since a delinquent is a young person apprehended and convicted of a criminal act, the delinquent category is the result not only of individual characteristics, but also of law enforcement practices. Therefore, being "predelinquent" might mean "on the verge of commiting a criminal act" or "on the verge of getting caught and convicted for a criminal act," or both.

occur in PINS cases, their predictions were incorrect more than 50 percent of the time [120].

Can Court Processing Solve Anything? The Limits: Part II. To justify the existence of the PINS jurisdiction, the court must be presumed able not only to predict the path a youth will follow without its intervention, but also to predict that court "treatment" will lead him to develop in a more desirable manner. Yet it is doubtful that any "supervision" at the court's command could have a major positive impact upon young people.

First, any positive impact must be discounted by the negative effect court processing may have upon youths and their families. Research on stigma shows that adjudications tend to alter one's image not only in the eyes of others but also in one's own eyes [121]. This perception of oneself as "tarnished" and less valued than others is accompanied in the long run by a loss of respect for the institutions of law, the legal process, and authority in general [122]. More immediately, such court proceedings may exacerbate intrafamily hostilities, and even increase an embattled parent's already heavy burden by treating the parent as the *only* source of rationality and competence within the family unit. And, by presuming the child helpless and incompetent, the court process cuts off the strength and support which the child might bring to the family were he or she treated as a responsible and contributing member of it. Thus, rather than strengthening the parent-child relationship in the child's interest, the PINS jurisdiction may weaken the family by isolating the child-respondent from it [123].

Second, the problems which the youth manifests in many cases simply cannot be remedied by means available to the court: it cannot supply a missing father, treble family income, or give a youth a second start on life with different parents.

Third, even where problems are not so all-encompassing, it is doubtful that even a vast commitment of resources could provide effective "treatment."* Judge Dembitz of New York, a strong apologist for the PINS jurisdiction, has recently said that "Despite the general upsurge in social science research during the past twenty or thirty years, there are no systematic data or reliable followups as to whether and when state intervention proves beneficial in the lives of beyond-lawful-authority youths" [124]. Indeed, little positive success (as marked by a lack of recidivism) has been demonstrated for any treatment, and it has been observed, "a very large number of studies of the effectiveness of punishments and treatments have negative results" [125]. A variety of social factors

---

*While a vast inflow of funds would no doubt improve staffing and physical conditions at the various facilities on which the court relies (however improbable such an inflow may be), improved conditions would not necessarily guarantee the *effectiveness* of the services. Science is not yet able to predict accurately what will "cure" individual problems, especially in dealing with needs revealed in complex parent-child conflicts. Hence, it is an open question whether, even with a commitment of funds, these institutions could surmount the limitations of human insight and leave the youths sent to them in a state substantially less detrimental than similar but "untreated" youths.

have been found to have great predictive power regarding recidivism, but none of these ordinarily relate to treatment [126].

Moreover, studies indicate that treatment, unless undertaken voluntarily, is not likely to be successful for such problems as those manifested by PINS. Those youths who do volunteer are more likely to "open up," and engage in verbal interaction with counselors [127]. Compulsion, on the other hand, often generates resistance [128], and not only is PINS treatment received under compulsion, but this compulsion is perceived by many youths as unjustified [129].

Briefly put, PINS jurisdiction is rooted in assumptions which, though emotionally compelling, are factually dubious. The failure of the jurisdiction stems from an overestimation of the capacities of the law. As an eminent authority in the related field of child placement recently observed:

[O]ur capacity to predict is limited. No one—and psychoanalysis creates no exception—can forecast just what experiences, what events, what changes a child, or for that matter his adult custodian, will actually encounter. Nor can anyone predict in detail how the unfolding development of a child and his family will be reflected in the long run in the child's personality and character formation. Thus the law will not act in the child's interests but merely add to the uncertainties if it tries to do the impossible —guess the future and impose . . . special conditions for the child's care [130].

Abolition

We recommend, therefore, that PINS jurisdiction be abolished. We base this recommendation on two principles. First, legal intervention in any situation must be tempered by a realistic assessment of its potential to achieve intended aims. The law is a blunt instrument with all the limitations of its imperfect creators. Our ability to predict is slight, and to intervene in the lives of non-criminal youths because of possible later misconduct is to put too much faith in limited instruments of prediction and treatment.

Second, the law should make the developmental needs of juveniles paramount over adult desires that run counter to them. It is to young people that society must turn to realize its hopes for ending the recurrent generational cycles of poverty and family breakdown which produce most PINS [131]. This means that the aim of giving "surcease to embattled parents" [132] is *not* an adequate justification for the PINS jurisdiction. For even though law cannot create human relationships or predict their growth, it can often destroy them and damage individual development—a cost too high to pay for such "surcease." It is likewise indefensible to put the development of important members of the next generation in the hands of decisionmakers whose decisions often are and must be based on idiosyncratic predilections or on bureaucratic pressures.

Moreover, abolition of the PINS jurisdiction does not imply that those youths now processed as PINS who are in fact neglected or criminal would be removed from the court. Indeed it might yield an increase in services, at least for neglected youths.* And while use of the delinquency jurisdiction for criminal PINS might appear to be a harsh measure, it would in fact provide greater protection for some respondents by affording them the constitutional protections to which alleged delinquents are entitled.

In addition, youths who use force against a parent could also continue to be processed by the court, just as adults are when they go beyond the bounds of accepted behavior in a family controversy. When a husband beats a wife in a family argument he is susceptible to adjudication as a family offender [133]. There is no reason why a child who goes so far as to use force against his parents should not be brought before the court as a family offender as well [134].

Hence, though judges protest any move to abolish the PINS jurisdiction with the plea, "We simply can't walk away from any responsibility to help" [135], abolition of PINS charges would not entail such abandonment. Judicial intervention would remain an option for the majority of those desperately in need of the sort of help that is usually difficult to obtain without the intervention of the family court.

However, those non-criminal, non-neglected youths now brought in as PINS to be "helped" because of truancy or disagreements with their parents would, of course, not receive such "help." Instead, parents who now turn to the court expecting what one judge characterized as "a panacea for all the ills of the family" would be forced back upon their own family resources and upon the range of community resources that often go underutilized in the rush to bring children to court. Schools would be required to fully work through their own procedures before referring "problem kids" to the court. In the end, such private, voluntary procedures might well be more effective for the youths than court processing.

There are, of course, some youths who need help and might not receive it from these sources. But their number is likely to be a few because research indicates that those in need of help frequently do seek it out [136]. Moreover, it must be remembered that many of the PINS cases which come to court involve issues of passing rather than ultimate significance in the lives of youths. Finally, 85 percent of PINS youths are thirteen years old or over, while more than 40 percent are over fifteen, with developed competencies to care for themselves in many ways.†

---

*Even with no increase in overall services, provisions for neglected youths might still be likely to improve. For example, in detention facilities neglected youths currently form only a minor proportion of the juvenile jurisdiction, and as a consequence, they are detained in facilities with youths charged with serious criminal actions. If neglect petitions were brought in the many PINS cases where neglect is present, there might be sufficient demand to designate some detention facilities exclusively for neglected youths.

†This might seem to imply the necessity of retaining jurisdiction for younger juveniles up through age twelve or so. However, it must be remembered that the sort of serious harm which would threaten these youths would derive primarily from abandonment by their parents, which would open the door to state succor of the youth in a neglect proceeding. It must also be remembered that whatever the age of the youth concerned, the effects of court processing will be equally detrimental; indeed, the effects of delay, detention, removal from the home, and stigma may be more harmful to younger youths than to the thirteen, fourteen and fifteen year olds with whom the court normally deals.

It is important that juveniles be "helped," of course, but the help the PINS jurisdiction now provides some youths is far outweighed by the harm it does to others. Non-criminal youths should be left alone by the law.

NOTES TO CHAPTER 2

1. This figure includes all those cases which are brought to intake including those adjusted there. Cases of the latter sort are considered in this study because they too have substantial consequences for the youth's life: Time is occupied, behavior probed, and frequently, the youth is led to accept "voluntary" counseling under the threat of being sent to court in the future.

The numerical estimate in text is derived by adding to the figure of 8,113 PINS petitions brought in New York State in fiscal year 1973 (*State of New York, The Judicial Conference, Eighteenth Annual Report* 329 (1974)) an estimated 5,300 cases adjusted at intake (based on an extrapolation from our finding that approximately 40 percent of PINS cases are adjusted) to yield a total of about thirteen thousand cases. Although the number of PINS is now declining slightly in New York City (*see* Family Court of the State of New York, City of New York, *Statistical Report* 1973, 1974 (monthly series)), ten thousand is a conservative estimate of the present number of PINS cases processed annually.

2. The precise figures for actions described in this introduction are reported in "New York County" and "Rockland County," *infra*.

3. *See N.Y. Family Court Act* §§754(d), 756, 757 (McKinney Supp. 1973–74). Probation supervision may also be ordered as part of a "suspended judgment," *see, N.Y. Family Court Act* §754(b) (McKinney 1963), and in Rockland County at least, as part of "informal supervision."

4. *See* Comment, " 'Delinquent Child': A Legal Term Without Meaning," 21 *Baylor L. Rev.* 352 (1969) for a useful survey of state laws in this area, including comparative tables, *id.* at 369–71, and Teitelbaum and Harris, "Some Historical Perspectives on Governmental Regulation of Children and Parents," *supra* Ch. 1, for a discussion of the development of PINS jurisdiction. *See also*, I. Solet, Report on State Laws Concerning Detention of Children, September 1973 (unpublished report of Yale Legislative Services in Yale Law Library).

5. *President's Comm'n. on Law Enforcement and the Administration of Justice, Task Force Report: Juvenile Delinquency* 4 (1967).

6. Klapmuts, "Children's Rights: The Legal Rights of Minors in Conflict with Law or Social Custom," 4 *Crime and Delinquency Literature* 449, 470 (1972). Klapmuts goes on to note: "PINS are more likely to receive harsher dispositions and to be sent to correctional institutions; they are more likely to be detained (54 percent) than serious delinquents (31 percent) and twice as likely to be held for more than thirty days; and the median length of institutional stay for PINS is thirteen months, compared with nine months for serious delinquents." *Id.* at 471.

7. *N.Y. Family Court Act*, Art. 7 (McKinney 1962); *Cal. Welf. and Inst.*

Code §601 (West 1961), *as amended, Cal. Welf. and Inst. Code* §601 (West 1972).

8. *See N.Y. Joint Legislative Committee on Court Reorganization*, pt. 2, at 7 (1962), noting that the PINS category is recommended to reduce instances of stigma and at the same time permit the court to use appropriate resources in dealing with persons in need of supervision.

The Association of the Bar of the City of New York, at the time the PINS classification was proposed, expressed doubt "whether this change in labelling will have the intended beneficial effect." *Special Committee on the Reorganization of the Courts of the N.Y. City Bar Ass'n., Reports on the Family Court Act Proposed by the Joint Legislative Committee on Court Reorganization*, Mar. 1, 1962, at 23.

9. Dembitz, "Ferment and Experiment in New York: Juvenile Cases in the New Family Court," 48 *Cornell L. Rev.* 499, 506 (1963) (emphasis supplied) [hereinafter cited as Dembitz].

10. *N.Y. Family Court Act* §712(b) (McKinney Supp. 1973–74).

11. *E.g., Ill. Rev. Stat.* ch. 37, §702–3 (1972) ("Minor in Need of Supervision"); *Fla. Stat. Ann.* tit. 5, §39.01 (11) (a)–(c) (Supp. 1974) ("Child in Need of Supervision"). Within the last few years, still more states have followed this trend. *E.g., Mass. Ann. Laws*, ch. 119, §21 (1975); *N.J. Stat. Ann.* §2A: 4–45 (1975–1976).

12. *E.g., Committee on Mental Health Services Inside and Outside the Family Court in the City of New York, Juvenile Justice Confounded: Pretensions and Realities of Treatment Services* (1972) [hereinafter cited as *Juvenile Justice Confounded*]; Office of Children's Services of the Judicial Conference of the State of New York, The PINS Child, A Plethora of Problems, November, 1973 [hereinafter cited as *OCS: Plethora*]. *See also*, Note, "Nondelinquent Children in New York: The Need for Alternatives to Institutional Treatment," 8 *Colum. J.L. & Soc. Prob.* 251 (1972) [hereinafter cited as *Nondelinquent Children*]; Note, "Persons in Need of Supervision: Is There a Constitutional Right to Treatment?" 39 *Brooklyn L. Rev.* 624 (1973) [hereinafter cited as *Right to Treatment*].

13. Subcommittee on Legal Representation of Indigent and Limited Income Groups, 1st and 2d Jud. Dept. Committees for Court Administration, Task Force (Hon. Florence M. Kelley, Chairman), Report on Legal Representation of Indigents in the Family Court within the City of New York, (August, 1973), p. 24 [hereinafter cited as *Kelley Report*].

14. *Cf.* Dembitz, "Justice for Children—For Now and For the Future," 60 *A.B.A.J.* 588 (1974) [hereinafter cited as Dembitz, *Justice*].

15. *See, e.g., In re* Gault, 387 U.S. 1 (1967); *In re* Winship, 397 U.S. 358 (1970).

16. *In re* Ellery C., 32 N.Y. 2d 588, 300 N.E. 2d 424, 347 N.Y.S. 2d 51 (1973). *Cf. In re* Lavette M., 35 N.Y. 2d 136, 316 N.E. 2d 314, 359 N.Y.S. 2d 20 (1974), upholding the legality of incarcerating PINS in training schools if an individualized treatment program is in effect.

17. *See* pages 81–85, "Criminal Allegations," *infra*.

18. Selection at random—that is, by chance rather than by any necessarily fallible method of personal selection—was used to assure, as far as possible, that the cases actually studied were representative of the entire population of cases processed in New York County. The validity of this device has long been recognized. *See, e.g., D. Campbell* and *J. Stanley, Experimental and Quasi-Experimental Designs for Research* 2 (1963).

19. *See State of New York, The Judicial Conference, Seventeenth Annual Report* 388 (1973) for the raw numbers for the year. The statistical breakdown for this judicial year was the only one available when the sample was chosen in the early summer of 1973. For the succeeding judicial year (July 1, 1972 th ough June 30, 1973) 43 percent of PINS petitions in the state came from New York City and 57 percent from outside it. *See Annual Report, supra* note 1 at 329, for the raw numbers for that year.

20. *See* pages 73—76, "Evidence of Neglect," *infra.*

21. For the importance of these precautionary measures, *see* Becker, "Problems of Inference and Proof in Participant Observations," 23 *Am. Soc. Rev.* 652 (1958); Maccoby and Maccoby, "The Interview: A Tool of Social Science," 1 *Handbook of Social Psychology* 449 (G. Lindzey, ed., 1954).

22. *N.Y. Family Ct. Act* §734 (a)(ii) (McKinney 1963). Adjustment efforts can only extend for an initial period of two months, however, and then may be extended an additional sixty days only with the judge's permission. *N.Y. Family Ct. Act* §734 (c) (McKinney 1963). Information gained therein may not be used at adjudication. *Id.* §735.

23. *Id.* §741.

24. *Id.* §738.

25. *N.Y. Family Ct. Act* §§728(b) (iii); 720(a) (McKinney Supp. 1973—74). The latter states that a secure facility is "characterized by physically restricting construction, hardware, and procedures." *Id.* §720(a) (ii).

26. *In re* W., 28 N.Y. 2d 589, 590, 268 N.E. 2d 642, 643, 319 N.Y.S. 2d 845, 846 (1971). In New York, unlike many jurisdictions, PINS allegations must be proved beyond a reasonable doubt. *N.Y. Family Ct. Act* §742 (McKinney Supp. 1973—74); *In re* E., 68 Misc. 2d 487, 327 N.Y.S. 2d 84 (Fam. Ct. 1971).

27. *N.Y. Family Ct. Act* §§711(b), 756 (McKinney 1963).

28. Placement at a training school is initially limited to a period of eighteen months. *N.Y. Family Ct. Act* §756(b) (McKinney 1963).

29. *Kelley Report, supra* note 13 at 24. This report concludes that "The physical conditions are demeaning to the court system and the people it serves." Happily, unlike most urban American court buildings, this is soon to be replaced by a building now rising in Foley Square. That building will at least be newer, and air-conditioned, and somewhat more rationally planned; for example, in contrast to present practice, the offices of the law guardians and those of the Assistant Corporation Counsel (between whom there is constant professional interchange) will be on the same or adjacent floors. Telephone interview with Judge Joseph Williams, Administrator of the N.Y. Family Ct., Aug. 5, 1974.

30. *N.Y. Family Ct. Act* §734(d) (McKinney 1963) provides that probation may not compel the appearance of any person at intake proceedings.

31. Letter from Ronnie Moskowitz, Research Assistant, Juvenile Justice

Standards Project, to R. Hale Andrews, Jr., September, 1973, p. 3 (on file with authors) [hereinafter cited as Moskowitz].

32. *N.Y. Family Ct. Act* §741(b) (McKinney 1963).

33. Many non-secure shelters have been found to be seriously overcrowded. *Nondelinquent Children, supra* note 12 at 266. This population was, moreover, broken down by a recent New York Assembly investigative committee report as follows: "Twenty percent are mentally disturbed, 10 percent retarded, 3 percent actively homosexual, 30 percent seriously misbehaved and 10 percent physically handicapped." N.Y. Times, Dec. 15, 1973, at 35, col. 8. The committee substantiated reports that youths at the facility were confronted with "homosexual attacks, sexual solicitation, extortion and homicide," *id.*, and depicted the facility "as a place from which youngsters easily sortie to commit muggings and return 'bedecked' in stolen finery and from which youths once left to perpetrate a rape and a murder." N.Y. Times, Dec. 14, 1973, at 51, col. 1. As for secure facilities, a recent case found the following conditions: youths being locked up as punishment even though the PINS youths had not harmed anyone, understaffing and inadequately trained staff, and lack of any bona fide effort to treat the detained youths. Martarella v. Kelley, 349 F. Supp. 575 (S.D.N.Y. 1972). Officials in charge of both secure and non-secure facilities in New York City admit that conditions are so poor as to harm the youths in them. N.Y. Times, April 4, 1973, at 86, col. 1.

34. Silver, "New York City Family Court: A Law Guardian's Overview," 18 *Crime and Delinquency* 93, 96 (1972).

35. Interview with Ms. Polly Whitney, Social Worker, Juvenile Rights Division, Legal Aid Society, N.Y. Family Court, at 135 E. 22nd St., New York City, August 29, 1973.

36. *Juvenile Justice Confounded, supra* note 12 at 22, 23. Agencies admit as much. In a recent suit brought by the Civil Liberties Union and the Legal Aid Society, seventy-seven children's services agencies in New York City and State joined in a consent judgment in which the agencies agreed that "the religion-based system of placing children in need of help in New York City and State has the effect of discriminating against black Protestant youngsters." N.Y. Times, January 6, 1974, §1 at 68, col. 1.

37. N.Y. Times, November 25, 1973, at 57, col. 1.

38. *Id.*

39. Interview with Mr. A.H. Gross, New York County Branch Chief West for Investigation and Supervision, New York City, July 6, 1973. *Cf.* the discussion of such placements in *OCS: Plethora, supra* note 12 at 58–61. A recent study reveals that of the ninety-one PINS children remanded to the Department of Social Services in the city of New York in 1971, only 18 percent ever were actually placed in an agency. Forty-one percent stagnated in shelters, 25 percent were returned to court. *Juvenile Justice Confounded, supra* note 12 at 113. Though the Department of Social Services is required to report to the court on these children within four months, and return them if no placement has been secured, such activity is rare, and children are often left for months in shelters while no action is taken on their cases.

40. Originally only delinquents were to be allowed in training schools. Act of April 24, 1962, ch. 686, §756, 2 [1962] *Session Laws* of *N.Y.* 2301 (McKinney). As a "temporary" measure, in 1963, some months after the Family Court Act was passed, an amendment to it permitted incarceration of PINS in the training schools for a year. Act of April 26, 1963, ch. 809, §10, [1963] *Session Laws of N.Y.* 1336 (McKinney), *as amended by* Act of April 23, 1963, ch. 811, §4, [1963] *Session Laws of N.Y.* 1339 (McKinney). Additional temporary one-year extensions occurred until 1968 when the measure was made permanent. Act of June 22, 1968, ch. 874, §§2, 3, 2 [1968] *Session Laws of N.Y.* 1784 (McKinney). In 1973, the Court of Appeals prohibited the incarceration of PINS in training schools for delinquents, *In re* Ellery C., 32 N.Y. 2d 588, 300 N.E. 2d 424, 347 N.Y.S. 2d 51 (1973), but it recently upheld PINS' incarceration in training schools just for PINS, *In re* Lavette M., 35 N.Y. 2d 136, 316 N.E. 2d 314, 359 N.Y.S. 2d 201 (1974). Now segregated PINS-only and delinquent-only training schools have been established. *OCS: Plethora, supra* note 12 at 77.

41. N.Y. Times, Dec. 2, 1973, §1, at 49, col. 1.

Finally, a small group of PINS children are more or less obviously mentally disturbed. For these children, as another recent study has shown, the state provides no facilities for care; they are shuttled between city psychiatric units and state facilities, which have suffered drastic personnel cutbacks and admit only a few of those who seek and need placement there. Even if a child gains admission, treatment tends to be short-lived, as many children either escape or are dismissed from the hospital, usually without notifying the court. *Office of Children's Services of the Judicial Conference of the State of New York, Desperate Situation—Disparate Service: Psychiatric Hospital Care for Court Related Children in the City of New York*, July, 1973 (available at Office of Children's Services of the Judicial Conference of New York).

42. Twenty-three percent of those adjusted return as PINS, 7 percent as delinquents, and 7 percent as neglect cases. Of those who have gone to court, only 20 percent return at least once. Half of this group reappears as alleged delinquents, while 8 percent reappear as alleged PINS and 2 percent return involved in neglect cases. Two percent of these youths are also charged with failing to comply with the terms of disposition, *see N.Y. Family Ct. Act* §§777, 778, 779 (McKinney 1963).

43. Half way through our sampling period, application of the statute to girls sixteen and over was declared unconstituionally discriminatory because it was not applied to boys of the same age. *In re* Patricia A., 31 N.Y. 2d 83, 286 N.E. 2d 432, 335 N.Y.S. 2d 33 (1972). Cases in our sampling involving juveniles sixteen and over were those involving girls prior to this decision.

44. "Quasi-criminal behavior" is behavior which would be either a crime or a violation if committed by an adult. Though only activity which would be criminal warrants a delinquency petition, *see* Carter v. Family Court, 22 A.D. 2d 888, 255 N.Y.S. 2d 385 (1964), we view youths who have committed quasi-criminal behavior as a group in order to get a sense of the extent to which PINS jurisdiction encompasses anti-social conduct.

For purposes of this and subsequent analysis, runaways are characterized as either short (less than a week) or long (a week or more).

The following table indicates the frequency of each allegation at intake in percentage terms. It should be remembered that there are 108 cases.

New York County: Frequency of Intake Allegations
(N = 108)

	Percent
Refuse to Obey	36
Truancy	48
Late Hours	39
Overnight	22
Short Runaway	46
Long Runaway	17
Disorderly Conduct	1
Vile Language	6
Verbal Abuse	5
Bad Companions	15
Bad Religion	1
Unlawful Assembly	
Harassment	
Assault	9
Malicious Mischief	2
Auto Theft	
Larceny	6
Shoplifting	2
Drug Possession	19
Possession to Sell	1
Glue Sniffing	
Alcohol	4
Illegal Auto Use	
Dangerous Weapon	1
Gambling	
Homicide	
Arson	3
Rape	
Other Sex Crime	
Robbery	
Burglary	1
Illegal Entry	2
Burglar Tools	
Possession Stolen Property	
Homosexuality	
Incest	
Other	24
Bad Boyfriend	14
Prostitution	1
Promiscuity	2
Group Sex	
Cohabiting	1
Found in Sex Acts	
Night with Male	3
Sex Innuendo	4

45. Moskowitz, *supra* note 31 at 17—18.

46. Wallace states, "The jurisdiction of the Family Court as to juveniles should be reduced," noting, "We know very little about how to effectively assist people to make a better adjustment to the world." Interview at 2 Lafayette Street, New York City, July 20, 1973.

47. Moskowitz, *supra* note 31 at 18.

48. *See* pages 73—76, 81—85, *infra.*

49. Each of the intake officers has had at least three years experience and holds at least a middle rank in the probation department. Interview with Mr. Felix J. Subervi, Case Supervisor, Room 616, 135 E. 22nd St., July 12, 1973. There is also a supervisor, who maintains that at least two more officers are needed to handle the job. Anne Mahoney, Interview with Marion Goldberg, Juvenile Intake Supervisor, May 31, 1973, at Room 126, 135 E. 22nd St., N.Y.C.

50. *N.Y. Family Ct. Act* §734(b) (McKinney 1963).

51. One recently observed interview was reported as follows: "When the intake officer asked the girl how she liked her new step-father, she started to say she thought he was O.K., but the mother interrupted by shouting, 'She's lyin' I know she's lyin'." Often the child is not asked whether the allegations are true, just why he or she did them. Moskowitz, Interview Observation, August 23, 1973.

52. Forty-three percent of *all* juvenile cases are referred to court. Annual Statistical Report of the Family Court of the State of New York, City of New York, 1972, p. 17, Table 17 (Probation Services, Intake, Juvenile Cases—By Counties). In contrast, 59 percent of PINS were referred to court.

53. "[The law guardian] will get a case dismissed, all right, but they won't say 'Let's be sure this kid gets treatment'," commented Mr. Felix J. Subervi, Case Supervisor, in an interview at 135 E. 22nd St., New York City, July 12, 1973.

The hostility to the law guardians among the probation personnel in the building—intake officers and CLOs—often leads them to make their recommendations more extreme in order to counter the law guardian's demands for leniency. Thus intake officers overstate the seriousness they see in a case if they think a youth should be detained, in order to counter an expected plea by the youth for probation. Moskowitz, *supra* note 31 at 18.

54. Some 40 percent are late each day and 5 percent never appear at all. Interview with Mr. Felix J. Subervi, Case Supervisor, New York Probation Department, at 135 E. 22nd St., New York City, July 12, 1973.

55. This may not always have been so. When the probation officer who was working on a case was in the same building as the child when the case came to court, as he or she usually was when all juvenile operations were together on 23rd St. (before November of 1971), the probation officer was often the person before the court who had the closest and most immediate contact with the child. This enabled probation to exercise a great deal more power in the courtroom. The current law guardian domination is dated by an observer from the time of the geographical separation of the courtrooms from the probation department. Interview with Ms. Polly Whitney, Social Worker, Juvenile Rights Division, Legal Aid Society, at 135 E. 22nd St., New York City, August 29, 1973.

56. Interview with Ms. Katherine McDonald, Attorney-in-Charge, Legal Aid Society, Juvenile Rights Division, New York County, together with Steven Hiltz and Steven Tarshis, law guardians, at George Washington Coffee House, 23rd St. and Lexington Ave., New York City, July 26, 1973 [hereinafter cited as McDonald, Hiltz, Tarshis interview].

57. Steven Tarshis, in McDonald, Hiltz, Tarshis interview, *supra* note 56.

58. The success of the law guardians in PINS cases increasingly has led CLOs to demand and judges to appoint Assistant Corporation Counsel to represent the parental complainants. This move has been spurred by what judges consider bullying of the mothers in PINS cases by law guardians, and at least some Corporation Counsel welcome the opportunity: "In most of the cases the mother has a legitimate grievance," Larry Schwarzstein, Attorney-in-Charge of the New York County Branch, told a recent interviewer. "She brought the kid into the world, nurtured him, is worried about him . . . so I think she has a right to have him cared for." Interview with Larry Schwartzstein, Attorney-in-Charge, Corporation Counsel's Office, 135 E. 22nd St., New York City, August 22, 1973.

The New York County Family Court Corporation Counsel's Office has several problems, however. It is badly understaffed, compared to the law guardians. Also, the job pays lower salaries. An Assistant Corporation Counsel's starting salary is $9,800, while law guardians have a starting salary of over $12,000. Interview with Tom Donnegan, Institute of Judicial Administration, Corporation Counsel Project, at 100 Bleeker St., New York City, July 3, 1973. In contrast to the average law guardian, for whom this is the first job out of law school, most of the Assistant Corporation Counsels have had several jobs, and their quality varies from competent to very incompetent. They pose, therefore, little threat to the law guardian's courtroom dominance.

59. *See, e.g., N.Y. Family Court Act* §747 (McKinney Supp. 1974–75): "A fact-finding hearing shall commence not more than three days after the filing of a petition under this article if the respondent is in detention."

60. Cases were observed in July, 1973, which had been in an intake part for over six months as the result of law guardian maneuvers. Court observation, New York County Family Court, 135 E. 22nd St., New York City, July 12, 1973.

61. McDonald, Hiltz, Tarshis interview, *supra* note 56.

62. Such a request may occur, for example, when the youth wants to get out of the home and a residential placement has been arranged, but a formal court adjudication is required by the *agency* before it will physically accept the youth. If agencies are willing to take any children with court contacts on PINS allegations at all, they prefer to take children who have been adjudicated; although over 90 percent of the costs of each child in agency care is paid by the state in any case, payment is quicker and generally surer when court adjudication has been made than when the child is just accepted off the streets. *Id.*

63. *In re* W., 28 N.Y. 2d 589, 590, 268 N.E. 2d 642, 643, 319 N.Y.S. 2d 845, 846 (1971).

64. One judge complains of feeling cut off because no prominent members of the bar ever practice in the Family Court. Interview with a N.Y. Family Court Judge, at 135 E. 22nd St., July 23, 1973.

65. One judge with eleven years service explained to us the process of disillusionment, from his request that Mayor Wagner appoint him to this court "because I believed it had more exciting possibilities than any other" to a point where the paperwork seems overwhelming (the eight sitting judges in the city share one secretary) and nothing seems to offer much hope: "We've had more studies of this court than you have hairs on your head. And every year it is the same: the report is issued, there's a lot of breast-beating in Albany, and . . ." Interview with a N.Y. Family Court Judge at 135 E. 22nd St., New York City, July 10, 1973.

66. *N.Y. Family Ct. Act* §712(b) (McKinney 1963).

67. Interview with a N.Y. Family Court Judge at 135 E. 22nd St., New York City, August 16, 1973.

68. Interview with a N.Y. Family Court Judge at 135 E. 22nd St., New York City, July 24, 1973.

69. Observation in the New York Family Court, at 135 E. 22nd St., New York City, August 17, 1973. With another youth the charge ran as follows:

I want you to promise me to obey your mother, to have perfect school attendance and not miss a day of school, to give up these people who are trying to lead you to do wrong, not to hang out in candy stores or tobacco shops or street corners where these people are, and to be in when your mother says: if it's 6:00 it's 6:00, if it's 7:00 it's 7:00, if it's 8:00 it's 8:00, but by 9:00 I don't want to see you on the streets of this city except with your parents or with your clergyman or to get a doctor. Do you understand?

Yes.

Court observation, New York County Family Court, August 17, 1973.

70. Court observation in New York Family Court, at 135 E. 22nd St., New York City, July 12, 1973.

71. Interview with Hon. Florence M. Kelley, Administrative Judge of the Family Court of N.Y., at 135 E. 22nd St., New York City, August 8, 1973.

72. Interview with a N.Y. Family Court Judge at 135 E. 22nd St., New York City, August 16, 1973. Asked about her ability to relate to PINS youths, the judge went on to say, "I think you can empathize without knowing the culture." Though admitting "there are good schools and bad schools," and "I have no idea what a bad school is like," the judge manifested confidence in her ability to understand. "I don't think it's necessary to take time off to go to schools." *Id.*

73. Court observation in New York Family Court, at 135 E. 22nd St., New York City, June 29, 1973.

74. *Id.*

75. For statewide percentages of suspended judgment and other types of supervision in New York, *see Judicial Conference Report 1972–73*, 412–15 (1974).

76. One judge remarked in this regard: "I won't do probation's job for them; they'll have to learn to screen these cases at intake." Interview with a judge, Rockland County Family Court, Rockland County Office Building, August 9, 1973.

77. Information on race was obtained for 91 percent of the sample. Court observation and interviews suggest that these statistics would apply as well to the remaining 9 percent. Rockland County's population (1970 census) is 5.7 percent black, 1.6 percent Puerto Rican, and over 90 percent white. The black and Puerto Rican populations are growing at a faster rate than the rest of the population. Thus, the percentages for these groups were probably slightly higher in 1973. Demographic Information, Appendix #1; Volunteer Counseling Service, Director's Report, March 1, 1973.

78. The following table indicates the number and percentage of Rockland allegations at intake.

Rockland County: Frequency of Intake Allegations
(N = 126)

	Percent	(No.)
Refuse to Obey	26	(33)
Truancy	53	(67)
Late Hours	5	(6)
Overnight	2	(2)
Short Runaway	29	(37)
Long Runaway	3	(4)
Disorderly Conduct	12	(15)
Vile Language	4	(5)
Verbal Abuse	8	(10)
Bad Companions	3	(4)
Bad Religion		
Unlawful Assembly	1	(1)
Harassment	6	(7)
Assault	9	(11)
Malicious Mischief	2	(3)
Auto Theft	1	(1)
Larceny	1	(1)
Shoplifting	2	(3)
Drug Possession	10	(13)
Possession to Sell	2	(2)
Glue Sniffing	1	(1)
Alcohol	1	(1)
Illegal Auto Use		
Dangerous Weapon	1	(1)
Gambling		
Homicide		
Arson	2	(2)
Rape		
Other Sex Crime		
Robbery		
Burglary		
Illegal Entry		
Burglar Tools		
Possession Stolen Property		
Homosexuality		
Incest		
Other	10	(13)

(Table continued overleaf)

Note 78. continued	Percent	(No.)
Bad Boyfriend	10	(13)
Prostitution		
Promiscuity	3	(4)
Group Sex		
Cohabiting		
Found in Sex Acts		
Night with Male		
Sex Innuendo	2	(2)

79. The opinion of probation officers about PINS cases as opposed to delinquency cases is instructive. For example, Mr. Michael Frenchak, Supervisor of the Juvenile Section, comments: "PINS cases are more problematic," JD's are just "acting out," PINS grow up to be greater criminals than JD's; PINS are "more sociopathic," PINS more frequently "refuse help," and more often rationalize and justify their acts; "9 out of 10" are "hung up on juvenile rights," "most have anti-authority hangups." Interview with Mr. Michael Frenchak, Supervisor, Juvenile Section, Rockland County Probation Department, in Rockland Family Court, June 26, 1973.

80. Exclusion of such information appears to be endemic to probation investigations. *Cf. R. Hood and R. Sparks, Key Issues in Criminology* 185 (1970).

81. Interview with three probation officers, Juvenile Section, Rockland County Probation Department, Rockland County Office Building, July 19, 1973.

82. Confidential conversation with probation officer, Juvenile Section, Rockland Probation Department, July 17, 1973.

83. *N.Y. Family Ct. Act* §§243(b) and 244(b) (McKinney 1963).

84. There are a few attorneys who do not rely on the probation department for information and assistance; interviews with these men indicate that they tend to look upon the probation department somewhat more negatively than those law guardians who rely extensively on it. Attorneys who occasionally take juvenile cases (almost always on delinquency charges) on a private-fee-basis feel that probation does not thoroughly check out all the alternatives available for a particular child. Interview with Mr. Everett J. Johns, at 123 Park Ave., New City, Rockland County, New York, July 19, 1973.

85. See page 85, *supra.*

86. Interviews with probation officers who often were called upon to interpret this information for a judge indicate that even such limited labelling is misunderstood. For example, "passive aggressive" is seen as depicting a youth liable at any moment to break into hostile, aggressive physical violence from a state of quiescent passivity, whereas the term actually denotes a personality disturbance in which the individual feels he dare not express hostility openly, but only by passive measures. *American Psychiatric Ass'n., Diagnostic and Statistical Manual of Mental Disorders* §3 (2d ed. 1968).

87. In-chambers observation of a judge of the Rockland County Family Court, at the Rockland County Family Court, June 26, 1973.

88. Interview with a judge of the Rockland County Family Court, Rockland County Office Building, August 16, 1973.

89. Judge Dembitz expressed concern about this problem in 1963:

It is the broad discretion in both phases of the proceeding—both in adjudicating whether the child is within the court's jurisdiction as well as in his disposition—which gives the judge an extraordinary and troubling degree of power over children who are before the court though they have not broken any law.

Dembitz, *supra* note 9 at 508.

90. *See N. Nie et al., Statistical Package for the Social Sciences* 116—17 (1970); *cf. M. Rosenberg, The Logic of Survey Analysis* (1968).

91. *See W. Hays, Statistics for Psychologists* 492—93 (1963); *R. Fried, Introduction to Statistics; Selected Procedures for the Behavioral Sciences* 177—78 (1969).

92. The following table presents rates of adjustment/referral to court for each allegation by percentage and by number.

Both Counties: Percentage of Intake Allegations Adjusted/Referred to Court

	Adjusted		Referred	
	Percent	(No.)	Percent	(No.)
Refuse to Obey	33	(24)	67	(48)
Truancy	29	(34)	71	(95)
Late Hours	40	(19)	60	(29)
Overnight	42	(11)	58	(15)
Short Runaway	32	(28)	68	(59)
Long Runaway	32	(7)	68	(15)
Disorderly Conduct	19	(3)	81	(13)
Vile Language	27	(3)	73	(8)
Verbal Abuse	20	(3)	80	(12)
Bad Companions	50	(10)	50	(10)
Bad Religion			100	(1)
Unlawful Assembly	100	(1)		
Harassment	100	(8)		
Assault	43	(9)	57	(12)
Malicious Mischief			100	(5)
Auto Theft			100	(1)
Larceny	50	(4)	50	(4)
Shoplifting	100	(5)		
Drug Possession	30	(10)	70	(23)
Possession to Sell	33	(1)	67	(2)
Glue Sniffing			100	(1)
Alcohol	20	(1)	80	(4)
Illegal Auto Use				
Dangerous Weapon	100	(2)		
Gambling				
Homicide				
Arson	60	(3)	40	(2)
Rape				
Other Sex Crime				
Robbery				
Burglary	100	(1)		

(Table continued overleaf . . .)

Note 92. continued	Adjusted		Referred	
	Percent	(No.)	Percent	(No.)
Illegal Entry	50	(1)	50	(1)
Burglar Tools				
Possession Stolen Property				
Homosexuality				
Incest				
Other	42	(16)	58	(22)
Bad Boyfriend	32	(9)	68	(19)
Prostitution			100	(1)
Promiscuity	17	(1)	83	(5)
Group Sex				
Cohabiting			100	(1)
Found in Sex Acts				
Night with Male			100	(1)
Sex Innuendo	33	(2)	67	(4)

93. *N.Y. Family Ct. Act* §728(b) (iii) (McKinney 1963).

94. The following table presents rates of detention for each petition allegation by percentage and by number.

Both Counties: Percentage of Respondents Detained by Petition Allegations *(N = 142)*

	Percent	(No.)
Refuse to Obey	47	(16)
Truancy	30	(27)
Late Hours	36	(8)
Overnight	50	(10)
Short Runaway	59	(26)
Long Runaway	25	(4)
Disorderly Conduct	33	(4)
Vile Language	29	(2)
Verbal Abuse	40	(4)
Bad Companions	55	(6)
Bad Religion		
Unlawful Assembly		
Harassment		
Assault	10	(1)
Malicious Mischief	20	(1)
Auto Theft		
Larceny	67	(6)
Shoplifting		
Drug Possession	46	(5)
Possession to Sell	100	(1)
Glue Sniffing		
Alcohol	100	(3)
Illegal Auto Use		
Dangerous Weapon		
Gambling		
Homicide		
Arson	100	(1)

Note 94. continued	*Percent*	*(No.)*
Rape		
Other Sex Crime		
Robbery		
Burglary		
Illegal Entry		
Burglar Tools		
Possession Stolen Property		
Homosexuality		
Incest		
Other	50	(7)
Bad Boyfriend	43	(3)
Prostitution	50	(1)
Promiscuity	50	(1)
Group Sex		
Cohabiting		
Found in Sex Acts		
Night with Male		
Sex Innuendo	33	(1)

95. The following table presents rates of adjudication for each petition allegation by percentage and by number.

Both Counties: Percentage of PINS Adjudications by Petition Allegations *(N = 142)*

	Percent	*(No.)*
Refuse to Obey	38	(13)
Truancy	53	(47)
Late Hours	36	(8)
Overnight	40	(8)
Short Runaway	46	(20)
Long Runaway	6	(1)
Disorderly Conduct	75	(9)
Vile Language	71	(5)
Verbal Abuse	70	(7)
Bad Companions	27	(3)
Bad Religion		
Unlawful Assembly		
Harassment		
Assault	40	(4)
Malicious Mischief	20	(1)
Auto Theft		
Larceny	33	(3)
Shoplifting		
Drug Possession	18	(2)
Possession to Sell	100	(1)
Glue Sniffing		
Alcohol	33	(1)
Illegal Auto Use		
Dangerous Weapon		
Gambling		
Homicide		
Arson	100	(1)

(Table continued overleaf . . .)

Note 95. continued	Percent	(No.)
Rape		
Other Sex Crime		
Robbery		
Burglary		
Illegal Entry		
Burglar Tools		
Possession Stolen Property		
Homosexuality		
Incest		
Other	36	(5)
Bad Boyfriend	57	(4)
Prostitution		
Promiscuity	50	(2)
Group Sex		
Cohabiting		
Found in Sex Acts		
Night with Male		
Sex Innuendo	33	(1)

96. The following table presents in percentage form the rates of dispositions for each petition allegation.

97. *N.Y. Family Ct. Act* §1012(f) (McKinney Supp. 1973–74) provides:

(f) "neglected child" means a child less than eighteen years of age

(i) whose physical, mental or emotional condition has been impaired or is in imminent danger of becoming impaired as a result of the failure of his parent or other person legally responsible for his care to exercise a minimum degree of care

(A) in supplying the child with adequate food, clothing, shelter or education in accordance with the provisions of part one of article sixty-five of the education law or medical, dental, optometrical or surgical care, though financially able to do so or offered financial or other reasonable means to do so or

(B) in providing the child with proper supervision or guardianship, by unreasonably inflicting or allowing to be inflicted harm, or a substantial risk thereof, including the infliction of excessive corporal punishment; or by using a drug or drugs; or by using alcoholic beverages to the extent that he loses self-control of his actions; or by any other acts of a similarly serious nature requiring the aid of the court; or

(ii) who has been abandoned by his parents or other person legally responsible for his care.

98. *See N.Y. Family Ct. Act* §1052 (McKinney Supp. 1974–1975).

99. Both authors evaluated these data, and a check on the comparability of their independent codings of neglect revealed agreement in more than 90 percent of all cases.

The following examples of case information led to classification as neglect in this study:

Difficult family situation—Father arrested on incest charge against Respondent's sister. Serious conflicts between mother and son. So serious that she is

(Table for Note 96)

Both Counties: Petition Allegations by Disposition

	Total (No.)	Withdrawal	Dismissal	Probation	Suspended Judgment	Informal Supervision	DFY Facility	Training School	Private Residential Placement	Non-Resident Placement	Department of Social Services	Transferred	Other
Refuse to Obey	(29)	35%	31%	3%	10%	4%	3%	3%	10%	1%	3%	3%	
Truancy	(74)	23%	18%	19%	24%			1%	5%		1%		
Late Hours	(18)	22%	50%	11%	6%				6%				6%
Overnight	(18)	28%	44%	17%					6%		6%		
Short Runaway	(38)	32%	32%	17%	11%	3%			11%		3%		
Long Runaway	(11)	54%	46%										
Disorderly Conduct	(11)		27%	9%	18%		9%	9%	18%			9%	
Vile Language	(6)	17%	17%		17%				33%			13%	
Verbal Abuse	(8)		38%	13%	13%			13%	13%			17%	
Bad Companions	(9)	22%	56%	11%								13%	11%
Bad Religion													
Unlawful Assembly													
Harassment													
Assault	(7)	57%	14%									14%	14%
Malicious Mischief	(5)	40%	40%		20%								
Auto Theft													
Larceny	(8)	38%	38%	13%					13%				
Shoplifting													13%
Drug Possession	(8)	25%	63%									13%	
Possession to Sell	(1)								100%				

(table cont'd overleaf . . .)

Both Counties: Petition Allegation by Disposition (continued)

	Total (No.)	Withdrawal	Dismissal	Probation	Suspended Judgment	Informal Supervision	DFY Facility	Training School	Private Residential Placement	Non-Resident Placement	Department of Social Services	Transferred	Other
Glue Sniffing													
Alcohol	(3)		67%	33%									
Illegal Auto Use													
Dangerous Weapon													
Gambling													
Homicide													
Arson	(1)							100%					
Rape													
Other Sex Crime													
Robbery													
Burglary													
Illegal Entry													
Burglar Tools													
Possession Stolen Property													
Homosexuality													
Incest													
Other	(13)	39%	31%	23%									8%
Bad Boyfriend	(5)		60%	40%									
Prostitution	(1)		100%										
Promiscuity	(2)	50%	50%	50%									
Group Sex													
Cohabiting													
Found in Sex Acts	(1)	100%	100%										
Night with Male													
Sex Innuendo	(3)	67%		33%									

afraid of him. He was referred to St. Luke's Psychiatric Center after previous PINS charge.

Father abuses child's privacy and seems to have sexual interest in her. He also requires her to keep house for him.

Girl was apparently beaten, not fed properly, filthy home, generally abused.

Brother has enormous record, has been in Bellevue, violent [threatened mother with kitchen knife]. Mother beats children with a belt. Intense sibling rivalry between Respondent and brother. Mother is an epileptic.

Father dead—mother ill, chronically, may not be able to care for the kid—girl boards between mother, aunt, mother's niece (a cousin) and at times a "Community House" residence.

Parents divorced—father an alcoholic—when girl was 3 and 4 before divorce, he'd come home, and "act like an animal"—breaking things, banging on walls, eating with bare hands. Father says mother takes tranquilizers—takes pills and falls asleep after dinner. Mother says father kidnaps kid when drunk and takes her to his hotel. Mother sent girl to live with an aunt and uncle in Connecticut, but the girl returned in 3 weeks. Later the girl's mother tried to get girl to move to Pa. to live with her grandparents—girl refused. —Then she took her to BCW asking for placement. Despite all this girl wants to go home. Mother is trying to dump her—Neglected by man she's with (been living with 49-year-old ex-con for 1 year). Both parents in methadone program—Grandmother is 80, but she has raised and is raising the 6 kids.

Girl's mother mental patient in Rockland for several years—two other kids placed in Willowbrook long ago—girl says father ejected her from house for hours at a time—that she slept with knife because afraid of him—had only 1 set of clothes, in rags. Also alleged (father denies) that he'd leave her without money for food. Father also attempted to place her with an uncle in P.R.—whose kids tried to molest her sexually and get her to inject heroin.

"Walk in Clinic" said girl beaten fairly consistently by mother and sister, and this why she ran—mother been in and out of Bellevue—mother diagnosed as heading for a paranoid breakdown.

Child been tossed between father-stepmother and mother-stepfather-boyfriend. She has never been made to feel wanted. Every parent figure rejects her. Mother admits doesn't want daughter around.

100. On this problem, Judge Dembitz's suggestion, made in 1963, remains valid:

> From the standpoint of statutory improvement, there perhaps should be a device in the nature of a custody proceeding—blaming neither the child as "ungovernable" or "delinquent" nor the parent, who may be exerting all his abilities, as "neglectful"—to determine whether the child needs custody other than parental. Dembitz, *supra* note 9 at 508.

101. Telephone interview with Polly Whitney, Social Worker, Juvenile Rights Division of the Legal Aid Society, New York Family Court, March 20, 1974. *See The Comm'n. on Mental Health Services Inside and Outside the Family Ct. in N.Y.C., Juvenile Justice Confounded: Pretensions and Realities of Treatment Services* 105 (1972): "[V]oluntary agencies have increasingly accepted more

dependent and neglected children . . . ." The report goes on to note that agency placement is most difficult for PINS when a child appears neglected and is in mid or late adolescence.

The present study confirms that it is especially difficult to place neglected PINS. These youths receive placement rejections in a greater proportion of sampled cases—17 percent—than do non-neglected youths, who are rejected by a placement institution in only 10 percent of cases. The 17 percent rejection figure for neglected cases does not include the numerous placement institutions that observations and interviews indicate probation officers automatically exclude from consideration because of the knowledge that the agency simply will not take youths with the double curse of parental neglect and a PINS adjudication.

102. Interview with Intake Officer, Rockland County Probation Department, Juvenile Section, June 20, 1973.

103. Interview with A.A. ("Gus") Poppalardo, Home-School Counselor, Clarkstown Jr. High School, Rockland County, New York, July 31, 1973. A home-school counselor is a social worker attached to the schools.

104. Much of the following discussion is based on earlier work by the authors, "Ungovernability: The Unjustifiable Jurisdiction," 83 *Yale L.J.* 1383 (1974).

105. Youths in such cases tend to be older than youths in non-parentally initiated cases: 44 percent are over fifteen, compared to 39 percent of those youths accused by persons other than their parents. They are also more often female. While 53 percent of all youths brought to intake are girls, 61 percent of girls accused by parents are older (and more sexually mature) than the boys so brought: 51 percent of the girls are over fifteen and only 34 percent of the boys; 74 percent of girls are over fourteen and only 60 percent of boys. Parents apparently are more concerned with girls' behavior and set a stricter standard for it. This is especially so in the 52 percent of cases involving a daughter's sexual behavior. Many judges cite as the typical parentally-initiated case a battle between mother and daughter over a "man." Interview with Administrative Judge Florence M. Kelley of the N.Y. Family Court, at 135 E. 22nd St., New York City, August 8, 1973.

106. Interview with Mr. Guy DiCosola, Branch Chief, Manhattan Intake, at 135 E. 22nd St., New York City, June 26, 1973.

After conducting three weeks of observations and interviews one of our associates reported: "All the I.O.'s [intake officers] spoken with feel that PINS mothers . . . either consciously or repressedly want to humiliate and punish their kids." Moskowitz, *supra* note 31 at 17.

107. The statute defines a PINS not in terms of the legality of the youth's acts, but in terms of whether the youth has gone "beyond the lawful control of [the] parent." *N.Y. Family Ct. Act* §712(b) (McKinney Supp. 1973—74).

108. *N.Y. Family Ct. Act* §739 (McKinney 1963), Committee Comments.

109. *N.Y. Family Ct. Act* §733(a)—(d) (McKinney 1963).

110. *N.Y. Family Ct. Act* §716(a) (McKinney 1963) permits a judge to substitute a PINS petition or finding for a delinquency petition or finding at any time, although the step is usually taken immediately after an adjudication of

delinquency. Its effect is to abolish completely the delinquency finding, leaving the youth with a record as a PINS and not as a delinquent.

111. Many of those PINS cases with delinquent allegations which are processed through to a conclusion may represent a conscious determination by court personnel to obtain dispositional power over a youth with the comparative ease afforded by the PINS jurisdiction—it is only necessary to prove that the youth disobeyed his parents on more than one occasion. (*See* text at note 63, *supra*). One judge stated, for example, that it was easier to use a PINS than a delinquency proceeding to handle a "pusher" who she was convinced had sold heroin in violation of the penal statutes: "If we have to prove this [penal violation], it requires exact evidence that on such and such a date, at 6:02 P.M., he did such and such," she said, while noting that this burden of proof is easily avoided when the youth is alleged to be a PINS. (Interview with a judge of the N.Y. Family Court, in New York City, July 24, 1974).

112. The comparable figure in Rockland is only 15 percent. In 1972 Rockland saw a 66 percent drop from previous numbers of such cases, as judges interpreted the Court of Appeals ruling in *In re* W., 28 N.Y.2d 589, 590, 268 N.E.2d 642, 643, 319 N.Y.S.2d 845, 846 (1971) to bar adjudicating a youth a PINS when he or she had committed only one (delinquent) act.

Although reduced delinquents represent only 12 percent of all youths sampled, they represent 32 percent of all cases ultimately labeled PINS which receive findings, since all reduced delinquencies are sent to court and all have findings. In New York, extrapolating from our 10 percent sample, 150 cases which originated as PINS would have had findings in 1972. By comparison, there were 120 reduced delinquency cases in New York by our count in 1972.

113. The following table gives the percentages and raw data for the petition allegations involved in these cases.

Delinquencies Reduced to PINS: Frequency of Petition Allegations *(N = 31)*

	Percent	*(No.)*
Refuse to Obey	3	(1)
Truancy		
Late Hours		
Overnight		
Short Runaway		
Long Runaway		
Disorderly Conduct		
Vile Language	3	(1)
Verbal Abuse	3	(1)
Bad Companions		
Bad Religion		
Unlawful Assembly		
Harassment	3	(1)
Assault	48	(15)
Malicious Mischief	7	(2)
Auto Theft		
Larceny	10	(3)
Shoplifting		

(Table continued overleaf . . .)

Note 113. continued	Percent	(No.)
Drug Possession	5	(1)
Possession to Sell		
Glue Sniffing		
Alcohol		
Illegal Auto Use	3	(1)
Dangerous Weapon	19	(6)
Gambling		
Homicide		
Arson		
Rape		
Other Sex Crime	3	(1)
Robbery	32	(10)
Burglary	13	(4)
Illegal Entry	7	(2)
Burglar Tools		
Possession Stolen Property		
Homosexuality	3	(1)
Incest		
Other	32	(10)
Bad Boyfriend		
Prostitution		
Promiscuity		
Group Sex		
Cohabiting		
Found in Sex Acts		
Night with Male		
Sex Innuendo		

114. All reasons which the records contained for reductions in New York were summarized and recorded as follows:

The facts were rather weak, and did not justify a finding of delinquency.

Law guardian agreed with probation officer to have kid go on probation, so probation supported the reduction.

Mother complained at intake of truancy, late hours, overnights—there were thus PINS type complaints too, and law guardians got this case reduced.

Child's demeanor—kid's very intelligent and working above his grade level in reading and mathematics; law guardian admitted to possession of a dangerous weapon, got a reduction at disposition.

Kid was sixteen and one-half, and it was felt case should be terminated (was one year from intake)—judge reduced to PINS then placed on probation.

Law guardian got court to agree to a PINS because boy was very young and had mental condition, had been in hospital for it.

Probation felt girl was adjusting well living away from home with aunt and urged that it was an isolated incident.

Arresting officer didn't want a hearing—so there was a deal—the judge was impressed by the lack of a previous record.

Law guardian arranged an acceptable plea, assault in the third degree. Probation was enthused about the kid's progress.

Probation recommended the reduction.

Co-respondent was blamed for all the planning, so kid's involvement did not look serious.

Sympathetic probation report.

Good probation report.

Admission traded for reduction. Probation was annoyed that child showed no remorse.

Probation requested that it would be good to have boy under supervision for a year and change it to a PINS.

115. A phrase used by *A.* and *J. Skolnick, Family in Transition* 310 (1971).

116. Children are seen as only interested in playing, and not in work and the more serious affairs of adults. There is a paradox in these adult assumptions about youths: they are somewhat self-fulfilling prophecies. "Even if a child or adolescent wants to take part in serious concerns, he may find himself excluded." Denzin, "The Work of Little Children," in *A.* and *J. Skolnick, Family in Transition* 319 (1971).

When the focus turns to the problems of children and youths, the handicap of adult conceptions may be most troublesome. As child psychologist Jean Piaget notes, "we must beware of letting adult logic mislead us" as to the nature of the "mind of the child." *J. Piaget, The Child's Conception of Physical Causality* 2 (1966).

117. "Adults have deeply engrained irrational reservations about the primacy of children's needs. These reservations—ambivalent feelings—cannot be guarded against except by clear and compelling priorities. . . . Adults universally experience children as representatives of their mortality as well as their immortality." *J. Goldstein, A. Freud,* and *A. Solnit, Beyond the Best Interests of the Child* 106 (1973) [hereinafter cited as *Goldstein*].

118. *E. Schur, Radical Non-Intervention: Rethinking the Delinquency Problem* 46–51 (1973).

119. Research Memorandum on "Status Offenders" of the Legal Action Support Project, Bureau of Social Science Research, Inc. (March, 1972) at 22. (On file at ABA–IJA Juvenile Justice Standards Project).

120. *E. Schur, Radical Non-Intervention* 47 (1973).

121. Studies of the stigmatizing effect of contact with the law in the role of the accused indicate that the degree of stigma felt is affected by the amount of "protective insulation" available in one's social environment. Schwartz and Skolnick, "Two Studies of Legal Stigma," in *The Other Side: Perspectives on Deviance* 103 (H. Becker, ed. 1964). It need hardly be said that adolescents are among the most lacking in such insulation and are likely to be seriously affected.

Though it might seem that little or no stigma would accrue to a PINS youth because the societal diagnosis as manifested in the juvenile court is that he or she should be "helped" and "saved," adolescents, unlike adults, do not pay much attention to the degree of "reprehensibility" of the bad things they are accused of. If an adolescent is adjudicated a "PINS," he does not care that he is less "bad" than being a delinquent. Rather, he focuses on his being *not* normal, not as good as others of his age. Erik Erikson has described the adolescent's reasoning in this regard: "An adolescent feels that to be a little less of one means to be much more of the other—or, rather to be a little less of one means to be *all* of the other. If . . . something happens that psycho-socially marks him . . . he may develop a deep fixation, connected with a negative identity." *Dep't. of HEW*, Pub. No. 356, *New Perspectives for Research on Juvenile Delinquency* 10 (H. Witmer and R. Kotinsky, eds. 1956). For a detailed analysis of stigmatization in the context of the juvenile court, *cf.* A. Mahoney, "The Effect of Labeling Upon Youths in the Juvenile Justice System: A Review of the Evidence," 8 *Law & Soc. Rev.* 583 (1974).

122. *Cf. D. Easton* and *J. Dennis, Children in the Political System* (1969).

123. Even the length of court processing may have negative effects for PINS youths. As pointed out by *Goldstein, Supra* note 117 at 31—34, periods of delay in court processing that are of no moment to adults may well have substantial, and possibly negative, effects on young people for whom these periods may encompass significant developmental change.

124. Dembitz, *Justice, supra* note 14 at 589. Although Judge Dembitz goes on to note, "A judge unfortunately must rely on personal impression," *id.*, this fact does not seem to give her, or any other judges, doubts about the jurisdiction.

125. *R. Hood* and *R. Sparks, Key Issues in Criminology* 191 (1970). With respect to the effect of court-ordered treatments, it has been said that youths who have experienced probation supervision and institutionalization have approximately equal rates of recidivism. *Id.* at 186. But the reader is cautioned against assuming that they "cure" anything: "It must be emphasized, however, that the research . . . *cannot* be interpreted as showing that probation is especially effective as a method of treatment." *Id.* at 187—88.

126. *Id.* at 193—214.

127. Hayes, Meltzer, and Lundberg, "Information Distribution, Interdependence and Activity Levels," 31 *Sociometry* 162 (1968). Those who volunteer are bound to yield a greater response to attitude change attempts than non-volunteers. Horowitz, "Effects of Volunteering, Fear Arousal, and Number of Communications on Attitude Change," 11 *J. Personal and Soc. Psychol.* 34 (1969).

128. Argyris, "Some Unintended Consequences of Rigorous Research," 70 *Psych. Bull.* 185, 186 (1968). The author also reports that students *required* to participate in psychology experiments manifested "very critical, mis-trustful, and hostile [attitudes] to the requirement." *Id.* at 188.

129. Testimony of Ms. Rena Uviller, Director, Juvenile Rights Project, ACLU, Public Hearings before Judiciary Committee, New York State Assembly, Albany, New York, March 28, 1974.

130. *Goldstein, Supra* note 117 at 51—52.

131. *Cf. id.* at 111: "[B]y and large society must use each child's placement as an occasion for protecting future generations of children by increasing the number of adults-to-be who are likely to be adequate parents. Only in the implementation of this policy does there lie a real opportunity for beginning to break the cycle of sickness and hardships bequeathed from one generation to the next. . . ." Judge Dembitz also agrees with the importance of elevating a young person's interests "regardless of competing adult claims," and points out there

is a "social stake in effectuating this right. . . ." Dembitz, Book Review, 83 *Yale L. J.* 1304, 1313 (1974).

132. Dembitz, *supra* note 9 at 506.

133. *N.Y. Family Ct. Act* §812 (McKinney Supp. 1973—74).

134. Indeed, youths are already subject to such charges, *see id.*, though PINS charges are generally used instead.

135. *E.g.*, Interview with N.Y. Family Court Administrative Judge Florence M. Kelley, New York, August 8, 1973.

136. Research studies of persons volunteering for experimental psychological programs have found that those who volunteered did so because "[they] hoped to find professional advice [or] help. . . ." *J. Katz, Experimentation with Human Beings* 624 (1972). And research indicates that those who do come to volunteer for experimental psychological programs are actually in need of help, as evidenced by their higher rates of clinically-diagnosed problems than the general population. For example, a New York State Psychiatric Institute report on volunteers for psychiatric studies noted: "On the basis of our clinical impressions the prevalence of psychopathology in the volunteer group seemed quite high." *Id.* at 623.

However, it should be noted that studies have also indicated there are certain types of individuals who are less likely to volunteer, such as persons with a high fear of failure and those who score high on tests for authoritarian personality. Interview with Dr. Neil Vidmar, Russell Sage Fellow in Law and Social Science, Yale Law School, New Haven, Conn., April 2, 1974.

Chapter 3

Law and Practice Concerning the Counterparts of "Persons in Need of Supervision" in Some European Countries with a Particular Emphasis on the Netherlands*

Fré LePoole

INTRODUCTION

This chapter is a comparative study of the law in a number of European countries relating to what in New York State are called "Persons in Need of Supervision" (PINS) [1]. I shall discuss the bases on which juveniles may become the object of state-imposed measures as a result of their own "misbehavior" not amounting to a criminal offense, in five Western European countries—Holland, France, West Germany, England, and Sweden; the measures which may be imposed; and the procedures which apply in proceedings to impose such measures. I shall also describe in detail what each of these measures may entail in one of the countries concerned, the Netherlands, and give an account of some new approaches in that country towards handling some of the most common problems of young people—such as running away from home—which in the United States often give rise to juvenile court jurisdiction.

It might have been interesting to study the ways in which such problems are handled in countries, such as Mali or the USSR, with cultural backgrounds and economic, social and political systems quite different from those prevailing in the United States. This study is nevertheless limited to Western European countries only. This seemed a reasonable selection for present purposes, because the family arrangements, social organization, and state of economic development of Western Europe are relatively similar to those prevailing in the United States.

*Several people have been very helpful to me in the research for and the writing of this chapter. I should like to acknowledge in particular the help of the staff of the library of the Workgroup Integrated Youth Welfare in the Netherlands ("WIJN" at Utrecht; formerly called National Federation for Child Welfare and located in the Hague), the cooperation of the Sosjale Joenit in the Hague, Netherlands and the helpful comments of my husband, John Griffiths.

While the insights to be derived from a study of the law and practice in these countries might be less innovative than those resulting from a study of more culturally-distant countries, at the same time the problems experienced by juveniles and the problems of state intervention in the lives of juveniles and their families in the countries of the study are probably more similar to those of American juveniles, and the ways in which these are handled more directly relevant to American concerns. Furthermore, as a practical matter, I am personally more familiar with these countries and their legal literature. Thus my interpretations of their law and practice are more likely to be accurate. Finally, literature on these countries is more readily available.

The countries whose law and practice I have drawn upon for some or many sections of the following account are West Germany, France, the Netherlands, the United Kingdom, and Sweden. My discussion of Dutch law and practice is far more extensive than that of any of the other countries. This is due to the fact that the research for this study was largely carried out in the Netherlands and I therefore had access to more information on the Netherlands than on any other country. Otherwise, the extent to which each country appears in the following account reflects the availability of literature in Dutch, English, French and German. This explains, in particular, the scarcity of information on Sweden, for which very little such literature exists.

STATUTORY CRITERIA FOR STATE INTERVENTION IN THE LIVES OF JUVENILES [2] WHO HAVE NOT COMMITTED A CRIMINAL OFFENSE

Of the five countries covered by this study, two (England and Sweden) have statutes quite comparable to New York's PINS statutes and other status offense statutes in the United States [3]. Thus, in England and Sweden, state agencies [4] have the power to intervene in the lives of juveniles on the basis of misbehavior that would not be a criminal offense if committed by an adult. France, West Germany, and the Netherlands, on the contrary, do not have a special body of juvenile offenses, such as truancy, running away, etc. [5]. Misbehavior not constituting a criminal offense is not as such a basis for state intervention. The only distinction made by the statutes is between juveniles who are subject to juvenile court jurisdiction for alleged criminal behavior, and those who are so on the basis of statutory criteria most comparable to those governing neglect and dependency proceedings in the United States.

In this section I shall first discuss the basic statutory framework in France, West Germany, and the Netherlands governing the kinds of situations in which minors who have not committed a criminal offense can be subject to compulsory measures on the part of the state, as well as the main implications of such measures. Then I shall do the same for England and Sweden. Thereafter I shall discuss statutory and other guidelines for the control of discretion in implementing the basic statutory criteria. Finally, I shall present some statistics concerning the extent to which the measures I have described are in fact imposed in the countries concerned.

Statutory Framework in Continental Europe

Holland and France. Until the end of the nineteenth century the state had no power to interfere with the way in which a child was brought up by its family, unless the child had committed a criminal offense. Under the original French and Dutch Civil Codes, parental—or at that time, rather, paternal—authority was practically unqualified. During the second half of the nineteenth century, while the juvenile court movement was gaining force in the United States, the idea also developed in Europe that in certain situations the state ought to be able to protect the child from the harmful consequences of his family milieu [6]. The initial result was the enactment of provisions authorizing termination of parental authority where parents failed to fulfill their rights and duties towards the child in a minimally acceptable way, whether or not this failure was deemed to be due to their own fault. Later on, forms of state intervention less drastic than total forfeiture of parental authority were developed. The present Dutch and French statutory schemes are more or less parallel. Two basic kinds of encroachment on parental authority are authorized in order to protect a juvenile: measures amounting to a limitation of parental rights and duties may be imposed, or parental authority may be terminated. Legislation in the two countries now clearly implies that termination is a measure of last resort, generally to be used after lesser encroachments on parental authority have failed [7]. These less far reaching forms of control are in fact used much more often than termination of parental authority [8].

Limitation of Parental Rights. In the Netherlands, the juvenile court [9] may order "supervision" (*ondertoezichtstelling*) if a child is "threatened by moral or physical ruin" (*zedelijke of lichamelijke ondergang*) [10]. Initially "supervision" may be ordered for at most one year but one-year renewals are authorized until the juvenile reaches majority [11]. In France, the juvenile court may order "assistance in upbringing" (*assistance éducative*) if a minor's health, security, or morality are endangered or if "his chances of receiving a proper upbringing are seriously jeopardized" [12].

The Dutch "supervision" mainly entails the appointment of a "family guardian" whose duties are described as follows by the relevant statute:

> The family guardian seeks personal contact with the child and its family, insofar as he can. He promotes the child's moral, physical and future material well-being. He counsels the parents concerning the care and education [of the child] and he attempts to persuade them to do what is necessary therefor [13].

The parents must follow his directions concerning the care and raising of the child. If they disagree they can appeal to the juvenile court. If they persistently fail to follow the family guardian's directions, termination of parental authority may follow [14]. The family guardian is roughly comparable to the American probation officer.

In principle, the child subject to "supervision" stays at home, but placement out of the home is possible without termination of parental authority. The Code authorizes the juvenile court to order out of home placement either for purposes of observation and diagnosis or if necessary for purposes of care and education. The former placement is for a maximum of three months, which may be extended for another two months at most, if absolutely necessary. The duration of the latter may initially be fixed by the court at one year at most which may be extended for a second year; further extensions for one-year periods are only authorized in a few circumstances [15].

The implications of the French "assistance in upbringing" are similar to those of the Dutch "supervision," in that the child in principle stays with its family, but some form of intervention in its upbringing is imposed. Thus the juvenile court [16] may appoint either an individual or an agency to provide the child's family with help and counseling; the court may also impose specific conditions concerning, for example, school attendance. If necessary, the juvenile court may place the child outside of its home. The French Civil Code does not set any specific time limits on the duration of "assistance in upbringing"—whether or not involving outside placement—nor does the Code require renewal at regular intervals. However, the juvenile court may modify or revoke all decisions at any time, at the request of either parent, of the child's legal guardian, the juvenile himself or of the government (*"ministère public"* [17]) [18].

Termination of Parental Authority. Both the Dutch and the French Civil Codes permit termination of parental authority on a number of grounds, all involving parental failure to care for the child in a minimally acceptable way or presumptively indicating the parents' unwillingness or inability to do so. The Dutch Code distinguishes between cases in which this is attributable to fault of the parents, and in cases in which the parents are not regarded as at fault [19]. "Forfeiture" of parental authority for fault (*ontzetting*) is authorized, if the district court [20] determines that it is necessary in the interest of the child, on grounds of:

(a) abuse of parental power or gross neglect of the care or upbringing of one or more children;
(b) bad way of life;
(c) final conviction:
    1. of intentional participation in a crime with a juvenile under the parent's authority;

2. of one of a number of serious offenses against such a juvenile (*e.g.* rape, incest, homicide, assault, etc.);

3. followed by a sentence of imprisonment of two or more years;

(d) serious disregard of the directions of a family guardian, or obstruction of a placement out of the home ordered by the juvenile court in the framework of a "supervision" measure [21];

(e) well-founded fear for neglect of the child's interests, because the parent demands or takes back the child from others who are caring for and rearing the child [22].

"Release" from parental authority in the absence of fault (*ontheffing*) may be sought, unless this would be against the child's interest, on the grounds of the parent's unfitness or inability to fulfill his duty of care and upbringing. In principle, such termination in the absence of fault is possible only if the parent concerned agrees. Nevertheless, it may be ordered against the parent's wishes:

(a) in case of insanity of the parent;

(b) if it appears after at least 6 months of "supervision," in the absence of placement out of the home, or after at least 18 months of placement out of the home ordered by the juvenile court in the framework of a "supervision" measure, that "supervision" is insufficient to save the child from moral or physical ruin, because of the inability of the parent to fulfill his or her duties toward the child;

(c) if "release" of the parent is necessary to make a "forfeiture" order against the other parent effective [23].

The grounds for "forfeiture" are presumed to indicate "fault" on the part of the parent; the grounds for "release" are presumed to indicate incompetence. "Forfeiture" under present law is dishonorable and entails a mandatory loss of franchise and right to be elected [24]. The greatest number of "forfeitures" in recent years have been on the first ground (abuse or gross neglect of parental power); a substantial number have been on the ground of "bad way of life." The other grounds have rarely been invoked [25]. Most "releases" have been on the ground that "supervision" turned out to be insufficiently protective [26].

The usual effect of termination of parental rights, for whatever reason, is placement of the child outside of the parental family, either in a foster home or in an institution. However, if only one of the parents is subject to the measure, the child may stay at home, if that is possible, i.e., if it would not reduce the effectiveness of the measure [27]. Unlike termination of parental rights in the United States, termination of parental authority in the Netherlands is not necessarily final. Either a parent or the Child Protection Council [28] may petition the juvenile court for restoration of parental authority, and this must be granted if the court is convinced that the child can again be entrusted to the parent. In order to facilitate such a decision a probationary restoration period of up to six months may be granted [29] .

The French Civil Code does not distinguish different modes of termination of parental authority depending on whether or not the parents are at fault. Rather the Code distinguishes between "delegation" (*délégation*) of parental authority, which may be voluntary and "forfeiture" (*déchéance*) which is conceived as a measure which takes place against the parents' wishes [30] . A district court [31] order pronouncing "delegation" of parental authority may issue in three cases:

(1) when the parents have placed the child with a reliable private person, an approved institution, or the Child Protection Service of the *Département*, and agree to renounce all or part of their parental authority;

(2) when the child has been abandoned by its parents and is being cared for by an individual or institution, or the Child Protection Service, and there is a request for "delegation" to which the parents do not object within three months of being notified;

(3) when the parents have not shown any interest in the child for over a year, and a person willing to exercise parental authority requests "delegation" [32] .

"Forfeiture" of parental authority may be ordered by the court in the following cases:

(1) if the parent concerned is convicted of a crime committed against the person of the child, or for being an accomplice in a crime committed by the child, the criminal sentence imposed may provide for "forfeiture";

(2) in the absence of a criminal conviction, if the parent "either by ill-treatment or by pernicious examples of habitual drunkenness, notorious misconduct or criminality, or by failure to take proper care of the child or to guide it, poses a manifest danger to the security, the health or the morality of the child," or

(3) if, after an order of "assistance in upbringing" has been imposed, the parents for over two years voluntarily fail to exercise the rights and to fulfill the duties that the statute leaves them, "forfeiture" may be ordered without any criminal conviction [33] .

The French provisions on termination of parental authority were revised in many respects in 1970 [34] . Until 1970, "forfeiture" had been mandatory in case of conviction for certain crimes (including those listed under (1) above. The 1970 law also attempts to limit judicial discretion in ordering "forfeiture" on the grounds listed under (2) by requiring that the parents pose a "manifest danger" to the child's well-being. The statute had previously required only that the child be "endangered" [35]. Even now, the statute's wording is flexible. In practice, most "forfeitures" are ordered on one of the grounds listed under (2) [36].

In France, unlike the Netherlands, both "delegation" and "forfeiture" may be partial rather than complete, depriving the parents of only some attributes of parental authority. For instance a parent might be deprived of his right to take care of the child, but retain formal authority. This possibility was authorized by a law of 1921, to make it possible for courts to attempt to protect the child without going so far as to terminate parental authority. Even partial forfeiture, though, proved to be too intrusive to be very popular which led eventually to the introduction of "assistance in upbringing" [37].

The child of a parent whose parental rights have been terminated may stay at home, if the other parent is alive and not affected by the measure. Otherwise, the child may be placed with a foster family, a private agency, or the Child Protective Service of the *Département.*

Parents may petition the district court to order a reinstatement on a showing of changed circumstances. Such a petition may not be filed earlier than one year after the termination and, if denied, may not be repeated in less than a year's time [38].

West Germany [39]. In West Germany a slightly different statutory scheme prevails. Two different statutes provide for two overlapping schemes both authorizing state intervention in the exercise of parental authority. In the first place, there is article 1666,1 of the Civil Code [40] which reads:

> If the mental or physical welfare of the child is threatened by the fact that the father or the mother abuse the right to take care of the person of the child, neglect the child or are guilty of dishonorable or immoral behavior, the Guardianship Court shall take the measures required to avert the danger. In particular, the Guardianship Court may order that the child shall, for purposes of its upbringing, be placed in a fit family or in an institution.

Under this provision, the guardianship court [41] may order all measures it sees fit, ranging from admonition of the parents to termination of all rights to take care of the child [42]. Apart from the two possibilities referred to in the last sentence of Article 1666,1 the Civil Code does not spell out any particular measures the Guardianship Court may order.

The second relevant statute is the Statute on Child Welfare [43]. This statute became effective in 1922, but has since been the object of several major revisions, most recently in 1961. It was deemed a necessary complement to Article 1666 of the Civil Code because the latter provision was commonly thought to require fault on the part of the parents, thus precluding intervention by the guardianship court in the absence of such fault. Furthermore, the Civil Code provided no organizational framework or funding for the purpose of taking care of the children concerned [44]. The Statute on Child Welfare authorizes several distinct measures, each of which may be ordered in the absence of fault on the part of any person involved. Thus "assistance in upbringing" (*Erziehungsbeistand*) which involves the appointment of an "assistant in upbringing" may be ordered for a minor whose "physical, mental or moral development is endangered or has been damaged" when such a measure seems required to avert the danger or to undo the damage and sufficient to do so. The measure may be ordered by the Municipal Youth Bureau [45] at the request of a parent or guardian or, in the absence of such a request, by the guardianship court on motion of the Municipal Youth Bureau [46]. The "assistant in upbringing" seems more or less comparable to the Dutch family guardian. A juvenile subject to this measure stays in his own home.

Furthermore, the State Youth Bureau [47] may render "voluntary help in upbringing" (*Freiwillige Erziehungshilfe*) for a juvenile who is not over twenty and whose "physical, mental or moral development is endangered or has been damaged," when such a measure is necessary to avert the danger or to undo the damage and when the minor's parents or legal guardians file a written request that such help be rendered [48]. Finally, when it is necessary "because a minor threatens to be neglected," the guardianship court may order "remedial upbringing" (*Fürsorgeerziehung*), but "remedial upbringing" may be ordered only if no other measure suffices [49]. Both "voluntary help in upbringing" and "remedial upbringing" may and often will result in placement away from the family.

Although the statutory language used to define the jurisdictional basis for the appointment of an "assistant in upbringing" and for the rendering of "voluntary help in upbringing" is different from that used to define the basis for "remedial upbringing," jurisdiction in both cases is in fact interpreted as depending upon the same condition of imminent or existing neglect [50].

Absence of Status Offense Jurisdiction in Continental European Countries. Thus, in France, the Netherlands and West Germany child protection measures are authorized only on criteria most comparable to those applicable in neglect or dependency proceedings in the United States. Of course, the kinds of noncriminal juvenile misconduct which in the United States would per se confer jurisdiction upon the juvenile court, might often in these European countries be considered symptoms of the presence of the state of danger required by law to impose child protective measures [51]. It is not considered impossible in these countries that the required state of danger be primarily due to the juvenile himself, but the question as to whether the juvenile is at fault is irrelevant where a child protective measure is to be imposed. It has been pointed out in the United States that it is hard to distinguish hard-core status offenders for whom some form of intervention is truly necessary from neglected or dependent children [52]. The European statutes discussed thus far do not attempt to make the distinction. The basis for court intervention is the diagnosis of a family problem, not juvenile misbehavior which may or may not indicate the presence of such a problem.

Apart from the general bases for state intervention described above, none of the three continental countries discussed provides for specific juvenile offenses, such as truancy, running away, or drinking. However, this does not mean that there are no instances of different legislative norms with regard to juvenile and adult behavior. For instance, in West Germany juveniles under sixteen may not smoke in public [53].

But to the extent that sanctions may be imposed where undesired juvenile behavior is engaged in, the persons subject to these sanctions are the *adults* who are held responsible for not preventing its occurrence. Thus, in Holland a child's parents or legal guardians must see to it that he attends school regularly, and are subject to minor penalties if he does not. Directors of schools must report regular non-attendance to an official of the municipal government, who interviews the juvenile and tries to induce him to attend school. In case of repeated non-attendance, the municipal official reports the case to the Child Protection Council [54]. This agency may decide to initiate "supervision" proceedings, but an allegation of repeated truancy would not suffice by itself to justify such a measure.

Statutory Framework in Great Britain and Sweden

In England and Sweden, statutes conferring powers upon state agencies to make compulsory measures with regard to juveniles do distinguish between juveniles who require help in the absence of misconduct and those who have misbehaved (without necessarily having committed a criminal offense), making the latter an independent basis for state intervention. Thus in England, the Children and Young Persons Act confers jurisdiction over a juvenile upon the juvenile court if any of the following conditions is satisfied:

(a) his proper development is being avoidably prevented or neglected or his health is being avoidably impaired or neglected or he is being ill-treated; or

(b) it is probable that the condition set out in the preceding paragraph will be satisfied in his case, having regard to the fact that the court or another court has found that that condition is or was satisfied in the case of another child or young person who is or was a member of the household to which he belongs; or

(c) he is exposed to moral danger; or

(d) he is beyond the control of his parent or guardian; or

(e) he is of compulsory school age within the meaning of the Education Act 1944, and is not receiving full-time education suitable to his age, ability and aptitude; or

(f) he is guilty of an offense, excluding homicide [55].

The distinction between children who are the victims of misbehaving parents and children who misbehave themselves is expressed even more clearly in the Swedish Child Welfare Act of 1961:

The Child Welfare Board shall take action . . . . :

(a) if a person, not yet eighteen years of age, is maltreated in his home or otherwise is treated there in a manner endangering his bodily or mental health, or if his development is jeopardized because of the unfitness of his parents or other guardians raising the child or of their inability to raise him, and

(b) if a person not yet twenty-one years of age, needs special corrective measures by the community because of his criminal act, immoral manner of life, failure to support himself honestly according to his ability, misuse of intoxicating beverages or narcotics or for some other comparable reason [56].

Children subject to the jurisdiction of the Child Welfare Board on the basis of non-criminal misconduct are treated in one breath with those having committed crimes. Both of them may in some respects be treated differently from children who are abused or neglected [57]. Thus, Sweden of all European countries covered by this study has legislation most closely comparable to that concerning PINS and their counterparts in the United States. As in the United States, a juvenile's freedom may be interfered with on the basis of his own misbehavior, not only when it amounts to a criminal offense. Also as in the United States, the norms defining what amounts to misbehavior are very vague. As in many American states, Swedish legislation treats non-criminal misbehavior cases and criminal cases alike. In the light of all these similarities, it is regrettable that the available literature does not permit research much beyond the actual text of the Child Welfare Act and some statistical data from the Swedish Statistical Yearbook.

Control of Discretion in Implementing the Statutory Criteria

The criteria for application of child protective measures to juveniles are as vague in Europe as in the United States and leave a wide area of discretion to the state agencies concerned. This discretion appears hardly limited in the law as it is, with but a few exceptions. One limit to agency discretion, found in the English and West German statutes, is the requirement that a protective measure must be necessary [58]. In the Netherlands, one of the few reported cases in this area holds that "supervision" may be ordered only if positive result is to be expected [59]. Insofar as child protection measures are based on parental inability or unwillingness to cope, use of the measure is in some countries limited by a statutory requirement that the measure be required by the best interest of the child [60].

The relevant authorities in the five countries appear to have almost complete discretion to evaluate whether the facts in question amount to the statutorily-required state of danger of the child. There is a certain amount of reported case law, in Germany and France, on the proper legal interpretation of that criterion. Certain minimal standards have been set; e.g., the court must indicate the precise fact or facts on which its judgment that the child is in need of a child protective measure is based [61]. But generally speaking, the statutory criteria are flexible, and deliberately so, and the relevant authorities may impose child protective measures in a variety of circumstances in which voluntary assistance to the child and its family does not appear to them sufficient [62].

In recent Dutch legal writing some concern with the vagueness of the statutory criteria is noticeable. It has been pointed out that this vagueness must be at least one factor in the enormous difference in the extent to which courts in various parts of the country impose "supervision" [63], and it has been suggested that standards for the interpretation of the criteria should be developed [64]. It has been argued that the courts have made too much use of "supervision," that it has been used in cases where help was only desirable, not absolutely necessary to avert great harm to the child [65], and that use of mandatory state power is justifiable only in the latter situation. Nevertheless, few writers have tried to formulate standards to guide the use of judicial discretion or to indicate the circumstances which should be present, in addition to the state of danger required by statute, to impose "supervision." One Dutch juvenile court judge has suggested that "supervision" should be imposed if the statutory criterion—that a child is threatened by moral or physical ruin—is satisfied and:

(a) the parents cannot cope with their child's upbringing themselves and are not capable of asking for help voluntarily; or
(b) the parents stop voluntary help before the proper time; or
(c) voluntary help is impossible because of the personality of the minor or the parents or the functioning of the parental milieu; or
(d) the parents are absolutely incapable of bringing up their children, but refuse to cooperate in a release of parental authority [66].

The Professor of Juvenile Law in Rotterdam proposes the following criteria:

(a) cooperation may not be expected;
(b) cooperation may be expected, but its stability is doubtful;
(c) there is no cooperation, but a family guardian is likely to obtain cooperation;
(d) use of judicial authority is likely to be the kind of help needed (some people need authoritarian help) [67].

**Statistics Concerning the Imposition
of the Measures Described**

A useful comparative statistical analysis of the extent to which courts or other agencies use their powers to intervene with respect to children is impossible. The basis of jurisdiction, available statistical data, etc., are too diverse.

Some data concerning trends in individual countries may be of interest, to give some indication of the way in which discretion is used. In the Netherlands, possibly in reaction to criticisms of the too frequent use of "supervision," the number of "supervision" orders has recently been decreasing (see Table 3–1). The same is true for the number of families subject to termination of parental authority. This trend is expected to continue [68]. Most of these terminations are "releases"—i.e., no fault is attributed to the parents. Thus, in 1971, 64 parents were subject to a termination for fault and 890 to a termination in the absence of fault.* The statistics confirm the proposition discussed above that termination is not necessarily final: Table 3–3 indicates the number of cases in

Table 3–1. Number of "Supervisions" in the Netherlands

	Number of Civil "Supervision" Orders[a]	Percent of Population of 0–20 Years[b]
1965	4,811	not available
1966	4,787	not available
1967	4,759	not available
1968	4,249	not available
1969	4,272	0.088
1970	3,984	0.082
1971	3,256	0.066
1972	3,034	not available
1973	3,002	not available

[a]As distinguished from criminal "supervisions"; "supervision" may also be imposed if a juvenile has been proved to have committed a criminal offense.
[b]I.e., the age group potentially subject to civil "supervision."

Table 3–2. Number of Families Subject to Termination of Parental Authority in the Netherlands

1966	1,323
1967	1,289
1968	1,148
1969	1,257
1970	1,210
1971	925

Table 3–3. Number of Restorations of Parental Authority in the Netherlands

1967	177
1968	183
1969	190
1970	186
1971	158 [69]

*The total number of terminations thus arrived at is different from that given in Table 3–2 because the latter counts cases in which one parent's authority is terminated for fault and the other parent's in the absence of fault as only one case, whereas the present statistic counts them as two cases.

which a restoration of parental authority with respect to one or both parents was granted.

In France, the number of cases in which "assistance in upbringing" was imposed went up tremendously during the first few years in which the measure existed in its present form, i.e., since 1958. The most recent available data— concerning 1968—suggest a certain stabilization now. Simultaneously, the number of "forfeitures" has apparently been going down [70]. In 1968 "assistance in upbringing" was imposed in 42,455 cases and .24 percent of the relevant age group was involved [71].

In West Germany, as in the Netherlands, the use of child protection measures has also been decreasing in recent years, as is shown by the statistics in Table 3—4. The total number of children subject to child protection measures has decreased by 26.7 percent between 1967 and 1971 [72]. The statistics in Table 3—4 reveal a tendency to rely less and less on the most intrusive measure, "remedial upbringing," and more and more on the other child protective measures.

Table 3—4. Numbers of Minors at End of Year in West Germany Placed in "Assistance in Upbringing," "Voluntary Help," and "Remedial Upbringing"

	"Assistance in Upbringing"		*"Voluntary Help in Upbringing"*		*"Remedial Upbringing"*			
		% of court actions		*% of court actions*		*% of court actions*	*Total*	*%*
1967	9,060	15.5	26,458	45.0	23,200	39.5	58,718	100.0
1968	8,809	15.1	26,713	45.9	22,703	39.0	58,225	100.0
1969	8,581	15.2	26,146	46.5	21,531	38.3	56,258	100.0
1970	8,203	15.6	25,186	48.2	18,901	36.2	52,290	100.0
1971	7,804	16.5	23,487	49.8	15,906	33.67	47,197	100.0
1972	7,723	17.9	22,349	51.9	12,974	30.2	43,046	100.0

REMEDIAL IMPLICATIONS OF THE VARIOUS MEASURES

This section will consider:

1. The possible remedial implications of the existence of a situation justifying intervention under the statute.
2. What, if any, legal criteria govern the decision as to what disposition should be made in a particular case.
3. Some statistics concerning the actual use of the various available dispositions.

Available Measures

The forms which state intervention in a child's and a family's life may take are all variations on a familiar theme: Referral over to parent or guardian [73], aid, admonition, warning, directives [74], supervision of the child or the family [75], placement in a foster family or in a home or institution. One interesting form of treatment—in the light of recent American interest in focusing on the family [76] —is the appointment of a family guardian. This is the normal consequence of a Dutch "supervision" order and a German "assistance in upbringing" order [77]. The Dutch family guardian may give the parents directives concerning the raising and care of the child subject to "supervision" [78]. The German "assistant in upbringing" helps those in charge of the child and counsels and aids the child and also gives him advice on the use of his income [79]. In all countries, institutionalization of children subject to child protective measures is possible; not infrequently they may be placed in the same kinds of institutions in which juveniles having committed criminal offenses are placed [80].

Criteria for Choice of Disposition

In all countries, legislation leaves the competent authorities a wide area of discretion to choose the course that seems to them most desirable in a particular case. However, sometimes an attempt is made in the authorizing statute to set certain minimal standards.

Thus, in many countries the relevant laws, either expressly or by implication, attempt to make sure that the interference with the child's and family's life is kept to a minimum. For instance, Section 26 of the Swedish Child Welfare Act states that if the Child Welfare Board has jurisdiction on the basis of one of the grounds described above [81] it "shall attempt, insofar as possible, to produce a remedy by one or more preventive measures, namely:

1. aid, including advice and support;
2. admonition and warning;
3. directives concerning the minor's living conditions; and
4. supervision."

The minor may "be taken in social care," (that is, placed outside of his own home) only "if preventive measures are judged profitless or if such measures have been taken without resulting in correction" [82]. Sections 36.2 and 39 of the Act provide that if placement outside of the home is necessary, placement in a private home should be sought rather than in an institution if at all possible. German legislation similarly indicates in several provisions that the child's and family's life ought to be interfered with as little as possible. For instance, Section 64 of the Statute on Child Welfare provides that "remedial upbringing" (the most severe child protective measure, often involving placement outside of the juvenile's own family [83]) should be ordered only when no other sufficient measure is available. In Holland, the relevant Civil Code provisions are thought to imply the rule that "supervision" ought normally to be ordered rather than termination of parental rights [84], and the Code somewhat limits the purposes for which a juvenile subject to "supervision" may be placed outside his own home [85]. In France, the provisions dealing with "assistance in upbringing" indicate that, if possible, the child should remain at home [86].

Within the contours of the statutory limitations, the criteria for use of one or another child protection measure are primarily social work criteria, although practical possibilities often limit the extent to which a theoretically-indicated measure can in fact be carried out [87].

Some Statistics Concerning Implications in Practice

As I pointed out before, it is not possible to find statistics for the different countries involved which are comparable to each other in most senses. Here again, though, some information based on the available data may be of interest:

Child Welfare Measures in Sweden. In Sweden, we have seen that the Child Welfare Act provides that the Child Welfare Board should attempt preventive remedies if at all possible, rather than placing a child out of his home [88]. In practice, in recent years, the Child Welfare Boards exercising jurisdiction on any of the grounds listed above in fact took preventive action in about twice as many cases as they "took a child in charge for social care" (Table 3–5). When placement outside the child's home is necessary, the Act provides that care in a private home should be given first consideration [90]. In practice, the statistics (Table 3–6) show that a far greater proportion of those subject to a Child Welfare Board's jurisdiction under Section 25(a) (roughly, "neglect") are placed in a private home than is the case with those subject to the Board's jurisdiction under Section 25(b) (roughly, "delinquents" and "PINS"). Even so, about 20 percent of the latter group are placed in private homes. On the other hand, most placements in a youth welfare school concern children in the latter group, although there are also children from the former group in such schools.

Extent of Placement Out of the Home in Holland and West Germany. As we have seen, both in the Netherlands and in West Germany the applicable law favors avoiding placement of a child out of its own home if at all possible. Nevertheless, the available statistics indicate that the number of such placements is

Table 3–5. Action Taken by Swedish Child Welfare Board

	1964	*1965*	*1966*	*1967*	*1968*
Preventive Action	22,420	20,197	20,657	19,621	18,547
Social Care (placement out of home)	10,572	10,719	10,647	10,583	10,948 [89]

Table 3–6. Placement of Children Taken in Charge for Social Care
in Sweden on December 31, 1968 [91]

Number Placed in →		Private Homes	Children's Homes	Youth Welfare School	Other Inst.	Other Place	Not Placed
Total number in social care:	9,112	4,680	701	1,652	261	557	1,261
On basis of §25A:	5,369	3,961	490	78	137	139	654
On basis of §25B	4,019	811	235	1,647	138	452	736

Table 3–7. Placement Outside the Family of Children Subject to
'Supervision' in the Netherlands

	Number of Terminated "Supervisions"	Placed Outside Family (percent)
1966	4,908	52.4
1967	4,740	53.4
1968	4,737	56.5
1969	4,799	52.5
1970	4,503	58.4
1971	4,771	56.2
1972	4,016	66.0
1973	3,667	65.1

substantial. Thus, Table 3–7 shows that in the Netherlands more than half of
all children whose "supervision" was terminated during recent years had been
placed outside of their home either for observation or "in the interest of care
and education" or for both [92]. Placement out of the home may be in a foster
family or in an institution. In recent years, about 27 percent of all children
subject to a "supervision" order were placed in an institution [93]. About 44
percent of children of parents whose parental rights had been terminated were
placed in institutions in recent years [94].

In West Germany, we have seen there is a noticeable trend towards the use of
the less intrusive measures of "assistance in upbringing" and "voluntary help in
upbringing" rather than "remedial upbringing" [95]. Those subject to "assistance in upbringing" cannot be placed outside their own home [96], but with
regard to the other two groups, in particular those subject to "voluntary help in
upbringing," the percentage of placements outside of the family is high. Of all
children in "remedial upbringing" on December 31, 1972, 50.2 percent were in
institutions; 3,500—of a total number of 12,974—were in their own family;
1,090 were in a family other than their own. Of all children (22,349) subject to

"voluntary help in upbringing," 67.5 percent were in an institution; 3,218 were in their own family; 1,237 were in a family other than their own [97].

In both the Netherlands and West Germany, the number of children institutionalized has decreased in recent years more or less proportionately with the number of child protection measures imposed [98]. Thus, in both countries, the decrease in use of child protection measures has not meant a higher rate of institutionalization of the children subject to these measures. If cases are now more hard-core, recourse to institutionalization has, nevertheless, been avoided to the same extent as before [99].

Duration of Child Protective Measures in Holland, West Germany and France. Statistics on the duration of child protective measures show that in both the Netherlands and West Germany the courts make extensive use of their power to extend the duration of the measures they impose, and that in both countries these measures usually extend over several years. Thus, in the Netherlands, out of all "supervisions" imposed in the absence of conviction for a criminal offense which were terminated in 1973, 10 percent had lasted less than one year, 18 percent between one and two years, 20 percent between two and three years, and 51 percent over three years. The number of "supervisions" that had lasted less than one year gradually decreased from 15 percent in 1962 to 10 percent in 1973; the number of "supervisions" that had lasted more than three years increased from 42 percent in 1962 to 51 percent in 1973 [100].

In West Germany, out of all "remedial upbringing" orders terminated in 1972, 11.8 percent lasted up to one year, 16.0 percent from one to two years, 24.0 percent between two and three years, 28.1 percent from three to five years, 15.6 percent from five to ten years, 4.5 percent more than ten years. Of all "voluntary help in upbringing" orders terminated in 1972, 24.4 percent lasted up to one year, 21.6 percent from one to two years, 19.6 percent from two to three years, 17.9 percent from three to five years, 14.0 percent from five to ten years, 2.5 percent more than ten years [101]. It is noteworthy that the duration of the latter measure, which is imposed with the consent of the parents or legal guardians, tends to be shorter than that of the coercive "remedial upbringing."

In France, the average duration of treatment of both children convicted of crimes and those subject to civil law protective measures is about three years [102].

Duration of Placement Outside the Home in Holland and West Germany. In Holland, out of all children placed outside their own home while subject to a "supervision" order and whose "supervision" was terminated at the end of 1973, 13 percent of the boys and 16 percent of the girls had been away for less than six months, 12 percent of the boys and 14 percent of the girls between six months and one year, 75 percent of the boys and 70 percent of the girls for over a year. These percentages do not appear to have changed much over the last six years [103].

In West Germany, out of all children released from "remedial upbringing" in 1972, 9.9 percent had been in an institution for less than six months, 10.8 percent for between six months and one year, 28.6 percent between one and two years, 20.0 percent for two to three years, 14.4 percent for three to five years, 8.8 percent for five to ten years and 2.3 percent for more than ten years. For children released from "voluntary help in upbringing," the respective percentages are: 12.8, 13.8, 24.8, 17.7, 13.3, 9.8, and 1.8 [104]. A commentator on similar statistics for 1971 in the German professional journal for child welfare workers complains about the number of children institutionalized for over three years: two or three years should, he says, suffice to do all that can be done [105].

PROCEDURE

In the United States, recent judicial decisions have displayed great concern for the procedural position of juveniles brought before the juvenile court. This section will examine some questions concerning the particular institution which has jurisdiction, and the procedure it follows, in order to shed some light on the procedural position of children involved in somewhat comparable proceedings in Europe.

Legal Institutions with Child Protective Jurisdiction

In the Scandinavian countries jurisdiction over all matters within the jurisdiction of American juvenile courts, often including cases in which a criminal offense has been committed by someone under eighteen, is with local administrative agencies called Child Welfare Boards [106]. In most other European countries, jurisdiction over the kinds of problems we are concerned with is vested in a court [107].

In the Netherlands decisions concerning "supervision" are made by a judge specializing in juvenile matters who is a member of the district court. Decisions concerning termination of parental rights lie with the normal district court, sitting with three judges [108], as it does in other cases. It is the practice in these types of cases to have one of the three be a judge specializing in juvenile matters. In France, similarly, "assistance in upbringing" matters are within the jurisdiction of a specialized children's judge, while cases involving "termination" of parental rights are committed to the normal district courts. The children's judge is a member of the district court, and under the Code he may be assigned to sit with two other judges in a "termination" case, although this is not required [109]. In West Germany, the power to order any of the measures discussed previously against the wishes of the parties concerned belongs to the "guardianship court," a court specializing in family matters [110]. With the parents' consent, "assistance in upbringing" may be ordered by the "Municipal Youth Bureau" and "voluntary help in upbringing" by the "State Youth Bureau" [111]. In England, jurisdiction is with the juvenile court [112]. The merits and demerits of boards versus courts have been discussed at great length elsewhere [113], and I will not go into this matter. It should be noted, however, that even where final power to take compulsory measures with regard to juveniles lies with a court, there is in several countries discussed in this article—e.g., the Netherlands and Germany—a substantial involvement of administrative agencies somewhat comparable to the Scandinavian Child Welfare Boards in the preparation of the court's decisions [114].

Procedure in Child Protection Cases

In European countries, as in the United States, the basic concept of the juvenile court or similar agency having jurisdiction in child protection cases is one of an agency acting to protect the best interests of the child. In Europe, as here, this has often led to a weakening of the procedural position of the parties concerned, the child himself in particular [115].

On the continent of Europe, especially, the rights of children involved in child protection proceedings (other than those involving the accusation of a criminal offense*) are not always adequately protected. In the Netherlands in particular, the proceedings are conceived as directed against the parents, for the protection of the child. The rights at stake are those of the parent to bring up the child themselves as they see fit, and the parents are the parties whose procedural rights the law seeks to insure. Recently, there has been an increasing awareness in the literature of the need to protect the procedural position of the child himself [116]. This awareness seems gradually to be reflecting itself in some recent legislation concerning procedure in child protection cases. This will be illustrated by the following discussion of a few procedural questions.

Who May Initiate Proceedings? In all continental countries one or both of the parents may petition the court to impose child protection measures [117]. In some countries close relatives are also empowered to petition the court [118]. Only in France, under recent amendments to the Code sections concerning "assistance in upbringing," is the juvenile himself entitled to bring proceedings [119]. While cases brought by juveniles themselves are relatively infrequent, they do occur. In 1966, 908 requests for "assistance in upbringing" were made by juveniles (24,913 by the prosecutor's office, 21,445 by the judge on his own motion, 6,328 by parents or guardians) [120].

Finally, official agencies such as a prosecutor's office [121] or a child protection agency [122] may petition the court or the court may have authority to

---

*In juvenile court proceedings involving a child who has committed a criminal offense, procedural guarantees are generally not much unlike those applicable in criminal proceedings against adults.

order child protection measures on its own motion [123]. The information available on France and Holland shows that in practice most child protection cases are initiated by official agencies [124]. There is no reason to believe that the situation is any different in West Germany.

In England only official agencies, such as the local children's or education authority, the police, or officers of the National Society for the Prevention of Cruelty to Children are authorized to initiate proceedings in juvenile court [125]. In Sweden, proceedings are initiated by the Child Welfare Board on its own motion [126].

✻ Rights of Parties During Proceedings. In the Netherlands, the juvenile himself has barely any rights during proceedings concerning measures to protect him. The court may hear the juvenile in proceedings concerning "supervision" or "termination" of parental authority, but has no duty to do so [127]. The juvenile has no right to counsel. The parents' rights are better protected. They must be adequately notified of the proceedings, and must be heard, unless they fail to appear after such notification; have a right to see the petition (which must contain its grounds and, if possible, be documented); and they must be notified of the grounds on which the petition is based [128].

In West Germany and France, the procedural position of parents and children is somewhat less unequal. Thus in Germany, the court must hear both the juvenile and his parents in proceedings concerning "assistance in upbringing" [129] and "remedial upbringing" [130]. However, a hearing of the juvenile is not required concerning decisions taken with consent of the parents, such as "voluntary assistance in upbringing." Section 1666 of the Civil Code prescribes that the parents be heard before decisions are rendered under that provision, but only allows the child to be heard [131].

In France, the court must notify the parents and the juvenile if they have not initiated the proceedings themselves [132], in "assistance in upbringing" matters, but only the parents in "forfeiture" cases [133]. The court must hear the parents [134]. It must hear the juvenile in "assistance in upbringing" matters during its investigation of the case, and also at the trial, unless "his age or condition do not permit [it] to do so," and it may hear the juvenile in "forfeiture" matters if it considers it useful to do so [135]. French legislation, unlike West German and Dutch law, specifically provides that the parents and child have a right to be represented by counsel or to have a counsel assigned by the court. The court must notify adult parties of this right at their first hearing and the juvenile also "whenever this is required in his interest" [136]. Counsel has a right to see the file of the case at the clerk's office and must be notified of the day of the hearing and be heard.

In England, the juvenile must be notified of an application for juvenile court proceedings, if notification appears appropriate to the applicant having regard to the juvenile's age and understanding. The child's parents must be notified if their whereabouts are known [137]. If the child is not legally represented, and unless the proceedings result from a request of the parents, the court must allow the parents or in their absence some other responsible person to conduct the case, unless the juvenile involved otherwise requests [138]. The court may hear evidence in the absence of the juvenile if the evidence likely to be given is such that it should not be given in his presence, unless he is conducting his own case. Evidence relating to his character or conduct must be heard in his presence. The court may require the parent to withdraw from the court while the juvenile gives evidence or makes a statement, but it must then inform the parent of the substance of allegations made against him and give him an opportunity of meeting these [139]. The juvenile has a right to counsel and legal aid, but no provision expressly requires the court to inform him of this right [140].

The Child Welfare Act of Sweden contains rather detailed provisions on the procedure to be followed by the Child Welfare Boards. It gives several procedural guarantees to the "person whom the matter concerns." Before the Board decides a matter, the person concerned must be informed of what the investigation disclosed and must be given an opportunity to comment on it, unless such a comment is obviously needless or there is no time to wait. The person concerned must be informed of his right to request an oral hearing, which shall be granted unless special reasons warrant some other procedure. He may plead his case and present evidence. He may request that another investigation be produced, which request must be honored unless it can be assumed that further investigation would have no significance. He may bring counsel to the hearing, but a Board may reject the counsel if he shows lack of skill of judgment [141]. The Act seems to assume that the interests of parents and children coincide, since it provides that where a child under fifteen years is involved the procedural guarantees shall apply to his parents [142].

The Judgment: Right to Appeal

In a number of countries, there is specific provision that the judgment must be supported by reasons [143]. In West Germany, France, and the Netherlands, at least, the case law has established minimal standards that the reasoning must satisfy. In particular, a general formula such as "because required in the best interest of the child" is not enough [144]. Juveniles over a specific age have a right to notification of the reasons in France, Germany, and Sweden [145], but there may be limitations on this right in order to protect the child from harm [146].

In continental countries, there usually lies an appeal on both fact and law and one upon law only [147] against judicial decisions concerning child protective measures. Here again the relevant legislation in several countries assumes more or less identity between parental and children's interest. In the Netherlands, the juvenile has no right to appeal at all; in West Germany only if he is fourteen years or older. Only in France has the juvenile himself an unqualified right to appeal [148]. In England, the juvenile may appeal to the Crown Court against any order made in respect of him except one requiring his parent or guardian to enter into a recognizance to take proper care of him and exercise proper control over him [149]. In Sweden, any person to whom a decision applies* has a first appeal to the County Administration with regard to most decisions taken by a Child Welfare Board, and a final resort to the Supreme Administrative Court [150]. A decision to take a person in social care is subject to automatic review by the County Administration unless every party concerned (i.e., a juvenile of fifteen and over, and the parents) agrees [151].

Available statistics on France indicate that in practice appeals are rare and reversals even more so [152]. I doubt that the situation is any different in the Netherlands, although I could not find any statistics. I cannot make any reasonable estimate with regard to the practice in other countries covered by this study.

TREATMENT OF THE COUNTERPARTS
OF PINS IN THE NETHERLANDS†

An attempt to describe the actual practice of treatment of those subject to child protective measures in all the countries whose laws have been discussed above would be a huge undertaking. For essentially practical reasons I therefore decided to concentrate on the situation in the Netherlands. The choice is not purely arbitrary, however, since some of the Dutch approaches towards troublesome juveniles, despite the manifold criticism to which child protection services are subject in the country itself, are widely regarded as particularly innovative and "enlightened" [153].

PINS and their counterparts in the various American states are a heterogeneous group. We have seen that there is no formal category like them in the Netherlands. On the other hand, we have seen that some children with problems more or less comparable to those of PINS are subject to the child protective measures provided for by the Dutch Civil Code. Others receive help outside of the court context. This section will first consider the treatment of the former—those subject to "judicial child protection"—and will then examine some of the more or less experimental programs carried out with regard to the latter. Because—as in the United States—many different agencies are involved in the treatment of the juveniles concerned, it is extremely difficult to get a comprehensive view of what is actually being done. The picture I draw therefore often has to be superficial or incidental.

---

*It is not clear whether this implies an independent right of appeal for the juvenile.

† The following description of Dutch practices is based mainly on the available literature, but also on discussions with people more or less directly involved in the field.

Treatment in the framework of "supervision" is carried out primarily under the aegis of the "family guardianship associations." These are private agencies, some organized on a denominational and others on a nondenominational basis, all of them almost entirely subsidized by the government. They employ professional staffs who in their turn are responsible for the recruitment of the actual family guardians. In many cases these are volunteers, who receive some initial training from their association and some support in their work with the families. The associations are responsible for proposing a particular family guardian for appointment by the judge in a particular case [154]. Comparable agencies—the "guardianship associations"—carry responsibility for children whose parents' parental authority has been terminated. Some agencies are involved in both guardianship and family guardianship work [155].

As has been described above, "supervision" orders in principle do not involve placement, and the "family guardian" role is basically limited to what can roughly be described as social work with the child and its family. Many "supervision" and most "termination" orders, however, do involve placement.

Foster families are the preferred possibility in the case of placements outside the home, and there have been some notable developments with respect to the foster care arrangements available to the associations [156], in particular the development of specialized forms of foster care. For example, in some cities there now are agencies for "therapeutic foster care" whose goal it is to make it possible for extremely difficult juveniles to be treated in foster families with intensive guidance from a team of experts [157]. Another example are the foster families who specialize in the treatment of particular kinds of juveniles with whom they have acquired extensive practical experience. Yet another form of specialized foster care is provided by foster families in which professionals, such as social workers, fill the adult roles [158].

Placement in institutions takes place primarily in private institutions, which again are almost entirely subsidized by the government. On December 31, 1969, there were 263 institutions which had been "approved" [159] by the government for placement of juveniles subject to "supervision" or "termination" orders. Of these, eight were public institutions.

Both public and private institutions differ in size, but all are small compared to the usual American institution. The largest public institution, the reception and observation house for boys in Amerongen, had in 1970 a capacity of 84 and an average daily population of 66 [160]. On December 31, 1969 there was a total population of 14,666 in 263 institutions—an average population of 55. By contrast, in the United States only 66 of 325 public institutions for delinquents had a capacity in 1970 of under 50, and more than 40 percent exceeded a capacity of 150 [161]. Moreover, in the United States 31 percent of these institutions had a population larger than their rated capacity [162], whereas in the Netherlands the population of the institutions appears generally to be less than capacity [163].

The Basic Act on Child Protection of 1961 divides private institutions into four groups: reception homes, observation homes, institutions for "upbringing," and institutions for special treatment. The last are meant for the treatment of very difficult, socially maladjusted children who cannot be placed in an institution for "upbringing" [164]. The institutions for "upbringing" are also divided into several categories depending on the group to which they cater, e.g., normal children, working youths, retarded children, children receiving trade or professional training, etc. [165]. Forty-one percent of all placements are of "normal" children, 10.5 percent retarded children, and 12.3 percent children in need of psychiatric treatment [166].

The public institutions include three which among other functions serve as institutions for children in need of special discipline [167], roughly comparable to American "training schools" or English "borstals" in that they are the most "correctional" of all the institutions. Otherwise, the public institutions are divided into the same categories as the private institutions and serve a back-up function in catering to children who cannot be privately placed [168]. There are no institutions intended exclusively for juveniles who have committed criminal offenses. Many institutions have a mixed population of both voluntary and court placements [169]. I have not seen any criticism of the mixing of non-criminal and criminal juveniles. The trend seems, on the contrary, to be toward a greater integration of the care of children subject to judicial child protection, i.e., roughly speaking, delinquents, PINS, dependent and neglected children, into general youth welfare work [170].

What actually is done in terms of treatment, within the organizational framework described, varies a lot in nature and quality. The family guardian may be an old-fashioned authoritarian "child protector" or a permissive, rather "hip" staff member of one of the "alternative" agencies described below [171]. Foster families vary along similar lines, as does the expert guidance they receive. The institutions vary from small, innovative, well-staffed homes to old-fashioned children's warehouses [172]. The whole institution of "judicial child protection" has been subjected to an enormous variety of criticism, from both insiders and outsiders. It is in the process of continuous change and possibly an entire reorganization in the near future. Some of the most prevalent criticisms are:

1. Too much recourse is had to compulsory measures. Help should be offered as much as possible on a voluntary basis. The most extreme position in this respect is taken by one of the "alternative help agencies" arguing that "supervision" should be abolished and that *all* help to the kinds of juveniles now subject to the measure should be offered on a voluntary basis [173]. To some extent, these criticisms may have had effect on recent practice, and have been a factor leading to the decrease of the yearly number of "supervisions" [174].

2. The irrational, diffuse organization of child protection work has some

clear drawbacks from the point of view of treatment. One consequence, for instance, is the lack of continuity of personnel having contacts with a family from the time of initial consultation to that of the appointment of a family guardian [175]. Two government reports have recently proposed a reorganization of child protection work [176], and changes are likely in the not too distant future.

3. There is excessive use made of institutionalization, it often lasts too long, and children are transferred from one institution to another too frequently [177]. One factor which is generally thought to have an unfavorable impact on the extent and length of institutionalization is the organization of government subsidies. Subsidy is given per child. If an institution does not have enough placements, it cannot survive [178]. There has been a recent downward trend in institutionalization [179]. This has resulted in, and is evidenced by, the closing of a number of institutions [180]. It is not clear from the available data whether the duration of institutionalization has declined, and whether transfers have become less frequent.

4. A factor underlying many of the other criticisms is the lack of evidence that child protection measures have the desired beneficial effects. The most elaborate study, published in 1952 and concerning a group of people who had been subject to "supervision" in the years 1930–1936 [181], did not find any obvious effect from the measure. Since that time the practice of child protection has changed considerably, but while it has become considerably more sophisticated, it is not clear that it has become any more effective. Of course, it would be extremely difficult to determine precisely what success of these kinds of interventions would entail, let alone measure it. There have been no more recent systematic studies of the effectiveness of child protection measures.

Recent years have seen a great deal of experimentation with new forms of help to juveniles and to families with problems. Some of this has occurred within the framework of judicial child protection measures—or at least of traditional child protection agencies. For instance, the oldest guardianship and family guardianship association is running several advisory centers for "child and family" which offer voluntary help to children and their parents, together or independently, in an effort to avoid the need for eventual court interference [182]. The same association is experimenting with new techniques, such as family therapy [183]. The use of therapeutic foster care described above might also be cited as an example of use of a new approach within the traditional framework.

Possibly the most interesting development is the appearance in recent years of the so-called "alternative help agencies." To these I will devote the rest of this section. These agencies started to appear in the nineteen-sixties contemporaneously with the dramatic flowering of new anti-authoritarian ideas proclaimed by political groups such as the "Provo's" and the "Gnomes" [184], and with new trends in traditional social work and psychiatric thinking [185]. By August

1975, these organizations appeared to be generally accepted as an integral part of social welfare work in this area [186]. Their stated goals are: "To give active support to people who are in trouble because their rights and liberties are encroached upon or because they are the victim of intolerance of 'deviant behavior' " [187]. "To give information, advice and help on individual and social questions to young people and groups of young people" [188]. "To give social help in the Hague undergound; to promote structural changes of society" [189].

The approach of these "alternative" agencies differs more or less from the traditional types of help available to young people with similar types of problems in a number of ways. The "alternative" agencies are interested more in social involvement and less in expertise than the traditional social work agencies are. They are staffed partly by volunteers, partly by professionals. Many of them are organized along strictly democratic lines, policy being made by all members equally. All of them to a greater or lesser extent emphasize the need for fundamental change and for social action to achieve this. All of them emphatically reject current social norms. All of them stress the need for crisis intervention and try to be prepared to offer immediate help. For instance, they do not have the waiting lists which often characterize the work of more traditional agencies [190], and their opening hours often differ from those of traditional agencies. In light of their views on the need for radical social change, it is interesting that many of them receive considerable or complete government or city subsidy [191].

In a recent pamphlet published by the National Council on Social Welfare, the three "alternative" agencies whose stated goals were quoted above are briefly described [192]. The two main organizations in terms of geographical distribution are *Release* and *JAC* (short for *Jongeren Advies Centrum*, which means Youth Advisory Center).

Release is connected with the "Civil Liberties Union" set up in 1970 to undertake social action to promote human liberty and respect for individual rights and liberties. *Release* was deliberately set up separately as an agency to give individual help, so as not to be hampered in that effort by the "Union's" social action. However, it is financed by the "Union" from membership dues (all of its local departments except one refuse government subsidy as a matter of principle), and Board membership of the two organizations overlaps to some extent. The name *Release* is taken from a similar organization in England, and the same type of organization exists in other European countries. In April, 1972, there were *Release* offices in fifteen Dutch cities. One of these, the Amsterdam office, has since decided to fold, because it found that rendering of individual help was so time-consuming that no time was left for more important work on structural social change [193]. *Release* is staffed by lay volunteers who handle first contacts and anything they can do without the advice of professionals. In case of need for professional help, they refer cases to one of *Release*'s specialized sections which rely on volunteer professionals such as lawyers, doctors, psychologists. *Release Amsterdam*, while it still existed, had the following sections: general (planning, organization, secretarial); aliens (problems concerning aliens staying in the Netherlands); minors (child protection cases; finding of "alternative," nonauthoritarian foster families); drugs (legal and medical help; information); contraception (including abortion referrals); housing; job counseling; social affairs (problems "resulting from repression by bureaucracy and concerning social welfare law"); military service (help and information concerning draft refusal and desertion); legal affairs; medical affairs; after-care (checking of referrals, treatment of cases, following the later development of all types of cases); publicity; and funding/representation [194]. In the period from May 1970 to July 1971 all *Release* offices in the country together received a total of 11,000 requests for help which were handled by about 250 intake staff members. In *Release Amsterdam* the largest number of cases concerned problems of aliens. In other cities, housing problems were at the top of the list (41 percent in Haarlem, 28 percent in the Hague). In Amsterdam, Haarlem, and the Hague problems of minors constituted the second largest group (Haarlem 14 percent, the Hague 14 percent). Some of these cases concerned runaways from child protection institutions.

In April 1972, there were *JAC*s in forty Dutch cities. Some of these are publicly subsidized. Almost all of them operate on the following basic principles:

1. help should be given with an aim of self-determination;
2. the helping person must be a professional, as well as feel solidarity with the person receiving help;
3. help should be immediate and short term—normally *JAC*s do not give long-term help themselves, referring cases to existing agencies, but where the latter are not adequate *JAC*s either provide help themselves or try to set up the needed facilities;*
4. help should be easily accessible—free, at convenient times for young and working people, and given anonymously if desired. In *JAC Amsterdam*, there is no official waiting room. Consultation and waiting takes place in the same room, unless the client expresses a desire for privacy. There are no waiting lists and the office does not specialize in particular kinds of problems. It is open evenings until 1 A.M., and on Saturday afternoons.

In 1972, *JAC Amsterdam* received 8,726 requests for help, 71 percent of these during office visits, 29 percent over the telephone: 27 percent of these were

---

*Thus, for instance JAC Amsterdam set up an Experimental Employment Office to help people who do not fit the pattern of the normal labor market (look differently, want to work different hours, etc.). It also set up a center for people who have urgent short-term housing needs, and an abortion clinic. In cooperation with *Release*, some probation/parole agencies and others it set up a center to find housing for difficult cases, such as difficult youths, people who have problems in establishing relationships, etc.

requests for general information (29 percent in 1971). Otherwise the requests for help came into the following categories:

medical	10%
drugs	3%
runaways	4%
family problems	4%
sex	5%
abortion	11%
legal	19%
psychological	8%
work/school	4%
religious	1%
permanent visitor	2%
various	2%

In its 1972 Report *JAC Amsterdam* states that it has had little success in attracting working class youths. In 1972 the *JAC* began a number of activities which do not involve direct help to individuals. Several of these attempt to reach the groups of young people who thus far have not contacted the *JAC*, e.g., a project concerning employment possibilities for unemployed youths and a project concerning schools, especially those involved in trade education.

The third important alternative help agency is the *Sosjale Jóenit* in the Hague.* This is in many ways the most radical of the agencies discussed. It is most militantly critical of present-day capitalist society and most deliberately seeks confrontation with the establishment. Its organizational structure is the most democratic in that policy is made at plenary meetings open to the public. In particular, this means that clients and staff, as well as anyone else who has an interest, can participate in policy-making. The staff consists of professionals, together with "laymen" having experience with a particular type of problem— drugs, for example. The *Sosjale Joenit* receives a subsidy from the city of the Hague. The *Joenit* refers cases to regular welfare agencies, or handles them by itself. It has developed its own list of "alternative" families that are willing to receive runaways while a more permanent solution is being worked out. In 1973 it received 1,783 requests for help, 1,399 of which were for one time only. In 1973 and 1972, the problems at intake of those with whom only one contact was had were:

	1973	1972
runaways	94	83
psychological/		
social problems	301	290

*The name is a "Dutchification" of the English word "social unit."

	1973	1972
legal problems	40	35
job problems	163	121
housing	243	216
problems with parents	24	—
drugs	64	45
child protection	98	90
welfare	169	114
abortion	18	23
homosexuality	8	—
sex	24	31
military problems	31	42
help to helpers	12	—
medical	66	78
aliens	38	15
education	—	5
Total	1,399	1,188

The problems of people with longer lasting contacts concerned:

	1973	1972
runaways	109	98
psychological/social	35	36
divorce	5	19
child protection	20	16
family problems	15	18
welfare problems	41	18
job problems	24	20
housing problems	51	40
aliens	20	2
drugs	20	16
education	1	13
sex	12	12
abortion	7	15
unwed mothers	—	1
legal	7	3
medical	12	5
military	4	3
help to helpers	7	10
unknown	—	1
Total	390	326 [195]

Finally, it should be reported that in 1971 a "Union for the Interests of Minors" was set up. This consists of minors who are in institutions and other people interested in their situation. Its aims are to improve conditions in institutions. One of its main concerns has been the selection of institutions to be closed in recent years [196].

In spite of the severe criticism of present society by many of the alternative help agencies and their express willingness to seek confrontation with the "establishment," public conflicts have been few. On the contrary, the established agencies often have been very open to their ideas and willing to cooperate with them. The major conflict which has arisen a number of times concerns the hiding of runaways by staff members of the agencies who by doing so violate a section of the Criminal Code prohibiting the hiding of a minor who has run away or the interference with a police search for such a minor [197]. Several attempts were made to challenge the applicability of this provision to cases in which a runaway juvenile had sought help from an agency and the agency had refused to reveal the minor's whereabouts to the police, claiming that police intervention at that time would interfere with the juvenile's best interest. The major test case is the *Sosjale Joenit* case which is worth an extended description, because it illustrates rather well the different and often ambivalent attitudes prevailing in Dutch society toward the alternative help agencies and the philosophy they represent.

In 1971, two staff members of the *Sosjale Joenit* were arrested and eventually prosecuted for hiding a runaway. The defendants had found temporary shelter for minors who had run away from home and had come to the *Sosjale Joenit* for help. They had informed the parents and the police of their contacts with the minors, but had refused to reveal the address where the minors were because the latter did not want this address revealed. In doing so they acted as they had done in many previous cases and in accordance, so they thought, with an agreement the *Sosjale Joenit* had with the police.* One of them was eventually acquitted for lack of evidence. The other accused was acquitted in the first instance and on appeal on legal grounds which I will discuss later; the Supreme Court quashed the original court of appeal's decision and referred the case back to another court of appeals, which convicted the defendant and imposed a fine of fl. 250 (about $90); the conviction and sentence were confirmed by the Supreme Court on October 16, 1973 [198]. The court of the first instance held that the accused could not be punished because his behavior, although formally inconsistent with the Criminal Code, was not unlawful, since it was a reasonable means towards a reasonable goal, *viz.* the protection of the interests of the runaway minor and those of her parents—the same interests which the relevant provision of the Criminal Code attempts to protect. The court added that such behavior is lawful only for short periods of time and that its lawfulness also depends on (1) the existence of clear cooperation agreements between the agency concerned, the juvenile court, the prosecutor's office, the police, the Child Protection Council, etc.; (2) whether these agreements have been loyally adhered to; (3) whether the

---

*The police denied that the agreement was valid for children under sixteen; the merits of the argument are not clear.

person rendering help has made himself externally responsible and controllable; (4) whether adequate help had actually been rendered.

The court of appeals acquitted on different grounds. It agreed that the accused's goal had been reasonable but it did not think that he had used reasonable means to achieve it. In particular, the court objected to the fact that when the accused, under pressure of an unexpected police search, had revealed the children's home where the girl was hiding, he had done so only after phoning the home to inform them that the police were going to come so that when the police arrived the girl had been taken elsewhere. Thus, the accused had deliberately foiled the police. However, the court of appeals held that the accused was in excusable error concerning the lawfulness of his behavior and therefore lacked the *mens rea* required for the offense.

The Supreme Court did not think that either of the grounds for acquitting the accused relied upon by the two lower courts was right. However, it left open the possibility of an acquittal on grounds of necessity before the court of appeals in Amsterdam to which the case was referred. For procedural reasons, the Supreme Court found that it could not consider the defense of necessity itself. The Amsterdam Court of Appeals held that acting in violation of article 280 of the Criminal Code may be justifiable if certain conditions are fulfilled, to wit if the immediate return of the juvenile is obviously inconsistent with or endangers seriously the moral or psychological interests of the juvenile or his health or that of one of his immediate relatives, provided that (1) the social worker reveals to the police what is the basis for his belief that this may be the case and (2) at the same time promises that as soon as he has further investigated the matter, and on the basis of his further investigation has become persuaded that the juvenile should not return home, he will inform the Child Protection Council and the juvenile court judge and will not prevent their intervention. The court held that in the case in question the conditions for justifiability had not been fulfilled, since the social worker had only had a superficial contact with the minor that would not enable him to determine if there were serious problems involved in a return home. Therefore, the court convicted. At the same time it imposed a light sentence, since obviously the defendant thought that he acted in a morally responsible manner and in the interest of the juvenile concerned.

The case then again went to the Supreme Court which not only confirmed the conviction, but also held that even the circumstances outlined by the Amsterdam Court of Appeals would not suffice to justify a violation of article 280 of the Criminal Code.

On the one hand, the case shows the extent to which the activities of the alternative help agencies are accepted by more established Dutch society. There was in existence an agreement with the police that the *Sosjale Joenit* would contact them and inform them of their dealings with a runaway minor and that the police in return would leave the *Sosjale Joenit* time to work out a solution and would explain to the parents, if necessary, that the child was in reliable hands.

The police, in other words, had accepted and in fact continue to accept the usefulness and legitimacy of the work done by the *Sosjale Joenit* [199].

Several agencies of government also have shown their basic acceptance of the new modes of help. In the first place, the *Sosjale Joenit* and other alternative agencies receive public subsidies. Also, and the accused in the *Sosjale Joenit* case relied on this in his defense, Cabinet Ministers in response to questions in Parliament or otherwise have on several occasions expressed support for the alternative help agencies in general and their way of handling runaways specifically [200]. Finally, the working methods of the *Sosjale Joenit* and other alternative agencies have been accepted and to some extent adopted by many of the established agencies. Several representatives of established social work agencies testified before the various courts that the *Sosjale Joenit* had acted properly in refusing to reveal the hiding place of the juvenile concerned until an acceptable solution had been worked out and the juvenile herself wished to inform her parents or other relevant adults [201]. Several made statements, e.g., to the newspapers, to the effect that they themselves did the same thing or at least considered the *Sosjale Joenit*'s method acceptable [202].

On the other hand, established society's doubts on the acceptability of alternative forms of help are also reflected in the case. It was clear that several people in the police office concerned were not very sympathetic to the work of the *Sosjale Joenit*. They objected to the fact that the *Joenit* helped minors regardless of age (i.e., even those under sixteen), and that minors were sometimes housed in so-called "kraakpanden" (unoccupied buildings that people have moved into without consent of the owner). Both the police and the courts seemed to be puzzled and troubled by the organizational structure of the *Sosjale Joenit*—an open democratic organization in which all significant decisions are made by the plenary meeting consisting of anyone who is interested in coming [203]. Then, of course, in final resort the *Sosjale Joenit* lost its case.

It does not seem that the outcome of the case before the Supreme Court has had a significant impact on the practice of the *Sosjale Joenit* or other such agencies. Mostly, the police continue to let them proceed as they see fit. The police's policy is however, inconsistent and a few more prosecutions have taken place [204].

The main impact of the *Sosjale Joenit* decision has been to increase the momentum for law reform. In August 1975 a Labor party member of Parliament introduced a bill proposing a revision of article 280 of the Criminal Code [205]. Shortly afterwards, the Minister of Justice who had opposed law reform for several years announced that the government would soon introduce its own proposals for revision [206]. Thus, a revision of the Criminal Code in the near future appears likely.

Furthermore, in a recent decision in a similar case, the court of appeals in Amsterdam reiterated its position that refusal to inform the police of a runaway's whereabouts may be justified in certain conditions, because to do so may be the only way for a "helper" to do his duty. For this reason, the court reversed a conviction of a staff member of *JAC* Utrecht [207]. An appeal to the Supreme Court is expected and it is not considered impossible that this court may overrule its decision in the *Sosjale Joenit* case.

CONCLUSION

The immediate applicability of comparative legal research to problems of New York PINS and their counterparts in other states is very limited. Possibly the most interesting discovery is that in many other countries there is no special category of juvenile—only offenses. Even taking into account the many relevant differences, the experience of other countries in this respect gives some support to a theory having current expression in the United States: that the juvenile court could fulfill all its functions with regard to children without having any PINS or similar jurisdiction. Those now treated as PINS who really need juvenile court supervision can receive it on the basis of other more narrowly drafted statutes, such as those conferring jurisdiction in the case of neglect [208].

In several of the countries studied we have found a consensus that a juvenile should receive care, protection, and treatment through the intervention of a court, upon whatever jurisdictional basis, only in cases where the parents or the child really need such help; are likely to benefit from it; and are not likely to receive it but for the coercion exercised by the court. In these countries a development very parallel to one seen in the United States has taken place. One sees initial enthusiasm for and overconfidence in the possible effectiveness of the juvenile court, followed more recently by a growing concern that this initial enthusiasm was excessive and a growing belief that juvenile court intervention should be limited.

There are different ways in which it is sought to limit such intervention by statute. In Germany, the Child Welfare Act stresses the preferability of voluntary, rather than court-imposed treatment. For instance, a court may impose "remedial upbringing" only where "voluntary help in upbringing"—"voluntary" at least on the part of the parents—is not sufficient. Of course, one may wonder what real benefits flow from the theoretical voluntariness of treatment when in fact the pressure on the parents to agree to it must be tremendous, and the *child's* will is legally not relevant. In the United Kingdom, it is sought to restrict court intervention to cases in which it is absolutely necessary by limiting the right to initiate cases to official agencies, such as the police or the National Association for the Prevention of Cruelty to Children. These must to some extent fulfill the screening function fulfilled by the intake division of juvenile courts in the United States. Parents may request the court to direct proceedings if they see fit, as they may (and do) in many of the United States. In France, the most recent relevant revision of the Civil Code limited the kinds of cases in which "assistance in upbringing" may be imposed by changing the wording of the provision concerned. Whereas prior to 1970 "education in upbringing" could be ordered if the juvenile's "health, safety, morality or upbringing" were "endangered," after 1970 intervention on the basis of danger to the juvenile's "upbringing" is no longer permitted unless "his chances of receiving a proper upbringing are seriously jeopardized" [209].

In practice, I am convinced that self-restraint on the part of all those responsible for deciding which cases the court should hear based upon a realistic assessment of what the court has to offer, is the most satisfactory way to restrict court intervention. I think that such growing self-restraint, based on healthy skepticism more than anything else, is responsible for the decrease in the number of cases before the courts in those countries in which it has occurred.

In all the countries studied, as in the United States, courts deciding matters concerning juveniles have a large discretion as to what implications a decision for intervention should have. There is in many codes an effort to establish rudimentary guidelines in order to assure that state intervention be kept to a minimum and that juveniles be kept in their own families whenever possible [210]. Such principles seem wise, but here again one may wonder whether their codification makes much difference. In practice, in the countries for which statistics could be found, the most far-reaching form of state intervention—institutionalization—has been on the decline in recent years without any concomitant change of the law.

A noteworthy feature of practice with regard to minors subject to court jurisdiction in some countries is the tendency not to differentiate, after the stage of adjudication, between those convicted of criminal offenses and others. In the United States, attacks upon the practice of treating PINS and delinquents alike in this stage has been one of the recent focuses of juvenile court reform [211]. The tendency to treat PINS like delinquents—even if in many states they no longer *are* delinquents—is one of the many criticisms of current law and practice with regard to PINS in the United States. In several European countries, on the contrary, it appears that the trend is towards less rather than more differentiation among different groups of juveniles before the juvenile court. One of the aims of the United Kingdom 1969 Children's and Young Persons Act was to end the distinctions among juveniles who have committed crimes and those subject to juvenile court jurisdiction for other reasons, so as to avoid undue stigmatization of the former group [212]. The only respect in which the statute distinguishes among delinquents and others after adjudication is that it provides specifically that only the former may be sent to borstals. In the Netherlands as well, the same kinds of treatment and the same institutions are available for the two groups [213]. There is concern with stigmatization, but the solution sought has not been to separate out those who have not been convicted, but rather to decrease distinctions among facilities for those subject to court supervision and other juveniles who are brought up outside the parental home or receive some form of professional help on a voluntary basis [214].

In the United States at the present time, keeping PINS out of training schools may be desirable as the most feasible short-term way of benefiting at least one group of juveniles. As a long-term policy, emphasizing the distinction between delinquents and other juveniles appears to be short-sighted. Delinquency itself is often a symptom of family problems. A far more reasonable, but also considerably more difficult approach, would be to attempt to create facilities decent enough to treat or care for all or almost all juveniles who cannot stay in their own home for whatever reason, and to attempt to minimize the stigma attached to any court adjudication.

The countries studied show a variety of approaches to procedure. In a country like the Netherlands, procedural rules on civil proceedings [215] still entirely reflect the belief that the court's beneficial intention makes procedural protections for the juvenile superfluous. In the United Kingdom, on the other hand, proceedings in juvenile court are conducted almost entirely like proceedings concerning adults [216]. Law reform in this respect may be expected in other countries in the near future, as a result of modern ideas which seem to prevail in all the countries studied, often as a result of influences from American thinking. One of the most interesting issues in procedural reform is the question of whether it ought to be possible for a juvenile to have recourse to a court to settle conflicts with his or her parents. The same question is currently under study in the United States [217].

In the Netherlands, a majority of the Commission on revision of Child Protection Law in its 1971 report proposed to give the minor over sixteen years old a right to address the proposed youth judge independently in case of conflicts with his/her parents or guardians; in some cases he/she may do so directly, in others, a negative decision by the proposed Council for Youth Protection is first required [218].

In France, *"assistance in upbringing"* proceedings may be initiated by a juvenile.

In practice, it is not clear that the system providing the most extensive procedural guarantees produces the fairest results in practice. A reasonable exercise of discretion and a willingness to provide the financial support necessary for adequate services seem far more essential than procedural guarantees in producing a more or less decent system [219].

Comparative research does not provide any easy answers as to the best ways of treating those PINS who need help. In the Netherlands there has been little evaluation of what has been done thus far, which I have described in some detail. In recent years, there has been great effort to offer help to young people on their own terms, by approaching them on a non-authoritarian basis and by accepting their own norms as valid, even if these norms are not the same as those of older generations. Many PINS—truants, runaways, drug users—do not deserve punishment and do not need elaborate treatment. But they may profit from advice and short-term help aand will use it if offered on acceptable terms.

"Alternative" programs in the Netherlands have shown at the very least that there is a felt need for such help, and that if offered it will be accepted.

NOTES TO CHAPTER 3

1. Juvenile courts in most other American states exercise similar jurisdiction under a variety of different names. Andrews and Cohn, "Ungovernability: The Unjustifiable Jurisdiction," 83 *Yale L.J.* 1383 (1974).

2. I use the term "juvenile" to refer to the persons to whom such legislation applies. In France, it applies to "minors," *i.e.*, persons under twenty-one unless emancipated. *See* Art. 372, 375, 388 *Code Civil* [French Civil Code; Hereinafter C.C.]. In Great Britain, it applies to persons under eighteen. *See* §§ 1 and 70 Children and Young Persons Act [hereinafter C.Y.P.A.], 1969. In the Netherlands, it applies to "minors," *i.e.*, persons under twenty-one unless emancipated. *See* Art. 233, 246, 258 *Burgerlijk Wetboek* [Dutch Civil Code; hereinafter B.W.]. In West Germany, it applies to "minors," *i.e.*, persons under twenty-one. *See* §§ 55, 62, 64 *Jugendwohlfartgesetz* [Statute on Child Welfare, hereinafter JWG], § 2 Burgerliches Gesetzbuch [German Civil Code, hereinafter BGB]. In Sweden, the age limit is eighteen for children who are abused or neglected; twenty-one for children subject to state intervention because of their own misconduct.

3. *See* discussion of English and Swedish law at p. 123 *et seq.*, *infra*.

4. For discussion of the kind of agency having jurisdiction in each of these countries, *see* pages 132–33, *infra*.

5. This does not mean that there is no attempt to enforce certain standards with regard to juvenile behavior different from those applicable to adults. *See infra*, text at notes 53–54.

6. For the history of current provisions, *see*, *e.g.*, de Langen, *Recht voot Jeugdigen* 54–117 (1973) (Netherlands); I. Mazeaud, *Lecons de Droit Civil*, 3rd Part at 550, 551 (5th ed., 1972) (France).

7. On the Netherlands, *see Prins, Van de Werk*, and *Zeylstra-van Loghem, Inleiding in Jeugdrecht en Vormen van Zorg voor Jeugdigen*, 74 (1972); on France, *see Colombet, Commentaire de la loi sur l'autorite parentale, Recueil Dalloz, Chroniques*, 1, 18 (1971).

8. For France, *see* statistics in 26 *Rééducation* 6–8 (1971); for Holland, *see* Centraal Bureau voor de Statistiek, *Toepassing der Kinderwetten* 1971, p. 34 ff. *Compare* Tables 3–1 through 3–3, *infra*.

9. *See* pages 132–33, *infra* for discussion of the court having jurisdiction.

10. Art. 254, *B.W.*

11. Art. 258, *B.W.*

12. Art. 375 ff. *C.C.*

13. Art. 259, *B.W.*

14. *See* pages 118–19, *infra*.

15. *See* Art. 255–264 *B.W.* on the implications of "supervision."

16. *See* pages 132–33, *infra* for discussion of the court having jurisdiction.

17. *See Herzog* and *Weser, Civil Procedure in France* at 120–124 (1967) for an explanation of the role of the French government in civil proceedings.

18. Art. 375 (2) − 375 (6) *C.C.*
19. Art. 266−268 *B.W.*
20. *See* pages 132−33, *infra.*
21. *See* text at note 20, *supra.*
22. Art. 269, *B.W.*
23. Art. 266, 268, *B.W.*
24. Constitution (*Grondwet*) Art. 90, 94. This provision is inconsistent with current ideas and law reform is likely in the near future, but had not yet occurred as of August 1975.
25. *See* Centraal Bureau voor de Statistiek, *Toepassing der Kinderwetten,* 1970, p. 40.
26. *Id.*
27. *Prins* et al., *Supra* n. 7 at 74. The number of cases in which parental authority is terminated with regard to only one parent is very small. *See* Central Bureau voor de Statistiek, *supra* note 8, at 37.
28. Each judicial district in the country has a Child Protection Council. It consists of a board of non-salaried members and a permanent staff. The Council is intended as a center of child protection activities in the district. The Council does social investigations for the court in matters involving juveniles and may initiate the kinds of proceedings described in this chapter. *See Rood-de Boer, Child Care in the Netherlands* 32 (1971).
29. *See Prins et al., Supra* note 7 at 75.
30. *Colombet, Supra* note 7.
31. For discussion of the court having jurisdiction, *see* text at notes 81−86, *infra.*
32. Art. 377, 377−1, *C.C.*; *Colombet, Supra* note 7 at 19.
33. Art. 378, 378−1, *C.C.*
34. Law of June 4, 1970.
35. *See Colombet, Supra* note 7 at 21.
36. *Ibid.*
37. *See Mazeaud, Supra* note 6 at 556.
38. *See* Art 376−381 *C.C.*; *Mazeaud, Supra* note 6 at 1144 ff.; *Colombet, Supra* note 30 at 18−23.
39. The West German law in this area is in the process of being revised. A revised law will be introduced sometime within the next few years. Some significant features of the most recent draft I am familiar with−the April 1974 so-called Referentenentwurf−are the strengthening of the position of young people, *e.g.,* the giving of increased rights to appeal from decisions taken with regard to them; greater degree of participation; the abolition of the distinction between "voluntary help in upbringing" and "remedial upbringing"; and the organizational structure for rendering aid to youths is changed in a number of ways. *See* Hasenclever, "Information uber den stand der Jugendhilferechtsreform," Internationales Expertengesprach zur Jugendhilfe (27.10−1.11. 1974).
40. *Bürgerliches Gesetzbuch* [hereinafter *BGB*].
41. *See* text at note 113, *infra.*
42. Dolle, II *Familienrecht* 264 ff. (1965).
43. *Jugendwohlfartgesetz* [hereinafter *JWG*].

44. *Cohn*, I *Manual of German Law* 245, 253 (2d ed., 1968).

45. The JWG provides for municipal and state Youth Bureaus, administrative agencies with central responsibilities for child welfare work in the municipality or state. (*See* art. 1—23 *JWG*; *see also Cohn, Supra* note 44 at 250, 251.)

46. Art. 55—57 *JWG*.

47. *See* note 45, *supra*.

48. Art. 62, 63 *JWG*.

49. Art. 65, 71 *JWG*.

50. *Riedel, Jugendwohlfartsgesetz* 605, 606 (4th ed., 1965).

51. *See*, as to the intent of the Dutch legislature, *Kluwer, Personen-en Familierecht*, comments on Art. 254 *B.W.*; *Compare*, on France, Robert, *Droit des Mineurs*, 137 *et seq.*; on West Germany, *Riedel, Supra* note 50 at 600 *et seq.*, 678 *et seq.*

52. *California Assembly Interim Committee on Criminal Procedure, Report on Juvenile Court Processes* 33 *et seq.* (1971).

53. Art. 9 *Jugendschutzgesetz* [Child Protection Statute—hereinafter *JSchG*].

54. *Leerplichtwet* (Compulsory Education Act) 1969. *Compare* section 22 of the German *JSchG*.

55. *Children and Young Persons Act*, 1969, Sec. 1, [hereinafter C.Y.P.A.].

56. Child Welfare Act, 1961 (Thorsten Sellin, transl.) Sec. 25 [hereinafter C.W.A.].

57. For instance, the latter may not be committed to a 'youth welfare school'—the most severe form of institutionalization available for juveniles in Sweden—whereas the former, whether or not they have committed a criminal act, may be so committed. Sec. 36 C.W.A.

58. C.Y.P.A., 1969, s. 1: "... and also that he is in need of care or control which he is unlikely to receive unless the court makes an order under this section in respect of him"; art. 55 *JWG* (*see* pp. 121—22, *supra*), Art. 1666 *BGD* (*see* p. 121, *supra*); *cf. Uniform Juvenile Court Act, 77 Handbook of the National Conference of Commissioners of Uniform State Laws* 248, 249 (1968) and Sheridan, *Legislative Guide for Drafting Family and Juvenile Court Acts* [Children's Bureau Pub. No. 472 (1969)].

59. Kinderrechter [Juvenile Judge]'s Gravenhage, 21 Jan. 1958, *Nederlandse Jurisprudentie* [hereinafter: *NJ*] 1958, 480.

60. *See, e.g.*, the Netherlands, Art. 266, 269 *B.W.*

61. *Riedel, Supra* note 50 at 616; Robert, *Supra* note 51 at 136, 137.

62. *See* Robert, *Supra* note 51 at 134—152; *Prins et al., Supra* note 7 at 85; *Riedel, Supra* note 50 at 605—620.

63. The country is divided into nineteen judicial districts, each with its own district court as the first instance court of general jurisdiction. Each district court has its juvenile court judge(s). In 1971, the number of "supervisions" per 100,000 children of 0—20 years varied from 32 in Groningen to 125 in Alkmaar. In the country as a whole there were 66 "supervisions" per 100,000 children of 0—20 years. *See* Centraal Bureau voor de Statistiek, *Maandstatistiek van politie en justitie*, p. 255 (1972).

64. *E.g.*, *de Langen, Supra* note 6, at 198—201. The author hardly attempts to draft such standards.

65. *de Ruiter, Hulp en Recht* 16, 17 (1972); *Hoefnagels, Recht en Maatschappelijk Werk* 55–82 (2d ed., 1965).

66. Bröcker, "Mogelijkheden en onmogelijkheden van de ondertoezichtstelling," 25 *Tijdschrift voor Maatschappelijk Werk* 139 (1971).

67. Hoefnagels, *Supra* note 65 at 110.

68. Ellink-de Boer, *Enkele Kwantitiatieve Gegevens over Kinderbeschermingsmaatregelen*, (mim. ed. 1972); Centraal Bureau voor de Statistiek, *Supra* note 8 at 36 ff.; *id.*, *Maandstatistiek van politie en justitie*, 258 ff. (1974).

69. Centraal Bureau voor de Statistiek, *Supra* note 8 at 39.

70. Robert, *supra* note 51 at 205, 206.

71. *See* 26 *Rééducation*, *supra* note 8.

72. *Mitglieder Rundbrief der Arbeitsgemeinschaft fur Erziehungshilfe*, 59 ff. (July 1974).

73. England: *C.Y.P.A.*, S. 1 (3).

74. Sweden: *C.W.A.*, S. 26.

75. England C.Y.P.A., 1969, ss. 1 (3), 11–19, France Art. 376–1 *C.C.*, Holland Art. 254, 255, 260 *B.W.*, West Germany, *JWG* §§55–61; Sweden, *C.W.A.* ss. 26, 28.

76. *See e.g.*, *Ackerman* (ed.), *Family Process* (1970), *Boszormey-Nagy* and *Framo*, *Intensive Family Therapy* (1965).

77. *See* text at notes 9–15, 44–46, *supra*.

78. Art. 260 *B.W.*

79. Section 58 *JWG*.

80. *See* text at notes 164–172, *infra*.

81. *Supra*, text at note 56.

82. *C.W.A.* s. 29.

83. *Supra*, text at notes 49–50.

84. *Prins* et al., *Supra* note 7 at 86.

85. *See* text at notes 14–15, *supra*.

86. Art. 375–2, *C.C.*

87. *See*, *e.g.*, Doek, *Vijftig Jaar Ondertoezichtstelling* at 197; almost 30 percent of all children subject to "supervision" are placed in institutions, only 5 percent in foster families, despite theoretical preferences for the latter form of care.

88. *Supra*, text at notes 81–82.

89. From 58 *Statistical Abstract of Sweden* 263 (1971). The available statistics do not differentiate between different grounds of Board jurisdiction in each of these cases.

90. *Supra*, text at note 82.

91. *Statistical Abstract*, *Supra* note 89 at 262. Same person may occur in more than one category.

92. 16 *Maandstatistiek van politie en justitie* 257 (1972), 18 *id.* 261 (1974). In most of these cases, the placement was for purposes of care and education— either alone or in addition to observational placement.

93. Ellink-de Boer, *Enkele Kwantitatieve Gegevens over Kinderbeschermingsmaatregelen*, p. 12 (mim. ed. 1972).

94. *Id.* at 13.
95. *Supra*, Table 3—4.
96. *Supra*, page 122.
97. *Mitglieder Rudbrief*, *Supra* note 72 at 60.
98. *Mitglieder Rundbrief* p. 30 (April 1973); Ellink-der Boer, *Supra* note 93 at 12, 13.
99. However, it does seem that the duration of "supervision" has gradually increased—*see infra*, text at note 100.
100. *Maandstatistiek*, *Supra* note 92 at 256, 18 *id.* 260 (1974).
101. *Mitglieder Rundbrief*, *Supra* note 72 at 67, 68.
103. 26 *Rééducation* 8 (1971).
103. 18 *Maandstatistiek*, *Supra* note 92 at 262.
104. *Mitglieder Rundbrief*, *supra* note 72 at 68, 69.
105. Spitta, in *Mitglieder Rundbrief*, *supra* note 72 at 30.
106. In Sweden the Boards have exclusive jurisdiction over offenses committed by children under fifteen. With regard to children fifteen to eighteen years old, the Boards obtain jurisdiction if a prosecutor decides to suspend prosecution or if a court decides to suspend sentence. Offenders from eighteen to twenty-one are under the jurisdiction of the ordinary court which may order them to be committed to the care of a Child Welfare Board. *See* Grobe, "Juvenile Delinquency in Sweden," 53 *Ken. L.J.* 247, 248 (1966). For an elaborate description of the conflict generated by the sharing of decision-making power between prosecutor and the Child Welfare Board as to fifteen to eighteen year olds, *see* Britt-Mari Persson Blegvad, "A Case Study of Interorganizational Conflict," 2 *Scan. Stud. in Criminology* 19 (1968).
107. United Nations, *Comparative Survey on Juvenile Delinquency* (ST/ SOA/SD/1), Part 2: Europe, 11—14, 47 ff. (1952).
108. Arts. 266, 269, *B.W.*
109. Arts 889—2, 889—4, *C.C.*
110. Text at notes 39—50, *supra.*
111. *Id.*
112. *C.Y.P.A.*, 1969 s. 1(1).
113. *See Comparative Survey*, *supra* note 107; *see also* "The Competent Authorities" in *Proceedings of the Fifth International Congress on Social Defense*, (Stockholm 1958).
114. *See* Tappan, "Jurisdical and Administrative Approaches to Children with Problems," in *Rosenheim* (ed.), *Justice for the Child*, 144 at 159—166, for a brief description of administrative boards in Scandinavia and some other countries.
115. *See, e.g.*, Griffiths, "Ideology in Criminal Procedure," 79 *Yale L.J.* 359 (1970) for a discussion of the ideology of the juvenile court movement and its practical consequences.
116. *See de Langen, Supra* note 6; *Nota Jeugdbeschermingsrecht, Rapport van de Commissie voor de herziening van het Kinderbeschermingsrecht*, (1971); *Doek* and *Slagter, Meer rechten voor minderjarigen* (1974).
117. *Netherlands*: Art. 254 *B.W.* ("supervision"), Art. 270 *B.W.* ("forfei-

ture") A termination of parental rights in the absence of fault may not be granted upon the request of the parent—apparently the legislature feared that parents would be all too willing to liberate themselves of the rights and duties of parenthood. *See Luijten* and *Jonkers, Het Personen en Familierecht in het Nieuwe Burgerlijk Wetboek*, p. 252 (1970); *France*: Art. 375 *C.C.* ("assistance in upbringing"); *West Germany*: section 63 *JWG* ("voluntary assistance in upbringing"), section 65 *JWG* ("remedial upbringing").

118. *Netherlands*: Art. 254 *B.W.* ("supervision"), Art. 270 *B.W.* ("forfeiture"); *France*: Art. 378 *C.C.* ("forfeiture"). In the Netherlands, recent proposals for law reform recommend eliminating this right, in view of the allegedly decreased role of the extended family. *See Nota Jeugdbeschermingsrecht, supra* note 116 at 172, 122.

119. Art. 375 *C.C.*

120. Robert, *Supra* note 51 at 404.

121. *Netherlands*: Art. 254 *B.W.* ("supervision"), Art. 267 *B.W.* ("release"), Art. 270 *B.W.* ("forfeiture"); *France*: Art 375 *C.C.* ("assistance in upbringing"); Art. 378 *C.C.* ("forfeiture").

122. *Netherlands*: Art. 254, 267, 270 *B.W.*; *West Germany*: section 57, 65 *JWG*.

123. *France*: 375 *C.C.* ("assistance in upbringing"); *West Germany*: section 57, 65 *JWG* ("assistance in upbringing" and "remedial upbringing").

124. *France*: see note 120, *supra*; *Netherlands*; see de Langen, *Supra* note 6, at 166, 167.

125. S. 1 (1) *C.Y.P. Act*, 1969; *see* also *Watson, The Juvenile Court—1970 Onward* 6 (1970).

126. S. 14 *C.W.A.*

127. Art. 936—3, 947 *Wetboek van Burgerlijke Rechtsvordering* [Code of Civil Procedure hereinafter: *W. Rv.*]. *See de Langen, Supra* note 6, for discussion and proposals for change.

128. *de Langen, Supra* note 6, at 211—213.

129. Art. 57 *JWG* "if they can be reached."

130. Art. 65 *JWG* "personally if possible."

131. Text at note 40, *supra*.

132. Art. 888—1, Code de Procédure Civile [Code of Civil Procedure—hereinafter: *C.P.C.*].

133. Art 889—4 *C.P.C.*

134. Art. 888—2, 888—7, 889—6 *C.P.C.*

135. Art. 882—2, 888—8, 889—6 *C.P.C.*

136. Art. 888—5, 889—8 *C.P.C.*

137. *Magistrates' Courts (Children and Young Persons) Rules* 1970, s. 14.

138. *Id.*, s. 17.

139. *Id.*, s. 18.

140. Unless this would be considered part of the court's general duty to inform the child of the nature of the proceedings. *Id.*, s. 16(1); *cf. Watson, Supra* note 125.

141. Sec. 19, 20, *C.W.A.*

142. Sec. 19, *C.W.A.*

143. *Netherlands*; Art 909, *W.Rv.*; *West Germany*: Art. 57, 67 *JWG*; *Sweden*: sec. 21 *C.W.A.* ("to the extent not found needless"). In France, there is no specific statutory requirement, but reasons seem to be required by case law. *See* Robert, *Supra* note 51 at 136.

144. *France*: Robert, *Supra* note 51 pp. 136, 137; *Netherlands: de Langen, Supra* note 6 pp. 214, 215; *West Germany: Riedel, Jugendwohlfartsrecht* 712 (6th ed. 1965).

145. The juvenile does not have such right at all in the Netherlands, nor in Sweden if under fifteen (sec. 15, *C.W.A.*), nor in West Germany if under fourteen (Art. 57, 65 *JWG*), nor in France if under seventeen. In France, the child's counsel must be notified (Art. 888−9 *C.P.C.*).

146. *E.g.*, *France*: not "if his state does not permit it" (Art. 888−8, *C.P.C.*); *West Germany*: not "if harm to his upbringing" likely (Art. 57, *JWG*).

147. This is the normal system of appeals in most continental European countries. *See e.g.*, on France, *Herzog* and *Weser, Supra* note 17, chapters 8 and 9; on West Germany, *Cohn, Supra* note 44 at 37, 38.

148. *Netherlands: de Langen, Supra* note 6 at 203−211; *West Germany*: Art. 20, 59, *Reichsgesetz über die Angelegenheiten der Freiwilligen Gerichtsbarkeit* [Law on Matters of Non-Contentious Jurisdiction; this statute governs procedure in guardianship cases among others]; *Riedel, Supra* note 144, at 643, section 65, *JWG*; *France*: Art. 888−12, 889−8 *C.P.C.*

149. Sec. 2(12), 1(3) (a) *Ch. and Y.P. Act 1967.*

150. Sec. 80, 84, 87 *C.W.A.*

151. Sec. 24 *C.W.A.*

152. Robert, *Supra* note 51, at 513−526.

153. For comments of foreign observers contrasting favorably the Dutch programs with those going on in their own countries, *see Cusky*, *Klein*, and *Krasner*, *Drug-Trip Abroad* (1972); Hulster, "Innovationsorientierte Jugendberatung in den Niederlanden," *Neue Praxis*, Nr. 3, p. 366 (1972); Tollemache, "Alternatives to Prison in Holland," 3 *Social Work Today* 13 (1972).

154. *Rood-de Boer, Child Care in the Netherlands* 34, 35 (3rd ed., 1971). For criticism by volunteers of the "system," in particular the way they used to be treated and often still are treated by the professionals in the family guardianship associations, *see* Pollmann, "De kritische vrijwilligers," in Stichting voor het Kind, *De Jeugd Zal Ons een Zorg Zijn* 44 (1972).

155. *Gids voor de Kinderbescherming*, Vol. I (loose-leaf service of VUGA publishing house).

156. The "family guardianship" and "guardianship" associations used to be responsible for the recruitment of foster families, but recently special regional agencies have been set up for this purpose. *Prins et al., Supra* note 7 at 65.

157. *Hart de Ruyter* and *Hubertus, Gezinsverpleging* 27−33 (1970).

158. *van Spanje, Kind en Pleeggezin* 86 (1968).

159. Under Art. 3 and 5 of the *Kinderbeginselenwet*, 1961 [Basic Act on Child Protection], children may be placed in private institutions that have been approved by the Minister of Justice. In order to receive approval, the institution

must file a written statement that it will comply with the conditions concerning staff, buildings, size of wards and groups, physical and mental health of the minors, their number, sex, age, education, and length of stay, their supervision and the administration of the institution, contained in the relevant regulations. (For these regulations, *see* Art. 53—105 *Uitvoeringsbesluit Kinderbescherming*, 1964 hereafter "Regulations." The institution must also submit information permitting the Minister to evaluate its compliance with the above conditions. On the basis of this information, and having regard to the question of whether there is a need for such an institution, and having heard the recommendations of several relevant advisory bodies, the Minister decides whether or not to approve (*See* Art. 54, 55 of the regulations).

Lack of approval by the Minister is not a total bar to receiving placements. However, institutions that have not been "approved" are subject to special subsidy regulations and, if the government is to bear the costs of a particular placement (as it normally does), special authorization for the placement is needed from the Minister of Justice. (Art. 123, 124 of the regulations.)

160. Centraal Bureau voor de Statistiek, *Supra* n. 25, at 49.

161. United States, Department of Health, Education and Welfare, *Statistics on Public Institutions for Delinquent Children* 57 (1970). The statistics on the two countries are only partly comparable. Those for the United States only concern public institutions, whereas the Dutch ones include private institutions too; the size of private institutions in the United States may be smaller. The American statistics only concern institutions for delinquent children, while the Dutch institutions also accept neglected and dependent children and are not even limited to court commitments.

162. *Ibid.*

163. Mulock Houwer, "Noodzaak van een anders georienteerd inrichtingswezen," in *Hoefnagels* et al., *Kinderbescherming, Jeugdbescherming of Welzijnszorg* 36 (1971). On December 31, 1969, total capacity was 16,369 (population: 14,666). It is quite possible that the difference between capacity and population has decreased since that date, since a number of institutions have been closed in recent years.

164. Regulations, Art. 100.

165. Regulations, Art. 96.

166. Mulock Houwer, *supra* note 163 at 48.

167. Regulations, Art. 18. Such an institution is known in Dutch as a "tuchtschool."

168. *See* Basic Act on Child Protection, Art. 6—9, 15—19. In principle, they thus fulfill the same function as state institutions often do in fact in the United States, that is, as repositories of those children considered least desirable by private institutions.

169. *Gids voor de Kinderbescherming*, *Supra* note 155, *passim.*

170. *See, e.g.*, Keizer, "De Kinderbescherming Kan nu reeds veranderen," in *Kinderbescherming, Jeugdbescherming of Welzijnszorg*, *Supra* note 163 at 57; Werkgroep "de Langste Dag," *Veldnota*; *Welzijn Voor de Jeugd* (1971). The trend in the United States seems to favor segregation of the different groups of

juveniles subject to juvenile court jurisdiction. *See Andrews* and *Cohn, Unruly Children: the Juvenile Non-criminal Offender* at 112, 113. (Study prepared for Juvenile Justice Standards Project, October 1, 1973.)

171. Personal conversation and observation.

172. *Hart de Ruyter* and *Hubertus, Supra* note 157 at 1, 2; personal conversations.

173. Release, "Opstel" in *De Jeugd Zal Ons een Zorg Zijn, Supra* note 154 at 64—67. For arguments in favor of limited use, *see e.g.*, Werkgroep "de Langste Dag," *supra* note 170 at 7; van Amerongen, "Goud voor de Kinderrechter en de ondertoezichstelling; ook goud voor de hulpverlening?" in *De Jeugd Zal Ons een Zorg Zijn* 36, and *passim*; Hoefnagels, "Kan de Kinderbescherming veranderen?" in *Kinderbescherming, Jeugdbescherming of Welzijnszorg, Supra* note 163 at 9 and *passim*. *Compare,* Juvenile Justice Standards Project (ABA—IJA), *Standards Relating to Non-Criminal Misbehavior* (Tent. Dr. 1976).

174. *See* page 126, *supra*.

175. *See e.g.*, Hoefnagels, "Analyse en plan," in *Hoefnagels* et al., *Een Nieuw Plan voor de Kinderbescherming* 16—22 (1970).

176. Nota, *Jeugdbescherming en Justitie* (1971); Nota, *Jeugdbeschermingsrecht* (1971).

177. *See, e.g., Een Nieuw Plan voor de Kinderbescherming, Supra* note 175 *passim; Kinderbescherming, Jeugdbescherming of Welzijnszorg, Supra* note 163, *passim*.

178. *Id.*

179. *See* pages 124—132, *supra*.

180. *De Volkskrant*, July 10, 1973, p. 7.

181. *Clemens Schröner, Gezinsvoogdij en Levensloop* (1952).

182. For a description of crisis intervention in the framework of such a project and favorable evaluation of its effects, with the conclusion that similar techniques ought to be used with regard to families subject to judicial child protection measures, *see* Memorandum van pro Juventute, "Van Kinderbescherming naar jeugdwelzijnszorg," 26 *Tijdschrift voor Maatschappelijk Werk* 367 (1972).

183. For a description and favorable evaluation, *see id.* at 370.

184. Elaborate reports on these groups and their ideas appeared in the American press (*e.g.* the New York Times and the Village Voice) at the times.

185. Dotinga, "Vijrheid en verantwoordelijkheid," 26 *De Koepel* 368 (1972).

186. *See, e.g.*, Gemengde interdepartementale werkgroep jeugdwelzijnsbeleid, *Startnota Jeugdwelzijnsbeleid* 18 (December 1973); *Prins* et al., *Inleiding in Jeugdrecht en Enige Vormen van Zorg voor Jeugdigen*, Ch. 1, 2, 3 (12th ed., 1975).

187. Stated goal of *Release* in National Raad voor Maatschappelijk Welzijn, *Alternatieve Hulpverlening* 7 (2nd ed., 1973).

188. Stated goal of *Jongeren Advies Centrum [JAC]*, in *id.*

189. Stated goal of *Sosjale Joenit* in *id.*

190. The traditional social work agencies have also tried to respond to this problem. *See* Nationaal Protestants Centrum voor de Geestelijke Volksgezondheid, *Projekt Andere Jeugd, Andere Hulp*, mim. ed.

191. *See Alternatieve Hulpverlening, supra* note 187 at 8, 9, 10. On Dutch

subsidy policies in this field, *see* Hulster, "Innovationsorientierte Jugendbera-tung in den Niederlanden," *Neue Praxis*, nr. 3, at 366 (1972). *But see* "Subsi-dievoorwaarde maakt JAC's te afhankelijk," 27 *Maandblad voor de Geestelijke Volksgezondheid* 149 (1972). *Alternatieve Hulpverlening, supra* note 187 at 15— reporting an allegation that *Release Haarlem* was refused subsidy by the provin-cial government because of its radical criticism of society.

192. *Alternatieve Hulpverlening, supra* note 187.

193. For criticism of this decision, see Arendhorst, "Release-Amsterdam laat vacuum achter," 4 *Jeugdwerk Nu* 3 (1972).

194. *Projekt Andere Jeugd, Andere Hulp, supra* note 190.

195. The above description of the alternative help agencies is based on the following materials: *Projekt Andere Jeugd, Andere Hulp, supra* note 190; *Alter-natieve Hulpverlening, supra* note 187; Symposium, in 25 *Tijdschrift voor Maat-schappelijk Werk* 275—290 (1971); unpublished materials provided the author by the Sosjale Joenit. *JAC Jaarverslag* 1972; *Sosjale Joenit, Jaarverslag* 1973.

196. *See, e.g.*, Jea Kiers, *Inbraak of Doorbraak*, 29 *Tijdschrift voor Maat-schappelijk Werk* 101 (1975).

197. Art. 280 *Wetboek van Strafrecht* [Criminal Code]. This provision is a nice illustration of the approach discussed earlier (p. 123, *supra*)—running away is not an offense for which the minor is subject to court jurisdiction, but adults facilitating the minor's act are punishable.

198. *See* note 147 *supra* for literature on continental European appellate procedure. The various *Sosjale Joenit* decisions have been reported as follows: District Court the Hague, Nov. 2, 1971, *N.J.* 1972, 13; Court of Appeals the Hague, March 17, 1972, *N.J.* 1972, 262; Supreme Court July 3, 1972, *N.J.* 1973, 78; Court of Appeals Amsterdam Dec. 28, 1972, *N.J.* 1973, 79; Supreme Court, Oct. 16, 1973, *N.J.* 1974, 29. For elaborate discussion of the case, *see*, *e.g.*, Hulsman, "Sosjale Joenit Arrest," 21 *Ars Aequi* 511 (1972).

199. In the beginning of 1974, the *Sosjale Joenit* did a survey among alterna-tive help agencies concerning agreements and cooperation with the police. It appeared that at that time eight of the thirty-three answering agencies had an agreement concerning runaway cases with the police; in five of these cases the existence of such an agreement was confirmed by the police. Eighteen of the alternative agencies said they did not cooperate with the police in any way in runaway cases, either because they themselves did not want to or because the police refused to. A number of arrests in cases where there *were* in fact agree-ments with the police did not help to promote trust in their effectiveness. *See Nota inzake de Moeilijkheden rond Art. 280 Wetboek van Strafrecht* (mim. ed. 1974).

200. *See* statement of Minister of Culture, Recreation and Social Work, as quoted in 25 *Tijdschrift voor Maatschappelijk Werk* 371 (1971); Memorandum accompanying proposed budget of Ministry of Justice, as referred to in *De Volks-krant* November 3, 1971.

201. Bunnik, member of the Board of Dutch Association of Social Workers, expert witness at court of first instance; Noyon, president of Dutch Association of Social Workers, expert witness before Court of Appeals. *See* case file, *supra* note 195.

202. Pro Juventute Groningen; Dutch Association of Social Workers. *See* case file *supra* note 195.

203. *See* case file, *supra* note 195.

204. *See Nota inzake de moeilijkheder rond Art. 280 Wetboek van Strafrecht* (mim. ed. 1974).

205. *De Volkskrant*, August 22, 1975, p. 1.

206. *Id.*

207. *De Volkskrant*, November or December 1975.

208. *See, e.g.*, Report of the California Assembly Interim Committee on Criminal Procedure, *Juvenile Court Processes*, p. 7—40 (1971). Proposals of Juvenile Justice Standards Project as reported in New York Law Journal, December 1, 1975, pp. 1 and 12. Massachusetts, in fact, recently abolished the "crimes of truancy, running away from home and being a stubborn child." *See* the *New York Times*, November 28, 1973, p. 24.

209. *See* Colombet, *supra* note 7 at 24.

210. *See* p. 18 *et seq., supra*.

211. Thus the New York Court of Appeals in *In re C.*, 32 N.Y.2d 588, 300 N.E.2d 424, 347 N.Y.S. 2d 51 (1973) held that PINS could not be sent to training schools for children.

212. *See eg.*, White Paper "The Child, the Family and the Young Offender" (Cmnd 2742, 1965).

213. *See* text at notes 167—170, *supra*.

214. *See, e.g., Keizer, De Kinderbescherming Kan nu reeds veranderen in Kinderbescherming, Jeugdbescherming of welzijnszorg, supra* note 163.

215. Juveniles have far more adequate safeguards in proceedings adjudicating their guilt of an offense. *See* Art. 486 ff. *Wetboek van Strafvordering* (Code of Criminal Procedure). Unlike American law, Dutch law does not consider all proceedings against juveniles even theoretically as "civil."

216. *See Clarke Hall* and *Morrisons Law Relating to Children and Young Persons* 3 (7th ed. 1967).

217. *See* Institute of Judicial Administration, Juvenile Justice Standards Project, *Final Report, Planning Phase*, pp. 77, 78 (February 1973).

218. *Nota Jeugdbeschermingsrecht, supra*, note 176 at 102, 103.

219. *Cf.* Griffiths, "Ideology in Criminal Procedure," *supra* note 115.

❄ *Chapter 4*

PINS and Parents*

Anne R. Mahoney

✳ The relationship between juvenile court proceedings and intrafamily
conflict in PINS cases has received relatively little attention [1].
Doubtless, both parents and court personnel expect some constructive result from juvenile court action, although their perceptions of what is constructive may differ. In most cases, both probably expect that resort to official
authority will strengthen the family by demonstrating the vitality and legitimacy of parental power or by gaining access to needed services to ameliorate
disruption. Yet, court action may seriously intensify rather than alleviate parent-
child alienation. This is particularly true of cases involving so-called status offenses, such as running away, unruliness, habitual disobedience, or truancy, which
would not be crimes if committed by adults, but which nevertheless bring a child,
because of his or her status as a minor, within the jurisdiction of the juvenile
court.

The focus of this chapter is on the significance of using the juvenile court procedure to regulate parent-child relationships. The first section addresses the eti-
ology of this process: it includes a discussion of the PINS petition as a signal of
family crisis and several hypotheses concerning why parents resort to court
action to control their children. The second considers issues relating to the effect
of the court process upon the relationships within families who come before it.
In the third section, data are presented to show that juvenile court intervention
through a PINS proceeding has potentially serious long-range effects on a child's

*This chapter was prepared for the Institute of Judicial Administration–American Bar
Association Juvenile Justice Standards Project. The project is supported by funds from the
National Institute of Law Enforcement and Criminal Justice, Andrew W. Mellon Foundation, the American Bar Endowment, the Vincent Astor Foundation and the Herman Goldman Foundation. This latter, in particular, provided support for social science input into
the project.

life, not only because he or she may be detained, referred to court, and institutionalized in a correctional facility, but also because the process may produce deterioration in family relationships.

PARENTAL USE OF A PINS PETITION

The acts of children who are adjudicated status offenders are not very different from the acts of most adolescents [2]. Yet some adolescents come to court and others do not. One important difference between the two sets of youth is the fact that in PINS cases, the complainant typically is a parent or relative of the respondent rather than someone external to the family. In New York City, for example, the overwhelming majority of PINS petitions—over 80 percent—are brought by parents or guardians [3]. In Rockland County, a suburban area near New York City, nearly a third of the PINS cases in 1972 were initiated by parents [4]. Statistics for New York State for 1964 through 1970 show that petitions by parents, relatives or guardians accounted for approximately 43 percent of all male PINS adjudications and between 65 percent and 70 percent of the PINS adjudications for girls [5].

The PINS Petition as a Signal of Family Crisis

Parental use of a PINS petition—involving subjection of one's own child to the juvenile court process and to the possibility of being institutionalized in a correctional facility—signals a crisis in parent-child relationships. Some theoretical and empirical work has been done on family response to certain kinds of crises, such as unemployment, alcoholism, separation because of war, and mental illness [6], but surprisingly little attention has been focused upon family response to juvenile misbehavior. Nevertheless, general theory about family reaction to stress provides a starting point in an attempt to understand why a parent might seek juvenile court intervention.

Family reaction to crisis has been described as a process of adaptation and reorganization [7]. Initially a family may attempt to deny the existence of a crisis by denying the behavior or events which threaten the family, and try to handle the matter within the existing family structure in the hope that the situation is temporary and will soon resolve itself. Some families, in this effort, seek to protect the status of both the family and its individual members by concealing information about the deviant behavior of family members from a potentially critical community [8]. Mentally ill or alcoholic members of a family may, in consequence, be denied rehabilitative treatment because of the family's fear of public reaction. This strategy will in some circumstances be successful. It is, however, more difficult for a family to conceal youthful "ungovernability" from the community than it is to conceal some other kinds of deviant behavior. Attendance records, for example, are kept on youths under a certain age; they are supposed to be in school and accounted for. If they are not, inquiries are made. In addition, community members often feel freer to complain about a youth's behavior than they would about similar behavior by an adult. The child's behavior may precipitate recognition of a crisis when attempts at concealment fail and deviant behavior has become so visible that non-family members begin openly to react negatively to it [9]. In many instances, the crisis—once so defined—is resolved at this point. If it is not, a second stage of family response is reached in which the child's conduct is defined formally as a problem. One intake worker in Manhattan noted that parents tend to bring their children to court after they have received calls about the child's disruptive behavior from schools, teachers, or recreation centers. In such cases the youth's behavior may be defined as a problem by the family *because* it has become public.

In other instances, the family's own definition of the youth's behavior as a crisis may lead family members to make it public. Parental initiation of court action against a child may be viewed as a public acknowledgement of family alienation—the breaking of family solidarity and public airing of the parent-child split. As the crisis progresses, it creates a new set of mutual expectations between family members. A cyclical process of alienation between parents and adolescent children occurs, which has much in common with the alienation found in disintegrating relationships between marital partners. In this process, each response leads to the next and the motive for each new step is furnished by the experiences of the process up to that point. At each step, the relationship is redefined upon a level of greater alienation and greater instability [10]. It is characteristic of such processes that they cannot easily be arrested, especially after family or couple solidarity is broken and the disputing parties begin to share their troubles with others.

Although almost every PINS petition signals a crisis, setting in motion the process just described, it should not be assumed that all families attach the same meaning or expectations to the initiation of court proceedings. Some parents may use the petition to coerce children into compliant behavior. Other parents may hope to employ it as a dumping device to remove the youth physically from the family. Others may bring a PINS petition because they seek help for their child that they cannot themselves provide. To understand the significance of PINS proceedings for the families that use them, it is important to identify the motives and expectations that lead parents to file complaints against their children.

PINS Petition as Parental Use of Force

The family, like other social units or systems, is a power system. Force or its threat, money, respect, and love underlie the family structure and are the four major sources of power by which people can move others to serve their ends [11]. Socialization and control of children involves a pattern of exchange in which the adult gives positive rewards to the child for compliant behavior. Parents constitute the primary source of rewards for young children. As the child's network of social relationships expands, however, alternative sources of rewards become available [12].

Some families have greater resources with which to control their children than others. Certain control mechanisms available to the middle class—economic rewards, influence, and social contacts—are less available to the poor.* The goods and services that are provided by the lower class family often cannot compete, especially in the urban ghetto, with opportunities for illegitimately obtained goods and services provided by peer and neighborhood groups [13]. Especially at the stage of adolescence, peer group rewards take on crucial significance and parental approval declines in importance. At this point parents either expand the reward system or turn to coercion. It is difficult to expand the reward system when resources are limited. Goode suggests that parents of the lower class may be impelled to use overt force because they lack other resources that provide power to parents of higher status [14]. Most people do not willingly choose overt force when they command other means of control because the costs of using force are high, especially in the family where its use can destroy spontaneous affection and respect. Furthermore, the utility of physical force diminishes when children begin to approach their parents in size and strength. One of the few resources available to lower class or minority parents is the legal power to take a child to court, with its threat of limitation of freedom. The parent, himself, may be unable to restrict his child's movement, but he has access to a coercive community agency—the juvenile court—which can. Access to legal coercive power may thus serve as a powerful resource for otherwise powerless parents [15]. No one knows how many harassed and frustrated parents use this threat or how often they do so. Nor is there any systematic evidence to show whether or not such threats are effective. It may be, however, that for some youths the threat of court is sufficient to maintain parental control.

PINS Petition as a Dumping Device

Some parents may seek a PINS petition against a child because they want to be rid of him. Difficult adolescents cause problems in families. They often cause strain in a parent's relationships with other adults, provide "bad" models for younger siblings, and limit parental ability to move upward. The initiation of a PINS petition may represent a family's attempt to legalize a parent-child split, much as a petition for divorce legalizes the split between husband and wife.

As a child approaches adolescence he becomes less dependent on parents as models for self-image and identity. He can begin to shape his parents' image of themselves and to play on their vulnerabilities by labeling them as bad parents or failures in life [16]. Sometimes a child's maturation to a new stage of development, especially adolescence, has significance for one or both parents. A maturing child may refuse to continue to allow himself to be used for the satis-

*It may be that the increasing concern among affluent parents about their inability to control adolescent children flows from the decreased value placed by some middle class young people upon these traditional middle class control devices.

faction of a parent's intrapsychic needs, thereby creating disequilibrium in the family role structure [17]. Parents who are unable to cope with this movement toward autonomy may retaliate with overt or covert hostility. They may convey their belief that the youth is innately "no good" or "too dumb" to amount to anything on his or her own. The youth may realize that the best way to get back at his parents is to live up to their image of him. The ensuing hostility may exacerbate other conflicts between family members, and parents and siblings may perceive the youth as pushing the whole family toward breakdown. The parent may not only want to remove the child from the home, but may wish to punish the child for creating family problems and/or rejecting the parent.

There is some evidence that youths in trouble are more likely than other youths to express dissatisfaction with their families, from which it can further be inferred than their families show less ability to cope with problems than other families. One study of 312 delinquents and 100 nondelinquents, the latter sample including sixteen siblings of the delinquents, reveals that those youngsters with the greatest degree of commitment to delinquent values and the least response to treatment displayed almost total indifference to expectations and disapproval of their parents and were almost completely uninterested in family activities and problems [18]. A study of the family concepts of disturbed and normal children, including siblings of the disturbed youths, traced a similar pattern of youthful dissatisfaction with family life [19]. The youth in trouble was more likely to consider his family less satisfying than were either his "normal" sibling or youths from a similar background in the control group. These studies, although not specifically addressed to PINS families, suggest that families of youths in trouble may maintain a fragile family balance which can adjust less well than others to the developing autonomy of a maturing adolescent.

It is also often true that the families from which PINS children come are less stable or otherwise less well suited to handling an adolescent than the norm. A sizable number of children who come to court on PINS petitions have moved around among several relatives and may actually have had less contact with their mother or father than with other family members or with foster families. Sometimes a parent, suddenly faced with the reappearance of a child who has been living with someone else, will bring the child to court and seek placement. Puerto Rican women, especially, feel the burden of constant child care when they move from the extended family system in Puerto Rico to the smaller family in New York. In Puerto Rico there are family members close at hand to relieve a mother in the care of her children. In New York, such a pattern is harder to maintain and children become more of a bother and a strain [20]. The change from extended to nuclear family may cause similar problems for black women who move to urban areas from the rural South or from the West Indies. Middle-class parents who feel overburdened with children can hire "help" to take over responsibility for child care, or they can send their children to camp or boarding school. Such relief is less available to the poor.

Blood relationship may carry legal responsibility, but the assumption that, in and of itself, it carries affection and a sense of emotional involvement and responsibility is open to question [21]. A youth's rejection of the family or behavior which causes distress or public embarrassment to family members may lead to the parental desire to "dump" the youth onto the court system. Court intervention may seem a welcome relief. It provides an opportunity for the family to publicly disassociate itself from the youth's behavior, and brings about a physical separation from an unsatisfying and unsatisfied family member. The problem for the family, of course, is that the juvenile court's revolving door returns the child back to the family in a few hours, weeks, or months.

PINS Petition as a Call for Help

Many parents go to family court because they genuinely want help for their children and do not know where else to go. The child's behavior has reached crisis proportions and family members neither know how to cope with the behavior themselves nor have the informational or economic resources to gain help from others. Families who seek PINS petitions tend to be poor, members of minority groups, and from structurally broken families. In the 1972 sample of PINS cases in Manhattan studied by Andrews and Cohn, the respondents' families had an average income of $5,200 for five and six people. Over half of the youths came from families supported by welfare. More than 85 percent of the youths were from racial minority groups. Seventy-nine percent of the youths came from "broken" families, and 14 percent of them lived with neither parent [22]. Families such as these have limited access to resources to help them cope with difficult adolescents [23]. One way to get help is to seek court intervention. They do not comprehend how meager the court's own resources are nor that the main resources available to the court are of questionable value.

Many of the parents, in the midst of a crisis in the relationship with their child, seek immediate relief. Many expect the court to support their efforts at discipline and control [24]. Puerto Rican or Mexican-American parents, for example, often express the desire that their children should be sent away someplace where they may learn discipline, manners, and respect [25]. Such parents hope perhaps that the court will scare the youth into obedience. Some come seeking the magic of psychiatric help or counseling for their children. Whether parents get satisfaction from the court depends upon what jurisdiction they come into and what intake worker or judge they appear before. Sometimes they find a probation officer, referee or judge who is sympathetic to parental desire for authority and obedience. Occasionally, they find that court sympathy lies with the child. Often they are processed in a hurried and routine manner. The parents may come to talk about the family's troubles, but find little chance to do so. Instead, they spend much of their time with an intake worker providing information for the family case record—address, names and ages of children, where they work, how long they have worked, how long they have been married.

Often parents and child are sent home together and told to come back another day. Nothing seems to have changed, no remedies have been provided, and neither parent nor child feels that he has really had a chance to explain his side of the story to anyone.

THE COURT'S ROLE IN PROMOTING
OR INHIBITING ALIENATION BETWEEN
FAMILY MEMBERS

Families that bring PINS petitions come to court with some kind of expectations. They want the court, through its coercive power, to change their child's behavior, or they want to get rid of their child, or they want help in coping with difficult behavior. The family is usually in a state of crisis, and conflict between the parents and the child is great. Ideally, the court's role in such situations lies in helping the family work through its crisis and in developing constructive techniques for coping with both the troublesome behavior of children and the alienation which exists between parents and children. There is, however, reason to question the capacity of a coercive agency to reduce family tension, especially when that agency provides a public forum in which family laundry is washed. A parent called by a detention facility intake worker may refuse to come to take the youth home, a fact that will usually be learned by the child. During court hearings, the parent may berate the child in front of the judge and other court officials, sometimes with great vehemence. Such public denunciation also has its effects. One study of youths' subjective reactions to their court experience asked boys what "made them feel worst" during their appearance before the judge. A substantial number mentioned their parents' reactions, especially the negative remarks the parents made about them in front of others [26]. Children, for their part, often humiliate their parents in court through their general behavior or by obvious manifestations of disrespect for their parents. It is hard to envision how such public displays of family hostility and rejection can improve relationships among family members.

Court intervention may also intensify competition among family members. There is evidence that in some cases the attention given to delinquent children in therapy intensifies the parents' competitive strivings with their children and even causes parents to sabotage the therapy [27]. Even though the parents genuinely wish for changes in their child's behavior, they can not tolerate attention to their child at the expense of their own gratification.

Negative effects upon youths may also be produced by court labeling of the respondent as a deviant. This concern usually centers upon the disadvantage for employment or other purposes that may flow from a juvenile court record and the impact upon the youth's self-concept of being officially labeled as a deviant. There is another aspect of this labeling process that has not been much discussed but which may have the greatest effect upon a youth's development: the labeling of a youth by his own family [28]. This is especially relevant in the case of a PINS proceeding, in which the parent selects his own child for public labeling and is, therefore, publicly committed to an adverse perception of the child's behavior or worth. At the same time, the child is forced to recognize publicly his parent's perception and to reject or accede to it. In consequence, the parent may find himself bound to his public characterization of the child as "incorrigible" or worse, and the child to acceptance of that label or rejection of both the label and its instigator. Court confrontation may in this way harden rejection and intensify hostility between parent and child.

Other family relationships may also be modified. Intake and court investigations often bring out information about members of the family other than the status offender. Some of this information may have been unknown to the family or, if known, never acknowledged. Public exposure obviously may reduce family solidarity and create additional alienation between family members, and perhaps thereby increase the possibility that the family will reappear in court. Moreover, family members often take sides in a PINS case. An indignant mother brings her son to court for staying out late and hitting her. In some situations, other children and perhaps the father sympathize with the son, isolating the mother. In other situations, siblings may side with the mother and isolate the PINS youth. The positions taken are made even sharper if the family members are required to testify formally on these issues. A family dispute which might blow over if it remained in the confines of the home takes on added significance because of the court's involvement.

Such conflict may not only increase the likelihood that the PINS child will commit more status offenses, but may as well increase the likelihood that the child will become involved in delinquent activities. Nye, in an examination of the mutual acceptance-rejection pattern between parents and children, found a direct relationship between the incidence of delinquency and the level of mutual rejection [29].

The court's potential for intensifying family alienation might be discounted if there were adequate resources and knowledge to provide meaningful family crisis intervention, individual and family counseling, and constructive emancipation alternatives for youths who would be better off away from their families. As Gough and Grilli note, "The need is to develop the family's effective internal controls, not to undercut its hegemony, as the exertion of juvenile court jurisdiction almost inevitably does in such cases" [30]. However, resources are most meager and knowledge is most scant in precisely this connection. For most PINS the salve of reconciliation is not likely and the relief of divorce is not possible. Even if they are sent away to an institution, they eventually return home again to live with their families. The juvenile justice system usually is able to do little to change a youth's family situation or to improve his or her ability to cope with it. But it may intensify alienation between the youth and his family and make any positive adaptation to that alienation even less likely than before.

THE LONG-RANGE EFFECTS OF PINS PETITIONS

The initiation of the PINS petition is not merely a scare tactic. It has real potential for substantially affecting a child's life. Children alleged to be in need of supervision may be deprived of their liberty before trial, subjected to formal adjudication as "incorrigibiles," "runaways," or the like, and then restricted in their liberty or removed from home after trial. Indeed, they are in some jurisdictions more likely to be so affected than children charged with delinquency. One study of delinquency and PINS cases in New York Family Court from July 1, 1965 to June 30, 1966 shows that PINS were more likely than delinquents to be detained before their hearing and were more likely to be detained lengthy periods. Fifty-four percent of PINS were detained compared to 31 percent of the delinquents, and 50 percent of the detained PINS were held for more than thirty days compared to 25 percent of the detained delinquents. The study also showed that PINS were more likely than delinquents to be adjudicated and committed to training schools. Eighty-one percent of the children on PINS petitions were found involved and adjudicated, compared to 58 percent of the children on delinquent petitions. And of those subject to an adjudication, 26 percent of the PINS, compared to 21 percent of the delinquents, were sent to institutions [31].

An exploratory study of Family Court records in New York County in May, 1973 provides additional empirical support for the proposition that PINS are dealt with more severely than delinquents. A random sample of 100 families who have had at least one contact with Intake since the beginning of 1970 was drawn from the intake card file. These cards include information on each contact any child in the family has with Intake involving delinquency, PINS, or neglect petitions.*

The primary unit of analysis used was the family instead of the individual, because the juvenile court emphasizes, at least in theory, that decisions about children are based upon the family situation as well as upon the child's specific acts. Families were put into three categories: families with only PINS petitions, families with only delinquency petitions, and families with some combination of PINS or delinquency petitions. The findings described here should be viewed with caution because the study was an exploratory one and the sample is small.

Table 4–1 shows the number of instances in which a complaint was filed and an Intake contact (hearing) recorded for each family. Of those families where only delinquency petitions had been filed, 21 percent had further contact with the court. Multiple contacts occurred, however, in 36 percent of the sample PINS cases. In other words, a PINS family (a family with an Intake record of PINS petitions, but no delinquency or neglect petitions) is considerably more

---

*The cards are filed by family name and name of the mother, and they include the following information on all children known to be a part of the family who have had contact with Intake: child's name, birthdate, date of contact, disposition at Intake (e.g., adjusted, court, withdrawn), kind of petition (e.g., Supervision, Delinquency, Neglect).

Table 4-1.　Number of Intake Contacts Per Family Type

Number of Contacts with New York Intake	Family Type			Total Families
	PINS Only	Delinquency Only	Mixed PINS & Del.	
One	64%	79%	–	61%
Two	24	12	7	15
Three	8	2	14	6
Four	4	5	28	9
Five	–	–	43	7
Six or more	–	2	7	2
	100%	100%	99%	100%
Total number of Families	(25)	(43)	(14)	(82)*

*Eighteen families came to Intake on petitions involving neglect or some combination of neglect and other kinds of petitions, or on petitions which were not specified as PINS or delinquency in the card file. These cases are not included in this table.

likely to reappear in Intake a second or third time than is a delinquency family (one with an Intake record of delinquency petitions but no PINS or neglect). Although the majority of both PINS families and delinquency families experience only one petition, the PINS family is more likely to reappear on a new petition, either for the same or a different child, than is the delinquency family.

One explanation for these data is offered by intake workers and court officials who say that the PINS children are more seriously troubled than the delinquent and, moreover, that the families from which they come have deeper problems. Other possible explanations should, however, be considered. PINS families may not necessarily be more pathological than delinquency families, but simply more regular users of the juvenile court. We have little idea about how parents learn about or decide to use the court; however, if the hypotheses discussed earlier are valid, it may be that, once a family determines to seek force, authority, or assistance from the court, return to that source seems natural and perhaps easy. The initial decision to seek judicial action might be difficult but, once made, subsequent appeals for court intervention are less so. A family may, in a sense, become a "juvenile court consumer." Another, related explanation for the findings set forth in Table 4-1 is that a PINS petition represents an important step in a process of parent-child alienation, and once that first step has been taken, subsequent steps resulting in further alienation and further PINS petitions either against the same child or other children in the family become more likely.

Table 4-1 showed that the PINS family who comes into court is more likely than the delinquency family to return again to court. Table 4-2 shows that, not only is the PINS family more likely to come back to court, it is more likely to proceed further into the juvenile system than is the delinquency family. Petitions involving PINS families are less likely to be adjusted informally or withdrawn than petitions involving delinquency families. Indeed, petitions involving PINS families are referred to court 22 percent more often than petitions involving delinquency families.

It might plausibly be thought that the difference in severity of PINS treatment can be attributed to the greater frequency of court contacts found in these cases. Such an interpretation is wholly consistent with the juvenile court's traditional emphasis on individualization of treatment. However, as Table 4-3 reveals, the pattern of more formal treatment holds even where the number of intake contacts is held constant for PINS families and delinquency families. Among PINS families with only one Intake contact, 62 percent are referred to court, whereas among delinquency families with only one Intake contact, 29 percent are referred to court—a difference of 33 percent. Thus, almost two-thirds of the PINS families who appeared in the Intake unit for the *first* time were sent to court.

Table 4-2. Disposition at Intake by Type of Family and Type of Petition

Disposition at Intake	PINS Only Family	Delinquency Only Family	Mixed PINS & Delinquency Family		Total
			PINS Contacts	Delinquency Contacts	
Adjusted	39%	48%	19%	31%	25%
Withdrawn	3	15	10	10	10
Referred to Court	58	37	71	59	65
	100%	100%	100%	100%	100%
Total Number of Contacts	(38)	(60)*	(31)	(29)	(60)**

*Total excludes one court transfer.
**Two contacts which did not indicate type of petition (not recorded in earlier cases) are not included in this total.

Table 4-3. Disposition at Intake by Type of Family and Number of Family Contacts with Intake

Disposition at Intake	PINS Only Family		Delinquency Only Family	
	One Contact	Two or More Contacts	One Contact	Two or More Contacts
Adjusted	38%	41%	53%	42%
Withdrawn	–	9	18	12
Referred to Court	62	50	29	46
	100%	100%	100%	100%
Total Number of Contacts	(16)	(22)	(34)	(26)*

*Total excludes one court transfer.

These tables, taken together, show that a family which comes in contact with the juvenile court intake unit on a PINS matter is more likely to reappear again in Intake than a family which comes into contact with the unit on a delinquency matter. They show further that the family which comes into Intake on a PINS complaint is more likely to be referred to court than the family which comes in on a delinquency complaint, even if it is the former's first contact with the Intake unit. Again, the frequently stated belief that PINS and their families are more troubled than delinquents and their families may explain these findings. And again, in the absence of any empirical evidence that this is the case, other explanations are also plausible. Third parties who file complaints in delinquency cases usually do not have to continue to cope with the youth on a day-to-day basis and may well be amenable to informal disposition of the matter. The parent does, and seeks the court's help precisely because he or she is no longer able to cope. Consequently, the parent may be less easily dissuaded than strangers from taking the case to court. Whether the parent comes to court in a generalized response to family crisis, in a power play against the child, in hopes of dumping the child, or in a search for help, an adjustment or a withdrawal at intake may be an unsatisfactory conclusion. Goode notes that although social customs dictate how to end conversations of different kinds, none may exist for ending conflict interaction [32]. Fighting conversation, because it exposes still more disagreements and hostility as it progresses, does not easily lend itself to a safe completion. Intake negotiations involving PINS cases, especially the cases initiated by parents, may more frequently be described as "fighting conversations" than negotiations involving delinquency cases. As such they may be harder to end. The problems brought to court by PINS families may require more time and require different intervention tactics than the problems brought by delinquents. PINS families may not necessarily be more troubled; they may, rather, require different handling because of the posture of the parties in the court process.

The possibility of the self-fulfilling prophecy must also be considered in evaluating the high rate of court referral in PINS cases, since intake workers believe that PINS families are often deeply troubled. They may, accordingly, be more inclined to conclude that court involvement is required whenever a PINS case is presented.

DISCUSSION

Research on juvenile offenders has recently begun to distinguish between children who commit acts which, if committed by an adult, would be a crime and children who commit acts that are non-criminal in nature but nevertheless bring them within the jurisdiction of the juvenile court. Data from New York show that one difference between these two categories of offenders lies in the identity of the complainant. Rather than someone external to the family, as is usually the case in a delinquency petition, the complainant in a PINS case is frequently the child's own parent or guardian. In this chapter, an attempt has been made to explore the meaning of this parent-initiated action against a child. The parent-initiated PINS petition can be viewed from several perspectives. It can be viewed as providing parents, who may otherwise be powerless in regard to their children, some legally constituted force, or threat of force, through which to control them. It can be seen as a dumping device available to parents who want to relieve themselves of difficult youths with whom neither they nor other relatives are willing to put up any longer. Or it can be defined as a genuine call for help by families with overwhelming problems and unmanageable children. There has been no systematic research, to my knowledge, of the frequency with which parents use a juvenile court PINS petition for any of these reasons. Information is needed, from a wide variety of jurisdictions, on the proportion of PINS cases which are initiated by parents and on the expectations with which these parents and their children enter the juvenile court.

A second focus of this chapter has been upon the court's role in intensifying or alleviating disputes between parents and children. This is of particular concern when it is observed that a substantial proportion of families with PINS petitions reappear in court on new complaints and that a high percentage of PINS cases are referred to juvenile court. It has been suggested that the initiation of a PINS petition against a child by a parent may increase family alienation and modify relationships among the child, his parents, and other members of the family. The cycle of alienation between a parent and a child may be similar to the alienation between marital partners in a dissolving marriage, except that there is no relief through divorce for parents and children. Research is needed on the specific significance to parents and children of court appearance and in the broader area of parent-child alienation.

We operate under the assumption that all parents and children really want to live together and "make it together" and that they should. This assumption may be not only unrealistic, it may be damaging to the individuals involved. Birdwhistell pleads for a more realistic view of the family:

It requires but little reflection to see that the American family, as idealized, is an overloaded institution. It is easy to see, too, that the goals set by the concept are unattainable and leave people failing both as spouses and as parents. This can have even more tragic results if the people who find it impossible to live in such a situation, because they are human and have human needs, seek help to escape and are directed back into the pathological situation. The counselor, the therapist, or the legal adviser who accepts the ideal becomes the reenforcer of the pathology [33].

Perhaps one of the most healthy and sensible things some adolescents can do is to leave parents whose lives and relationships are confused, who are out of touch with reality, or who attempt to use the youths to meet their own emotional needs. Such youths need institutional support to move out, to obtain a "divorce" in some acceptable way from parents. The courts are now stacked on the side of parents as they have been since the time that children and slaves were viewed equally as property [34]. And, while they provide a resource—albeit not a very successful one—for powerless parents, they provide none for powerless youth.

NOTES TO CHAPTER 4

1. There is a considerable amount of sociological and psychological literature available on family and delinquency, but most of the sociological material tends to focus on the outward structure of the family—whether it is broken, its size, and the like. Psychological studies have tended to focus on early family experiences such as material deprivation and superego lacunae. For useful discussions of recent empirical and theoretical work on family and delinquency, *see* Rodman and Grams, "Juvenile Delinquency and the Family: A Review and Discussion," in President's Commission on Law Enforcement and Administration of Justice, *Task Force Report: Juvenile Delinquency and Youth Crime* 188, 195 (1967); Walters and Stinnett, "Parent-Child Relationships: A Decade Review of Research," 33 *Journal of Marriage and the Family* 70 (1971); Friedman, "Delinquency and the Family System," in *Family Dynamics and Female Sexual Delinquency* 34 (O. Pollak and A. Friedman, eds., 1969).

2. Short and Nye, "The Extent of Unrecorded Juvenile Delinquency: Tentative Conclusions," 49 *Journal of Crim. L. & Crim.* 296 (1958); Williams and Gold, "From Delinquent Behavior to Official Delinquency," 20 *Social Problems* 209, 213 (1972); Murphy, Shirley, and Witmer, "The Incidence of Hidden Delinquency," 16 *Amer. J. of Orthopsychiatry* 686 (1946); A. Porterfield, *Youth in Trouble* (1946).

3. Andrews and Cohn, "PINS Processing in New York: An Evaluation," *supra* Ch. 2, Table 2−1, p. 55.

4. *Id.* at Table 2−2, p. 64.

5. *New York State Judicial Conference, Annual Report, 1965−66, 1968−69, 1969−70.* These statistics refer to PINS petitions which were referred to court and acted upon by a judge, and do not include cases which were subject to informal disposition at sub-judicial processing.

6. *See, e.g., E. Bakke, Citizens Without Work* (1949); Hill, "Generic Features of Families Under Stress," 39 *Social Casework* 139 (1958); *E. Koos, Families in Trouble* (1946); Vogel and Bell, "The Emotionally Disturbed Child as the Family Scapegoat," in *A Modern Introduction to the Family* 412 (N. Bell and E. Vogel, eds., 1968); Clausen and Yarrow, "The Impact of Mental Illness on the Family," 11 *Journal of Soc. Issues* 3 (No. 4, 1955); Jackson, "The Adjustment of the Family to Alcoholism," 18 *Marriage & Family Living* 361 (1956).

7. *B. Farber, Family: Organization and Interaction* 403−406 (1964).

8. Bryant, "Concealment of Stigma and Deviancy as a Family Function," in *C.D. Bryant* and *J.G. Wells, Deviancy and the Family* 391 (1973).

9. "The public appearance of any family member may be taken as evidence of the family's 'private' state and, given their common identification, the behav-

ior of any one member may reflect on the others." Voysey, "Impression Management by Parents with Disabled Children," 13 *J. of Health & Social Behavior* 80–81 (1972).

10. Waller and Hill, "The Process of Alienation," in *Family Roles and Interaction* 484 (J. Heiss, ed., 1968).

11. Goode, "Force and Violence in the Family," 33 *J. of Marriage and the Family* 624 (1971), reprinted in *S. Steinmetz* and *M. Straus, Violence in the Family* 25, 26 (1974).

12. Several authors have analyzed the parent-child relationship as an exchange system. *See, e.g.*, Edwards, "Family Behavior as Social Exchange," 31 *J. of Marriage and the Family* 518 (1969); Edwards and Braumburger, "Exchange and Parent-Youth Conflict," 35 *J. of Marriage and the Family* 101 (1973); Richer, "The Economics of Child Rearing," 30 *J. of Marriage and the Family* 462 (1968). Others have studied the relationship between parental discipline and delinquency, *e.g.*, Peterson and Becker, "Family Interaction and Delinquency," in *Juvenile Delinquency, Research and Theory* 63 (H. Quay, ed., 1965); Slocum and Stone, "Family Culture Patterns and Delinquent-Type Behavior," 25 *Marriage and Family Living* 202 (1963); *W. McCord, J. McCord, and I. Zola, Origins of Crime* (1959); *F.I. Nye, Family Relationships and Delinquent Behavior* (1958); Reiss, "Delinquency as the Failure of Personal and Social Controls," 16 *Amer. Soc. Rev.* 196 (1951).

13. Delinquency is much more common in the United States than in Mexico despite the greater incidence of poverty and family disorganization in Mexico. Maslow and Diaz-Guerrero attribute this difference to the fact that parental roles within the family, especially the father's role, are much more clear-cut in Mexico. This clarity of role might be viewed as a resource. Maslow and Diaz-Guerrero, "Delinquency as a Value Disturbance," in *J. Peatman* and *E. Hartley*, eds., *Festschrift for Gardner Murphy* 228 (1960).

14. Goode, *supra* note 11 at 629.

15. It is interesting to speculate whether parents who file PINS petitions are parents who, in different circumstances, might abuse their children. There is a fair amount of evidence to indicate that abusing parents demand far higher performances from their children than other parents. *See* Pollock and Steele, "A Therapeutic Approach to the Parents," in *C. Kempe* and *R. Helfer, Helping the Battered Child and His Family* 11 (1972); Lord and Weisfeld, "The Abused Child," in *Childhood Deprivation* 78 (A. Roberts, ed. 1974). "Essentially, they approach the task of child care with the wish to do something for the child, a deep need for the child to fill their own lacks," and to give them love, and a harsh demand that the child behave in a certain way. "The parents' high standards . . . create an inevitable failure on the part of the child to show his virtue, and thus his concern for the parent himself." Such a parent may use a PINS petition in the same way that a physically abusive parent may use his fists. It would be interesting to ascertain whether the recorded incidence of child abuse among parents who initiate PINS petitions is any higher than it is among parents of other youths in the juvenile court and to compare the psychological profiles of PINS petitioners with the profiles of physically abusive parents. *See*, Goode, *supra* note 11 at 633–34.

16. Stierlin, Levi, and Savard, "Parental Perceptions of Separating Children," 10 *Family Process* 411, 414 (1971).

17. Richmond and Lauga, "Some Observations Concerning the Role of Children in the Disruption of Family Homeostasis," 33 *Amer. J. of Orthopsychiatry* 757, 758 (1963).

18. Venezia, "Delinquency as a Function of Intrafamily Relationships," 5 *J. of Research in Crime and Delinquency* 148, 149 (1968).

19. van der Veen and Novak, "The Family Concept of the Disturbed Child: A Replication Study," 44 *Amer. J. of Orthopsychiatry* 763, 770 (1974).

20. *N. Glazer* and *D. Moynihan, Beyond the Melting Pot* 125 (2d Ed. 1970).

21. Birdwhistell is highly critical of the "ideal" American family and notes that "Unless the family unit can be expanded and its members supported in larger social relationships, we can give little more than first aid to its members." Birdwhistell, "The Idealized Model of the American Family," 51 *Social Casework* 197 (1970).

22. Andrews and Cohn, *infra* note 3 at Table 2–1, p. 55.

23. One study of family attitudes towards childrens' mental health services showed that children from lower-income and minority families "were among those least likely to have obtained services, although the concentration of problems was greatest within this group. Within the group of children judged to be moderately to severely impaired, only one black child in ten, as compared to one white child in four, received appropriate mental health assistance." Lurie, "Parents' Attitudes Toward Children's Problems and Toward Use of Mental Health Services," 44 *Amer. J. of Orthopsychiatry* 109, 112 (1974).

24. "We have largely operated upon the seldom-scrutinized assumptions that the standards of the parents are congruent with those of society, and that the interests of the parent, the child and the community converge." Gough, "The Beyond-Control Child and the Right to Treatment: An Exercise in the Synthesis of Paradox," 16 *St. Louis U.L.J.* 182, 187 (1971).

25. *N. Glazer* and *D. Moynihan, supra* note 20 at 124.

26. Snyder, "The Impact of the Juvenile Court Hearing on the Child," 17 *Crime and Delinquency* 180, 187 (1971).

27. Deykin, "Life Functioning in Families of Delinquent Boys: An Assessment Model," 46 *Soc. Service Review* 90, 99 (1972).

28. Mahoney, "The Effect of Labeling Upon Youths in the Juvenile Justice System: A Review of the Evidence," 8 *Law & Society Review* 583, 600–03 (1974).

29. *F.I. Nye, supra* note 12 at 69–76.

30. Gough and Grilli, "The Unruly Child and the Law: Toward a Focus on the Family," 23 *Juvenile Justice* 9, 11 (No. 3, 1972).

31. Lerman, "Beyond Gault: Injustice and the Child," in *Delinquency and Social Policy* 236, 243–45 (P. Lerman, ed., 1970).

32. Goode, *supra* note 11 at 624.

33. Birdwhistell, *supra* note 21 at 197.

34. "Magistrates could order that children and servants who behaved 'disobediently and disorderly towards their Parents, Masters and Governours' be whipped but not by more than ten stripes for each offense, or they could bind them over to the next County Court." Although cursing and smiting parents and being a stubborn or rebellious son were capital crimes, only those 'above sixteen years old, and of sufficient understanding' could be put to death." *E. Powers Crime and Punishment in Early Massachusetts* 443 (1966).

✳ *Chapter 5*

Sex-Based Discrimination and PINS Jurisdiction

Alan Sussman

INTRODUCTION

In 1925 Judge Ben Lindsey, drawing from his experience in the Denver juvenile court, wrote what was considered a revealing portrait of the wayward tendencies of "modern" youth [1]. It is significant that almost all of the troubled adolescents described—many of whom were saved by the protective judge—were girls whose sexual misconduct had led them astray.

The pattern of waywardness that appeared in Judge Lindsey's work is still observable, more than fifty years later. While adults are not as alarmed today about girls riding in motor cars or "going beyond petting," it remains true that statutes which extend juvenile court jurisdiction to persons in need of supervision (PINS) are applied far more frequently to females than to males. It is certainly still the case that, despite a rise in female delinquency [2], the majority of minor girls who appear in court are charged with non-criminal behavior while only one-fifth of the boys referred to family court are charged with status offenses [3]. Moreover, girls—who make up only 25 percent of those subject to delinquency and PINS charges together—appear in fully one-half of the PINS proceedings [4]. This phenomenon is now, as it was then, largely attributable to the vague standards of conduct that characterize PINS statutes. Their breadth invites discretionary application of their provisions and allows parents, police, and juvenile court authorities, who ordinarily decide whether PINS proceedings should be initiated, to hold girls legally accountable for behavior—often sexual or in some way related to sex—that they would not consider serious if commited by boys.

Virtually every juvenile court practice is justified in some degree by reference

179

to the protective function of the state in its relation to children. It is this protective function that explains why children are subject to closer regulation than adults. Juvenile court jurisdiction over non-criminal girls, however, also reflects a double standard whereby girls are subject to greater "protection" than boys. Female children, therefore, may well be subject to unequal treatment under law, not only in comparison with older women not liable to juvenile codes but also in contrast to male children similarly situated. This chapter will focus on the latter condition and on the ways in which PINS provisions place girls at an unfair disadvantage in the scheme of protective juvenile legislation.

SEX-BASED JURISDICTIONAL STATUTES

The most obvious differentiations between juvenile men and women occurs when they are made subject to juvenile court authority by formal statutory sex-based distinctions. Until recently, some state laws held girls subject to family or juvenile court jurisdiction by reason of non-criminal behavior until a later age than boys [5]. In New York, to take one example, children of both sexes could be found delinquent or in need of supervision until the age of sixteen, but only girls were subject to PINS jurisdiction between the ages of sixteen and eighteen [6]. The reasons supporting statutory distinctions of this kind have never been made clear. Virtually no significant data indicate that girls, either because of their behavior patterns or for any other reason, are more in need of continuing supervision than boys past a common age [7]. Rather, differential jurisdictional classifications appear to rest upon vague but commonly accepted notions that girls have special physical and psychological characteristics which require extension of protection and supervision for longer periods of time than is needed for boys. Perhaps the most familiar characteristic of this sort is the female's capacity to bear children, which evokes a societal interest in protecting itself and its female children from sexual promiscuity, unwanted pregnancies, and illegitimate births [8].

Recently—perhaps sparked by rapidly changing concepts of a woman's role in society and a growing awareness of the "special" status often afforded women under law [9]—such provisions have recently come under legislative and judicial attack [10]. These challenges have largely relied on the absence of convincing demonstrable reasons for treating males and females differently for purposes of PINS jurisdiction. In 1972 the New York Court of Appeals struck down that state's higher age limit for juvenile court power over non-criminal behavior by girls on constitutional grounds [11]. The challenge was brought by a sixteen-year-old girl charged with incorrigibility who was within the Family Court's jurisdiction as a PINS although a boy the same age could not have been so treated. In declaring the statutory distinction invalid, Chief Judge Fuld observed:

The object of the PINS statute is to provide rehabilitation and treatment for young persons who engage in the sort of conduct there proscribed. This affords no reasonable ground, however, for differentiating between males and females over 16 and under 18. Girls in that age bracket are no more prone than boys to truancy, disobedience, incorrigible conduct and the like, nor are they more in need of rehabilitation and treatment by reason of such conduct [12].

A similar case arose with respect to the Oklahoma Children's Code which extended juvenile court jurisdiction generally to females under the age of eighteen but only to males under the age of sixteen. As it happened, the Oklahoma statute was challenged, not by a girl seeking to avoid juvenile court, but by a seventeen-year-old *boy* who claimed that the law discriminated against males by rendering them subject to the jurisdiction of adult criminal courts at an age earlier than females [13]. This argument was rejected by the State Court of Criminal Appeals, which found that the statutory distinction exemplified "the demonstrated facts of life" [14]. The Tenth Circuit Court of Appeals, although "strongly disinclined to hold that the considered judgment of the Oklahoma Legislature . . . does not meet the measure of federal constitutional standards," held that the state had wholly failed to present a "rational justification" for the disparity in treatment of males and females of the same age and therefore found that the law violated the Equal Protection Clause of the Fourteenth Amendment. The circuit court noted that the "demonstrated facts of life" upon which the state court, and the government on appeal, relied were neither articulated nor apparent and could not, therefore, be weighed to determine if they might suffice to characterize the classification as reasonable rather than arbitrary and invidious [15].

Not all sex-based jurisdictional provisions differentiate by age. In some states, certain categories of *behavior* have been expressly defined as applicable only to one sex (usually girls). In Tennessee, for example, the law creates juvenile court jurisdiction and permits institutional commitment of females—but not males— who are "living a criminal life" [16]. A similarly discriminatory statute, which subjected an unmarried girl between the ages of sixteen and twenty-one who was "in manifest danger of falling into habits of vice" or who was "leading a vicious life" to the possibility of commitment, was operative in Connecticut until 1972 [17].

Most of these sex-based jurisdictional statutes for non-criminal acts have been repealed or declared invalid in recent years. That is, beyond question, an important step. However, it is plain that, while formal law has changed, traditional concepts of female misbehavior still persist in the administration and selective application of facially neutral PINS statutes. This circumstance will be explored in the following section.

SEX-BASED STANDARDS OF BEHAVIOR:
DISCRIMINATION IN PRACTICE

The terminology of PINS statutes has traditionally been ambiguous and conclusory. Words describing a child's behavior as "incorrigible," "unruly," or "wayward" are included in the definitional clauses of many PINS provisions, and phrases describing the child's status as "beyond control," "habitually disobedient," or "a danger to one's self or others" appear in others [18]. Such statutes have repeatedly been attacked on constitutional grounds because of their failure to state precisely what conduct they proscribe. Those who have challenged PINS provisions point out that statutory categories like those mentioned above fail to give a child adequate notice with respect to the nature of the behavior for which he or she may be deprived of liberty and that they vest an extraordinary range of discretion in the hands of parents, police and juvenile court authorities. Despite the accuracy of these objections, thus far PINS provisions have routinely been upheld as legitimate expressions of the public interest in protecting children under the *parens patriae* doctrine [19].

Beyond doubt, the vagueness of jurisdictional definitions places children of both sexes at considerable risk. The statutes neither clearly inform the youth of the limits to his or her conduct nor limit the circumstances under which he or she may be charged with wrongdoing. In addition, girls often suffer the further disadvantage of being subject to a stricter code of ethics or a "higher" level of acceptable behavior than boys, and thereby, to greater regulation by parents and courts. This is the case with specific charges of sexual behavior [20], and it has further been suggested that charges of "ungovernability" or "incorrigibility" also serve as euphemistic vehicles for complaints involving sexual misbehavior or promiscuity [21]. Given the breadth of most PINS provisions—under which nearly every child could be said to be culpable to some degree—and given the fact that most acts of a sexual nature involve partners of both sexes, there seems to be no rational explanation of the high percentage of female PINS respondents other than that the vagueness and broad scope of the statutes facilitate the application of a double standard of permissible behavior for young boys and girls.

This situation results from a variety of factors, including the following: (1) Parents and police are more prone to disapprove of expressions of female than of male sexuality; (2) Judges are generally more "protective" of girls than boys; and (3) Pregnancy is a uniquely female condition.

1. In great part, the PINS jurisdiction is intended to enforce parental authority over children. "Incorrigibility" does not describe specific conduct that is, per se, socially disruptive or otherwise harmful. Associating with a group of peers, for example, is not by itself conduct justifying juvenile court intervention; it becomes so only when that behavior is objectionable to the child's parents and the parents seek authoritative help in controlling the child [22]. It is inevitable,

therefore, that certain kinds of youthful behavior will be viewed as disruptive or incorrigible by one parent or set of parents and "normal" by another.

Nowhere is the potential for inconsistency greater than in questions of the appropriateness of moral and sexual conduct. Parents may consider late hours acceptable for teenage boys but unacceptable for girls; premarital intercourse may be regarded as part of "growing up" or "gaining experience" for a boy but as "immoral" behavior for a girl. Parents are permitted by PINS statutes to file petitions—and do, in great numbers [23] —against their daughters for acts which, if committed by their sons, would be overlooked [24]. Non-coercive *male* sexual misbehavior, on the other hand, usually comes to the attention of the court only when parents of the girl involved are offended [25].

For similar reasons, police are more likely to take females than boys into custody for sexually-oriented acts. Overbreadth in the range and definitions of prohibited behavior generally encourages selective police enforcement of the law [26] and, given the breadth of discretion that characterizes PINS statutes, it is not surprising that police often overlook male participation in sexual relations but consider themselves guardians of community standards in dealing with girls [27].

Divergent views of morality held by parents or community officials not only place girls at a greater disadvantage than boys, but exert an extra burden on lower status girls as well. Middle and upper class parents are likely to place a premium on the reputation of their children (as well as their own) which they are hesitant to risk by bringing their disobedient daughters into court [28]. Boarding schools and travel often serve as alternative remedies for parents with financial resources unavailable to lower-status families. The poor, in contrast, are often denied access to any option for dealing with disobedient children other than referral to court [29].

Vague and virtually undemonstrable charges also permit some parents to rid themselves of meddlesome or inconvenient children. It is not uncommon for a mother to be threatened by the presence of her daughter in the home when the teen-age girl may be making real or imagined sexual overtures to the mother's lover, paramour, or husband. In such cases, girls are often brought into court under the sweeping jurisdiction of PINS statutes and charged by the mother with ungovernability or immoral behavior [30].

2. Judges and probation officers, as well as parents and police officers, are subject to the pervasive double standard of youthful sexual behavior. Girls, especially those of the lower classes, are often regarded as persons to be condemned for or saved from their immoral ways, either of which typically involves drastic intervention in the female's life [31]. This attitude is regrettably reinforced by the available literature on female sexuality and crime, which tends to categorize girls as either emotionally weak (and therefore in need of guidance and protection) or sexually manipulative and calculating (and therefore in need of reformation) [32].

The notion that youthful sexual misconduct results from female manipulation or seduction of otherwise innocent boys is surprisingly prevalent. One study which examined 1,500 cases before a single metropolitan juvenile court judge revealed that:

> . . . the judge refused to treat any form of sexual behavior on the part of boys, even the most bizarre forms, as warranting more than probationary status. The judge, however, regarded girls as the "cause" of sexual deviation of boys in all cases of coition involving an adolescent couple and refused to hear the complaints of the girl and her family; the girl was regarded as a prostitute [33].

Acute judicial concern with female immorality, moreover, often results in a higher rate of adjudication for PINS petitions alleging sexual misbehavior than for those charging commission of criminal acts [34].

3. Fear of pregnancy and illegitimate birth exerts a certain influence on the attitudes and practices of those who consider girls to be in need of a higher degree of protection than boys [35]. This stems partly from the biological truth of the situation, but may also be attributed to an adult's simple embarrassment at the decidedly public nature of premarital pregnancy. This fear (and reaction to a visible challenge to traditional concepts of morality) also may tend to legitimate imposition of harsh sanctions upon girls who run away from home or keep late hours [36].

SEX-BASED TERMS OF CONFINEMENT

Girls subject to PINS charges may be treated differently from boys for dispositional as well as jurisdictional purposes. A special concern for women, which sometimes results in higher acquittal rates for adult female offenders and leniency in their sentencing [37], has come to be known as the "chivalry factor" in law [38]. The chivalry factor seems, however, to disappear or cut the opposite way in cases of female juvenile offenders. Perhaps because the primary purpose of intervention in cases involving children is considered protective rather than punitive, judges and probation officers in some jurisdictions are less hesitant to take drastic actions against females (particularly those in need of supervision). For example, the available evidence indicates that girls brought before New York courts on PINS petitions receive a somewhat lower percentage of suspended or discharged judgments than boys and are more often placed on probation [39]. Respondents of both sexes in PINS cases are kept in juvenile detention for what some believe to be unjustified reasons [40], but female PINS are detained even more frequently than males [41]. In fact, when juveniles are detained in *adult* jails, females are more likely to be held for status offenses than are males for similar conduct, and are detained for longer periods of time as well [42]. Moreover, juvenile status offenders, especially females, are detained in adult jails more often than those who are alleged to have committed crimes against persons or property [43].

With respect to dispositional decisions, it has been argued that females adjudicated for non-criminal misconduct (which may be as PINS or as delinquent, according to local law) are disproportionately represented in state training schools and reformatories [44]. In New York, for example, such a trend was found in 1972—1973 [45]. What is generally true is that the proportion of girls committed for non-criminal behavior, whether as delinquents or PINS, is far greater than the proportion of boys committed for that reason. This fact becomes significant when duration of commitment to training schools and reformatories is considered. Moreover, there is reason to believe that girls as a group spend longer periods in institutions than boys, despite the fact that their conduct, again as a group, is far less likely to have been law violative (and therefore seriously threatening) than that of boys [46].

The reasons for this pattern are never clearly stated, but the following explanation has been offered:

Although there is no clear reason for this disparity, it may stem from fear that the young girls may become pregnant or morally depraved. Since they are seen to be weaker than males and less able to care for their moral beings, they are kept incarcerated for their own protection [47].

A similar explanation has been given for a Pennsylvania law that rendered adult female criminals liable to longer sentences than men. The Philadelphia District Attorney, urging that differential treatment should be held unconstitutional, offered the following observation by an early criminologist to illustrate the philosophy behind the statute:

There is little doubt in the minds of those who have had much experience in dealing with women delinquents, that the fundamental fact is that they belong to the class of women who lead sexually immoral lives. . . .
[A long-term detention statute for women] would remove permanently from the community the feebleminded delinquents who are now generally recognized as a social menace . . . [48].

That such a view has been accepted is further supported by the existence of statutes that expressly authorize commitment of female PINS until a later age than is allowed for males. Under the New York Family Court Act, girls adjudicated in need of supervision may be placed in a state institution until the age of twenty-one, but boys may be similarly committed only until the age of eighteen [49]. And in Maine, a seventeen-year-old male offender may serve a maximum of three years, but a seventeen-year-old girl may be confined indefinitely [50].

In most jurisdictions, disparate periods of commitment are the product of the indeterminate dispositional scheme characteristic of juvenile court laws and of parole practices in the jurisdiction. Indeterminate dispositions for juveniles have routinely been upheld against constitutional attack, even though they permit and perhaps even contemplate that some children receive longer "terms" for certain behavior than either adults or other children who engage in the same kinds of misconduct [51]. Since the focus of juvenile justice has traditionally been directed to the treatment or rehabilitation of the offender, the logic of the system supports the individualized (and therefore variable) degree to which a child may be confined. As stated by a Texas court:

> If the purpose of permitting longer periods of detention for children was to punish youthful offenders more severely than adult criminals, the application of a strict standard of review would seem justified. But where the legislative purpose is to *benefit* the affected class, a less strict standard would seem proper. . . . The purpose of our juvenile law is *benign*, rather than invidious [52].

That good intentions can continue to insulate juvenile court sentencing procedures from constitutional scrutiny is, however, by no means clear. Although limited in its holding to the adjudicative rather than the dispositional phase of juvenile proceedings and to delinquency matters in particular, the Supreme Court's decision in *In re* Gault [53] clearly reflects a realization that the benign purposes claimed by the juvenile justice system are in fact not being realized and that commitment, for whatever purpose, still results in the deprivation of liberty of young people [54]. Whether for reasons of treatment or punishment, the institutionalization of female PINS for longer periods of time than males can be said to deny members of one sex due process and equal protection of the laws. This question will be further explored in the following section.

SEX DISCRIMINATION, PINS, AND
THE CONSTITUTION: STANDARDS
FOR REVIEWING DISCRIMINATION

Prevailing Standards for Review of Sex-Based
Classifications

Over the course of the last century, the Supreme Court has reviewed the constitutionality of a number of statutes which affect women differently from men. Initially, the decisions were uniform in finding that differential treatment was founded on some rational basis and that the laws did not, therefore, deny women equal protection of the laws [55]. In the last several years, however, a variety of state statutes discriminating against persons on the basis of sex have been found unconstitutional [56]. In each of these cases, the Court overturned legislation which presumed that certain social and legal roles—including the administration of estates and the guardianship of minors—could best be performed by members of one sex without regard to individual ability or fitness. While the reasoning of the Supreme Court in sex discrimination cases has not been consistent [57], it and other courts have generally considered such statutes unconstitutional if they create distinctions based on sex when no pervasive difference between men and women exists to justify dissimilar treatment [58].

This does not mean, of course, that every law that treats men and women differently is unconstitutional. Statutes involving a sex-based classification will only be declared unconstitutional when dissimilar treatment lacks a "rational relationship" to some legitimate governmental interest [59]. This places a heavy burden on the party challenging such legislation and certainly makes successful challenge difficult, although surely not impossible. It is worth noting, however, that limitations placed on review of legislative classifications under the Equal Protection clause may not obtain if suit is brought under a state Equal Rights Amendment (or, if adopted, the federal amendment) [60]. An Equal Rights Amendment may be interpreted to make legislative distinctions on the basis of sex wholly impermissible [61]. At the least, it should make sex a "suspect classification" which would, in turn, require that distinctions be not only rationally related but necessary to achievement of some legislative purpose and, moreover, that the purpose served be not merely one the government could legitimately choose but one of "compelling" importance. Classifications by sex would thus be subjected to the same "strict scrutiny" imposed on laws involving racial classifications [62]; they would be presumed unconstitutional and the state would be required to establish the existence of a compelling interest for so classifying persons and the necessity of such classification to accomplish that compelling interest [63].

Proving Sex Discrimination in PINS Cases

As we saw in the first section of this chapter, there have been a number of decisions specifically addressed to sex discrimination in juvenile court laws [64]. In recent years, for example, courts have regularly found differential age provisions violative of equal protection, even under the "minimum rational basis" test. It further seems likely that statutes allowing either longer terms of commitment or commitment to a later age for members of one sex will receive similar treatment by most courts, and their invalidation is virtually certain in states that adopt an Equal Rights Amendment. There is at this point no reliable evidence to suggest that rehabilitation requires longer periods for one than another sex or that females (for example) will benefit from juvenile institutions until a later age than males. Without such information, overt sex-based standards for confinement cannot rationally be related even to the legitimate governmental goal of rehabilitation and surely cannot meet the higher requirements of strict scrutiny that an Equal Rights Amendment would import.

Most of the statutes that have thus far been reviewed, however, subject men and women to unequal burdens through express legislative classification; therefore, locating the classes of persons disadvantaged by the law is a simple matter. Once the disadvantaged class is identified, the process of analysis described in the preceding discussion will apply. Matters are far less simple, however, when the questioned statute in both language and operation affects some members of all classes but in its impact weighs disproportionately on one of those classes. It was earlier suggested that this is true of PINS statutes with respect both to jurisdictional definitions and dispositional practices. Specifically, the earlier discussion has presented evidence that, among other things, vague jurisdictional standards such as "incorrigibility" expose more girls than boys to juvenile court jurisdiction and that indeterminate dispositional schemes result in disproportionate use of commitment for girls found to be PINS.

It is, therefore, important to consider the constitutional posture of statutes that are neutral in terms but unequal in effect. An initial obstacle to claims based on discriminatory impact lies in establishing the fact and nature of the unfairness. That "discrimination" exists is a conclusion drawn from facts which demonstrate that one class of persons is treated differently, to their disadvantage, from another class of persons similarly situated with respect to the purpose of the statute. Proof that a law actually does affect people differently is an obvious precondition to a charge of discrimination. Ordinarily, the burden of so proving can be met, but even here difficulty may arise. Certainly small statistical differences, which may be a function of chance, are weak evidence unless large numbers, accurate reporting, and consistent trends can be shown.

Even more troublesome is proof that a facially neutral statute in practice discriminates against a particular class which is similarly situated to the non-disadvantaged population. Brief reference to recent Supreme Court cases illustrates the nature of the difficulty. In *San Antonio Independent School District v. Rodriguez* [65], plaintiffs were public school children from poor, Mexican-American families. Under Texas law, public schools are financed on a district basis and the amount of financing available in each district depends in part on real estate property tax collected in the district. The plaintiffs claimed that such a method of local finance discriminated against the "poor" as a class and against minority groups, membership in which was said to correlate with family income. The Supreme Court, however, held that—despite considerable evidence of these relationships—plaintiffs had not proved that the Texas scheme disproportionately affected an identifiable suspect class (minority racial group or, perhaps, indigents). *Jefferson v. Hackney* [66], decided the year before *Rodriguez*, further suggests the difficulty of proof that is correlational in nature. That case involved the administration of welfare, again in Texas. As it happened, the state made available less support to one social security categorical assistance program (AFDC) than to others (aid to the blind, the aged, and the permanently disabled). Appellants presented evidence that AFDC recipients are more likely to be Black or Mexican-American than recipients under other programs and urged that the Texas plan discriminated, in its effect, against minority racial group members. Had appellants succeeded in persuading the court that Texas law did discriminate by race, a high standard of justification would have been required by the "strict scrutiny" standard discussed above and, almost certainly, the law would have fallen. The Court, however, was not satisfied by what it called a "naked statistical argument" and, finding no racially discriminatory element, sustained the statute.

It would not be right to say that statistics can never establish a pattern of specific discrimination. Indeed, they have been so used successfully, most often in cases alleging racial discrimination in jury selection procedures [67]. However, it is clear that evidence merely establishing that a law affects more girls than boys, without more, will not support a finding of discrimination by sex. Consider, for example, data showing that female PINS are less likely to receive suspended judgments than males. Such information may not justify a finding that sex per se accounts for the differences. Before that conclusion could safely be reached, it would first be necessary to show that boys and girls were charged with offenses similarly difficult of proof in court, that both groups had comparable court and police histories, that their ages at adjudication were comparable, and that any other facts that might account for differential treatment were comparable or irrelevant to decisions. Absent such a showing, the court cannot conclude that differential treatment was a function of sex rather than, for example, number of prior adjudications. Given such ambiguity, there is insufficient basis for resort to strict scrutiny (where that test would be applied to sex discrimination cases) or for finding that the dispositions were related to irrelevant factors (such as sex) rather than to appropriate factors (prior court history). The same point can be made with respect to a variety of other adjuative and dispositional decisions; available data simply do not adequately control for variables other than sex that might account for observed results.

This should not imply, of course, that sex-based discrimination in the impact of PINS statutes can never be demonstrated. Rather, it means that careful study must be made of the evidence supporting the charge and, perhaps, that attention should be directed to gathering evidence of the kind that would support such a charge. There are, as well, areas in which the evidence of sex-specific impact is, while perhaps not conclusive, relatively clear and, from time to time, even recognized by judicial pronouncement. One such area is the disproportionate percentage of girls prosecuted—either formally or in fact—for their sexual conduct. There seems to be good reason to conclude that PINS statutes do bear more heavily on girls than boys in this respect, and for reasons specifically associated with their sex [68]. Assuming this is established, the questions initially discussed can finally be addressed: Is such a distinction rationally related to legitimate legislative goals or, perhaps, is it necessary to attainment of some goal of compelling importance?

It is submitted that, even under a rational relationship standard, the over-inclusion of girls within the administration of PINS statutes bears no substantial relation to the laws' objective—the supervision of wayward youths for their protection or reformation—without relying on the very same presumptions which have been unsuccessfully invoked to justify express legislative discrimination by sex. These presumptions imply that girls are, by virtue of their sex, (1) more prone than boys to be led astray by keeping late hours, associating with undesirable friends, truanting from school or demonstrating incorrigible or ungovernable behavior; (2) more prone than boys to reap undesirable consequences from involvement in sexual activity; (3) in greater need than boys of pre-trial detention when charged with non-criminal behavior; and (4) in greater need than boys of post-adjudication supervision, training, and institutionalization for commiting non-criminal acts.

Only presumption (2) could be said to have any rational basis, and this is only due to the fact that pregnancy and motherhood are purely feminine phenomena. Presumptions (1), (3), and (4) are, in the first instance, simply unsupported by any known evidence. They rely, moreover, on unalterable sex role concepts that bear no necessary relationship to an individual's needs, abilities or life situation [69]. It is precisely these sex-role presumptions [70], customarily invoked by legislatures and courts to classify women, which have recently been determined irrational and arbitrary when used to justify differential treatment of the sexes [71].

Presumption (2), however, warrants closer examination since the biological distinction between the sexes may be claimed to justify differential treatment or even qualify as an exception to the constitutional mandate that males and females be treated equally, since young men and women are not "similarly situated" in this respect. While it is true that only females may become pregnant or give birth to illegitimate children who, in turn, may become financial burdens upon the state, that leaves for consideration the degree to which a statute may constitutionally permit the enforcement of a double standard of morality, based on traditional or generalized sex roles [72]. Pregnancy and fear of impregnation may also be viewed from a perspective radically different from that in currency when most PINS provisions were legislated. The last decade has witnessed a sexual revolution of sorts, partly sparked by the availability of birth control devices and, more recently, by the legalization of abortions. These two developments deflate to some extent the argument that girls need to be protected from their own sexual misbehavior. If birth control devices and abortions are available to prevent or discontinue pregnancies, the law should take account of the fact that the ability to avoid or undo a previously irreversible condition is now within the realm of choice of female children [73]. Furthermore, another possible harmful consequence of sexual intercourse, venereal disease, poses a danger that affects male and female partners equally.

Perhaps the most compelling analysis of the "special" condition of girls with regard to sexual behavior, pregnancy and illegitimate births is that of former Chief Judge Fuld of the New York State Court of Appeals [74]. In striking down a provision holding girls subject to PINS jurisdiction for two years longer than boys, he observed:

> The argument that discrimination against females on the basis of age is justified because of the obvious danger of pregnancy in an immature girl and because out-of-wedlock births which add to the welfare relief burdens of the State and City is without merit. . . . Even if we were to assume that the legislation had been prompted by such considerations, there would have been no rational basis for exempting, from the PINS definition, the 16 and 17-year-old boy responsible for the girl's pregnancy or the out-of-wedlock birth. As it is, the conclusion seems inescapable that lurking behind the discrimination is the imputation that females who engage in misconduct, sexual or otherwise, ought more to be censured, and their conduct subject to greater control and regulation, than males [75].

If this assumption cannot rationally be indulged by legislatures, as Judge Fuld suggests, then it should not be allowed to justify similar results at the hands of courts and parents.

CONCLUSION

PINS statutes, perhaps by their nature, are vaguely worded and fail to provide children adequate notice of the behavioral standards they are legally obligated to uphold. The inexact definitions vest an inordinate amount of discretion in the hands of parents, community officials and judicial officers who often reflect traditional standards of morality by petitioning and punishing for conduct which, if demonstrated by boys, would be overlooked. Furthermore, female PINS are deprived of their liberty more frequently than their male counterparts, and are often committed or held subject to the jurisdiction of the court for longer periods of time as well. While no evidence or data exist which demonstrate that young girls are more in need of supervision or treatment than are young boys, customary fears of sexual promiscuity, pregnancy, and illegitimate childbirth as well as unreasonable concepts of women as the weaker and less stable sex often serve to rationalize their discriminatory treatment under law. It is likely that such sex-based generalizations and presumptions are unconstitutional since no pervasive difference between male and female children can be nor has been offered to justify their dissimilar treatment pursuant to the existence and operation of PINS statutes.

NOTES TO CHAPTER 5

1. *B. Lindsey* and *W. Evans, The Revolt of Modern Youth* (1925).

2. *U.S. Dep't. of Health, Education and Welfare, Juvenile Court Statistics 1970*, Pub. No. 72–03452 at 3–4 (1972). The boy-girl ratio of referral to court for delinquent behavior has been reduced from four to one to three to one. *Id.*

3. In New York State, for the fiscal year 1972–1973, 11,466 delinquency petitions were lodged against boys and 1,514 against girls. PINS petitions, however, were almost equally distributed between the sexes: 3,784 were filed against boys and 3,750 against girls. Approximately three times as many boys were brought to court on delinquency charges as were brought on PINS petitions, while approximately two and one-half times as many girls appeared on PINS petitions as on delinquency charges. *State of New York, The Judicial Conference, Nineteenth Annual Report* at 329, 408, 410, 416, 418 (1974) [hereinafter cited as *Annual Report*]. *See also* E.S.G. v. State, 447 S.W. 2d 225 (Tex. 1969); *President's Commission on Law Enforcement and the Administration of Justice: The Challenge of Crime in a Free Society* 56 (1967).

4. Andrews and Cohn, "Ungovernability: The Unjustifiable Jurisdiction," 83 *Yale L.J.* 1383, 1387 (1974). *See also Annual Report, supra* note 3.

5. *E.g.*, 10 *Okl. Stat. Ann.* §1101 (Supp. 1969); *Vernon's Tex. Civ. Stat.* Art. 2338–1, §3 (1971); *N.Y. Fam. Ct. Act* §712(b) (1963). In Illinois, girls were subject to be declared delinquent for one year longer than boys, but both sexes were liable to be held in need of supervision until the age of eighteen. *Ill. Rev. Stat.* ch. 37, §§702–2, 702–3 (Supp. 1971).

6. *N.Y. Fam. Ct. Act* §712(a) & (b) (1963).

7. Gold, "Equal Protection for Juvenile Girls in Need of Supervision in New York State," 17 *N.Y.L. Forum* 570, 590 (1971).

8. Davis and Chaires, "Equal Protection for Juveniles: The Present Status of Sex-Based Discrimination in Juvenile Court Laws," 7 *Geo. L. Rev.* 494, 499–501 (1973); Gold, *supra* note 7 at 591.

9. *See, e.g.*, Harrigfeld v. District Court of Seventh Judicial District, 95 Idaho 540, 511 P. 2d 822 (1973) in which a state law declaring eighteen the age of majority for females and twenty-one the age for males was declared unconstitutional as violative of the equal protection clause of the Fourteenth Amendment.

10. *Ill. Rev. Stat.* ch. 37, §702–2 (1972); *Vernon's Tex. Ann. Fam. Code* §51.02 (1973), Tex. Acts 1972, 62nd Leg., p. 43, ch. 20, §§1, 2. The Illinois revision was followed by the case of People v. Ellis, 10 Ill. App. 3rd 216, 293 N.E. 2d 189 (1973), which declared the previous differential classification unconstitutional. The Texas repeal was aided by two important cases, both of which reflected that state's confusing statutory scheme which applied jurisdictional age limits at the time of trial rather than at the time of the offense. In Broadway v. Beto, 338 F. Supp. 827 (N.D. Tex. 1971), a seventeen-year-old boy was held subject to prosecution as an adult for an offense he committed at age sixteen, even though a seventeen-year-old girl in his situation would still be subject to juvenile court jurisdiction. In *Ex parte* Matthews, 488 S.W. 2d 434 (Tex. Ct. Crim. App. 1973), the differential sex-based jurisdictional definition contained in Article 2338–1, §3 was struck down as violative of the equal protection clause of the Fourteenth Amendment since the court could find no rational objective for its existence.

11. *In re* Patricia A., 31 N.Y. 2d 83, 286 N.E. 2d 432, 335 N.Y.S. 2d 33 (1972).

12. *Id.* at 88, 286 N.E. 2d at 434–35, 335 N.Y.S. 2d at 37.

13. Lamb v. State, 475 P.2d 829 (Okl. Crim. App. 1970).
14. *Id.* at 830.
15. Lamb v. Brown, 456 F.2d 18 (10th Cir. 1972).
16. *Tenn. Code Ann.* §37−440 (1955).
17. *Conn. Gen. Stats. Ann.* §17−379; Repealed, Pub. Act No. 28, S.Bill No. 14 (April 10, 1972). Before legislative repeal, this provision was held constitutional since it was not "penal" but rather was concerned with the protection of females. Connecticut v. Mattiello, 4 Conn. Cir. 55, 225 A. 2d 507 (1966), *cert. den.*, 395 U.S. 209 (1969). The *Mattiello* case dealt with a young woman charged with acts including "lascivious carriage."
18. These terms, including truancy and running away from home, constitute the general scope of most PINS statutes. Some states, however, extend the supervisory power of the court to include behavior such as frequenting pool halls or taverns, being in a disreputable place, keeping late hours, begging, associating with bad companions, being profane, or leading an immoral life. *See, e.g., Okl. Stat. Ann.*, tit. 10, §101 (1966); *Ind. Stat. Ann.* §31−5−7−4 (1973); *Code of Laws of So. Car.* §16−1103 (9) (1962).
19. A few qualified exceptions to this trend have been established. In 1973, the Superior Court for the District of Columbia held unconstitutionally vague and violative of the Fifth Amendment parts of the District's PINS law which granted jurisdiction over "habitually disobedient" and "ungovernable" children. The court found the language so imprecise as to make it impossible for one to be aware of how to obey the law. *In re* Brinkley, Docket No. J−1305−73, Sup. Ct. D.C., June 14, 1973, 5 *Juv. Ct. Digest* 34 (No. 3, 1973). In 1971, a federal court held unconstitutionally vague that portion of the California Welfare & Institutions Code that conferred jurisdiction over a child leading or in danger of leading an "idle, dissolute or immoral life." Gonzalez v. Mailliard, Civ. No. 50424 (N.D. Cal., Feb. 9, 1971), 4 *Juv. Ct. Digest* 4−5 (No. 3, 1972). The court did not rule out the right of a state to provide protective custody for troubled children, but held that it must so provide upon reasonably clear and definite standards. The final outcome of the case is in doubt, however, since the United States Supreme Court recently ordered the Federal District Court to "reconsider" its decision. Mailliard v. Gonzalez, 416 U.S. 918 (1974). The strongest objection to ambiguously written protective legislation was handed down by a federal court in Gesicki v. Oswald, 336 F. Supp. 371 (S.D.N.Y., 1971), *aff'd.* 406 U.S. 913 (1972). The court held that a New York Criminal Procedure Law which defined a "wayward minor" as "any person between the ages of sixteen and twenty-one who either . . . is wilfully disobedient . . . and is morally depraved or in danger of becoming morally depraved . . . " was unconstitutionally vague. While the statute in question did not apply to and, indeed, sought to distinguish juvenile court cases, the language the Court used to strike it down provides a persuasive standard for measuring PINS provisions of similar scope. Judge Kaufman stated (at 374):

> It is clear to us that the terms 'morally depraved' and 'in danger of becoming morally depraved' fall far beyond the bounds of permissible ambiguity in standards defining a criminal act. . . . The concept of morality has occupied men of extraordinary intelligence for centuries, without notable

progress (among even philosophers and theologians) toward a common understanding.
See also, People v. Fields, 388 Mich. 66, 199 N.W. 2d 217 (1972).

20. In a major study of PINS jurisdiction in New York, 13 percent of the girls composing the sample of respondents were charged with sexual promiscuity, while only 2 percent of the boys in the same sample were similarly charged. *Office of Children's Services of the New York Judicial Conference, The PINS Child—A Plethora of Problems* 45 (1973). In the Andrews and Cohen study, *supra* note 4 at 1388, n. 33, explicit allegations of sexual misbehavior appeared in 21 percent of the cases, mostly against girls.

21. Reiss, "Sex Offenses: The Marginal Status of the Adolescent," 25 *Law and Contemp. Prob.* 309, 311—312 (1960); Goldman, "Women's Crime in a Male Society," 22 *Juv. Ct. Journal* 33 (1971); Gold, *supra* note 7 at 591; Greene and Esselstyn, "The Beyond Control Girl," 23 *Juvenile Justice* 13, 16 (1972); Riback, "Juvenile Delinquency Laws: Juvenile Women and The Double Standard of Morality," 19 *U.C.L.A. L. Rev.* 313, 321 (1971).

22. According to Andrews and Cohn, *supra* note 4 at 1386: "[I]n ungovernability cases the Family Court allows itself to be used by angry parents to punish their children."

23. In New York State, parents and relatives of the respondent constitute the greatest single source of petitioners against female PINS. They also comprise a greater percentage of petitioners against female as compared to male PINS respondents. *Annual Report, supra* note 3 at 331; Andrews and Cohn, *supra* note 4 at 1395, n. 83. Andrews and Cohn also point out that there is a very low parental withdrawal rate of petitions lodged against daughters charged with sexual misbehavior. In such cases parents withdraw only 13 percent of the petitions while they withdraw 48 percent of the cases in which no such allegations were made. *Id.* at 1397, n. 95.

24. Goldman, *supra* note 21 at 33.

25. Reiss, *supra* note 21 at 314.

26. Riback, *supra* note 21 at 328—330.

27. Goldman, *supra* note 21 at 34; Reiss, *supra* note 21 at 314.

28. Reiss, *supra* note 21 at 314, 316.

29. Aidan Gough, "Memorandum of General Principles and Tentative Standards on Non-Criminal Misbehavior" at 12 (Manuscript prepared for Juvenile Justice Standards Project, March, 1974).

30. Andrews and Cohn, *supra* note 4 at 1395, n. 83.

31. Gough, *supra* note 29 at 12; Reiss, *supra* note 21 at 319.

32. William Thomas suggests, in *The Unadjusted Girl* (1967), that the potentially delinquent girl, often devoid of sexual feeling or passion, uses sex as a tool or "capital" by which she can gain amusement, material goods, and favorable notice. *Id.* at 109. Gisela Konopka, in *The Adolescent Girl in Conflict* (1966), finds a sexual basis to female crime which in turn is rooted in girls' greater need for dependency than boys. *Id.* at 40—41. Perhaps both the agressive-manipulative and passive-dependent viewpoints can be traced to Freud, whose theory of infant

sexuality holds that women's natural exhibitionistic and narcissistic tendencies are manifestations of the desire to compensate for their "loss" (castration). S. Freud, "Some Psychological Consequences of the Anatomical Distinctions Between the Sexes," 5 *Collected Papers* (1925). Men, according to Freud, channel their sexual desires into socially productive activities, while women have "little sense of justice, [and this] is no doubt related to the predominance of envy in their mental life . . . [W]omen [are] weaker in their social interests and [have] less capacity for sublimating their instincts than men." *S. Freud, New Introductory Lectures on Psychoanalysis* 134 (vol. 22, 1964). (The author is indebted to Diana Boernstein for the references to Freud, contained in her study "Women's Criminality" [Unpublished, 1974]).

33. Reiss, *supra* note 21 at 316. *See also*, comments of New York State judges regarding female sexuality in Andrews and Cohn, *supra* note 4 at 1303–1304, ns. 124–126.

34. Andrews and Cohn, *supra* note 4 at 1399, n. 102.

35. Goldman, *supra* note 21 at 33. A similar sentiment is ascribed to a New York Family Court judge in Gold, *supra* note 7 at 597. *See also*, Greene and Esselstyn, *supra* note 21 at 15.

36. G. Konopka, *Supra* note 32 at 125; Reiss, *supra* note 21 at 321. Medical examinations for signs of intercourse, venereal disease, and pregnancy are routinely given girls taken into custody for criminal and non-criminal behavior. *Id.* at 313, 314.

37. K. Burkhart, *Women in Prison* 73 (1973); O. Pollak, *The Criminality of Women* 4–5 (1950). The accuracy of the figures which point to lighter sentences for women is called into serious question by the fact that many jurisdictions permit indeterminate sentences for women criminals only, which often results in their serving a longer period of time in confinement or being eligible for parole later than men found guilty of similar acts. The policy of indeterminate sentences has lately come under successful challenge. U.S. *ex rel.* Sumrell v. York, 288 F. Supp. 955 (D. Conn. 1968); U.S. *ex rel.* Robinson v. York, 281 F. Supp. 8 (D. Conn. 1968); Commonwealth v. Daniel, 430 Pa. 642, 243 A. 2d 400 (1968), *reversing* Commonwealth v. Daniels, 210 Pa. Super. 156, 232 A. 2d 247 (1967). *Contra*, Wark v. Robbins, 458 F. 2d 1295 (1st Cir. 1972).

38. W. Reckless and B. Kay, *The Female Offender*, Consultant Report, Prepared for the President's Commission on Law Enforcement and Administration of Justice (1967).

39. *State of New York, The Judicial Conference, 19th Annual Report*, at 336 (1974).

(Table overleaf)

Specific Intervention Made With "Supervision" Adjudication, by Sex
1971–1972 and 1972–1973 Compared

Intervention	Boys		Girls	
	1971–72 Percent	1972–73 Percent	1971–72 Percent	1972–73 Percent
Judgment Suspended	10	11	9	8
Discharged with Warning	3	3	3	3
Probation	58	55	60	56
Placement in Private Facilities	11	13	10	13
Placement or Commitment in State Training School	6	2	5	4
Other Placement	9	14	12	15
Discharge to Mental Institutions	–	–	–	–
Discharge to Another Petition	3	2	1	1
Other	–	–	–	–
	100	100	100	100

40. *E.g.*, *see* West, "Juvenile Court Jurisdiction over 'Immoral' Youth in California," 24 *Stan. L. Rev.* 568, 577 (1972).

41. *R. Sarri, Under Lock and Key: Juveniles in Jails and Detention* 18, 19, 45 (1974). Nearly 75 percent of the detained females are charged with status offenses, compared with 25 percent of the males. *Id. See also Annual Report*, *supra* note 3 at 332, 333. Chesney-Lind refers to two studies which further illustrate this point. One report from Pennsylvania indicates that 45 percent of the girls charged with juvenile or sex role violations were detained prior to trial, compared to only 24 percent of those charged with misdemeanors and 35 percent of those charged with felonies. Chesney-Lind, "Juvenile Delinquency: The Sexualization of Female Crime," *Psychology Today* 43, 45 (July, 1974).

42. *R. Sarri, supra* note 41 at 10.

43. *Id.*

44. Gold, *supra* note 7 at 585; *State of New York, The Judicial Conference, Annual Report*, volumes 1965–1973.

More than 80 percent of the women institutionalized at the New Jersey State Reformatory in 1971 were placed for having violated non-criminal standards of behavior. Lerman, "Child Convicts," 8 *Trans-Action* 35 (No. 9–10, 1971). Nationally, 70 percent of adjudicated females are institutionalized for status offenses while only 23 percent of adjudicated males are in this category. Skoler and McKeown, "Women in Detention and Statewide Jail Standards," Clearinghouse Bulletin No. 7 at 7 (March, 1974). *See also, A.B.A. Commission on Correctional Facilities and Services, Survey and Handbook on State Standards and Inspection Legislation for Jails and Juvenile Detention Facilities* 72 (3rd ed. 1974).

Recently, a number of jurisdictions have restricted placement of PINS children, both male and female, in training schools. In New York, the Court of Appeals prohibited the Division for Youth from placing PINS and delinquents in the same institutions. *In re* Ellery C., 32 N.Y. 2d 588, 300 N.E. 2d 424, 347 N.Y.S. 2d 51 (1973). In Illinois, a recent legislative enactment prohibits PINS from being committed to the Youth Division of the Department of Corrections, *Ill. Rev. Stat.*, ch. 37, §705−2(1) (b) (1973), and in Maine a child who has not committed a crime may not be placed in a correctional or training center. *Me. Rev. Stat Ann.*, tit. 15, §2611(5) (Supp. 1975). California PINS cannot be delivered to the Youth Authority and locked up without a special court petition. *Cal. Welf. & Inst'ns. Code* §730 (1966). Nevertheless, placement in other institutions or programs (including "special" training schools for PINS only) is not prohibited in New York and a PINS child in California may be locked up if he or she runs away from a court-authorized non-secure original placement. *Id.*, §731.

45. *See* note 39, *supra.*

46. Haft, "Women in Prison: Discriminatory Practices and Some Legal Solutions," 8 *Clearinghouse Review* 1, 2 (May, 1974), citing *U.S. Dep't. of Health, Education and Welfare, Children's Bureau, Statistics on Public Institutions for Delinquent Children 1964* (1965); Gold, *supra* note 7 at 584, citing *W. Lunden, Statistics on Delinquents and Delinquency* 258 (1964); Skoler and McKeown, *supra* note 44 at 8.

47. Haft, *supra* note 46 at 2. The irony of the situation is compounded in that single-sex institutions are considered no answer to the problems of either boys or girls who are confined as sex offenders and placement therein may even foster deviate sex practices. Reiss, *supra* note 21 at 331.

48. Commonwealth v. Daniels, 210 Pa. Super. 156, 232 A. 2d 247, 255 n. 2 (1967), *reversed* Commonwealth v. Daniels, 430 Pa. 642, 243 A.2d 400 (1968).

49. *N.Y. Fam. Ct. Act* §756(c) (1963). In Oklahoma, on the other hand, female delinquents may be discharged from an institution three years earlier than males. *Okl. Stat. Ann.*, tit. 10, §1139(b) (Supp. 1973).

50. *Me. Rev. Stat. Ann.*, tit. 34, §§802, 853 (Supp. 1973).

51. *In re* Blakes, 4 Ill. App. 3d 567, 281 N.E. 2d 454 (1972); *In re* Sekeres, 48 Ill. 2d 431, 270 N.E. 2d 7 (1971). *See* Note, "Overdue Process for Juveniles: For the Retroactive Restoration of Constitutional Rights," 17 *How. L.J.* 402, 428−430 (1972).

52. Smith v. State, 444 S.W. 2d 941, 947−948 (Tex. Civ. App. 1969) (emphasis added).

53. 387 U.S. 1 (1967).

54. *See In re* Gregory W., 19 N.Y. 2d 55, 62, 224 N.E. 2d 102, 106, 277 N.Y.S. 2d 675, 680 (1966).

55. Goesaert v. Cleary, 335 U.S. 464 (1948), for example, upheld a Michigan statute that barred women from serving drinks in bars unless they were daughters or wives of male bar owners. Such discrimination was sustained on the theory that the Michigan legislature might reasonably have believed that women serving drinks would be in danger unless a father or husband were present to protect them. In reaching this result, Mr. Justice Frankfurter observed for the Court:

Michigan could, beyond question, forbid all women from working behind a bar. This is so despite the vast changes in the social and legal position of women. The fact that women may now have achieved the virtues that men have long claimed as their prerogatives and now indulge in vices that men have long practiced, does not preclude the States from drawing a sharp line between the sexes, certainly in such matters as the regulation of the liquor traffic. See the Twenty-First Amendment and *Carter v. Virginia*, 321 U.S. 131. The Constitution does not require legislatures to reflect sociological insight, or shifting social standards, any more than it requires them to keep abreast of the latest scientific standards.

Id. at 465–66.

Similarly, a Florida statute prohibiting selection of female jurors unless they specifically requested placement on a jury list was held constitutional. The Court found that the state had a valid interest in encouraging women to discharge their responsibilities in the home and that a law relieving women from jury service except when they themselves had decided that service was consistent with those responsibilities was rationally related to attainment of the governmental interest. Hoyt v. Florida, 368 U.S. 57 (1961).

56. Reed v. Reed, 404 U.S. 71 (1971); Frontiero v. Richardson, 411 U.S. 677 (1973); Weinberger v. Wiesenfeld, 420 U.S. 636 (1975); Stanton v. Stanton, 421 U.S. 7 (1975).

57. *See* Johnston, "Sex Discrimination and the Supreme Court—1971– 1974," 49 *N.Y.U.L. Rev.* 617 (1974).

58. *See* cases cited, note 56 *supra.* In Frontiero v. Richardson, 411 U.S. 677 (1973), it seemed that the Court was ready to treat sex as a "suspect classification," which would have invoked a higher standard of justification for statutes using such a classification. Four justices frankly took that view and a fifth did not expressly reject it. Recent decisions, however, have rejected the "suspect classification" approach and it seems that the optimism engendered by the plurality opinion in *Frontiero* is unlikely to be fulfilled.

59. Thus, several statutes which treat men and women differently have been sustained in recent years: when the Court found there existed a rational relationship between classification by sex and a legitimate governmental objective. *E.g.*, Kahn v. Shevin, 416 U.S. 351 (1974) (sustaining a Florida law giving a $500 property tax exemption, without regard to need, to widows but not to widowers); Geduldig v. Aiello, 417 U.S. 484 (1974) (sustaining state insurance law that excluded from coverage certain disabilities resulting from normal pregnancies and deliveries); Schlesinger v. Ballard, 419 U.S. 498 (1975) (sustaining regulations giving female naval officers a longer period in which to receive promotion or suffer mandatory discharge than was available to male officers).

60. The federal Equal Rights Amendment will provide, if ratified, that "Equality of rights under the law shall not be denied or abridged by the United States or by any State on account of sex." State Equal Rights Amendments closely approximate the wording of the proposed federal Amendment.

61. *See* S. Rep. No. 92–689, *Sen. Comm. on the Judiciary*, 92 *Cong.* 2nd *Sess.* (1972); Brown, Emerson, Falk, and Freedman, "The Equal Rights Amendment: A Constitutional Basis for Equal Rights for Women," 80 *Yale L.J.* 871, 893 (1971).

62. *Cf.* Loving v. Virginia, 388 U.S. 1 (1967); Korematsu v. United States, 323 U.S. 214 (1944).

63. This is a heavy burden indeed. The Supreme Court has only rarely found a governmental interest sufficiently compelling to meet that test. *See* Korematsu v. United States, 323 U.S. 214 (1944).

64. *See* text at notes 12—15, *supra.*

65. 411 U.S. 1 (1973).

66. 406 U.S. 535 (1972).

67. *E.g.*, Jones v. Georgia, 389 U.S. 24 (1967); Hernandez v. Texas, 347 U.S. 475 (1954).

68. *See* text at notes 23—36, *supra.*

69. *See* State *ex rel.* Watts v. Watts, 77 Misc. 2d 178, 350 N.Y.S. 2d 285 (Fam. Ct., N.Y. Co., 1973).

70. For discussion of the "irrebuttable presumption" rationale, *see* Johnston, *supra* note 57 at 630—35 (1974).

71. *See* Note 59, *infra. See also*, U.S. *ex. rel.* Robinson v. York, *supra* note 38, Seidenberg v. McSorley's Old Ale House, Inc., 317 F. Supp. 593 (S.D.N.Y. 1970).

72. "Role-typing" along sex lines, to the detriment of young women, was dismissed as an unjustifiable rationale by the Supreme Court in overturning a Utah statute under which girls reached majority at eighteen years of age and boys at twenty-one. Stanton v. Stanton, 421 U.S. 7 (1975). In the context of child support, the Court held that "no valid distinction between male and female may be drawn."

73. Eisenstadt v. Baird, 405 U.S. 438 (1972); Roe v. Wade, 410 U.S. 113 (1973); Doe v. Bolton, 410 U.S. 179 (1973); *In re P.J.*, 12 *Crim. L. Rptr.* 2549 (D.C. Sup. Ct., Feb. 6, 1973); Poe v. Gerstein, 517 F.2d 787 (5th Cir. 1975); Wolfe v. Schroering, 388 F. Supp. 631 (W.D. Ky. 1974); State of Washington v. Koome, Wash. Sup. Ct. No. 42645 (Jan. 7, 1975); Planned Parenthood Ass'n. of Southeastern Pa., Inc. v. Fitzpatrick, Civ. No. 74—2440 (E.D. Pa., Oct. 10, 1974); Baird v. Bellotti, 393 F. Supp. 847 (D. Mass. 1975).

74. *In re* Patricia A., 31 N.Y. 2d 83, 286 N.E. 2d 432, 335 N.Y.S. 2d 33 (1972).

75. *Id.* at 89, 286 N.E. 2d at 435, 335 N.Y.S. 2d at 37.

Chapter 6

PINS Jurisdiction, the Vagueness Doctrine, and the Rule of the Law

Al Katz
Lee E. Teitelbaum

INTRODUCTION

Statutes governing Persons in Need of Supervision (PINS) often include a wide variety of conduct or circumstances from which courts may infer the need for intervention in a child's career. The Ohio "Unruly Child" provision illustrates the breadth that such legislation may attain:

As used in . . . the Revised Code, 'Unruly Child' includes any child:
   (A) Who does not subject himself to the reasonable control of his parents, teachers, guardian, or custodian, by reason of his being wayward or disobedient;
   (B) Who is an habitual truant from home or school;
   (C) Who so deports himself as to injure or endanger the health or morals of himself or others;
   (D) Who attempts to enter the marriage relation in any state without the consent of his parents, custodian, legal guardian, or other legal authority;
   (E) Who is found in a disreputable place, visits or patronizes a place prohibited by law, or associates with vagrant, vicious, criminal, notorious, or immoral persons;
   (F) Who engages in an occupation prohibited by law, or is in a situation dangerous to life or limb or injurious to the health or morals of himself or others;
   (G) Who has violated a law applicable only to a child [1].

This statute, which is not unusual [2], covers conduct that is defined with great specificity (e.g., marriage without parental consent), with some specificity (e.g., failure to subject oneself to the reasonable control of one's parents), and entirely without specificity (e.g., so deporting oneself as to endanger one's own or another's morals). It is, moreover, addressed to a wide range of potential complainants, among them parents who think a child has failed to accept their control, neighbors who find a juvenile engaging in dangerous activity, police officers who see a child in company with criminal or notorious persons, and social workers who conclude that a young person is in circumstances dangerous to his health or morals. The statute further allows broad charges to operate as residual categories when narrower allegations cannot for some reason be proved; thus, if a child alleged to have been a party to burglary cannot be shown to have participated knowingly in the theft, the petition may be amended to charge her with associating with criminals [3].

It is also plain that the Ohio statute embodies not only broad and ambiguous but potentially inconsistent standards with respect to behavior that makes children "unruly." A child who conforms passively to her parent's expectations may nevertheless be said by police officers, social workers, or judges to be "in morally dangerous circumstances" where, for example, the parents are unmarried, drink heavily, or gamble in the home. The potential for inconsistency arises from the generality of the grant of concern to various sources of authority. Those subject to multiple grants of such authority can only hope that each grantee will construe similarly what is proper behavior on the subject's part.

The breadth, ambiguity, and potential inconsistency of the Ohio statute is not accidental. For reasons that will be discussed below, these characteristics have traditionally been thought necessary and desirable in juvenile court legislation. At the same time, these same characteristics have, of late, led to the claim that such laws violate due process because they are "void for vagueness." The following discussion will analyze the relationship between the legal notion of vagueness and one aspect of juvenile court jurisdiction over "unruly" children: that concerning respondents who are "ungovernable," "beyond the control of their parents," or the like. Such provisions are found in most juvenile codes, although in some states they are included within the definition of delinquency while in others incorrigible children are classified as "Persons in Need of Supervision" or some similar description [4]. Since we are concerned here with the regulation of parent-child relationships rather than with the jurisdictional category in which it appears, the following analysis is generally applicable to both delinquency and PINS statutes dealing with ungovernable children. At base, our conclusion is that legal supervision of the parent-child relationship cannot be undertaken consistent with the rule of law.

The argument will proceed as follows. In the first part we will review the relatively well understood connection between statutory definiteness, legal justice, and the rule of law. We will then compare this approach—the normal version of criminal justice—with a type of order characterized by imprecise directives, substantive justice, and status relationships, and argue that the juvenile court ideal reflected a belief in the need to do substantive justice and a vision of the parent-child relationship as essentially one of status. This comparison will reveal that the juvenile court undertook an inherently contradictory enterprise—to supervise the parent-child status relationship through forms drawn from legal justice and the rule of law while seeking at the same time to secure substantive justice. The effort to resolve this contradiction created, we submit, the problem of vagueness in PINS laws.

In the second part of this chapter, we work toward a similar point using a different method. The essence of the argument here is that there are contradictions within the parent-child relationship itself and within the rule of law. These contradictions confront each other within the PINS jurisdiction and generate an unbreakable paradox.

The paradox leads us to consider, in the final part, whether supervision of the parent-child relationship according to the rule of law has consequences fundamentally different from a similar effort at supervision by an inquiry directly into dangerousness. We will irreverently conclude that, traditional theory to the contrary, the two models are not antinomies and that the paradox discovered in our earlier analysis arises again at this somewhat higher level of abstraction.

STATUTORY DEFINITENESS, LEGAL JUSTICE, AND THE RULE OF LAW

It is a commonplace of Anglo-American law that a statute may not be so indefinite in its language "that men of common intelligence must necessarily guess at its meaning and differ as to its application" [5]. Failure to satisfy this requirement not only offends notions of wise legislative policy [6], but may lead to the invalidation of both civil and criminal laws as "void for vagueness" [7].

Imprecision offends a number of principles relating both to fairness to individuals who may run afoul of the law and to the manner of political organization. The rule of statutory definiteness is designed to assure that persons will be free from coercive intervention for their behavior unless their conduct has been previously proscribed and the fact of proscription was knowable. More generally, requirements of definiteness are related to the notion that governments operate by rules; that the rules are known or at least knowable provides security for the fact of their existence in the first instance. Correlatively, requirements of specificity serve to protect the autonomy of the governed by setting forth, publicly and in advance, the areas of proscribed activity. The proscription and the resulting ambit of autonomy together constitute the relationship of citizen to state [8].

Requirements of certainty, prior existence, and notice of rules are, indeed, a logical corollary of the rule of law or principle of "legal justice" which operates throughout Anglo-American law [9]. The rule of law implies that legal commands are uniform and general; that they cover all situations within the class they define and apply to all persons within those situations. The conditions of statutory definiteness serve these same functions. To the extent they are fulfilled, justice is impersonal and abstracted from the immediate source of authority. If a law is certain, the exercise of power can be considered separate from the person or the authority exercising the power; accordingly, individuals before the court may be satisfied that their conduct is punished because of previously established rules and not on the basis of rules fashioned on the instant for their particular disadvantage. By the same token, their punishment is not the product of the judge's greater social or political power but rather of rules that govern both the individual and the judge's exercise of power. If, however, a law is uncertain in its meaning, the distinction between law-maker and law-enforcer collapses. The process of interpretation becomes indistinguishable from the process of law-making and the exercise of authority (adjudication) becomes legislative in character [10]. Lack of specificity in the rules obscures the controlling force of those rules independent of the judge.

Rules which do not satisfy a minimum degree of specificity fail, therefore, to eliminate the experience and the fact of personal domination, because their application appears to and may in fact depend entirely on the subjective judgment of officials. The rule of law can be described as the contrary of government by the domination of persons, as the phrase "A government of laws and not of men" surely suggests. That government by personal domination is fundamentally inconsistent with our most cherished political values hardly requires stating. As the Supreme Court long ago remarked in striking down a statute giving certain officials an unlimited power to grant or deny licenses, "[T]he very idea that one may be compelled to hold his life, or the means of living, at the mere will of another, seems intolerable in any country where freedom prevails, as being the essence of slavery itself" [11].

Finally a regime of rules or of "legal justice" can be contrasted with "substantive justice," in which specific rules for decision-making do not preexist the time of decision and the rule applied at the time is wholly instrumental in character. Under substantive justice, each decision is justified because it is best calculated to advance some accepted objective, such as prevention of future wrongdoing by a person. By contrast, in a system of "legal justice" (under which the normal version of both civil and criminal law uniformly purport to operate), the function of law-making must antedate adjudication because the latter operates by applying previously established rules of prescriptive quality to a given case, whether or not reliance on those rules will under immediate circumstances best serve the general objective [12]. The contrast between law ordered by prescriptive rules and law ordered by instrumental rules is commonly understood as, at base, a contrast between the goal or value of individual freedom and the goal or value of social protection. An inquiry directly addressed to, for example, whether a person is dangerous rather than whether he has acted in a given way may in fact better facilitate discovery of persons who require intervention than a regime of prescriptive rules. It can only do so, however, at the price of great intrusiveness into the lives of those who are subject to the inquiry and of great insecurity as a result of the lack of notice of the circumstances that will lead to official intervention. In this respect, adherence to the rule of law is thought to define the distance between state and individual in such a way as to limit sharply the government's control over its subjects.

Requirements of definiteness preserve the relationship of individual to authority in non-judicial circumstances as well. An imprecise statute not only fails to define the appropriate scope of governmental intervention when a case comes to court but, regardless of the construction actually applied by courts, compromises the exercise of autonomy by citizens who wish to avoid arrest by the police and trial at the instance of prosecutors. The cautious person gives the law a wide berth, realizing that the costs of approaching the margin are very great. Moreover, the principle that laws be impersonal is severely compromised at the police level, since vague statutes are likely to be enforced against those whose personal characteristics excite official disapproval. This, too, has been recognized by the Supreme Court, which observed in connection with a vagrancy ordinance that "Those generally implicated by the imprecise terms of the ordinance—poor people, nonconformists, dissenters, idlers—may be required to comport themselves according to the life style deemed appropriate by the Jacksonville police and the courts. . . . It results in a regime in which the poor and the unpopular are permitted to 'stand on a public sidewalk . . . only at the whim of any police officer' " [13].

Substantive Justice and Status:
The Juvenile Court Ideal
The function of the vagueness doctrine—control of official power and provision of notice to citizens—thus appears as the antithesis of the experience of personal domination. The doctrine itself comes as close as law can come to a definition of what is not law [14]. In most contexts, both the rule of law and its corollary requirement of statutory definiteness are accepted without question, although their precise meaning in any given instance may be disputed. General acceptance flows, as we have seen, from the conviction that social order achieved by personal domination is intolerable. This conviction has not been, of course, universally held. Domination is the organizing principle of status relationships, in which law serves principally to confirm the existence of the relationship and perhaps to limit the exercise of domination in matters of detail. The archtypal status relationship was that of the early Roman father over his children [15], and it was this relationship which Sir Henry Maine used to identify the existence of status relationships in other areas [16]. The opposition of status or personal condition to the rule of law and to the doctrine of vagueness in particular was explicitly stated by Hayek:

In fact, as planning becomes more and more extensive, it becomes regularly necessary to qualify legal provisions increasingly by reference to what is 'fair' or 'reasonable'; this means that it becomes necessary to leave the decision of the concrete case more and more to the discretion of the judge or authority in question. One could write a history of the decline of the Rule of Law, the disappearance of the Rechtsstaat, in terms of the progressive introduction of these vague formulas into legislation and jurisdiction. . . . It means in effect a return to the rule of status, a reversal of the 'movement of progressive societies' which, in the famous phrase of Sir Henry Maine, 'has hitherto been a movement from status to contract.' Indeed, the Rule of Law, more than the rule of contract, should probably be regarded as the true opposite of the rule of status [17].

To the extent, then, that notions of personal domination are valued, the application of the rule of law is problematic, and it is clear that they have not wholly disappeared. The idea of status has certainly not been rejected in perceptions of the institution which typifies the rule of status: the family. Courts still use that term, albeit metaphorically rather than strictly, in talking about the marital relationship [18] and it is directly reflected in juvenile court jurisdictional provisions concerning children who behave so as to excite adult disapproval. The general domination of adults over children is firmly rooted in social theory and in juvenile court theory specifically. To be classified as a child, both in law and custom, is to fall into the somewhat ambiguous category of "non-" or "developing-person," in which one is dependent upon adults rather than autonomous in determining one's course of action [19]. Youth are, it has been observed, not only a minority group but, as for Maine, represent *the* minority group in the sense that their treatment has provided "a paradigm for imputations and policy regarding disliked ethnic factions" [20]. Equally important, this dependent status is most significantly political rather than social or economic [21]; it is a deficiency in citizenship before it is one of wealth or prestige. While it may be true that the dependent status of children has been ameliorated in some degree since the turn of this century, adult domination remains the principal characteristic of parent-child relationships [22].

This principle has been often stated, and was urged in justification for traditional juvenile court theory by the National Council of Juvenile Court Judges as recently as 1967:

Some of the vociferous critics of the juvenile courts seem to forget what the wise parent knows, for example, that children really are not adults. They do not come to life fully equipped with knowledge and wisdom, like Minerva springing full-panoplied from the brow of Jove. They are not like insects which are hatched complete with all the instincts they need to complete their life cycle. On the contrary, human children start life completely helpless and must come to the rights and privileges of adulthood by slow degrees. It is not difficult to see in this failure to recognize that there is a real difference between children and adults the explanation of much of the difficulty which underlies our present problems of delinquency and youth crime. If a child is to be accorded all the rights and privileges of adulthood, what necessity is there for the child to mature? Adults who are themselves immature, children who have never had to grow up, are unable to lead their own children to maturity, in a vicious circle which is nowhere so apparent as in juvenile courts [23].

Dependency places young people generally under the care and control of adults. In most instances, the superintending power lies with parents, whose power to regulate their children's lives as they see fit enjoys constitutional protection and is in theory subject to state regulation only in extreme circumstances [24]. The rule of law is by definition external to this relationship; it operates, if at all, only as an analogy.

The principle of the dependency of children to their parents, used by Maine to exemplify status, was adopted by proponents of the juvenile court as the operative model for its activity. In their view, the court would assume the traditional parental function of guiding and controlling the youth in the way that a "wise parent" should have done [25]. In all cases involving children—whether predicated upon criminal conduct, misbehavior wrongful only because of the actor's youth, or parental neglect—the court would assume responsibility for the respondent's socialization. As one court said of delinquency matters:

[T]he proceedings under this law are in no sense criminal proceedings . . . they are simply statutory proceedings by which the state, in the legitimate exercise of its police power, or, in other words, its right to preserve its own integrity and future existence, reaches out its arm in a kindly way and provides for the protection of its children from parental neglect or from vicious influences and surroundings, either by keeping watch over the child while in its natural home, or where that seems impracticable, by placing it in an institution designed for that purpose [26].

Reliance on family relationships as a model for official action was perhaps most regularly emphasized with respect to procedural matters. Since parents were not required to use formal process to discipline their children, juvenile courts were held similarly exempt from such requirements; since rules of evidence and procedure were not demanded of natural parents, their judicial surrogates were also free to decide matters without regard to strictures applicable in either civil or criminal cases [27]. But the notion of court as surrogate parent also had a substantive impact. Traditional juvenile court theory extended official concern beyond discrete misbehavior to the condition of the whole child. Those responsible for the creation of juvenile court legislation and a considerable number of persons administering juvenile courts believed that official action should reflect the necessities of the child's condition rather than a narrow legal conception of guilt or liability. This "new attitude toward human beings in conflict with the law" was articulated by Judge Miriam Van Waters, among others. The juvenile court, in her view, operated from the belief that "if the offender is *young* the object of court procedure is not to discover whether he has committed a specific offense; but to determine if he is in such a condition that he has lost or has never known the fundamental rights of childhood to parental shelter, guidance, and control" [28]. Accordingly, intervention could not depend on establishment of a narrow jurisdictional predicate. The exercise of power would adhere less to what is ordinarily considered the rule of law, but should reflect instead an assessment of dangerousness independent of violation of specific, previously announced norms.

In a real sense, the juvenile court was originally conceived as a system of "substantive justice" rather than of "legal justice" [29]. The difference between these two ideal types may be illustrated by supposing the case of a child who engages in disorderly conduct. If she is charged with delinquency, the court would do legal justice by determining whether her behavior violated some law and whether violation of that law constitutes delinquency as that category is defined in the juvenile code. Where delinquency is, for example, defined as conduct that would be a "crime" if done by an adult, the court would adjudicate the child a delinquent only if (1) it is satisfactorily established that she engaged in disorderly conduct, as that term is treated under the general law, and (2) if disorderly conduct is a "crime" if committed by an adult. If, however, disorderly conduct is a "violation" but not a "crime" (as is true in New York, for instance), a delinquency finding cannot be made [30]. In contrast, judicial action engages in substantive justice when its direct focus is on the welfare of the child and the safety of society and is unconstrained (not mediated) by prior rules. The respondent in our hypothetical case would be adjudicated delinquent under such a system if that decision would promote the welfare of the public or the child, without resort to technical statutory requirements. It is plain that the latter mode—substantive justice—reflects the expectations of those who urged creation of the juvenile court.

Vagueness and the Mediation of Standards

Had the juvenile court frankly been established as its proponents wished, it would have presented a significant reconstitution of the justice system. The jurisdictional inquiry and scope of material proof would have been radically broadened. As it happened, however, this conception was never fully implemented. The statutes ultimately enacted were the work of lawyers who defined the occasion for intervention conventionally: that is, in terms of specific conduct rather than in terms of general dangerousness [31]. The drafters did, however, go some distance toward accommodating the goals of their constituents by employing expansive definitions of delinquency and neglect. Open-ended categories such as "incorrigibility" or "growing up in idleness" were added to virtually exhaustive lists of specifically proscribed behavior in an effort to stretch as broadly as possible the conventional conduct requirement [32]. In practice, the combination of expansive statutory language and relaxed rules of evidence and procedure combined to approximate a system of substantive justice of the kind initially contemplated but not formally enacted. Allegations that a child was "incorrigibile" or "growing up in idleness" made relevant at adjudication evidence bearing on the child's general history; moreover, reception of such evidence was not constrained by rules of first hand knowledge and the like [33]. This information, in turn, would support an adjudication of wardship which did not reflect any special concern for the strength of proof of particular misconduct. For most juvenile courts, Judge Mack's dictum was literally followed: "The problem for determination by the judge is not, Has this boy or girl committed a specific wrong, but What is he, how has he become what he is, and what had best be done in his interest and in the interest of the state to save him from a downward career" [34].

The discussion thus far demonstrates that PINS jurisdiction embodies a set of fundamental conceptual contradictions, which it seeks to resolve through the mediating device of general standards. On the one hand, PINS laws attempt to apply the rule of law to a relationship of status governed essentially by personal domination. On the other, it reflects a desire to do substantive justice without abandoning the formal requirements of legal justice. Broad, imprecise legislative standards were introduced in an effort to mediate these contradictions.

In view of the conceptual inconsistencies underlying PINS jurisdiction, the "vagueness" of PINS statutes can not be considered accidental. Whether the resulting breadth and imprecision of some PINS statutes is of constitutional dimension has been the subject of considerable discussion [35] and a number of decisions [36]. If ordinary vagueness tests are applied, many of these laws are subject to challenge. Returning to the Ohio statute quoted above, a rule prohibiting a person from behaving so "as to injure or endanger the health or morals of himself or others" can guide neither the conduct of citizens nor of officials. Jurisdictional categories such as "vagrancy" and "immorality" have regularly been held unconstitutionally indefinite [37], and a statute allowing the jury to assess a civil penalty if it found an acquitted criminal defendant nevertheless guilty of "some misconduct" has been similarly treated [38]. A law that purports to attach sanctions, not only to immoral conduct but also to conduct that "endangers the morals" of the actor or of others, is even more unclear in its meaning. The same can be said of the provision in the Ohio statute recognizing jurisdiction over a child who is in a "situation dangerous to life or limb or injurious to the health or morals of himself or another." It is unclear whether anything more than wholly innocent conduct by the child is required to make him "unruly," and the "situations" injurious to health or morals may, in the eyes of the police and possibly the courts, include presence at rock concerts, Unification Church meetings, busing demonstrations, pool halls, street corners, or in the limb of a tree. Thus the child, like an adult under a vagrancy statute, may be suffered to engage in a great number of activities "only at the whim of any police officer."

That this circumstance is no more tolerable with respect to children facing substantial deprivation of their freedom than it is with respect to adults has occasionally been recognized [39] but, more commonly, denied by state and lower federal courts [40]. This rejection of vagueness challenges, especially in connection with statutes covering "immorality" or the like, has been severely criticized by a number of authorities [41]. These critics convincingly apply usual vagueness standards to provisions of the kind just mentioned, and we do not propose to repeat their arguments. There are, however, some incorrigibility statutes that could, if one looks only to ordinary vagueness standards, survive a constitutional challenge or could, without violence to the overall legislative design, be amended so as to satisfy usual constitutional standards. Because our concern is with the function of the rule of law in connection with state regulation of parent-child relations, we propose to examine in the second part of this essay the consequences associated with adopting a PINS law that in terms will probably or certainly survive an orthodox vagueness challenge, even assuming—as we think is surely true—that the consequences of delinquency or PINS proceedings on the ground of incorrigibility are such that ordinary vagueness standards apply despite the "non-criminal" denomination of such proceedings [42]. We will consider three such formulations for this purpose. The first defines incorrigibility in terms of disobedience to parental commands, without further qualification. A provision so phrased removes ambiguity from the definition of misconduct. Children are effectively placed on notice concerning the behavior expected of them: that they obey *all* parental commands. Judges, police, and other officials are likewise informed of the occasions for legitimate intervention; they may act when it is claimed or proved that the child has disobeyed her parents. Thus, the criteria upon which statutes are upheld against constitutional vagueness attacks seem to be satisfied.

Our second formulation qualifies the child's duty of obedience by introducing a requirement that legal intervention occur only when the command disobeyed was *reasonable*. Although introduction of such a condition, which is commonly found in existing laws [43], imports a degree of ambiguity into the definition of wrongdoing, statutes penalizing "unreasonable" conduct have often been sustained. In *United States v. Ragen* [44], the Supreme Court upheld the conviction of a taxpayer for violation of a provision making illegal the taking of an "unreasonable allowance" for salaries on an income tax return. In the course of its decision, the Court remarked that "The mere fact that a penal statute is so framed as to require a jury upon occasion to determine a question of reasonableness is not sufficient to make it too vague to afford a practical guide to permissible conduct" [45]. Perhaps even more closely in point is *Edgar A. Levy Leasing Co. v. Siegel* [46], sustaining rent control legislation which treated reasonableness as a matter of excuse in allowing a tenant to defeat his landlord's action by showing that the rent charged was "unjust and unreasonable." And, of course, statutes proscribing "negligent," "careless," or "reckless" behavior have routinely been upheld [47].

While some statutes employing reasonableness as the test for legality have been invalidated [48], the impossibility of achieving true precision in incorrigibility statutes, together with the general knowledge of children that they are obliged to obey their parents, suggest that the degree of indefiniteness may not be fatal. As Fuller has remarked, "To put a high value on legislative clarity is not to condemn out of hand rules that make legal consequences depend on standards such as 'good faith' and 'due care.' Sometimes the best way to achieve clarity is to take advantage of, and to incorporate into the law, common sense standards of judgment that have grown up in the ordinary life outside legislative halls" [49]. We will return to this point in the next section.

The third formulation we will discuss, also currently employed in a number of laws [50], defines incorrigibility as *habitual* or *persistent* disobedience to parental commands. In some jurisdictions, this qualification has been interpreted to mean only that more than one instance of misconduct be proved [51]. Where this is so, the definition is as precise as that of the unconditional rule discussed above, and no vagueness problem arises. Even if a less precise meaning is given to the term "habitual," it does not follow that the statute is constitutionally vague under traditional doctrine. The nature of the duty expressed is known to those affected by it and is generally accepted by society as important. While the court may be required to make judgments of degree under this rule, standard doctrine suggests that such judgments may constitutionally be incorporated into a penal or regulatory statute [52].

THE RULE OF LAW AND PINS STATUTES:
A DIALECTIC OF FORM AND SUBSTANCE

We have argued that the problem of vagueness arose as a consequence of attempting to apply the rule of law to a relationship governed essentially by personal domination—a relationship of status. Vagueness appeared in the form of those imprecise standards which carried the burden of mediating between the demands of legal formality and the desire for substantive justice. The remedy for vagueness in PINS statutes, as the three formulations mentioned demonstrate, lies not in narrow specification of proscribed conduct but in global regulation of children. Two factors make it impossible to achieve statutory definiteness by specifying the kinds of behavior giving rise to need for supervision. The first is that the particular forms of misbehavior are virtually infinite since the particular commands that parents may give—disobedience to which justifies intervention— are virtually infinite. The second is that the particular commands uttered by various parents to their children may be inconsistent. One parent might tell his child to come home after school to do her homework; another may order the child to help mind the store after school: failure to do either may found an incorrigibility complaint. Since it is youthful disobedience rather than an act itself that causes the social concern expressed in PINS laws, definiteness concerning the underlying conduct cannot be had.

Achieving statutory definiteness through increasing the ambit of control in this global way could be contemplated only with respect to children and is accepted in their case only because of their dependent status. Significantly, analogous control over adults is found only in association with institutionally recognized and general deprivations of citizenship, such as imprisonment for crime and commitment as an insane or mentally deficient person. It is not otherwise attempted because liberal political principles and the rule of law demand that persons be left free except to the extent specific justification for infringement is present and the nature of this infringement is thought sufficiently clear that persons may avoid official intervention in their lives. The following discussion will address the problem of definiteness in PINS laws by considering in more detail the nature of the parent-child relationship and the consequences—both inside the family and in society generally—of attempting to supervise that relationship through forms derived from the rule of law.

Socialization to Authority
and Development of Autonomy

In its ideal form the rule of law in modern society mediates between the domination of personal authority and the experience of pure autonomy. Because it must rely on language, this mediation is generally unstable and problematic,* but in the context of a legal jurisdiction supervising the relations between parents and children the difficulty is particularly severe precisely because there are strong interests both in maintaining a regime of personal (parental) domination and in facilitating the development of the (child's) sense of and capacity for autonomy. The problem of the mediation of the rule of law in this context may be considered from several perspectives, each of which locates the doctrine of vagueness at the center of a legal regime concerned with relations between parents and their children. The first of these perspectives is one of socialization to authority and development of autonomy.

It is systematically expected that parents will acculturate and socialize their children [53]. Indeed, the perception that parents in any given case are not willing or able to do so is the principal occasion for juvenile court intervention. On the one hand, these processes imply that children will learn and accept cultural goals in general and will conform their conduct to rules in particular. At the same time, the end point of these processes is adulthood, upon which the person becomes a full citizen whose behavior is autonomous except as limited by

*The problem of language is considered in more detail *infra* at p. 222 *et seq.*

the rule of law. Proper child rearing must accordingly facilitate the development of a capacity for choice and autonomous action within existing norms. A child who does not learn social values and rules has not been properly raised; equally a person without capacity for autonomous behavior remains an infant. Thus, the complex of authority, rules, and autonomy is a fundamental aspect of parental responsibility for children.

Within the family, authority is essentially personal; for the child the experience of authority is the experience of the personal domination of parents. As the child grows, the level or degree of parental authority is reduced, and this reduction corresponds to growth in the child's capacity for autonomous action and choice. Unless both parents and children agree with respect to the appropriate ambits of control and autonomy, however, the parents will regard the child as ungovernable (that is, excessively or prematurely autonomous), or the child will regard parental authority as unjustified, or both.

This synchronous process is complicated by the principle that beyond early childhood the domination of personal authority is generally unjustified. Coercive authority in modern society must be embodied in rules. This means that the personal authority of parents must gradually be replaced by the impersonal authority of rules. That transition is necessary for reasons of socialization and for reasons of development. A child who does not learn that the exercise of personal domination is unjustified and that the experience of personal domination is oppressive has not been properly socialized. Similarly, the absence of a capacity for autonomous action and choice constitutes infantalization. Adults improperly socialized and/or undeveloped with respect to authority and autonomy are more likely than others to become social problems of one sort or another. Thus, the same general social interest that explains concern for the socialization of authority justifies emphasis on the development of autonomy.

It is important not to underestimate the significance of the introduction of rules in the relations between parents and children. This process undermines the personal domination of parental authority without replacing it, and facilitates the development of autonomy without literally requiring it. The period in the child's life when the mediation of rules is most consciously present is generally a difficult one, and it is at just this time that PINS jurisdiction tends to be invoked. The court under that jurisdiction intervenes in a family dispute by virtue of a rule which specifies the limits of parental authority, the level of obedience required of the child, or both [54]. The fact of intervention by rule, however, is as significant as the substance of the particular rule, and such intervention—occurring at that point in the history of the family when the distribution of emphasis within the complex of parental authority, rules, and child autonomy is most unstable—underscores the salience of rules at the expense of both parental authority and youthful autonomy.

To demonstrate why this is so, it is useful to consider the operation of an unconditional PINS statute. The parents complain that their child is ungovernable in that she refuses to obey their commands. The child asserts that her parents' commands are incoherent, unreasonable or oppressive. The judge informs the child of the legal requirement that she obey *all* parental commands, and that if she fails to do so she will be placed under some other form of supervision.

Viewed from within the family it is supposed to regulate, the consequence of intervention is that the obedience of the child is now a direct consequence of external rule—the rule of law which requires unconditional obedience by the child. Though the substance of the legal command reenforces the personal domination of parental authority, the form of a rule of law undermines that authority in favor of obedience to rules [55]. Intervention by rule of law moves the child in the direction of autonomy by undermining the personal authority of parents, while it supports that authority by ordering unconditional obedience.

If one turns from the meaning of intervention within the family to its meaning for a social order governed by the rule of law, the consequence of intervention is the converse of its effect within the family. The court has intervened by invoking a general and fairly precise rule. No substantial claim can be made that the application of the rule to this case is a result of uncontrolled judicial discretion or could not have been foreseen by the parties. To this extent the requirements of social order are satisfied by a formally adequate rule. According to traditional theory, such a statute facilitates the experience of autonomy by specifying the ambit of choice. In this instance, however, the rule in substance negates the experience of autonomy by stating that the child must obey her parents unconditionally. Thus, the experience of personal domination is only partially eliminated by this rule. The illustration makes clear that formal adequacy is a necessary but not a sufficient condition of autonomy within the social order [56].

The application of an unambiguous rule requiring unconditional obedience gives rise to a set of paradoxes. The substance of the rule supports parental authority at the expense of autonomy, while the fact that it is an external rule undermines that authority in the service of the development of autonomy. Simultaneously, although the unconditional rule satisfies the formal requirements set forth by the vagueness doctrine, its substance undermines the child's capacity for autonomous action and thus frustrates one of the principal values associated with a social order based on rules. If, as one assumes, it is preservation of those values which warrants invocation of the due process clause, our analysis collaterally suggests that reliance on the traditional vagueness doctrine may be dysfunctional, at least when the law seeks definiteness through global rather than specific description of the proscribed behavior. Certainly that seems to be the case here, where the most precisely drafted statute—the one which would most readily be sustained under ordinary vagueness standards—most directly compromises the values of the rule of law.

A "Reasonable Command" Rule and the Perspective of Control and Responsibility

The paradoxes revealed by the perspective of authority and autonomy arise, as we have seen, from the nature of the PINS enterprise itself: importation of the rule of law, which presupposes a relationship of the kind that exists between citizen and state to a relationship in which personal domination is valued and which resembles status rather than citizenship. The question now is whether this set of paradoxes may be eliminated by modifying the content of the rule within the bounds of the vagueness doctrine or whether any formulation consistent with the rule of law produces contradictions of the sort already observed. Initially, we will consider the result under a rule requiring obedience only to reasonable parental commands, and in the course of that inquiry will introduce a second perspective—one of control and responsibility—to that of socialization and development.

At first glance, a rule of obedience qualified by reasonableness seems to reduce the paradox demonstrated by the perspective of socialization and development. On the one hand, the substance of the rule supports only a limited ambit of parental authority and to that extent permits the development of autonomy. And, as was true of the unconditional formulation, the rule is external to the parental authority it supposedly asserts and therefore pushes in the direction of autonomy. On the other hand, while the substance of the rule supports the development of autonomy to a greater extent than an unqualified rule, it reduces both the general level of autonomy in society and the child's experience of freedom from personal domination by introducing a measure of uncertainty in the reach of the rule. The result of qualifying the requirement of obedience is not so much to remove the experience of personal domination but to substitute judicial for parental domination. A qualified rule accordingly perpetuates the initial paradox, but in somewhat different form. As between parent and child it intervenes on the side of developmental autonomy, but does so by sacrificing the clarity of rules upon which general social autonomy is said to depend.

The nature of this contradiction is clarified when attention is directed to the allocation of control and responsibility effected by the qualified rule of obedience. As a general proposition, control and responsibility are mutually exclusive notions. All members of society are deemed either capable of assuming responsibility for their acts or they are not [57]. In the latter event, they may properly be subjected to the control of others. Because control is predicated upon lack of capacity for responsible action (usually for reasons of mental disease or defect), those who are deemed subject to control will not be held responsible for their acts, at least when those acts relate to the sphere of control [58]. It is only the person who is not under control that may be held responsible for her acts in this scheme.

The position of children under incorrigibility laws of the kind discussed here falls, however, into neither category. An unconditional rule of obedience would say that all children are under parental control with respect to the infinite range of matters parents might choose to regulate. At the same time, most older children would be held responsible for precisely the same range of conduct; that is, they would be adjudicated delinquent or in need of supervision for choosing to act in a manner contrary to their parents' commands [59]. Thus, children are simultaneously subject to control and responsible for their acts relating to the potentially infinite sphere of control. Specifically, the child's wrongdoing lies in her failure to obey—an "omission" in standard criminal law terms—for which she will be held responsible.*

While the contradiction in ideas of control and responsibility is clearest in connection with an unconditional rule, its special significance becomes apparent in considering the rule of obedience to reasonable commands. Such a rule tells the child that the ambit of parental authority (control) is limited to commands which are reasonable—that is, which accurately reflect the child's own limitations. Implicitly, if not expressly, the qualified rule also tells the child that she is autonomous with respect to unreasonable parental commands—presumably, those which impose limitations more stringent than her own capacity justifies. She will be held responsible, therefore, for judging correctly whether a parental command was reasonable, which judgment must necessarily be independent of the parent's own determination implicit in the act of commanding obedience. The child will, in effect, be held responsible for going beyond the limits of her sphere of responsibility.

The relationship between the contradictions apparent under this perspective and those associated with socialization and autonomy is evident. The degree of autonomy available under a "reasonable command" rule is a function of the child's capacity for responsible action. While qualification of the duty of obedience formally provides the youth some sphere of freedom, that sphere is simultaneously limited by the nature of the decision she must make. A determination that a given command is "reasonable," after all, comprises all that there is to be said about both child and family—the former's age, maturity, prior experience, school history, psychological characteristics, and special needs; the latter's strength, mutual relationships, values, aspirations, psychological needs. The child cannot well rely on her capacity to assess these variables as the judge will and, therefore, cannot safely assert freedom from parental commands. Moreover, the less able she is to make such an evaluation, the more likely it is that she will be held properly under control and responsible for her omission to submit to that control. Nor will intervention under such a standard clarify the parent-child relationship for the future. The generality of the governing standard and the impermanent character of the circumstances taken into account suggest that each decision will be a new one.

---

*In the general criminal law, offenses characterized by omissions are problematic on two grounds: the character of the duty or its scope is frequently obscure and the absence of an affirmative act makes assessment of culpability difficult. Both of these are varieties of the problem of vagueness and hence give rise to analysis in terms of the rule of law.

The qualified rule also complicates the situation outside the context of the particular family. The court must intervene either on the side of the parent who complains that the child has disobeyed a reasonable command or on the side of the child who claims the command was unreasonable, but it can no longer do so with perfect assurance that it is mediating authority and autonomy with precise rules.* Consequently, intervention may be experienced by the losing party as an unjustified exercise of personal domination by the judge.

In summary, we have noted that the paradox of autonomy and authority tends to be ameliorated when an unconditional rule is made conditional; the modification pushes in the direction of autonomy. However, introducing the perspective of control and responsibility indicates that a qualified rule undermines the mediating capacity of rules both within the particular family and in society generally. Within the family, introducing a standard of reasonableness produces a direct confrontation of authority with autonomy by reducing the mediating power of a clear rule: it reduces that mediation by making the child responsible for determining the reasonable limits of control over her. Outside the particular family, the introduction of a qualified rule makes judicial discriminations more obviously subjective and idiosyncratic, and thus opens up the possibility that public authority will be experienced as personal (judicial) domination rather than as a social order open to autonomous action and choice within general, impersonal rules. While the qualified or conditional rule mitigates the paradox of authority and autonomy which the conditional rule generates by its contradiction of form and substance, it simultaneously undermines the child's development of rule-oriented autonomy within the family and the general social experience of freedom from unjustified authority which the rule of law otherwise assures.

An "Habitual Disobedience" Rule and the
Perspective of Character and Choice
We turn now to consideration of the third PINS formulation that appears facially consistent with the requirements of statutory definiteness: a rule which

---

*The characterization of the failure of obedience as an act of omission complicated the situation outside the family in yet another way. The PINS jurisdiction does not exist simply to resolve minor squabbles within the family, but to deal with behavior problems with which the parents appear unable to cope. This implies that the judge must distinguish those cases in which the child is in need of supervision from those cases in which she is not. The character of failure of obedience as a type of omission "offense," in combination with obscurity in the scope of the duty to obey *reasonable* commands, makes this distinction particularly difficult. Together they open up several possibilities: the child may have honestly and sincerely believed that the command was unreasonable, and otherwise stands ready to obey all reasonable commands; or disobedience may mean that the child never bothered to determine with any degree of care or seriousness whether the command was or was not reasonable; or the child may have known full well that the command was reasonable but chose to exploit the ambiguity of the qualified rule of obedience to her own advantage or simply to drive her parents crazy. The absence of an affirmative act and the absence of certainty in the rule combine to make judicial selection among these alternatives especially difficult.

subjects a child to coercive disposition only if she *habitually* disobeys the (reasonable) commands of her parents. In conjunction with this standard, a third perspective, that of character and choice, will be added for purposes of analysis.

The perspective of character and choice is directly related to an essential function of PINS laws—that of distinguishing those children who ought to be subject to coercive disposition from those who should not. If the original juvenile court theory had been formally adopted, this determination could have been reached by consideration of all information bearing on the respondent's character, without necessary reliance on concrete instances of behavior. The inclusion of an act requirement in both delinquency and PINS statutes requires, however, that dangerousness in children be predicted from behavior [60], and evidentiary rules further require that, where jurisdiction is defined entirely in terms of disobedience, only evidence related to the child's conduct or omission be admitted. Thus, a decision that a given child needs supervision beyond that to which she is accustomed must initially depend on proved misbehavior. But behavior by itself says little about the actor's character or particularly her dangerousness; it is neutral unless the actor was aware that her conduct was wrongful and chose nevertheless to engage in it. In this respect, the judgment which distinguishes children on the basis of behavior presupposes that children retain some general capacity for choice and have exercised that capacity on one or more occasions. Operationally, behavior is evidence that choices have been made, and the way choices are made says something but not everything about character. Thus, the perspective of character and choice is directly related to the judicial need to differentiate among children.

Since behavior is the basis for inferring choice, the importance of statutory definiteness is obvious. The area of proscribed activity must be sufficiently unambiguous that one may know its existence for any inference about choice to be permissible. This is important for the citizen, who is entitled to remain free of authority unless she could have chosen to stay within the law; it is equally important from an institutional perspective since, without adequate precision, the central inference justifying intervention cannot be made. The clearer the law, it is thought, the more confidence one may have that offenders knew what their choices were and chose to violate the law. Correlatively, the more confident one is that the actor so chose, the clearer the inference about her character.

The perspective of character and choice builds upon the two previous perspectives in the following way. It is related in an obvious way to the perspective of control and responsibility. To the extent the child chooses among options she may be held responsible for her choices. Holding her responsible for her choices means making an assessment of her character; making a judgment about the degree of control she needs must necessarily take her past choices into account. In turn, a judicial assessment of character and need for control will determine the distribution of authority and autonomy in the child's immediate future. Put another way, character and choice, control and responsibility, both determine and are determined by the socialization of authority and the development of autonomy. Socialization (authority), control, and character are thus related to each other in the way development (autonomy), responsibility, and choice are related to each other.*

The introduction of a requirement that the child must *habitually* disobey the reasonable commands of her parents before becoming subject to legal control may ameliorate the contradictions discussed above. The extent to which it does so is, however, inversely proportional to the clarity of the term "habitual." If that term means, as it commonly does, that there need only be more than one instance of disobedience, the resulting ambit of choice is virtually valueless. In order to supply a significant range of autonomy for children, the condition for intervention must be made not more precise but more ambiguous by, for example, interpreting it to mean an extended course of defiance or multiple occasions of serious wrongdoing. An "habitualness" qualification, so interpreted, does not communicate a mixed message of the sort which results from the unconditional or "reasonableness" rules. The unconditional rule substantively affirms parental authority while formally undermining it; the rule qualified by reasonableness tends to distribute its emphasis in the direction of developmental autonomy but undercuts this autonomy (within the family) by forcing the child to make judgments she is, by definition, poorly equipped to make. A rule qualified further to cover only *habitual* disobedience of reasonable commands distributes its emphasis in the direction of increased developmental autonomy by refusing to intervene except in the more extraordinary cases, and it lifts some of the burden of choice from the child by allowing her greater margin of error in making judgments of reasonableness before external coercive intervention will be regarded as necessary. Within the family, then, the doubly qualified rule may push in the direction of autonomy by refusing to intervene in what the rule describes substantively as instances of minor disobedience.

Outside the family context, however, the situation is not so hopeful. The doubly qualified rule indicates that when a child is made subject to the PINS jurisdiction, the appropriateness of coercive disposition is to be determined on the basis of a history of choices made over time. The doubly qualified rule does not permit any single choice to be made the basis of a judgment of character, and prior to actual litigation there is no way to predict which choices will be considered relevant to the assessment of character, or how many such choices are either necessary or sufficient.

The situation might be compared with profit to the adult criminal process.

---

*The relationship would appear as follows in tabular form:

Perspective	*Authority*	*Autonomy*
First	Socialization	Development
Second	Control	Responsibility
Third	Character	Choice

The criminal law presupposes that adults have a matured capacity for choice so that a discrete instance of behavior may be made the basis for a legal judgment which carries serious consequences for the adult. In a real sense the criminal law assesses character on the basis of one particular exercise of choice [61], but it may do so only so long as its presupposition of a mature cognitive and affective capacity for choice is firmly tied to reality.

This presupposed capacity for choice must be weaker in the case of children. An assessment of their character cannot and should not be made on the basis of isolated instances of behavior; one needs a history or pattern of behavior. However, reliance on a history or pattern of behavior reduces the relative significance of any particular exercise of choice. Where the criminal law demands that the facts which constitute a particular event be meticulously examined because all judgments depend on those facts, under the doubly qualified rule a rigorous factual inquiry with respect to any particular event is considerably less important precisely because no single event has dispositive significance.

The doubly qualified rule produces the following situation. Within the family it pushes in the direction of autonomy and places considerably less emphasis on socialization; it also reduces the child's burden of responsibility by eliminating the need for her to make an accurate assessment of reasonableness in each instance. But outside the family, the doubly qualified rule undermines the social level of autonomy within rules by fracturing the clarity and simplicity of rule-based judgments, leaving obscure which exercises of choice will be subsequently considered relevant in an assessment of character. Correlatively, this formulation makes impossible any confident prediction of the number or seriousness of acts which will occasion intervention; since the relative significance of any particular instance of behavior is reduced by its inclusion in a history or pattern of behavior, it makes unnecessary an accurate, careful or complete determination of the factual circumstances of each instance. In short, the doubly qualified rule intensifies the experience of personal (judicial) domination, and thus weakens the social sense of autonomy within impersonal, general rules. The measure of developmental autonomy within the family which the doubly qualified rule permits is reversed outside the family by a reduction of general social autonomy within the rule of law.

This analysis leads to the following observation. A PINS jurisdiction can maintain the rule of law only at the cost of communicating to parents and children an ambiguous social message regarding the proper mix of socialization and development, authority and autonomy within the family. This confusion can be reduced by introducing qualified rules which tend to push in the direction of developmental autonomy *within* the family, but simultaneously do violence to the rule of law in society. Consequently, these rules cut against the general social experience of autonomy within rules. A more concise formulation of this observation is that a PINS jurisdiction which respects autonomy is incompatible with the rule of law in society; a PINS jurisdiction based on the rule of law interferes with the socialization of authority and the development of autonomy mediated by rules within the family.

THE RULE OF LAW AND THE INQUIRY INTO DANGEROUSNESS

The foregoing analysis throws into serious doubt the traditional assumption that a social order based on rules necessarily provides those governed by it with a knowable area of autonomy, responsibility and choice. Indeed, it has appeared that the more PINS laws conform to the rule of law through definiteness of language, the more severely autonomy, responsibility, and choice are compromised. This conclusion leads to further doubt concerning a fundamental tenet of criminal law theory discussed throughout this essay: that a social order based on rules and one founded on an inquiry directly into dangerousness, not mediated by prescriptive rules, present an antinomy [62].

Normal version theory, as we have seen, assumes that a sharp contrast can be drawn between a society ordered by specific prescriptive rules and one in which rules are instrumental and directly oriented to goals. This is the political meaning of the difference between "legal" and "substantive" justice. As generally understood, the vagueness doctrine is a logical corollary of government by legal justice or by the rule of law. Statutory definiteness is thought to assure the uniformity and generality of legal rules which in turn are expected to mediate between the experience of personal domination and that of perfect autonomy. Rules which do not meet a minimum degree of specificity fail to eliminate the experience of domination because their application depends on the subjective judgment of those exercising authority. The vagueness doctrine attempts to identify those rules which are not law [63].

With this model we may contrast a PINS law that is facially inconsistent with the rule of law: one that focuses directly on the child's dangerousness. It has the same general goal as the three formulations discussed in the preceding part—identification of that excessive assertion of youthful autonomy which creates concern for the child's future behavior. Unlike those formulations, however, the proposed statute would abandon jurisdictional definitions referring to particular behavior (i.e., disobedience of parental commands of whatever quality and with whatever regularity) and authorize intervention upon a finding that the child is dangerous in the same sense assumed by current statutes: that her disobedience is manifested within a universe of circumstances which suggest that, without intervention, she is likely to become an adult deviant.

Lawyers will quickly say that such a statute is contrary to what we mean by law. The dangerousness inquiry gives no notice of the conduct that occasions official intervention, nor does it confine the exercise of authority by public officials. Moreover, the law provides no assurance of uniform and equal application, because the exercise of power in any individual case does not depend on objective behavior that can be evaluated for its similarity to behavior in other cases. All these objections are directed, ultimately, to a single claim: that the term "dangerousness," as used here, is vague.

Initially, it should be apparent that the difference between the rule of law and the dangerousness rule in this respect must be at most one of degree. The generality and uniformity of the rule of law depends heavily on language. The meaning of a rule must be sufficiently clear to citizens that they might exercise a margin of autonomy free of concern for the potential illegality of their conduct. The extent to which they may be secure in this freedom further depends on the degree of assurance that officials will not read the language of a rule in such a way that given conduct will be included within it. In general, acceptance of a regime of rules implies a belief that the language of rules exercises real control over the officials charged with their enforcement; in no other way can the experience of personal domination be eliminated. The rule of law is, therefore, weakened to the extent there is no substantial unanimity on the meaning of a particular set of words. That is the precise significance of the vagueness doctrine.

We know, however—intuitively or as a matter of common experience—that substantial unanimity on the meaning of a particular set of words is highly problematic. The problem cannot be avoided, moreover, by choosing words that are clear and avoiding words that are not. Ambiguity or vagueness is not a problem of language as such; some words are not inherently more clear or more ambiguous than others. Rather, the precision of language is relational [64] : if a given locution corresponds to a common experience or shared value, it is clear; otherwise it is not. Accordingly, adherence to the rule of law requires that a given locution correspond to common experience or shared values. This judgment of correspondence is what is required by the legal doctrine of vagueness.

Perhaps the most common method of dealing with the problem of determining the existence of shared meaning is to distinguish between the "core meaning" of a legal proposition expressed in words and its potential or "penumbral" meanings. The core meaning is said to be that reading of legal language which would produce substantial unanimity. The notion of core meaning serves, however, only to expose and not to remove the central difficulty posed by the rule of law's entire dependence on language.

In the first place, the determination of correspondence between statutory language and core meaning must be made by a judge, who initially must determine what the core meaning is and then decide whether that core meaning corresponds to common experience or shared values. Actually, however, what seem to be two steps is a single operation, for the judge cannot subjectively determine the core meaning of the language; he must determine whether the given set of words has a core meaning in common experience or shared values. Plainly this is an empirical question of some difficulty. There is no little irony in the observation that the most politically defensible method for resolving the question is through popular representation in the legislature: as representatives of the people, the legislature should be in the best position to know whether a set of words has a core meaning. But, of course, the problem of vagueness only arises in the context of legislative products.

If the doctrine of vagueness requires a judgment of correspondence between a set of words and common experience or shared values, and if there appears to be no way for the judge to have ready access to the information he needs to make this decision, on what basis are these decisions actually made? At best, the judgment must be made on the basis of a judicial assessment of the character of common experience or the nature of shared values. But the general absence of the data essential to the making of such an assessment leads one to believe that judgments of correspondence are entirely subjective.

We are left, therefore, with a fundamental weakness in the capacity of the rule of law to accomplish its fundamental purpose: the accurate and precise statement, beforehand, of the circumstances in which intervention is justified. Ultimately, judgments concerning the meaning and enforceability of a statute depend on subjective decisions by the judge concerning the nature of common experience or shared values. This is precisely what the rule of law is supposed to avoid, and precisely what—as the vagueness doctrine makes clear—it cannot successfully avoid.

It should also be observed that if a given set of words expresses a core meaning, the expression necessarily reflects very common experience or broadly shared values. To the extent an experience is common or a value broadly shared, it is fair to ask why a rule expressed in clear language is necessary at all. In this situation, it is surely not the language of the rule which provides citizens with notice and which constrains official behavior, but the shared understanding of the experience or value. In a real sense, therefore, adherence to the rule of law does not account for and is unnecessary to compliance: there is no reason to expect less obedience to a more imprecise rule or, perhaps, even to a non-prescriptive rule. Recall, for example, our earlier illustration of a relatively precise legal rule: a child must obey all parental commands. The duty of obedience children owe to their parents is surely within common experience and we may assume it is a shared value. To this extent, the language has a core meaning. But that meaning lies embedded in common experience and shared values; it is not elaborated by the legal language. Would the absence of a rule change anything of consequence? Plainly the common experience or shared value would not vanish. It may, of course, be said that, since not all shared experiences and values are legally cognizable, notice must be given that this one is and authority to enforce it must be conferred—hence, the necessity of a rule. But notice could be given and authority conferred by a rule which stated that the duty of children to obey their parents will be enforced. If youthful disobedience is the product of children's common understanding of their duty in this regard, as seems likely, they will comply with such a rule independently of technical legal specification.

Thus, because the rule of law is entirely at the mercy of the signifying capacity of language, its capacity and indispensability to achieve its own purposes is impeached. Statutory commands are neither objective guides to compliance with legal rules nor necessary to accomplishment of their social meaning. Furthermore, the doctrine of vagueness requires a judgment of correspondence between a set of words and common experience or shared values, and if there appears to be no way for the judge to have ready access to the information he should have to make this judgment, it must be made on the basis of a subjective assessment of the character of common experience or the nature of shared values. This is a critical point. The *attitude* which allows participants in the legal process to behave as though legal language is generally clear (i.e., that it corresponds to common experience or shared values) and as if, when there is doubt on the matter, an objective judgment can be made, *stands between* the application of legal terms to concrete cases and the actual existence of common experience or shared values. In other words, the *attitude* which assumes an ability to distinguish between those legal locutions which have a core meaning and those which do not *mediates* between the application of legal terms in concrete cases and the unknown common experience or shared values [65].

If, as it now appears, traditional vagueness doctrine claims too much for the rule of law, our analysis of PINS laws further reveals that even relatively definite statutes may fail to accomplish their purposes and, we would argue, relatively less definite statutes may be as well suited to that end. Given the values served by the rule of law, the following ought to be true if the distinction between it and an inquiry into dangerousness is valid: the PINS formulations consistent with the rule of law, discussed at length in this chapter, should (1) eliminate or ameliorate the experience of personal domination, whereas a dangerousness formulation should heighten it; (2) provide for a significant range of autonomy by citizens, whereas a dangerousness formulation should contract the ambit of autonomy; (3) limit the scope of governmental intrusiveness into individual and group activities, whereas the dangerousness approach should increase intrusiveness.

None of these propositions is true. The formulation that most closely conforms to the rule of law creates a duty of *absolute* obedience on the part of children. This statute has a clear meaning insofar as any has: none of its key terms (child, parent, obey, command) fails to correspond with common experience or shared values. Moreover, these terms are relatively precise, clearly notifying parents, children, and officials of what the law will enforce. This very clarity, however, increases for the child both the fact and the perception of personal domination. Within the family, it makes children subject to universal regulation of their activities by a source of authority identical to the source of its exercise. Parents are both rule-makers and rule-enforcers, and the rules they apply need not have general application. It would be no defense for the respondent to argue that, while she has to carry out the garbage, her siblings have no chores. Nor do qualified rules of obedience resolve this difficulty. A duty of obedience to *reasonable* commands only shifts the source of personal domination from parents to judge. While such a rule continues the presence of external rules governing parental domination, the condition of its operation is sufficiently unclear that no limits on judicial determination of deviance can be perceived. Thus, the judge becomes the maker and enforcer of rules, and the generality of the inquiry into reasonableness militates against the notion that the rules ultimately applied are necessarily uniform. Finally, reliance on a definition of *habitual* disobedience also raises serious problems. If habitual means only "more than once," it in no way relieves the child's experience of personal domination by parents. If, on the other hand, this formulation is taken to imply some higher level of deviance it goes well beyond the uncertainty of a reasonableness standard. Here judicial action is unpredictable; both formally and practically, intervention will turn on highly individualized rather than general criteria. Thus, the function of the rule of law in eliminating the experience of personal domination by separating authority from its exercise is incompatible with legal regulation of incorrigibility.

Precision of language in PINS laws also has the effect of increasing the law's intrusiveness into individual careers rather than of limiting such intrusion, as the rule of law contemplates. The more definite the formulation, the more this is true. Under a standard of unconditional obedience, any instance of defiance by the child, however trivial or atypical it may be, is sufficient to authorize societal intervention if the parent chooses to complain. Nor is this intervention simply that of a surrogate parent, since the court upon assuming jurisdiction may remove the child from its home, place her on probation, inquire into her entire history, or take any other statutorily authorized step, whatever the natural parents may have had in mind when they invoked that jurisdiction.

We now turn to the operational characteristics of an inquiry into dangerousness. An inquiry of this kind may, despite its lack of guidance to actors and officials, provide a greater range of autonomy to children than do incorrigibility statutes which attempt to comply with the rule of law. The dangerousness formulation itself conveys no particular duty to children and it can further be assumed that actual intervention under the rule will be limited to children with a significant history of ungovernable behavior or who engage in some particularly serious but isolated kind of misconduct. Minors, accordingly, have a range of choice concerning conduct within the family bounded by these limits rather than by each and every command given them. Correlatively, the judge is able to determine directly whether one or more instances of disobedience reflects a simple disagreement about a tolerable level of autonomy for the child and her capacity for responsibility, or a more serious problem in the child's socialization.

By the same token, a dangerousness statute without apparent limits may in fact be less intrusive than existing incorrigibility laws. The latter contemplate constant intervention; the former asserts openly that the public interest requires intervention only when matters are grave. Parental discretion to invoke the process will be reduced because no rational parent can expect judicial review of trivial complaints. Finally, while the substance of the provision is not directly addressed to parental authority, it implicitly supports that authority, but does so only at the point where the weakening of authority seems to involve serious consequences.

We conclude that, at least in the area discussed here, the rule of law and an inquiry into dangerousness are not antinomies. Rather, the real distinction between the two lies in their differential distribution of vagueness and precision [66]. The inquiry into dangerousness is less precise about the sort of conduct proscribed, but considerably more precise about how bad a child must be before she becomes an object of legal concern. The rule of law provision, on the other hand, is more precise about the sort of conduct proscribed but gives greater discretion to parents to invoke the legal process for trivial or improper reasons.

More generally, detailing the operational characteristics of these two types of PINS jurisdiction leads us to the same point as did our analysis from the three perspectives of socialization and development, control and responsibility, and character and choice: a PINS jurisdiction based on rules generates a paradox. On the one hand, it attempts to reenforce parental authority, but it must do so by rules; the child must obey the parent because the rule says so. This proposition has the alternative meaning that children are to be autonomous unless that autonomy is qualified by a rule. In attempting to reenforce the personal domination of parental authority, this type of PINS jurisdiction undermines it in favor of the authority of impersonal rules. On the other hand, in generating broad parental discretion to invoke the legal process and in requiring a broad range of dispositional alternatives scaled by severity, the rule of law model undermines the salience of rules and hence the development of autonomy. Children can never know when parents will decide to take them to court or how seriously the judge will regard their behavior.

A PINS jurisdiction based on dangerousness, in contrast, respects the autonomy of children because it withholds intervention until there is a serious problem of public order. In the meanwhile it leaves the family to work through its problems internally. However, the inquiry into dangerousness depends directly on the existence of common experience and shared values to give notice to parents and children, and to control official discretion. Since the statute does not rely on the mediation of legal assumptions regarding language, the inquiry into dangerousness appears inconsistent with the rule of law.

It is now clear from a variety of perspectives that PINS jurisdiction based on the rule of law interferes with the socialization to authority and the development of autonomy mediated by rules, whereas PINS jurisdiction which respects autonomy and a narrower vision of the public interest is inconsistent with the rule of law. The rule of law generates an unbreakable paradox of authority and autonomy, while dangerousness fails to satisfy the requirements of legal justice.

NOTES TO CHAPTER 6

1. *Ohio Rev. Code* §2151.022 (Supp. 1975).

2. As of July 1975, twenty-seven jurisdictions employed "omnibus clauses" making presentation of unspecified danger to oneself or others a ground for PINS jurisdiction and at least three included living an idle or dissolute life or being in danger of doing so. *See* Appendix.

3. Gonzalez v. Mailliard, No. 50424 (D.C.N.D. Cal., Feb. 9, 1971), judgment vacated and remanded, 416 U.S. 918 (1974) illustrates this strategy. Eight children were taken into custody in connection with an assault on a young girl, which would ordinarily make out a delinquency charge. They were, however, ultimately charged with being in "danger of leading a lewd and dissolute life" under California's equivalent of a PINS statute. Moreover, many juvenile codes freely allow amendment of petitions, not only from one charge to another, but from one jurisdictional category to another. On this practice, *see* W. *Stapleton* and *L. Teitelbaum*, *In Defense of Youth: A Study of the Role of Counsel in American Juvenile Courts* 128–29 (1972); Note, "Rights and Rehabilitation in the Juvenile Courts," 67 *Colum. L. Rev.* 281, 308 (1967); Note, "Minnesota Juvenile Court Rules: Brightening One World for Juveniles," 54 *Minn. L. Rev.* 303, 326 (1969).

4. *See generally*, IJA-ABA, Juvenile Justice Standards Project, *Standards Relating to Non-Criminal Behavior* (Tent. Dr. 1976).

5. Connally v. General Construction Co., 269 U.S. 385, 391 (1926).

6. *See, e.g.*, *L. Fuller, The Morality of Law*, c.2 (1964). *See also*, *E. Freund, Standards of American Legislation* 222–223 (2nd ed. 1965), for evidence that even a constitutional but vague statute may not serve the legislative purpose.

7. *See generally*, Note, "The Void-for-Vagueness Doctrine in the Supreme Court," 109 *U. Pa. L. Rev.* 67 (1960).

8. Fuller expresses this notion in *The Morality of Law*, *supra* note 6 at 39–40: "[T]here can be no rational ground for asserting a man can have a moral obligation to obey a legal rule that does not exist, or is kept secret from him, or that came into existence only after he had acted, or was unintelligible. . . . As the sociologist Simmel has observed, there is a kind of reciprocity between government and the citizen with respect to the observance of rules. Government says to the citizen in effect, 'These are the rules we expect you to follow. If you follow them, you have our assurance that they are the rules that will be applied to your conduct'."

9. *See R. Unger, Knowledge and Politics* 89 (1975).

10. *See id.* at 89–91.

11. Yick Wo v. Hopkins, 118 U.S. 356, 370 (1886).

12. *R. Unger, Supra* note 9 at 88–91.

13. Papachristou v. Jacksonville, 405 U.S. 156, 170 (1972). *See also*, Thornhill v. Alabama, 310 U.S. 88 (1940); Grayned v. Rockford, 408 U.S. 104 (1972).

14. *Cf.* L. Fuller, *Supra* note 6 at 63, n. 21.

15. Maine describes the Roman doctrine of *potestas* in the following way:

[I]n all the relations created by Private Law, the son lived under a domestic despotism which, considering the severity it retained to the last, and the number of centuries through which it endured, constitutes one of the strangest problems in legal history.

. . . [T] he parent, when our information commences, has over his children the *jus vitae necisque*, the power of life and death, and *a fortiori* of uncontrolled corporal chastisement; he can modify their personal condition at pleasure; he can give a wife to his son; he can give his daughter in marriage; he can divorce his children of either sex; he can transfer them to another family by adoption; and he can sell them.

H. Maine, Ancient Law 133 (1864).

16. *E.g., id.* at 156–57, 163–165. Relations within the family have also been offered as the model for the relationship between king and subject in feudal England. *See* Kettner, "The Development of American Citizenship in the Revolutionary Era: The Idea of Volitional Allegiance," 18 *Am. J. Legal History* 208, 208–09 (1974).

17. *F. Hayek, The Road to Serfdom* 78–79 (1944).

18. E.g., Bove v. Pinciotti, 46 Pa. D. & C. 159 (C.P. 1942) ("Marriage is not only a contract but a status and a kind of fealty to the State as well").

19. *See Matza,* "Position and Behavior Patterns of Youth," in *Handbook of Modern Sociology* 191 (R. Faris, ed., 1964).

20. *Id.* at *194.*

21. *Id.* at *193. See generally,* T. Marshall, *Citizenship and Social Class* (1950).

22. It has often been observed that techniques of parental domination have generally shifted from physical coercion to psychological manipulation of various kinds, and it may be that the shift coincides with the establishment of juvenile courts in the early part of this century. *See id.* at 193; Bronfenbrenner, "The Changing American Child," in *Values and Ideals of American Youth* 71 (1961). This trend has tended to produce greater indulgence and, consequently, greater freedom for children. However, such ameliorization does not remove their dependency nor, indeed, substantially modify it as a legal matter.

23. Brief for the National Council of Juvenile Court Judges as *Amicus Curiae, In re* Gault, 387 U.S. 1 (1967).

24. *See, e.g.,* Stanley v. Illinois, 405 U.S. 645, 651 (1972):

The private interest here, that of a man in the children he has sired and raised, undeniably warrants deference and, absent a powerful countervailing interest, protection. . . .

The rights to conceive and to raise one's children have been deemed 'essential' . . . , 'basic civil rights of man' . . . and [r] ights far more precious than property rights.

. . . 'It is cardinal with us that the custody, care and nurture of the child reside first in the parents, whose primary function and freedom include preparation for obligations the state can neither supply nor hinder'."

25. *E.g.,* Cabot, "The Detention of Children as Part of Treatment," in *The Child, The Clinic and The Court* 246, 249 (J. Addams, ed., 1925): "Remember the fathers and mothers have failed, or the child has no business [in the juvenile court], and it is when they failed that the state opened this way to receive them, into the court, and said, 'This is the way in which we want you to grow up'."

Similar expressions are found throughout the "child-saving" literature. *See generally*, A. Platt, *The Child Savers* (1969); W. Stapleton and L. Teitelbaum, *Supra* note 3, ch. 1.

This concern was not "libertarian" in complexion. The primary justifying goal of the movement was prevention of future misconduct; those espousing the juvenile court, like those who argued for use of reformatories rather than penitentiaries, assumed that this goal could best be accomplished by rehabilitative rather than retributive devices. Creation of special courts for children was expected to end the "miscarriages of justice" whereby, at the end of the 19th century, youthful offenders "were let off [in criminal prosecutions] because often justices could neither tolerate sending children to the bridewell nor bear to be themselves guilty of the harsh folly of compelling poverty-stricken parents to pay fines." Lathrop, "The Background of the Juvenile Court in Illinois," in *The Child, The Clinic and The Court* 290, 290—91 (J. Addams, ed. 1927). Moreover, reformation—implying resocialization in a broad sense—was a considerably more taxing process than simple, if highly unpleasant, incarceration in prison. As one of the leaders of the reformatory movement said, "In [many penitentiaries] it is far easier for a prisoner to adapt himself to rules and regulations, preserve correct deportment, and perform a certain amount of labor than to submit to the discipline of institutions which make a constant draft upon his mental, moral and physical powers." S. Barrows, *The Reformatory System in the United States* 9 (1900).

26. State v. Scholl, 167 Wis. 504, 510, 167 N.W. 830, 832 (1918).

27. The use of the parental model was frequently made explicit by courts reviewing juvenile legislation. The opinion of the Pennsylvania Supreme Court in Commonwealth v. Fisher, 213 Pa. 48, 53, 62 Atl. 198, 200 (1905), holding *inter alia* that a summons was not necessary to initiate juvenile court proceedings, can stand for many others: "The natural parent needs no process to temporarily deprive his child of its liberty by confining it in its own home to save and to shield it from the consequences of persistence in a career of waywardness, nor is the state, when compelled, as *parens patriae*, to take the place of the father for the same purpose, required to adopt any process as a means of placing its hands upon the child to lead it into one of its courts."

28. Van Waters, "The Juvenile Court from the Child's Viewpoint," in *The Child, The Clinic and The Court* 217, 218 (J. Addams, ed. 1925). *See also*, Mack, "The Juvenile Court," 23 *Harv. L. Rev.* 104 (1909).

29. For this distinction, *see* R. Unger, *Knowledge and Politics* 88—91 (1975).

30. This result is by no means hypothetical. In New York, a juvenile delinquent is a person of appropriate age "who does any act which, if done by an adult, would constitute a crime." *N.Y. Fam. Ct. Act* §712(a). Disorderly conduct is, like other offenses against public safety, classified as a "violation" by the Penal Code and not as a crime (which category is limited to felonies and misdemeanors). Accordingly, New York courts have consistently held that conduct which, if done by an adult, would amount to a "violation" cannot be made the basis of an adjudication of delinquency. *E.g.*, Carter v. Family Court, 22 A.D. 2d 888, 255 N.Y.S. 2d 385 (1964); *In re* M., 318 N.Y.S. 2d 904 (1971). Nor can a child who is charged with a single instance of a "violation" be found a "Person

in Need of Supervision," since the statute requires that there be more than a single incident to support such a determination. *In re* David W., 28 N.Y. 2d 589, 268 N.E. 2d 642, 319 N.Y.S. 2d 845 (1971).

31. *E.g.*, Law of April 21, 1899, *Laws of Illinois* (1899) §1; Missouri Laws (1909) §1, p. 423. *See* Teitelbaum, "Book Review," 4 *Fam. L. Q.* 444, 447–48 (1970).

32. The early definitions of neglect and delinquency in the Illinois juvenile court law illustrate both open-endedness and specificity as devices for achieving broad coverage.

§169 DEFINITION §2. [1] That all persons under the age of twenty-one (21) years shall, for the purpose of this act only, be considered wards of the State and their persons shall be subject to the care, guardianship and control of the court as hereinafter provided.

For the purpose of this act, the words "dependent child" and "neglected child" shall mean any male child who while under the age of seventeen years or any female child who while under the age of eighteen years, for any reason, is destitute, homeless or abandoned; or dependent upon the public for support; or has not proper parental care or guardianship; or habitually begs or receives alms; or is found living in any house of ill-fame or with any vicious or disreputable person; or has a home which by reason of neglect, cruelty or depravity, on the part of its parents, guardian or any other person in whose care it may be, is an unfit place for such a child; and any child who while under the age of ten (10) years is found begging, peddling or selling any articles or singing or playing any musical instrument for gain upon the street or giving any public entertainments or accompanies or is used in aid of any person so doing.

The words "delinquent child" shall mean any male child who while under the age of seventeen years or any female child who while under the age of eighteen years, violates any law of this State; or is incorrigible, or knowingly associates with thieves, vicious or immoral persons, or without just cause and without that [the] consent of its parents, guardian or custodian absents itself from its home or place of abode, or is growing up in idleness or crime; or knowingly frequents a house of ill repute; or knowingly frequents any policy shop or place where any gaming device is operated; or frequents any saloon or drama show where intoxicating liquors are sold; or patronizes or visits any public pool room or basket shop; or wanders about the streets in the night time without being on any lawful business or lawful occupation; or habitually wanders about any railroad yards or tracks or jumps or attempts to jump onto [any] moving train, or enters any car or engine without lawful authority; or uses vile, obscene, vulgar, profane or indecent language in [any] public place or about any school house; or is guilty of indecent or lascivious conduct; any child committing any of these acts herein mentioned shall be deemed a delinquent child and shall be cared for as such in the manner hereinafter provided.

Law of June 4, 1907, *Laws of Illinois* (1907), p. 70. For another instance, see *Missouri Laws* (1909), §1, p. 423.

33. *E.g.*, *In re* Holmes, 379 Pa. 599, 109 A. 2d 523 (1954), *cert. denied*, 348 U.S. 973; State *ex. rel.* Christiensen v. Christiensen, 227 P. 2d 760 (Utah 1951). It was common practice, for example, to prepare and submit a social investigation report to the judge prior to adjudication, which would contain virtually all available information concerning the child's behavior, his relations with his family, his record at school and with the police, and his attitudes in general. *See* Teitelbaum, "The Use of Social Reports in Juvenile Court Adjudications," 7 *J. Fam. L.* 425 (1967).

34. Mack, *supra* note 28 at 119–20. *See also*, Lindsey, "The Juvenile Court in Denver," in *S. Barrows, Children's Courts in the United States* 107 (1904).

35. *E.g.*, Stiller and Elder, "PINS–A Concept in Need of Supervision," 12 *Am. Crim. L. Rev.* 33 (1974); Note, *"Parens Patriae* and Statutory Vagueness in the Juvenile Court," 82 *Yale L.J.* 745 (1973); Note, "Juvenile Statutes and Noncriminal Delinquents: Applying the Void-for-Vagueness Doctrine," 4 *Seton Hall L. Rev.* 184 (1972); Note, "Juvenile Court Jurisdiction over 'Immoral' Youth in California," 24 *Stan. L. Rev.* 568 (1972).

36. *E.g.*, Gonzalez v. Mailliard, No. 50424 (N.D. Cal., Feb. 9, 1971), *vacated* 416 U.S. 918 (1974); State v. Mattiello, 4 Conn. Cir. 55, 225 A. 2d 507 (Conn. App. 1966); E.S.G. v. State, 447 S.W. 2d 225 (Tex. Civ. App. 1969), *cert. denied* 398 U.S. 956 (1970). And *cf.* Gesicki v. Oswald, 336 F. Supp. 365 (S.D.N.Y. 1971), *aff'd per curiam* 406 U.S. 913 (1972).

37. *See*, *e.g.*, Papachristou v. Jacksonville, 405 U.S. 156 (1972) ("vagrants," "lewd, wanton and lascivious persons," "dissolute persons"); Musser v. Utah, 333 U.S. 95 (1948) ("injurious to public morals"); Ricks v. District of Columbia, 414 F. 2d 1097, 1106–07 (D.C. Cir. 1968) ("leading an immoral and profligate life"); Goldman v. Knecht, 295 F. Supp. 897 (D. Colo. 1969) (defined a vagrant as a person who leads "an idle, immoral, or profligate course of life"); Gesicki v. Oswald, 336 F. Supp. 365 (S.D.N.Y. 1971), *aff'd per curiam* 406 U.S. 913 (1972) ("morally depraved;" "in danger of becoming morally depraved").

38. Giaccio v. Pennsylvania, 382 U.S. 399 (1966).

39. *E.g.*, Gonzalez v. Mailliard, No. 50424 (N.D. Cal., Feb. 9, 1971), *vacated* 416 U.S. 918 (1974).

40. *E.g.*, Commonwealth v. Brasher, 270 N.E. 2d 389 (Mass. 1971); E.S.G. v. State, 447 S.W. 2d 225 (Tex. Civ. App. 1969), *cert. denied* 398 U.S. 956 (1970); State v. L.N., 109 N.J. Super. 278, 263 A. 2d 150 (App. Div.), *aff'd per curiam* 57 N.J. 165, 270 A. 2d 409 (1970), *cert. denied* 402 U.S. 1009 (1971).

41. *See* authorities cited in note 35, *supra.*

42. Juvenile court proceedings have always been formally denominated civil rather than criminal in nature. Use of such a label should not, however, either remove incorrigibility statutes from the ambit of constitutional concern or significantly diminish the level of scrutiny to which they will be exposed. That civil laws may offend due process because of their vagueness has long been recognized and recently affirmed. Giaccio v. Pennsylvania, 382 U.S. 399 (1966); Baggett v. Bullitt, 377 U.S. 360 (1964); Jordan v. DeGeorge, 341 U.S. 223 (1951); A.B. Small Co. v. American Sugar Refining Co., 267 U.S. 233 (1925). If, as has sometimes been suggested, civil statutes are less likely than criminal laws to be struck down on this basis, that is because the sanction involved is ordinarily less oner-

ous and, concomitantly, the costs of ambiguity are lower. *See* Note, *supra* note 3 at 69–70, n. 16. Where, however, the civil penalty is severe, it will be measured by the same standard of definiteness that applies to criminal provisions. As the Supreme Court said in Jordan v. DeGeorge, 341 U.S. 223, 231 (1951), with respect to a civil deportation proceeding:

> Despite the fact that this is not a criminal statute, we shall nevertheless examine the application of the vagueness doctrine to this case. We do this in view of the grave nature of deportation. The Court has stated that deportation is a drastic measure. . . . We shall, therefore, test this Statute under the established criteria of the 'void-for-vagueness' doctrine.

The "drastic" nature of intervention in delinquency cases has been recognized by the Supreme Court and has been specifically equated with criminal conviction. *In re* Gault, 387 U.S. 1, 49–50 (1967). The consequences of adjudication as a delinquent by reason of incorrigibility are not materially different from those of adjudication by reason of conduct that would be criminal if done by an adult. Courts have available the same remedies for delinquent children, whatever the underlying charge. Where incorrigibility is treated as a PINS rather than as a delinquency offense, it remains the case that a child may be deprived of his liberty until he reaches majority. He may, as well, be placed in an institution that houses delinquents or which, although delinquents are not there committed, is indistinguishable in facilities and programs from institution for delinquents. *See*, *e.g.*, Institute of Judicial Administration, "The *Ellery C.* Decision: A Case Study of Judicial Regulation of Juvenile Status Offenders" (1975). The civil "label-of-convenience" will no more insulate PINS provisions from requirements of statutory definiteness than it insulated delinquency proceedings from procedural due process requirements.

43. *E.g.*, *Calif. Welf.* and *Inst. Code* §601; *Mass. Gen. Laws* c. 119 §21; *N.M. S.A.* §13–14–3 (M).

44. 314 U.S. 513 (1942).

45. *Id.* at 523.

46. 258 U.S. 242 (1922). *See also*, Nash v. United States, 229 U.S. 373 (1913) (sustaining a criminal conviction based on a statute penalizing "undue restraining of trade").

47. *E.g.*, People v. Garman, 411 Ill. 279, 103 N.E. 2d 636 (1952); State v. Beckman, 219 Ind. 176, 37 N.E. 2d 531 (1941); State v. Bolsinger, 221 Minn. 154, 21 N.W. 2d 480 (1946); State v. Wojohn, 204 Ore. 84, 282 P. 2d 675 (1955). On the matter of excuse, *see* n. 67, *infra*.

48. *E.g.*, Cline v. Frink Dairy Co., 274 U.S. 445 (1927); United States v. L. Cohen Grocery Co., 255 U.S. 81 (1921).

49. *L. Fuller, Supra* note 6 at 64.

50. *E.g.*, *Mass. Gen. Laws* c. 119, §21; *N.Y. Fam. Ct. Act* §712(b); *N.J. Rev. Stat.* §2A:4–45 (a).

51. *See In re* B., 18 Cal. App. 3d 782, 96 Cal. Rptr. 146 (1971); *In re* David W., 28 N.Y. 2d 589, 268 N.E. 2d 642, 319 N.Y.S. 2d 845 (1971). *And see* Andrews and Cohn, "PINS Processing in New York: An Evaluation," ch. 2, *supra*, at p. 58.

52. United States v. Ragen, 314 U.S. 513 (1942); Nash v. United States, 229 U.S. 373 (1913).

53. The second year is said to be the time when parents initiate major socialization training. "[As] agents of socialization, the parents direct the child's learning of what the culture defines as desirable characteristics and behavior, at the same time encouraging him to inhibit undesirable motives and behavior." *Mussen, Conger,* and *Kagen, Child Development and Personality* 259 (1969).

54. In New York, for example, two-thirds of the respondents charged with being in need of supervision are fourteen years of age or older, and almost half are fifteen years of age or more. Andrews and Cohn, "PINS Processing in New York: An Evaluation," ch. 2, *supra*, at Table 2−1, p. 55.

55. See *Slater*, "Social Change and the Democratic Family," in *W. Bennis* and *P. Slater, The Temporary Society* 20, 47 (1968).

56. *See generally*, the Hart-Fuller exchange contained in Hart, "Positivism and the Separation of Morals," 71 *Harv. L. Rev.* 593 (1958); Fuller, "Positivism and Fidelity to Law," 71 *Harv. L. Rev.* 630 (1958). *See also*, the trenchant demystification of these issues in Kennedy, "Legal Formality," 2 *J. of Legal Studies* 351 (1973).

57. *See Katz*, "Dangerousness: A Theoretical Reconstruction of the Criminal Law: I," 19 *Buff. L. Rev.* 1, 28−30 (1969).

58. Thus, the legal condition of an insane person will not change because he escapes and does harm. The same may be said of the incompetent who purports to enter into a business arrangement; he will not be held responsible for his act precisely because of his legal irresponsibility in business matters. This is, moreover, the situation in matters involving children apart from the juvenile court. Contracts entered into by minors are ordinarily voidable because of their presumed incapacity for responsible judgment in such transactions, and the same is true with regard to most other areas of law. See Lefstein, Stapleton, and Teitelbaum, "In Search of Juvenile Justice: *Gault* and Its Implementation," 3 *Law & Society Rev.* 491, 553−58 (1969).

59. At least where incorrigibility is included with delinquency statutes, responsibility in the ordinary sense seems to be required before an adjudication can be made. This is true even with respect to formal notions of responsibility derived from the criminal law; with few exceptions, courts that have recently considered the issue hold that children may raise defenses of mental incapacity in connection with delinquency prosecutions.

In *In re* Winburn, 145 N.W. 2d 178, 182 (Wis. 1966), the court rejected an argument that the rehabilitative purposes of the juvenile court made such defenses inappropriate:

Irrespective of what we call the juvenile procedure, and no matter how benign and well-intended the judge who administers the system, the juvenile procedures, to some degree at least, smack of 'crime and punishment'. While the primary statutory goal is the best interest of the child, that interest is, as it should be, conditioned by the consideration of the interest of the public. . . . The interest of the public is served not only by rehabilitating juveniles when that is possible, but the interest of the public is also served by removing some juveniles from environments where they are likely to harm their fellow citizens. Retribution, in practice, plays a role in the function of the juvenile court. The judgments of juvenile courts do serve as deterrents. . . .

Courts in California and Florida have held that statutory and common law defenses of infancy likewise operate in delinquency matters. *In re* Gladys R., 1 Cal. 3d 855, 464 P. 2d 127, 83 Cal. Rptr. 671 (1970); State v. D.H., 309 So. 2d 601 (Fla. Ct. App. 1975). *Contra*: Borders v. United States, 256 F.2d 458 (5th Cir. 1958). And *cf. In re* H.C., 106 N.J. Super. 583, 256 A. 2d 322 (1969).

No cases involving defenses of mental capacity in respect of PINS proceedings appear to be reported. The issue would only rarely arise because the imprecision of the definition allows courts to decide whether the child is in need of supervision by implicitly incorporating a scienter or wilfulness requirement—*e.g.*, that the child has intentionally or knowingly disobeyed his parents.

60. *See* discussion, text on notes 30—32, *supra*.

61. *See* A. *Katz, Studies in Boundary Theory* 45—51 (unpub., 1976) for a more intensive discussion of the Principle of Offense and the Principle of Character in the general criminal law.

62. A recent expression of this view can be found in Fletcher, "The Right Deed for the Wrong Reason," 23 *U.C.L.A. L. Rev.* 293, 301 (1975).

63. To the extent the rule of law seeks to eliminate the experience of personal domination, and vagueness is understood as the doctrinal specification of the point at which this effort has failed, it is doubtful that Professor Fletcher's distinction between "definitional" vagueness and "justification" vagueness is or should be persuasive. *Id.* at 308—16. Uncertainty as to whether or not an act which meets the formal definition of an offense is justified gives rise to the experience of personal domination no less than uncertainty in the definition of the offense. *See generally, R. Unger, Knowledge and Politics* 80, 92—94 (1975).

64. *See* Hill, "Reason and Reasonableness," in *C. Hill, Change and Continuity in Seventeenth Century England* (1974).

65. To the extent this attitude which assumes an ability to distinguish legal locutions which have a core meaning from those which do not mediates—outside the family—between the claim for autonomy of individual persons in concrete cases and the general authority of community consensus, it corresponds to the mediation of rules in the socialization of authority and the development of autonomy within the family. That is, the child's gradual movement from the personal domination of parents toward the development of autonomy is mediated by rules: the personal domination of parents is progressively replaced by the impersonal authority of rules; the development of autonomy takes place alongside a growing appreciation of the collective significance of rules. *See generally, J. Piaget, The Moral Judgment of the Child* (1932, 1965).

66. This notion is borrowed from *P. Diesing, Patterns of Discovery in the Social Sciences* 221 (1971). For a discussion of this idea in terms of the radical separation of universals and particulars, *see R. Unger, Supra* note 63 at 133 *et seq.*

✳ *Chapter 7*

Should Status Offenders
Go to Court?

Lindsay A. Arthur

Legal proceedings may be a means of compelling an uncooperative child and his family to accept the help they have refused on a voluntary basis. Or they may be a means of certifying need—a gateway to help—where resources are scarce [1].

INTRODUCTION

Various proposals have been introduced which, if accepted, would remove status offenders and others from the jurisdiction of the juvenile court. By and large, these proposals are said to be justified by the ambiguity associated with status offense provisions "which mean different things to different people" [2] and by the belief that the acts involved in this jurisdictional category do not call for juvenile court intervention.

True, "status offense" is broad and perhaps ambiguous, but then so are the terms "pornography," "breach of the peace," and "executive privilege," and the imprecision of past draftsmen is no reason not to essay new definitions and surely is no more reason to disregard whole concepts and remove all constraints from insecure children any more than from boisterous adults or imperious presidents. The court's functions of certifying need and compelling help are eminently desirable and important ones, and attention should be directed to their accomplishment in appropriate ways rather than to their wholesale abandonment because of real or imagined defects.

THE IMPORTANCE OF PINS JURISDICTION

The importance of retaining jurisdiction over status offenses is apparent when its purposes are considered. In the first place, the public has a stake in what happens to young people. It expects children to be educated, which means that they should not drop out of school in the second or third or seventh grade. It expects children to be healthy, not to be alcoholics before they start to shave. It expects children to be controlled until they learn self-control, which means they should not run the streets at night. It expects children to adhere to a moral code, at least to the extent of not producing their own children while they are themselves still going through puberty. No segment of the public, other than a few professors and other reformers, have been heard to say that compulsory education laws should be repealed, as they would effectively be if truancy jurisdiction were eliminated; or that children should not obey their parents, as they could if incorrigibility jurisdiction were eliminated; or that children should be allowed to smoke and drink to their heart's content, as they might if possession and consumption of cigarettes and alcohol were no longer unlawful for children.

It is, however, sometimes more generally argued that status offenders are brought to the bar of justice for conduct which adults can do with impunity. This is a denial of equal protection and thus unconstitutional—at least so goes the superficial argument. If nothing else, turn the argument around. Children should be as free as adults. They should not have to obey their parents, or go to the dentist, or go to school. They should be permitted to run freely, to live where they please, to refuse to learn to read or write or count or think—but then of course should anyone have to provide them with food, clothing, housing, or medical care unless they are paupers? This reverse argument is equally superficial.

"The fundamental justification for exercising power over children for their 'non-criminal behavior' is that children require adult guidance for their proper development (though there is obviously disagreement over the age at which a 'child' becomes a person who is free to make his own choices)" [3]. Children *are* unequal. They *are* incapable of making mature judgments, of looking beyond tomorrow, of selecting adequate food, shelter, or clothing, of supporting themselves. At some time they acquire these abilities, hopefully; possibly at fifteen, possibly at eighteen, possibly at twenty-one, possibly later. If a "maturity test" could be devised, like an I.Q. test, it would solve many problems: once the test was passed a person could vote, drive, marry—and not be held accountable for status offenses—but until then a person would be a child. Until such a test is devised, age, however arbitrary, is the only test generally acceptable, tempered by parents and schools and courts that substitute their own concepts of maturity.

Children cannot, therefore, be relied on to rear themselves. There are, of course, institutions other than courts that are relied on to facilitate realization of public expectations concerning the health, education, and conduct of children, among them parents, schools, and welfare agencies. We rely, for example, on the family for most child rearing purposes. We have rejected ancient and communistic wisdom according to which all children should be taken from their parents at birth and developed by experts [4]. We have not, as yet, subscribed to the new, fearsome logic that children should be cared for by psychological parents who may coincidentally, but not necessarily, be the same as the biological parents [5]. We still rely on natural parents to raise their children. There have been and will, however, be problems with this approach. Some parents are not smart enough to raise children and need guidance which, as well, they are too stupid or proud to accept. Some parents are too rigid and some too permissive; some too close and some too distant; some too frustrated and some too uncertain. Of these, many will seek help or accept it if someone brings it to them, but some will not. In all likelihood, the latter are the parents who most need help and whose children show that need by their status offenses. These children can be trained only if a court orders them to participate in some treatment form. Other parents know what to do and want to do it, but they lack the moral or psychological strength. They require external authority to support them, and by the time this becomes clear, the child may have become so wayward as to accept nothing other than judicial authority. Every juvenile court knows these parents: they come fearfully, proudly, tearfully, and confusedly seeking help, often too late. Such cases cannot be diverted to other channels.

It is well and good to say that school classes should be so attractive that no child would ever skip a class, but even law professors cannot approach this ideal with their highly motivated students. It is well and good to say that homes should be so pleasant that no child would ever run away, but when that day comes, the divorce laws can also be repealed. It is well and good to say that parents should prevent all drinking, smoking, and running loose, but parents do not, and many of them cannot. If the commonly accepted public expectations about the raising of children are to be realized, court enforcement of these expectations must be available to the extent that other responsible agencies need their assistance.

Court intervention in these matters plays a facilitative as well as a compulsory role in meeting social expectations about children. Some young people acknowledge the need for counseling but cannot bring themselves to accept on-going services of this kind. Some parents ridicule counseling, or fear it, or are too busy to become involved in it. Some children genuinely want to go to school but need some authority to override negative pressure from their peers. Some parents will drink to excess even if it impels their children to run away from home, unless a court impels the parents to visit Alcoholics Anonymous or some other community agency. Some families need court intervention in order to be able to compose themselves and talk rationally among themselves [6]. In these situations, courts serve to make possible the conditions under which useful work can be done—not necessarily by the court itself, but by other agencies who must, to be effective, be assured of the cooperation of child and family.

The Sacramento Project is a case in point. The principal thrust of that project was to shunt incorrigible children from juvenile court detention to intensive care counseling, in the belief that service in the community was preferable to detention home treatment [7]. Significantly, the project had two prerequisites for acceptance of a client for counseling: (1) the referral must come from detention, a process implying that the clientele were already subject to a form of court presence or threat; and (2) all members of the family must agree to counseling. Thus, the project—which generally enjoyed considerable success, although it experienced a 35 percent recidivism rate [8]—continued to rely on the court both for its facilitative function (that is, by threatening detention rather than release for counseling) and for treatment of those cases, presumably the most difficult, in which the entire family would not agree to participation. For the angry or hurt child, or the drinking, rejecting, or martinette parent, the Sacramento Project fell back on juvenile court resources as a last, but necessary, resort. As the project concluded, ". . . beyond control children should not be brought to court and subjected to the judicial process when their conduct does not infringe upon the criminal law, *unless there is a substantial showing that, even given all of the resources we can bring to bear, the family dysfunction is otherwise insoluble and the child cannot adequately function at home"* [9].

THE IMPORTANCE OF USING COURTS
IN PINS CASES

The preceding discussion shows why intervention is often necessary both to compel adherence by children and sometimes parents to public expectations concerning their conduct and condition and to facilitate assistance by other agencies concerned with children. It has been assumed that courts are the appropriate institutions for such intervention, but it is worthwhile to consider why this is so. If coercion is necessary, who would bring it to bear other than courts?

In the first place, constitutional due process was clearly established by *In re Gault* [10], but only for governmental intervention. Should due process be extended to the "community resources" so relied on by the reformers in order to protect a child who is dumped into a foster home by rejecting parents who mouth the right concerns, or a child who is chained to her bed to prevent her from running away, or a child who is denied participation in school activities because he drinks or smokes, or is truant from inappropriate classes and courses, or a child whose hair is shaved to make her unattractive to boys? Would schools and welfare agencies conduct trials? [11] Would they lock up those who disobeyed them? Or paddle them? Or take away privileges? Or rights? How would they apply coercion? How would they decide coercion was necessary? Or would coercion be applied by parents? Or should coercion be applied by the Boys Club, or the 4–H Club, or the "Y" or the Scouts? All of these alternatives are shocking to Americans. *Our whole American tradition and law has been that if coercion, force, lock-up, or compulsion is necessary, it should be imposed by the family and if the family cannot or will not, only the courts can adequately protect the child, and his inalienable rights.*

There is another, less important but still significant, reason for retaining judicial control over status offenders. There is just so much money and so many resources which can be used to help children in trouble. Some percentage of this will be spent by public agencies, some by community agencies. The percentages may vary from place to place and from time to time, but the total will not vary materially. If responsibility for a category of children is shifted from one agency to another, percentages may shift too, but no additional funds will become available. If the size of the shifted category is different from the amount of the shifted funds, as almost certainly will happen, some caseloads will be unduly relieved and some caseloads will be unduly loaded [12]. The argument that removing status offenders from public caseloads will make public resources more readily available to criminal offenders sounds fine if only one side of the equation is viewed. But these status offenders will be added to community caseloads, overloading them unless there is a significant underwriting by public funds shifted from public resources or a reduction of taxes with a substantial increase in charitable contributions, which are unlikely. *Public agencies are better able than community agencies to mobilize and maintain the funds needed to serve the needs of status offenders.*

It has, of course, recently been said that courts have not proved effective in dealing with status offense (and other) cases. One should, however, inquire into the basis for that claim. Are there any generally accepted means of evaluating? The police and the reformers point to recidivism figures but these are surely simplistic: they do not account for time lapse, or environmental influences, or relative severity of offenses, or experimentation in finding the right treatment, or arrest and referral policies. If a child is treated for measles in 1974 and recovers but contracts measles again in 1975, did the physician fail? Or did he fail if the 1975 problem is pneumonia, or a broken arm? If a person confesses his sins to a priest in 1974, and sins again and confesses again in 1975, did the priest fail?

Moreover, such criticism is often based on the assumption that the juvenile court has but four choices: to dismiss, to reprimand, to put on probation, or to commit to a horrendous training school. The assumption makes two errors: most courts have many more choices, and the horrendous training schools have existed largely on television or in Massachusetts, Texas, or Dickens. It is also assumed that juvenile courts enjoy detaining children, preferably in dark jails replete with felons, Fagins, and far-outs. Again the assumption overlooks both the procedural safeguards imposed by most statutes and most courts, and the separate and specialized facilities available to most of the metropolitan courts before whom the majority of both status and criminal offenders appear. But more pertinently, the juvenile courts do have and can develop options, good options [13]. While most training schools are campus-style, professionally staffed, and well-pro-grammed, there are alternative options in every state to the training schools, of which the Homes of the Good Shepherd, the George Republics, and the Boys' Town are the best known examples. Minnesota alone, with only four million population, has eleven privately operated and six publicly operated campus/cottage style residential treatment centers, staffed by graduate social workers, plus various medical and psychiatric facilities, and numerous professionally operated group homes in the community. Only the public facilities require court commitment. The others accept referrals from youth service bureaus and from private sources as well as from the court, intentionally mixing the children, treat-ing needs, not offenses or referral sources. On another level, "probation" is an adult word implying some kind of monitoring, with the ever present threat of incarceration. But, most juvenile courts use it rather as a potpourri of counseling services: one-to-one, group, family, chemical abuse, tutorial, and so forth, pos-sibly more extensive and better staffed than non-court facilities. Most juvenile courts have developed camping programs, employment programs, athletic pro-grams, volunteering programs, and the like, usually outside the court but relying on it for support and coordination. Most courts have access to and use and sup-port community mental health facilities in their many programs. Some courts use civil commitments, hospital programs and dependency related dispositions. *Most juvenile courts are imaginative, progressive, oriented to the needs of the children and the public, dedicated to improving themselves and the services for the children who cannot be diverted from them.*

IMPLEMENTATION OF PINS JURISDICTION

Having examined the reasons that justify, indeed demand, retention of court jurisdiction over juvenile status offenders, we should next turn to the principles according to which these goals should be implemented.

Definitions Should Be Clarified

We have remarked that some believe the term "status offense" is an exces-sively ambiguous one meaning different things to different people [14]. This is, to an extent, true and reason for concern, but it is not unique to juvenile courts and is not a reason to junk the jurisdiction [15]. Definitions *are* possible [16]. A status offense as a generic category is simply conduct unlawful for children but lawful for adults. Of these drinking, smoking, sniffing of glue and other sub-stances, curfew, and truancy are easy to define and to prove; leaving home with-out parental permission (though parental denial might be unreasonable in some cases) is no less definable than escape. Thus the only status offenders who have been imprecisely defined are children who have been in the past described as "wayward," "unruly," "incorrigible," "disobedient," "ungovernable," and sim-ilar vague terms. Recently, however, the prestigious National Conference of

Commissioners on Uniform State Laws has proposed words describing this category of offenses which are both readily understandable and subject to proof within the rules of evidence: a PINS is a child who is ". . . habitually disobedient of the reasonable and lawful commands of his parent, guardian, or other custodian and is ungovernable. . . ." [17].

Intervention Should Be Focused on the Child's Needs Rather than His Offenses

In dealing with status offenders—in dealing with *any* offenders—the "why" is more important than the "what." The particular misconduct is merely a surface indicium; the reasons for the misconduct will disclose far better what intervention, if any, is appropriate by either governmental or private agencies; what treatment, if any; what punishment, if any; what incarceration, if any, are appropriate. Proposals which would remove status offenders, dangerous offenders, and traffic offenders from the jurisdiction of the juvenile court are based only on what the child *did* or did not do, not on what the child or the public *needs*. In considering only the misconduct, one looks backward to a completed act which cannot be undone. In considering the reasons for the misconduct, one looks forward to acts not yet done which can still be prevented. More than most criminal offenders, the status offenders are acting for reasons where help *can* be rendered; often they are acting purely in a cry for help. Sometimes, as in absenting from home without consent, the child may actually be exercising good judgment by absenting an intolerable and destructive situation, needing court intervention to protect him from parents. If help is not forthcoming, these children may degenerate to criminal offenses, unnecessarily causing damage and fear to the public.

The Family's Problems, Rather than the Child's Faults, Should Be Considered. It follows that, when the juvenile court intervenes in status offenses, it should not do so simply to point an accusatory finger at the child and say, "You have been bad, you must be punished." Rather, the court will recognize that it is normal for a child to stay home, go to school, not run the streets at night, and experiment a bit with tobacco, alcohol, and sex. Deviation, from these norms usually have their roots in family dysfunction and loss or abdication of family control. It takes a lot of pressure for a child to be abnormal, and that pressure almost always originates in or could be controlled by the family.

We need to see the runaway youth not solely as a problem child in the family but as a signal that the family has a problem [18].

Court hearings may be necessary to "apprise parents of their primary responsibility to enroll and maintain their children in school" [19]. "The juvenile court should avoid demeaning and unnecessarily labeling a child, and when the family is the root of the problem, the court should direct its jurisdiction and authority towards the family and not merely towards the child, looking always to future needs rather than to past or superficial culpabilities" [20].

> ... serious thought should be given to the feasibility of an entirely new jurisdictional concept, the Family In Need of Service (FINS) which would subsume the existing jurisdictional categories of the neglected and the beyond-control child. While this new jurisdictional base would obviously pose both conceptual and operational difficulties which would require working-out, it would also afford many advantages. It would abate the stigma now attendant upon the handling of the beyond control child and avoid the consequences of labelling that child as delinquent. It could provide the court with a direct jurisdictional tie to the parents; at present, the only leverage upon parents and other family members is that provided by the juvenile court's jurisdiction over the individual child. Finally, it would direct the dispositional focus of the juvenile justice system where it belongs in cases of deprived and unruly children: upon the family unit [21].

The juvenile court can and should adjust and develop its jurisdictions and procedures so as to provide help for whole families instead of stigma for individual children, opening the whole gamut of its diagnostic and dispositional resources— and its constitutional protections—to the dysfunctioning interactions of the whole constellation of those who should be providing the child with guidance, stability, and control.

The Child Should Be Given the Maximum Liberty Feasible Under the Circumstances. Attention to the child's needs rather than specific conduct should also extend to all forms of disposition. There are many instances in which the child has committed an unlawful act but, in the circumstances, does not require formal intervention, and should not be referred to court regardless of his offense. *Instead of removing offenses from the juvenile court indiscriminately regardless of the nature of the offender, it is a wiser policy to remove offenders from the court discriminately regardless of the nature of the offense, if they do not need the court.*

In general, a child should be given the most liberty he can handle without injury to himself or to the public, whatever the nature of the wrong alleged or proved. He should not be detained, whether for a status or criminal offense, unless he will hurt or be hurt, or unless detention is necessary to insure his presence at judicial proceedings or for necessary medical or rehabilitative care. If a child can handle shelter care, he should not be held in secure care. If he can handle a foster home, he should not be held in shelter care. If he can handle living at his own home, he should not be held in a foster home. However, if it is judicially determined that he cannot handle any degree of liberty without injuring himself or others, or running loose, he should be held in security for the protection of himself and of the public. This of course requires a prognostication—a guess at what he will or would do—and prophecy is not a perfected science. It is better that liberty be granted or denied on the basis of the needs of a child's and the public's future safety than simply on the basis of what the child has been caught for in the past. Similarly, neither a public nor a private agency should restrict a child's liberty by unnecessary diagnoses, social work, group work, clinics, structured activities, or other restrictions on a child's or a family's freedom to determine for itself the use of its time and energies. Diversion from governmental intervention is desirable whenever possible, but so is diversion from private intervention whenever possible, however "voluntary" that intervention may be. If nothing will help, then nothing should be done, unless the child's or the public's safety requires [22].

Where Incarceration Is Required, that Should Be Determined by the Child's Needs Rather than His Acts. Much has been made of the mixing of status offenders with criminal offenders, as though the most naive shoplifter were somehow more vicious than the most angry runaway [23]. Much can be said for segregating children according to their sophistication and depravity, but such a segregation should be by the child's needs, not his offenses and surely not by any such indiscriminate standard as commission of a status offense. A program, whether school, counseling, or incarceration, should include those whose needs fit the program; excluding all whose needs do not fit, regardless of their offenses, and including all whose needs do fit, regardless of their offenses. If institutional segregation is desired, designation merely by status or criminal offenders is illogical. The violent, the angry, the manipulators, the economically motivated, the racially reacting, the status seekers, should more logically be kept apart than simply separating the runaways from the trespassers or those who have refused to obey their parents from those who have refused to obey the law, or those who drink in excess and stay out all night from those who drink to excess and drive someone's car.

Stigma Should Be Avoided as Far as Possible

A current adage says "Mention the word 'delinquency' and everyone thinks 'juvenile'." It is generally assumed that there is a stigma to juvenile court. But is there? Adopted children are not stigmatized, nor are dependent children, nor battered children, nor minor traffic offenders, nor younger marriage applicants, nor children involved in custody struggles; yet all of these are referred to juvenile court. The only group which is stigmatized are those labeled delinquent—so why not stop labeling them delinquent? Even PINS and CINS are acquiring an odor, so why not stop calling them PINS and CINS? Why do we need a label? Why not refer to *all* children in juvenile court as simply "children needing help" [24] — even if its acronym is not pronounceable, or maybe because it is not. All children who are involved in adoption, traffic, status offenses, marriage proposals, custody struggles, criminal offenses, battering, or abandonment need help. Why not say that, and no more? Civil courts got rid of the detinue, ejectment, and the other classic forms of action decades ago, substituting fact pleading. Why can't the juvenile courts? There would have to be allegation and proof of jurisdictional facts, whether the case be one sounding in adoption, burglary, custody, speeding, marriage, or neglect. Similarly, why should not all institutions be residential facilities, whether they are foster homes or detention centers or group homes or training schools or centers for children who are emotionally disturbed or who have learning disabilities; and why shouldn't all facilities be designed around needs of the children and the public, not around a jurisdictional base? Why should we not abolish probation officers and correctional workers and create family service practitioners, some employed by the public, some by the community, some in private practice the same as lawyers, doctors, and engineers. Labels can be abolished: job titles, institutional types, offense names, jurisdictional categories all define traditional packages developed in other days when they were handled in separate courts, or by separate proceedings, involving different people and different agencies. *With the consolidation of most proceedings affecting children in juvenile court, there is no need for labeling and name calling but rather all children needing help, whether for adoption, misconduct, or marriage, can be merged in the court's proceedings and the court can concentrate on discovering and remedying needs which cannot be satisfied without the court.*

CONCLUSION

Every juvenile court judge is reminded daily by the police, the schools, the prosecutors, and segments of the press that the juvenile court is too permissive, that it mollycoddles, that it slaps on the wrist and excuses the disobediences and flauntings of the young. These critics have their support and backing; their influence waxes with the public's fear of crime. Curiously they make common cause with those who think the juvenile courts are too punitive, too arbitrary, too untutored, and should be confined to proportionate sentencing and the trappings of ancient criminal courts. Their influence is felt in the legislatures where bills are regularly introduced to restrict juvenile courts, to force criminal procedures on them, to reduce or eliminate the socially oriented, rehabilitative approach and return to punishment [25]. Now the reformers would make the juvenile justice system even more permissive by allowing children to run freely, to sleep where and with whom they desire, to skip school, to disobey their parents.

The position of juvenile court judges who deal with these problems daily differs markedly and almost unanimously. In a recent survey by the Womens Crusade Against Crime, of St. Louis, 89 percent of the juvenile court judges did not believe status offenses should be removed from juvenile court jurisdiction; 65 percent felt that if they were removed there would be no agency capable of dealing with those who now come to court. Seventy-seven percent felt that the status offenders they now detain are held because no other resource would take them [26]. At its recent convention on July 17, 1975, the National Council of Juvenile Court Judges clarified its position:

WHEREAS the Council recognizes that [antisocial and self-destructive adolescent] conduct is contrary to the Welfare of the child, hinders his development to responsible adulthood, impairs the parent's ability to guide and regulate the child's behavior, and may also violate the rights of the community, and

WHEREAS the Council recognizes that such children, their parents, and the community have both rights and responsibilities under law which must sometimes be determined and enforced by legal means, and

WHEREAS a proper distinction must be made in the classification and treatment as between delinquent behavior and the Status Offender,

NOW, THEREFORE, BE IT RESOLVED:

That the Juvenile Court retain jurisdiction over Status Offenses; that said conduct be defined by law as non-delinquent, and that such children be classified as 'Children in Need of Supervision,' or other similar category;

That the determination that a child is in need of supervision be a judicial one, protected by the same due process afforded a child charged with delinquent conduct, including the same quantum of proof;

That children found to be within the jurisdiction of the Court as Children in Need of Supervision should be afforded such supervision and treatment as their needs require;

Further, that children alleged or found to be in need of supervision should not be held in any jail, and when placement is necessary, it should be in an appropriate facility with the custody and care necessary for their physical and mental well-being [27].

NOTES TO CHAPTER 7

1. This quotation is taken from an address by Winifred Cavenagh, Professor of Social Administration and Criminology, University of Birmingham, England, reprinted in *Ninth Congress of the International Association of Youth Magistrates, Final Report* 7 (1974).

2. J. Dineen, *Juvenile Court Organization and Status Offenses: A Statutory Profile* 33 (1974).

3. M. Paulsen and C. Whitebread, *Juvenile Law and Procedure* 43 (1974).

4. *See* Plato, The Republic, Bk. V.

5. *See, e.g., J. Goldstein, A. Freud,* and *A. Solnit, Beyond the Best Interests of the Child* (1973).

6. For a discussion of these family-related problem children and methods of helping them, including court involvement, *see* Traitel, *Dispositional Alternatives in Juvenile Justice: A Goal-Oriented Approach* (1974).

7. Center on Administration of Criminal Justice, University of California, Davis, *Report of the Conference on Family Counseling and Juvenile Diversion* (1975).

8. County of Sacramento, California, Probation Department, *The Sacramento Diversion Project: A First-Year Report* (1972). It says much about such projects that the Sacramento experiment can be called a success although it experienced a 35 percent recidivism rate.

9. Gough and Grilli, "The Unruly Child and the Law: Toward a Focus on the Family," 23 *Juv. Just.* 9 (No. 3, 1972).

10. 387 U.S. 1 (1967). See generally, N. Weinstein, *Legal Rights of Children* (1974).

11. A bill has been introduced in the California Legislature providing for "the creation of community youth boards in high school attendance areas. The boards would be given the *power* to establish rehabilitation programs for young offenders not involved in violent crime." Cal. A.B. 2385, Assembly Comm. on Criminal Justice, Reg. Sess. 1975. This report on the bill does not indicate any constitutional restraints, due process, or parameters of the "power" of these new mini-juvenile courts to be scattered apparently helter-skelter about the land.

12. Sarri, "Diversion—Within or Without the Juvenile Justice System," 2 *Soundings* 11 (1975).

13. *See* Traitel, *supra* note 6.

14. Dineen, *Supra* note 2 at 33.

15. *See* Note, "Juvenile Statutes and Non-Criminal Delinquents: Applying the Void-for-Vagueness Doctrine," 4 *Seton Hall L. Rev.* 184 (1972).

16. Cole, "The Arguments to Retain Status Offenses Within Juvenile Court Jurisdiction," 2 *Soundings* 5 (1975).

17. Uniform Juvenile Court Act §2(4) (1968).

18. Poliner, "A Profile of Runaway Youth," *Youth Reporter* (March, 1975).

19. Saccuzzo and Milligan, "Mass Truancy Hearings," 24 *Juv. Just.* 31 (1973).

20. Resolution, Minnesota Council of Juvenile Court Judges (1972).

21. Gough and Grilli, *supra* note 9 at 12 (emphasis supplied). *Compare* Arthur, "A Family Court—Why Not?," 51 *Minn. L. Rev.* 223 (1966).

22. *E.g.*, Uniform Juvenile Court Act §29(b) (1968) (requiring a court "to hear evidence as to whether the child is in *need* of treatment or rehabilitation. . . . If the court finds that the child is not . . . it shall dismiss the proceeding and discharge the child from any detention or other restriction . . . .") (emphasis supplied). It would be a salutary change to require the same standard of private agencies.

23. National Council on Crime and Delinquency, *Jurisdiction Over Status Offenders Should be Removed from the Juvenile Court—A Policy Statement* (1974).

24. *S. Wheeler* and *L. Cottrell, Juvenile Delinquency: Its Prevention and Control* (1966), reprinted in *O. Ketcham* and *M. Paulsen, Cases and Materials Relating to Juvenile Courts* 420 (1967).

25. Mack, "The Juvenile Court," 23 *Harv. L. Rev.* 104 (1909).

26. As reported in National Council of Juvenile Court Judges, *Juvenile Court Newsletter*, July, 1975, p. 2.

(27.) The Minnesota Council of Juvenile Court Judges clarified its position at its convention on September 8, 1972, by the following resolution unanimously adopted after a lengthy discussion:

RESOLVED

I

The Juvenile Court was created to provide treatment and supervision of children in trouble based on each child's needs. The philosophy of the Court has always been that it will base its jurisdiction on a child's problems and the treatment of those individual problems rather than on categories of misconduct;

II

All children in trouble, particularly those with the most deepseated needs which might show themselves through acts of truancy, absenting, and incorrigibility, should not be removed from judicial concern unless viable alternatives exist which will assure an education for unwilling children and a home for disrupted children;

III

No child should appear in the Juvenile Court unless he cannot or will not otherwise obtain essential treatment which is necessary for his welfare or for the protection of the public;

IV

Whenever possible the family, schools, and the various public, charitable, and private resources should be utilized for treatment rather than formal judicial process, and to this end the Juvenile Court should constantly support and encourage the development and improvement of non-judicial resources for a greater diversion of children from the Courts;

V

The Juvenile Court should avoid demeaning and unnecessarily labelling a child, and when the family is the root of the problem, the Court should direct its jurisdiction and authority towards the family and not merely towards the child, looking always to future needs rather than to past or superficial culpabilities;

VI

A child is entitled to as much constitutional protection as an adult, particularly for protection of his privacy from unwarranted invasion for however worthy a purpose, and for protection from unwarranted removal from his family unless truly beneficial. Only a Court can adequately provide these basic protections to children and families.

※ *Chapter 8*

The PINS Problem—A "No Fault" Approach

Floyd Feeney

One of the most troubling issues in juvenile justice today is that of the youth who has violated no general criminal law but who is a runaway, beyond the control of his parents, truant, or otherwise in conflict with the codes relating specifically to minors. In California, this kind of case makes up about 30 percent of all juvenile arrests, referrals to probation and the juvenile court, and detentions in juvenile hall [1]. While extremely common, many judges and probation officers have long felt this kind of case to be both difficult and inappropriate for the juvenile justice system. In addition, in recent years as the juvenile justice system has come under greater legal scrutiny, many have felt increasingly uncomfortable with the provision of essentially criminal handling for this kind of behavior.

Because of these concerns, there is widespread agreement on the need for developing alternatives to handling through the juvenile court. There is much less agreement, however, on what these alternatives should be. Some have seen the solution as lying in the creation of new social services—youth service bureaus, crisis clinics, or runaway centers [2]. Others would transfer the problem to other social agencies such as welfare departments or schools as in some foreign countries [3]. Still others have urged simply that the whole area be decriminalized [4].

To an important extent the choice among these competing suggestions rests upon differing perceptions of the underlying facts and values. Broadly, two positions seem to have been staked out: those based on an assumption that some underlying behavior problem exists, and those which assume there is no such problem.

The view at first blush, and the view of those urging retention of the present system, is that there clearly is an underlying problem [5]. Based on the premise that "pre-delinquent" acts often lead to later criminal behavior and that official intervention can head this off, this view is in many respects similar to that held by those who three-quarters of a century ago originated the legislation bringing this kind of behavior into the jurisdiction of the juvenile court in the first place [6].

Others, while agreeing that there is an underlying behavior problem, find that the present system has been unable to deal with it and consequently emphasize the ensuing need for improved system performance. More and better community services for youth is seen as the critical requirement. The youth service bureaus recommended by the President's Crime Commission in 1967, runaway centers such as Huckleberry and Runaway Houses in San Francisco and Washington, D.C., Senator Bayh's legislation encouraging more of these, and clinics, hot lines, and other such services in many cities have all resulted in increased responses to these concerns [7].

Still others, however, feel that the problem is not the youth involved but rather the law itself. Decriminalization follows rather logically from this view. If the laws requiring youths to obey their parents, to go to school, or not to run away are repealed, there will be no problem. No cases will come to court because no law will have been broken. Nothing else needs to be done because there never was any problem other than the law in the first place. Or they feel that if there is a problem, it is self-correcting and requires no intervention. In this view, there is no need for "child-saving" and if the youth can avoid being labeled delinquent (particularly by the legal system), he will be all right [8].

The proponents of these differing views tend to emphasize different parts of the underlying statutes and the caseload generated from them. Those who favor the decriminalization approach emphasize the portions of the statutes which relate to sexual conduct ("in danger of leading an idle and dissolute life"); the practice in some police departments of charging a Person In Need of Supervision (PINS)-type violation when they strongly suspect a juvenile of some criminal offense that they cannot prove; and the constitutional problems concerning vagueness [9]. Truancy also is emphasized, and the hint thrown out that Huck Finn would not have survived these unwarranted intrusions into childhood life.

What limited facts there are about PINS-type cases, however, suggest that while some cases fit this description, most do not. Perhaps the fullest data are from California. In 1970, truancies and sexual delinquency cases made up only

Initial Referrals to Probation—1970

Incorrigible	19,561
Sexual Delinquency	4,359
Truancy	5,578
Runaway	18,384
Total	47,882

20 percent or so of the total; the majority—over 70 percent of the PINS-type cases referred to court—were beyond parental control or were runaways [10].

Since that time the percentage of cases in the sexual delinquency and truancy categories appears to have become even smaller. The section of the California code dealing specifically with sexual delinquency was found unconstitutionally vague in 1972 by a three-judge federal court, and has since been removed from the code [11].

This does not mean that concerns about sexual behavior are not involved to some degree in PINS cases, particularly in cases involving girls. They are involved, however, largely only insofar as they contribute to family disagreements that lead to the invoking of legal action. For the most part, it is the failure of the family to resolve the problem rather than the sexual behavior as such which brings the case into court.

TWO EXAMPLES

In order to focus more clearly on what is involved in PINS-type cases, two recent examples are portrayed below:

Jane R. is a large, quiet 16-year-old girl, brought to Juvenile Hall, as a first-time runaway. Tomboyish with long blond hair, she lives with her father, a 47-year-old businessman, her stepmother of 4 years, and a 13-year-old sister, Debbie. Her real mother deserted the family when Jane was 12 after several involvements with other men and a series of mental breakdowns. She now lives in another city several hundred miles away. Jane indicates constant concern about the situation involving her real mother. She doesn't understand why her mother ran away, and hungers for some kind of contact. Her parents, however, particularly her stepmother, are fearful that Jane will only be hurt by learning the real character of her mother and seek to seal her off from any contact. They refuse to let Jane visit or write, intercept communications from the mother to Jane, and talk the mother down whenever her name is mentioned. Jane, who has made one feeble attempt at suicide, says little and mopes a great deal in her own room. Her stepmother, concerned that Jane "might go crazy" like her mother, hovers over her, asking questions, reading her diaries and coming into her room when she is alone. Jane, picking up her parents' concern, increasingly withdraws and worries that something is in fact wrong with her. Because of her quietness, virtually all the family attention focuses on Jane and very little on Debbie who is far more talkative and outgoing. While Jane feels very close to her father and enjoys fishing with him, he has a busy business schedule and is around very little.

Johnny G., a somewhat retarded and chubby 14-year-old with a smile and a winning way, was brought into the Juvenile Hall as being "beyond the control of his parents." This was his fourth time to the Hall for this "offense." Twice previously he had been placed on informal probation and had only recently completed his latest stint. Johnny's father is a 41-year-old truck driver and his mother a 38-year-old housewife. There are no other children. The father says the problem is that Johnny sometimes steals from his parents, never goes to sleep at a decent hour, rarely gets up in time for school, and "just doesn't listen." The father says that he has to go to bed early, usually by 10 P.M. because his work requires that he get up early in the morning. The mother, on the other hand, likes to stay up late and does not get up until after Mr. G. has gone to work and Johnny to school (on those occasions when he does get up in time for school). Mr. G. is critical of Mrs. G. and seems strongly to resent Mrs. G.'s hours. At one point he said, "If you got up, Johnny would." Mrs. G. lashed back with, "There's no reason you could not get him out of bed in the morning if you wanted to." Both mother and father indicate that Johnny has no specific bedtime and that virtually none of the family rules are consistently enforced with respect to Johnny.

While these descriptions cannot convey a full understanding of the depth of feelings involved, they do indicate something of the extent to which the problem in the PINS case is one of conflict and communication within the family unit. In California, at least, such cases involving family breakdown are much more representative than the cases involving vague allegations of sexual misconduct or unprovable criminal charges. The indications are that this is true in other states as well, but there is little solid information either way and it is known that practices vary greatly from jurisdiction to jurisdiction.

In one sense, runaway and incorrigible behavior are simply opposite sides of the same coin—the child initiating the action in the runaway situation and the parent in the incorrigible or beyond-control case. At the level of referral to the probation department, the numbers—in some jurisdictions at least—are about the same. The dynamics are not very well understood, however, because it is clear that many runaways are arrested and sent home without referral to court, and that at least some incorrigibility cases are based on the parents' reaction to an earlier running-away by the child. Generally parents initiate the incorrigibility charge by calling the police, but in some instances they may bring the youth to a juvenile detention center themselves. Runaway cases on the other hand are usually triggered by police arrest and referral.

Girls make up about half the PINS cases, and this is the principal way that they become involved with the juvenile justice system. Boys, on the other hand, while also constituting half of the PINS total, are much more heavily involved in violations of the regular criminal law [12]. For both groups, the problem centers at age fifteen and sixteen and in families in which there has been a divorce or separation [13]. Often the child appears to be playing one parent or set of parents off against the other. Parents, on the other hand, are often still trying to get even with each other through the medium of the child.

THE SACRAMENTO 601 PROJECT

One recent study which sheds some light on this problem is that of the Sacramento 601 Diversion Project [14]. This project was begun in 1970 in Sacramento County as a way of testing whether juveniles accused of being runaway, beyond the control of their parents, or otherwise in violation of Section 601 of the California Juvenile Court Law (the California PINS statute) [15] could be better handled through short-term family crisis therapy than by the traditional procedures of the juvenile court.

Established as an experiment in the probation department, the project staff consisted of specially-trained probation officers who handled cases four days a week while the regular intake unit handled the other three days as control group. Days were rotated monthly.

The project approach, when a 601 referral was received—whether from the police, the schools, the parents, or whomever—was to arrange a family counseling session to discuss the problem. Every effort was made to insure that the session was held as soon as possible, and most were held within the first or second hour after referral.

All members of the family living at home including other children were urged to attend this session, as well as grandparents, girlfriends or boyfriends, and significant others as well. Through the use of family counseling techniques, the project counselor sought to develop the idea that the problem was one to be addressed by the family as a whole and not just by the youth who has been arrested. The problem was treated as one involving the interaction of the family rather than as somebody's fault.

Locking up the youth as a method of solving problems was discouraged, and a return home with a commitment by all to try to work through the problem was encouraged. If the underlying emotions were too strong to permit the youth's return home immediately ("I'd rather stay in 'juvie' than go home with you." "We don't ever want him back."), an attempt was made to locate an alternative place for the youth to stay temporarily. This was a voluntary procedure which required consent of both the parents and the youth.

Families were encouraged to return for a second discussion with the counselor, and depending upon the nature of the problem, for a third, fourth, or fifth session. Normally the maximum number of sessions was five, and the average was closer to one and a half. Sessions rarely lasted less than one hour, and often went as long as two or two and a half hours.

Project Results

The intent of the project was to keep the child out of Juvenile Hall, keep the family problem out of court, and still offer counseling and help to the family. The results of the experiment indicated that to a great extent, these goals had been accomplished, and hence its practice was adopted as policy. During the first year of the project, 977 cases involving opportunities for diversion were referred to the project and only 36 petitions were filed. Court processing was thus necessary in only 3.7 percent of these referrals as opposed to 19.8 percent of the beyond-control referrals handled in the control groups.

Project cases also spent far less time in Juvenile Hall than did the control cases as a result of initial handling—an average of 0.5 nights per case as opposed to 4.6 nights for the control cases. Over 55 percent of all control group youths spent at least one night in Juvenile Hall, while the comparable figure for youths handled by the project was 14 percent.

Even more important are the data concerning repeat behavior. One reason for this project in the first place was the indication in prior studies of a very high degree of repeated problems for this kind of youth. Moreover, these repeated problems were found frequently to escalate into criminal offenses. Several different measures were consequently developed to test for repeated problems, and cases were followed for one year to determine the extent to which they had occurred.

At the end of this period, 54.2 percent of the control group youths had been rebooked for either a 601 offense or for violations of the penal code. The comparable figure for the project group was 46.3 percent. Thus, while the repeat rate for both groups was high, the project cases did noticeably better. Out of 100 youths handled, 7.9 fewer were found to repeat under project handling. The decrease is over 14 percent of the return rate for control cases.

Looking at only criminal conduct, the improvement was even greater. In this respect, only 22.4 percent of the project group moved on to criminal offenses, compared to 29.8 percent for the control group. Project cases committed subsequent criminal acts 24.8 percent less than control group cases; because of the greater consistency in classification among all agencies involved this is perhaps the best overall measure for the project.

Also extremely important in a practical sense is the fact that these results were accomplished at a lower cost than the cost of service provided prior to the beginning of the project. Based on the twelve-month follow-up data, the average total handling time for project youths was 14.2 hours as compared with 23.7 hours for the control youths. Including detention and placement, costs for the project youth were $274 as compared with $561 for the control group. Thus the cost to the probation department of regular intake care for this kind of case is more than twice as expensive as the cost of diversion.

Implications

What are the implications of this approach? Does it suggest anything about what ought to happen more generally in the handling of runaway and beyond-control cases?

Factually, it does seem clear that there is some kind of underlying problem in many of the cases. The feelings involved are intense and the clinical evidence, at least, is that these do not abate without some kind of intervention. Moreover, the form which these problems take in the absence of intervention is often that of criminal behavior. In Sacramento, nearly 30 percent of the control group 601s and over 20 percent of the project group later became involved in criminal conduct [16]. Other data suggest that these figures are not atypical [17].

Whether the Sacramento approach suggests anything new in terms of legislation is a difficult question, however. Given past failings in this area, this topic should be approached with a great deal of caution and uncertainty. What we know is very little compared to what we do not know. Several ideas, however, do seem to warrant consideration.

The first of these is based on the assumption that the Sacramento approach is now feasible almost anywhere. All that is required is the desire to go ahead. In Sacramento the program was taken over at the end of the three-year experimental period by the county. A number of other jurisdictions have also begun similar programs, including Alameda, Contra Costa, Fresno and Humboldt Counties in California; and Virginia Beach, Virginia; DuPage County, Illinois; and Camden, New Jersey. Selection of the Sacramento project by the United States Department of Justice as one of its first five exemplary criminal justice projects has encouraged yet other jurisdictions to consider the approach [18]. Recent federal emphasis on the deinstitutionalization of status offenders is likely to encourage even more [19].

Legislatures could, if they so desired, further this process of adoption by enacting new legislation authorizing use of the Sacramento procedure. Such legislation is of course not required for programs to begin, but would be helpful in encouraging the approach. Legislative scrutiny could also be of assistance in spelling out the ground rules under which the program operates in order to prevent the development of abuses.

New funds to accompany an authorizing statute would also be helpful, particularly insofar as training costs are concerned. While this kind of program is in fact generally cheaper than the programs it replaces, and can usually be created simply by reorganizing and shifting existing personnel and resources already devoted to the same general purposes, start-up monies are often hard to come by and the training costs involved, while not great, are often more than is available.

A NO FAULT APPROACH

A second suggestion is more tentative than the first. It is also more fundamental. While strong arguments can and are being made in favor of repeal of PINS-type jurisdiction, there are many problems in this solution [20]. Among the most important of these is the fact that this solution would radically alter the underlying legal relationships in the family without discussion or consideration. This problem can be illustrated by the case of runaways. What implications would repeal have for runaways? Would it mean that runaways are under no compulsion to return home and that a police agency or a probation agency finding a young boy or girl hundreds of miles from home would have no authority to return the child to the home and would in essence be limited to waving hello or yelling good luck?

Some undoubtedly would be willing to go this far [21]. Many who have advocated repeal, however, have not really considered this problem. Further, even if this solution is accepted for fifteen-year-olds, how about twelve-year-olds or eight-year-olds?

The result of total repeal would in effect be a further lowering of the age of majority—presumably to the age of birth. The child becomes a free agent, able to move or go wherever he or she chooses at any time. Repeal would affect the child's duty to obey the parents in the same way. The child would be free to go his own way.

This solution raises a great many complex economic and social questions. Aside from the many obvious issues involving younger children, it raises the highly important and by no means theoretical question as to what extent the parents remain obligated to provide support for the child. Obviously this is only one facet of the parent-child relationship—parents provide much more than money. It is an important facet, however, and until now, the duty of support has been a reciprocal of the duty of the child to obey the parent [22]. There is, of course, nothing in the nature of things which requires this, and it would be possible to require support without responsibility for discipline and control [23]. This would require a wholly different kind of personal relationship, however, than that which has generally existed until now.

In an age in which consensual living arrangements between males and females have become acceptable, or even fashionable, there is perhaps something to be said for a generally consensual relationship between parents and children. Successful relationships in a totally free market, however, generally require some equality of positions. And, as long as there is some economic dependency involved, even without discussion of any immaturity present, it seems clear that this equality is not present. One result could be increased conflict and hard feelings. There is, in addition, the very real question of parental supervision and guidance. While views may differ as to the value and need for such a role, most still believe it to be essential to the sound development of the child.

It is of course true that repeal of the duty to provide either economic support or parental guidance would not necessarily mean that these would cease. It may be, however, that removal of the principal legal supports for these actions could have that tendency. The relationships involved are extremely delicate ones, and a "damn the torpedoes" approach seems neither wise nor warranted.

Many other changes in legal relationships could follow from repeal, including changes in the tort and contractual responsibilities of both parent and child [24]. These changes do not necessarily follow automatically from decriminalization but are strongly related to the underlying factual and philosophical assumptions upon which repeal is based. At a minimum, there needs to be some awareness that these issues are involved. Ideally each should be thought through separately, and not decided *sub rosa* through the device of decriminalization.

More limited than repeal is the approach, taken by the courts in a number of states including California, to narrow the previously broad and ambiguous definitions of 601-type offenses [25]. This has the effect of restricting the law's support for parental authority. Courts in a few jurisdictions have gone so far as to find the statutory language so vague as to be constitutionally void [26]. Others have simply attempted to shift the responsibility for accommodating to conflict to the parent [27]. Thus a California court recently said:

The inquiry allowed when a minor is charged with being beyond the control of his parents must be a broad one. If, in connection with the normal frictions of family life, the minor is so disobedient as to warrant sustaining a petition under section 601 he is branded as a delinquent. . . . If, on the other hand, . . . the breakdown in parental control is because of failings in the parent rather than that in the minor, a section 601 petition could not be sustained. Given the identical complaints by a mother, against a son, if it was determined that she was the one who has lost control, a dismissal of section 601 charges would follow. A finding that the parent was at fault might support the determination that the minor was within section 600, but that section deals with dependent children in need of help and not with delinquent children in need of correction. We do not at all intimate that Henry's mother was the one at fault but his counsel should have been allowed to try to show that fact [28].

The issue, however, is not really whose fault the problem is, but rather what is to be done about it. How does it help to say that it is the father's fault rather than the son's? Can the court really do any more with a neglect (section 600) petition than with a runaway/beyond control (601) petition? It seems clear that a pronouncement that this party or that party is the one at fault does not solve anything and may very well make things worse.

The central questions in any 601 situation are: (1) Whether anything is to be done, (2) if so, what, and (3) by whom? The determination as to whether something is to be done or not depends upon whether someone, generally the child, did something that he should not have done. If the answer to this question is in the affirmative, then the court decides essentially between leaving the child in the home under some admonition to do better (with or without supervision) or taking the child out of the home either temporarily or permanently.

The situation seems in many ways parallel to that existing in the traditional divorce law. Under that law, a party was entitled to judicial relief from a marriage that was felt to be unsatisfactory if, but only if, the other party was at fault. The newer divorce statutes, however, take a much different approach. They are triggered not by a finding of fault but rather by finding that an irreconcilable conflict exists [29]. They thus avoid the requirement that the court make a determination concerning the acrimonious and destructive issue of fault [30]. These statutes thus not only have the advantage of recognizing the under-lying realities of the personal relationships involved, but also make it possible for breakups to be somewhat less contentious, particularly where there are no issues involving property or child custody [31].

It seems desirable that serious consideration now be given to similar treatment of the parent-child disputes which make up the bulk of the 601-type cases. The law should cease to weigh in automatically on the side of the parent. At the same time, it should avoid the Charybdis of automatically taking the side of the child. Rather, it should say that if there is a child in the family who runs away or if there is an irreconcilable conflict between the child and his parents, then the matter is within the jurisdiction of the juvenile court. The triggering event thus becomes the conflict rather than the fault and could be invoked by either party.

The statute should also contain a counseling provision, requiring each jurisdic-tion to establish a service capable of counseling with the family as a whole and providing that no order affecting the substantial rights of any family member can be entered by the court unless the counseling agency has certified its inabil-ity to deal with the situation. Under this kind of statute, the court would be directed to resolve the problem wherever possible within the context of the family unit and would be empowered to order the entire family, including the parents, to participate in counseling or to do or refrain from doing other things of importance in the situation. The court would be authorized as now to sepa-rate the child from the family if no other solution is feasible, but would not be authorized to send the child to reform school or other hard-core juvenile facilities.

The basic determinant of the authority structure within the family under present law is of course the family's own desires. By and large the law comes into play only when there is some problem or malfunctioning. To the extent that the law does come into play, however, it more or less automatically rein-forces the authority of the parent. To be sure, present statutes and decisions speak of obeying the parents' "reasonable orders," but the wording and the structure make clear the intent to uphold the parents' authority.

The kind of statute proposed would change this to a more evenhanded ap-proach. The family would still be free to make its own decisions about authority as before, but to the extent the law comes into play, there would be no auto-matic presumption of parental authority. Thus, in a legal sense, the statute would change the balance of authority somewhat, but not so radically as outright repeal [32]. It reaffirms the value of the family relationships as the best way for the child to grow and develop. At the same time, it recognizes the fact that the extreme reinforcement of parental authority inherent in the older statutes is to some degree out of tune with the mainstream of modern family life.

The standard to be applied by the court in reaching a decision concerning those matters certified to it can only be understood in the context of the counseling provision. This provision is not incidental to the statutory scheme but is its very heart.

Throughout the history of the juvenile justice system, lip service has been paid to the need for psychiatric and psychological services. By and large these services have been ignored to date, in major part because they really have not had all that much to offer. Within the last decade, however, powerful new tools have emerged from these disciplines, particularly the technique of family crisis counseling [33] . This technique has the capacity to make a substantial difference in the life of a juvenile, primarily through the mobilization of the family. While sociologists and others have long recognized the importance of the family as a determining influence on the life of the child, until recently no very satisfactory way of influencing the family for good or for ill was available [34] . Now, through family counseling, this possibility does exist to a much greater degree.

To be sure, family counseling is not a panacea. And as it deals primarily with the internal dynamics of the family, it does not affect the tide of external factors which place such great pressure and stress on the family. Nevertheless, the indications at this time are that it is a many times more potent force than has heretofore existed for bringing the weight of the family to bear on any given problem.

The power of this technique derives from several factors. First, it treats the issue not as the fault of the runaway or beyond-control child, but rather as a problem with which the whole family must deal. Secondly, it focuses on the general relationships and decision-making process in the family rather than the specific event which triggered the crisis. The theory here is that if the relationships and communication in the family can be placed in good working order, the family itself will be able to deal with the specific problem.

Perhaps the most difficult problem to be faced in the drafting of the new statutory scheme is the role of the juvenile court. The standard for intervention proposed is whether a conflict exists. Given the fact that "even in stable families there is a certain amount of child-parent conflict, particularly in relation to the older adolescent group" [35] , this can only be viewed as a very broad one. This breadth, however, is greatly reduced by the fact that the court is not permitted to act until the counseling agency has certified that it can do nothing with the case. The effect of the counseling requirement, and one of its intents, should be to drastically reduce the number of cases coming before the juvenile court, thus substituting family counseling for the court process wherever possible [36] . Intervention is nonetheless troubling and care must be taken to make it clear that the court is not intended to interject itself into those situations where the "storm can be weathered through the use of common sense and skilled handling or through the gradual process of maturation." Perhaps the operative terms should be "serious conflict" rather than "conflict" alone—although any such term begins to some extent to bring fault back into play through the necessity of proving seriousness.

Some court role is essential, however:

> Where parent-child relations reach an impasse, there must be some consti-
> tuted authority which can intervene in the child-parent relationship with
> or without the consent of the parties. Such intervention obviously involves
> some curtailment of basic personal rights and should conform to due pro-
> cess of law. In this country traditionally we have looked to the court to
> determine when, under what conditions, and to what extent the state may
> intervene in the private lives of its citizens [37].

Upon receipt of a case, the court's first effort necessarily must be to try to mediate the case, even though the counseling effort has previously failed. With skill in
the execution of this enterprise, the court should have some success. A different
intermediary with a different perspective should produce different results at
least some of the time.

In addition, under the new standards in which fault is irrelevant, the judge
should have authority to impose requirements—within reason—on the parents
as well as the child [38]. Thus, he might direct the entire family to continue
counseling or rule that the family's seventeen-year-old daughter should not be
required to be in by 9:30 on Saturday night. Generally, such matters should be
resolved voluntarily as far as possible and compulsory orders should be imposed
only upon a finding that such an order is "highly necessary." Orders imposing
counseling on the parties are particularly sensitive and should be used only as a
measure of last resort. Aside from whatever civil liberties issues there are involved, there is some serious question as to the efficacy of compulsory counseling [39]. It is preferable, however, to extended out-of-home placement and
should be used when it offers some hope of avoiding this.

In many instances, even after its best efforts, the court will not be able to
find a solution within the family. Some placement outside of the home then becomes necessary. Here the court should attempt to work out some consensual
solution if it can. Compulsion may be required, however, as to either one or
both of the parties. In this situation, the authority and procedures of the court
are needed to insure that the rights of all the parties are protected and to authorize the necessary action. Even where the parties have agreed, there may be some
need for court overview of out-of-home placements—at least for those to be
made for any extended period of time—to insure among other things that reconciliation efforts continue.

This still leaves the question as to when the judge should conclude that the
child should be separated from the family. Under the present law, except for
some largely hortatory language about the sanctity of the family, there is little
guidance on this point. Legally, "the best interests of the child" presumably

controls. Factually, however, the question is often determined by how "ornery" the child is perceived to be. As both parent and child often start out opposed to any continuing relationship, it seems clear that their initial positions should not necessarily be accepted on this point. Where both, after thorough exploration, want the relationship dissolved either permanently or for a time, however, the judge has little course but to concur. Where one party wants to continue the relationship and the other does not, the issue is a difficult one—perhaps best left to *ad hoc* decision in the particular case.

The pre-court counseling provided in the proposed statute would be essentially voluntary. No member of the family would be required to attend the session or sessions. No referral would be made to the court, however, unless every effort had been made to resolve the situation through counseling and no individual member of the family who had not participated in the sessions could demand that the matter come before the court.

In order to ensure the voluntariness of the proceedings, after the first counseling session the matter as a technical legal issue would be dismissed. Either the child or the family could request further sessions; and, if requested, the counselor would attempt to arrange these. Participation would continue to be voluntary, however. If the matter was eventually referred to court, the court would be empowered to order counseling on a mandatory basis. Presumably this would primarily be useful in those situations in which one or more parties had refused to participate in the earlier sessions, but might be used in some other instances as well.

The counseling agency involved could be a specially trained branch of the probation department, a private agency such as a family service agency, a mental health clinic, or some other group. Generally it would be preferable for the agency—at least insofar as short-term counseling is concerned—to be a probation department or some other agency which is responsive to the direction of the court. For longer-term counseling, referral to private agencies is a more practicable alternative.

Whatever the organization, however, care must be taken to insure that the counseling requirement is not simply a hollow routine. Many jurisdictions already have formal structures which could lay claim to satisfying this counseling function. The intake division, for example, of many present probation departments is instructed not to send cases to court until "everything possible" has been done to handle the matter outside of court. In a few jurisdictions there is already a legislative provision limiting the filing of a juvenile court petition to social agencies or the probation department, as opposed to the majority of states in which anyone may file. The limited filing provisions in effect encourage some kind of pre-court social work [40].

These efforts and those of the intake units described above are sensible and often, although not always, successful. What is proposed here, however, is a vast extension of this approach. To insure that this extension takes place, any new legislation should provide that the counseling agency must be certified to meet certain minimum requirements. The specific requirements for these standards can be built into the legislation itself or could be placed in administrative standards promulgated pursuant to the legislation. For metropolitan areas, these should include: (1) the capacity to provide immediate crisis service for a minimum of twelve hours a day for seven days a week, (2) no more than twenty new cases per counselor per month (if counselors are limited to five counseling sessions per case; and fewer than twenty cases if more counseling sessions are permitted), and (3) a requirement that counselors have a minimum of 100 hours of training in family crisis counseling including 30 hours of supervised counseling. Additional training, particularly on-going consultation, is highly desirable and should be encouraged, as should smaller caseloads.

The reasons for these standards should be apparent. Without the competence and the time that they provide for working with cases, the system suggested is little different from that which now exists. The changes suggested would probably still be worth making but would be unlikely to produce major new results.

SOME OTHER ISSUES

No mention has been made thus far of either detention or institutionalization under the proposed new statute. Both are, of course, substantial problems under existing law and practice. The pre-hearing detention rate of PINS cases is typically quite high—30 to 40 percent or more in many jurisdictions [41]. Similarly, there has in the past been a substantial amount of institutionalization associated with the PINS-type jurisdiction. In California, up to 10 percent of the commitments to the California Youth Authority at one time resulted from this kind of case; in New York 25 percent of the commitments were to reform schools [42].

Solutions to these problems are not necessarily dependent upon adoption of the proposals made in this chapter. There are a variety of ways of improving the present situation. Institutionalization—at least in secure facilities—can simply be banned, as several states have already done, and as the Federal Juvenile Justice and Delinquency Prevention Act mandates for states participating in its benefits [43]. Similarly, the practice—now followed in many states—by which violation of a court order entered under a PINS-type statute becomes a violation of the criminal code can also be banned [44]. Together these steps would essentially eliminate the institutionalization problem. They should be undertaken whether the proposed approach is adopted or not. In so doing, care must be taken not to create new forms of out-of-home placement that are more lengthy and more onerous than those being replaced.

Pre-hearing detention is more complicated [45]. Legal changes are introducing a whole new host of practical and financial problems. They would be greatly lessened, however, by adoption of the proposal. In the Sacramento 601 project, for example, the average number of detention days was reduced from 4.6 for control youths to 0.5 per project youth [46].

Another issue is that of truancy. Most PINS-type statutes include truancy within their ambit [47]. What constitutes truancy, however, seems to differ widely from school district to school district, and it is unclear how far the underlying dynamics resemble those of the runaway or beyond-control situation. Some truancy cases do seem to be related to parent-child conflicts. Others appear to be child-school conflicts, or even parent and child conflicts with the school. While it seems likely that many of the features of the system proposed would be appropriate for dealing with truancy, too little is known at this time to recommend that truancy be included in any new statute.

An even trickier issue is how the proposed system would relate to such legal requirements as the *Miranda* warnings [48]. Although the application to PINS cases of the requirements imposed by *Gault* [49] for notice, right to confrontation, and right to counsel is not as clear as it might be, on principle these requirements should and in some states clearly do apply to PINS cases [50]. While not altogether certain, it seems likely that these provisions would apply to the same extent to a no fault PINS statute as well [51]. It is also clear, however, that it is virtually impossible to counsel the family unless the parties are willing to communicate freely with each other and the counselor. So long as any information divulged is used solely for counseling, *Miranda* warnings may not be required as no court use of the information is involved. If counseling fails, however, and the case goes to court, any disclosures made might prove to be legally objectionable. Since the outcome of the counseling is not known in advance, this poses the question as to whether the full panoply of legal rights initiated by *Gault*, including *Miranda* warnings, should be afforded from the beginning of the counseling.

The answer to this is that they probably should. Although most may concede this result as legally desirable, some may see it as making counseling difficult, particularly insofar as it encourages youths not to talk and brings attorneys into the process. While this is something of a dilemma, it is not as great as one might think. Notice as to what is involved seems almost as important for the counseling as for an actual court appearance. Similarly if counseling information is to be available for later use in court, both honesty and fairness seem to require that that fact be made known at the outset so that the parties may make their decision in light of the real situation. An even better solution is that already adopted in Illinois of making any information brought forward in the counseling confidential and not admissible in court [52].

As far as attorneys are concerned, it seems clear that there is no real advantage to preventing or discouraging consultation. Most attorneys consulted in this situation would advise full and complete participation in the counseling. This would be even more true if a rule were adopted making any statements made in the counseling sessions not admissible later in court. It also seems clear that full knowledge of one's legal rights and obligations should be a help rather than a hindrance in any counseling undertaken. Moreover, advising the parties of their right to an attorney would not mean that the attorney himself would participate in the family counseling session. His role would normally be limited to explaining the rights and obligations involved and advising as to whether his client should participate.

Doubtless, many other details would have to be worked out in drafting a full-blown no-fault PINS statute. Enough has been set out here, however, to give the gist of the idea and some of the major considerations involved. Few would deny that the history of the present law in this area has been a dismal one, but many still doubt the advisability of total repeal. The approach suggested would certainly not end all problems in this area. It could establish a new and sounder framework for dealing with these issues, however, creating better solutions for many troubled youths and families.

NOTES TO CHAPTER 8

1. In 1972 there were 186,113 arrests in California for delinquent tendencies. California Bureau of Criminal Statistics, *Crime and Delinquency in California—1972*, 51. This is a decrease from 229,794 in 1969. The last year for which court and juvenile hall admissions data is available is 1970. *See Crime and Delinquency in California—1970*, 80, 97, 102.

2. President's Commission on Law Enforcement and Administration of Justice, *The Challenge of Crime in a Free Society* 83 (1967) [hereinafter cited as *President's Commission*].

3. *See* E. Lemert, *Instead of Court: Diversion in Juvenile Justice* (Natl. Inst. of Mental Health, Crime and Delinquency Series, 1971), for an excellent description of these alternatives. *See also* Bazelon, "Beyond Control of Juvenile Court," 21 *Juv. Ct. Judges J.*, No. 2, 43 (Summer, 1970), arguing for transferring this responsibility to the schools.

4. *See, e.g.*, Board of Directors, National Council on Crime and Delinquency, "Jurisdiction over Status Offenses Should Be Removed from the Juvenile Court," 21 *Crime and Delinquency* 97 (1975); California Legislature, *Report of the Assembly Interim Committee on Criminal Procedure, Juvenile Court Processes*, 1970 Interim Sess.

5. *See, e.g.*, Larson, "Identifying Court Needs, Programs to Meet Them," 20 *Juv. Ct. Judges J.*, No. 3, at 91 (Fall, 1970).

6. *See, e.g.*, Fox, "Juvenile Justice Reform: An Historical Perspective," 22 *Stan. L. Rev.* 1164 (1970); A. Platt, *The Child Savers* (1969). *See also* Teitelbaum, Book Review, 4 *Fam. L. Q.* 444 (1970).

7. *See President's Commission, Supra* note 2; Beggs, *Huckleberrys for Runaways* (1969); Juvenile Justice and Delinquency Prevention Act of 1974, 42 U.S.C.A. §§5701—51 (Supp. 1976).

8. *See, e.g.,* E. Schur, *Radical Non-Intervention: Rethinking the Delinquency Problem* 118–26 (1973).

9. *See, e.g.,* N. Morris and G. Hawkins, *An Honest Politician's Guide to Crime Control* 146–68 (1970); *Cf.* Note, "Ungovernability: The Unjustifiable Jurisdiction," 83 *Yale L. J.* 1383 (1974) (using the PINS label to cover delinquent acts). The specific statutory language quoted was a part of California Welfare and Institutions Code §601 until 1976; *see infra* note 26 for discussion of recent legal developments concerning this section.

10. California Bureau of Criminal Statistics, *Juvenile Probation and Detention, Reference Tables—1970,* at 16. This does not include violations of specific offenses applicable to juveniles such as curfew and liquor laws.

11. Gonzalez v. Mailliard, No. 50424 (N.D. Cal. 1971), *vacated and remanded,* Mailliard v. Gonzalez, 416 U.S. 918 (1974); A.B. 432, Cal. Legis., Reg. Sess. (1975), *infra* note 26.

12. *Supra* note 10, at 11.

13. *See, e.g.,* R. Baron and F. Feeney, *Preventing Delinquency Through Diversion, A Second Year Report,* Appendix A (July, 1973).

14. This project is described in greater detail in R. Baron and F. Feeney, *Preventing Delinquency Through Diversion, A First Year Report* (May 1972); *Baron and Feeney, A Second Year Report* (July 1973); Baron, Feeney, and Thornton, "Preventing Delinquency Through Diversion," 37 *Fed. Prob.* 13 (March 1973). It was suggested in part by a paper presented by former Denver Juvenile Court Judge Ted Rubin entitled "Law as an Agent of Delinquency Prevention," presented to the California Delinquency Prevention Strategy Conference in February, 1970. *See also* R. Baron and F. Feeney, *Juvenile Diversion Through Family Counseling* (1976).

15. Cal. Welf. and Instn's Code §601 (Supp. 1976).

16. *See* Baron and Feeney, *Supra* note 13.

17. *See, e.g.,* McKay, "Report on the Criminal Careers of Male Delinquents in Chicago," in President's Commission on Law Enforcement and Administration of Justice, *Task Force Report: Juvenile Delinquency and Youth Crime* 107 (1967) [hereinafter *Task Force Report*]. Given its importance, there is surprisingly little research available on this subject.

18. The purpose of selecting exemplary programs is to identify outstanding projects and assist other jurisdictions in implementing them. Selections are made by an advisory board of state and L.E.A.A. officials. Press Release, Law Enforcement Assistance Administration, April, 1974.

19. "Deinstitutionalization" means removing status offenders from secure custody. It is required by the federal Juvenile Justice and Delinquency Prevention Act of 1974 for states receiving funds under the act. Section 223(a)(12) [42 U.S.C.A. §5633(a)(12)(Supp. 1976)] requires states to:

[P]rovide within two years after submission of the (state) plan that juveniles who are charged with or who have committed offenses that would not be criminal if committed by an adult, shall not be placed in juvenile detention or correctional facilities, but must be placed in shelter facilities. . . .

20. *Supra*, note 4.

21. *See, e.g.*, Note, "Ungovernability: The Unjustifiable Jurisdiction," 83 *Yale L.J.* 1383 (1974). *See also, E. Schur, Radical Non-Intervention: Rethinking the Delinquency Problem* (1973); A.B. 3121, Cal. Stats., 1975 Reg. Sess. ch. 193; Comment, "The Juvenile Court and the Runaway: Part of the Solution or Part of the Problem," 24 *Emory L.J.* 1075 (1975).

22. *See, e.g.*, Roe v. Doe, 29 N.Y. 2d 188, 272 N.E. 2d 567, 324 N.Y.S. 2d 71 (1971). The origin of the parents' duty of support is of course not premised solely on the duty of the child to obey the parents' "reasonable regulations." The parents' right to earnings and to custody are also cited as bases for the duty. The duty is generally mandated by statute, *see, e.g.*, former *Cal. Civil Code* §196 (West 1954), but this seems to be treated more as a codification of the common law duty rather than an independent basis for the duty.

23. *See, e.g.*, County of Alameda v. Kaiser, 238 Cal. App. 2d 815, 48 Cal. Rptr. 343 (1965), in which a mother was held liable for the hospital bill of an "emancipated" son. *See also*, Katz, Schroeder, and Sidman, "Emancipating our Children—Coming of Legal Age in America," 7 *Fam. L. Q.* 211, 225–29 (1973).

24. For a description of current law, *see generally, H. Clark, Domestic Relations* 230–60 (1968).

25. *See, e.g., In re* D.J.B., 18 Cal. App. 3d 782, 96 Cal. Rptr. 146; People v. Grieve, 131 Ill. Ap. 2d 1078, 267 N.E. 2d 19 (1971); *In re K.*, 35 App. Div. 2d 716, 314 N.Y.S. 2d 1004 (1970). *See also*, Note, "California Runaways," 26 *Hastings L. J.* 1013, 1032 at note 134 (1975).

26. In Gonzalez v. Mailliard, No. 50424 (N.D. Cal., Feb. 9, 1971) a three-judge federal district court held the portion of the California statute dealing with "idle, dissolute, lewd or immoral life" unconstitutional on vagueness grounds. The court granted both declaratory and injunctive relief. On appeal, the United States Supreme Court, 416 U.S. 918 (1974), vacated and remanded "for reconsideration of the injunction in light of Steffel v. Thompson, 415 U.S. 452 (1974), and Zwickler v. Koota, 389 U.S. 241 (1967)." This disposition presumably left the declaratory judgment holding the provision unconstitutionally vague intact. *See* Note, "California Runaways," 26 *Hastings L. J.* 1013, 1030 (1975).

The California legislature subsequently removed the "idle and dissolute" language from the statute, A.B. 3161 Cal. Stats., 1975 Reg. Sess., ch. 193. *See also, In re* E.M.B., No. J1365–73 (D.C. Super. Ct., June 14, 1973), *rev'd. sub. nom.* District of Columbia v. B.J.R., 332 A.2d 58 (D.C. App. 1975); Gesicki v. Oswald, 336 F. Supp. 371 (S.D.N.Y. 1971), *aff'd without opinion*, 406 U.S. 913 (1972); *M. Paulsen* and *C. Whitebread, Juvenile Law and Procedure* 48–50 (1974). The vagueness issue was earlier presented to the United States Supreme Court in Mattiello v. Conn., 4 Conn. Cir. 55, 225 A. 2d 507 (App. Div. 1966), *cert. denied*, 154 Conn. 737, 225 A. 2d 201 (1966), *prob. juris. noted*, 391 U.S. 963, *petition for cert. dismissed*, 395 U.S. 209 (1969). In this case the Supreme Court first took jurisdiction, then dismissed the case without decision for want of a proper federal question. *See* Note, "Statutory Vagueness in Juvenile Law: The Supreme Court and *Mattiello v. Connecticut*," 118 *U. Penn. L. Rev.* 143

(1969). *See also* Note, "Juvenile Court Jurisdiction Over 'Immoral' Youth in California," 24 *Stan. L. Rev.* 568 (1972).

27. *See* Ganion, "Section 601 California Welfare and Institutions Code: A Need for a Change," 9 *San Diego L. Rev.* 294, 304 (1972); Los Angeles Superior Court, Special Committee on Judicial Reforms, *A Study of Current Problems Affecting the Administration of Justice*, at 26—27 (February 22, 1971).

28. *In re* Henry G., 28 Cal. App. 3d 276, 284, 104 Cal. Rptr. 585, 590 (1972).

29. One example of the futility of arguing about fault is provided in *In re* Lloyd, 33 App. Div. 2d 385, 308 N.Y.S. 2d 419, 421 (1970), where a New York Court reversed a finding that a youth was a PINS in favor of a neglect finding. The court then went on to show how little the whole procedure had accomplished:

> Is this child then to be relegated to the custody of his mother under conditions that the record shows have actually deteriorated since the original, and justified, finding of neglect? It is easy to say, as it is undoubtedly true, that it is not our problem. The court obviously cannot provide a facility where none exists. We do not give up, however, without a final gesture. . . . [W]e direct a new adjudicatory and dispositional hearing in the hope that with the lapse of time a place in some authorized agency may be found or that the Children's Center may be able to make a viable adjustment.

30. *Cf. Cal. Civil Code* §4506—07 (West 1970). Section 4507 provides that "Irreconcilable differences are those grounds which are determined by the court to be substantial reasons for not continuing the marriage and which make it appear that the marriage should be dissolved." *See also* Iowa Code Ann. §598.17 (Supp. 1976); *M. Wheeler, No-Fault Divorce* (1974).

31. The extent to which fault creeps into the courtroom depends in part upon the extent to which the court accepts the assertions of the parties as to "conflict" and the extent to which it seeks to make its own judgments as to this. See McKim v. McKim, 6 Cal. 3d 673, 493 P. 2d 868, 100 Cal. Rptr. 140 (1972). Even under the no fault concept as a basis for dissolution, fault issues tend to be involved where there is a dispute as to child custody or to property settlement.

32. Kleinfeld, "The Balance of Power Among Infants, Their Parents and the State," 4 *Fam. L. Q.* 409, 433 *et seq.* (1970) suggests that courts are less strict now than previously in interpreting the PINS jurisdiction. This seems very unlikely, however, given the looseness of the pre-*Gault* jurisdictional standard.

33. *See V. Satir, Conjoint Family Therapy* (revised ed. 1967). This technique has proved to be very powerful in mental health. See *D. Langsley* and *D. Kaplan, The Treatment of Families in Crisis Intervention* (1968).

34. Rodman and Grams, "Juvenile Delinquency and the Family: A Review and Discussion," in *Task Force Report, supra* note 17 at 188 (App. L.) (1967).

35. Sheridan, "Juveniles Who Commit Noncriminal Acts: Why Treat in a Correctional System," 31 *Fed. Prob.* 26, 28 (March, 1967).

36. In Gough, "The Beyond-Control Child and the Right to Treatment: An Exercise in the Synthesis of Paradox," 16 *St. Louis U.L.J.* 182, 195 (1971), it is

suggested that the emergence of the "right to treatment" principle may entitle a juvenile to a "right not to be removed from that setting in which the corrective therapy must be carried out—the family."

37. Sheridan, *supra* note 35 at 28.

38. This kind of authority already exists in a limited way under some statutes. *Cal. Educ. Code* §12410 (West 1969), for example, authorizes the court to order a parent to deliver a truant or disorderly child to school. Section 12454 provides penalties for failure to comply.

39. This matter has been debated considerably in the context of counseling at the time of divorce. *See, e.g.*, Hansen, "Three Dimensions of Divorce," 50 *Marq. L. Rev.* 1 (1966); Shakiverler, "Statutory Marriage Counseling," 45 *Florida B.J.* 1557 (1971). *See also* Bodenheimer, "New Approaches of Psychiatry: Implications for Divorce Reform," 1970 *Utah L. Rev.* 191.

40. *See, e.g., Colo. Rev. Stats. Ann.* §19−3−101(2) (1973); *Conn. Gen. Stats. Ann.* §17−61 (1976); Sheridan, *supra* note 33 at 29.

41. *Supra* note 1; see also Ferster and Courtless, "Juvenile Detention in an Affluent County," 6 *Fam. L. Q.* 3, 9 at note 38 (1972), showing detention rates of 16.5 to 68.5 percent in twelve major jurisdictions across country.

42. *See, e.g., California Youth Authority, Annual Report: 1968* at 16. This shows a high-water mark in California for incorrigibles and runaways—916 percent of first admissions. For a discussion of the New York data, *see* Gough, *supra* note 36 at 191−92.

43. *Supra* note 19.

44. The federal guidelines issued under the Juvenile Justice and Delinquency Prevention Act of 1974 provide that status offenders who violate the terms of their probation in ways other than through the commission of criminal acts continue to be status offenders for federal act purposes. Law Enforcement Assistance Administration, *Guideline Manual: State Planning Agency Grants*, at 117−21 (January 16, 1976).

45. This, too, is being affected by section 223(a) (12) of the Juvenile Justice and Delinquency Prevention Act of 1974, which requires participating states to eliminate secure detention in favor of shelter care or other alternatives. 42 U.S.C.A. §5633(a) (12) (Supp. 1976).

46. *Supra* note 14.

47. *See, e.g., Cal. Welf. and Inst. Code* §601 (West 1972); *Ill. Ann. Stat.* §37:702−3 (Smith-Hurd 1972). For an analysis of status offenses in the various states, *see J. Dineen, Juvenile Court Organization and Status Offenses: A Statutory Profile* (1974); *M. Levin* and *R. Sarri, Juvenile Delinquency; A Study of Juvenile Codes in the U.S.* (1974).

48. Miranda v. Arizona, 384 U.S. 436 (1965).

49. *In re* Gault, 387 U.S. 1 (1967).

50. *See* Stiller and Elder, "PINS—A Concept in Need of Supervision," 12 *Am. Crim. L. Rev.* 33, 39−44 (1974).

51. *In re* Gault, 387 U.S. 1 (1967) was itself a case in which the juvenile court judge who initially heard the case indicated that the youth involved had violated both the criminal code and the Arizona PINS statute [then *Ariz. Rev. Stat.* §8−201−6(a)]. *See* 387 U.S. 1, notes 1 & 2. In *Gault*, the Supreme Court

rejected the argument that juvenile court proceedings did not require notice, right to counsel, and other such incidents of due process because of the "civil" nature of the proceedings. Later cases have indicated, however, that juvenile court proceedings are not considered fully criminal. See, e.g., McKeiver v. Pennsylvania, 403 U.S. 528 (1971). While these later cases raise the possibility that a more genuinely "civil" PINS statute, such as one based on no-fault concepts, might not require the kind of due process spelled out in *Gault*, this seems highly unlikely.

52. *Ill. Ann. Stat.* §37:702−8(5) (Smith-Hurd 1972): "No statement made during a preliminary conference may be admitted into evidence at an adjudicatory hearing or at any proceding against the minor under the criminal laws of this state prior to his conviction thereunder."

Chapter 9

Beyond-Control Youth
in the Juvenile Court—
The Climate for Change*

Aidan R. Gough

The juvenile court's jurisdiction over children's non-criminal misbehavior has long been seen as a cornerstone of its mission. Indeed,
assertions of state power over unruly children far antedate juvenile
courts themselves; the laws conferring court jurisdiction over unruly children
have their roots in "early colonial concerns with the child's key role as a source
of labor for the family economic unit" and some early statutes punished filial
disobedience with death [1].

This jurisdiction over non-criminal misbehavior is both widespread and
widely invoked. Every American juvenile court law has some ground or grounds
extending the court's power of intervention to cases involving antisocial but non-
criminal behavior. Such cases probably comprise—though firm figures are not
available—no less than one-third and probably close to one-half the workload
of America's juvenile courts [2]. While the labels vary from state to state—
Person/Child/Minor/Juvenile in Need of Supervision (commonly abbreviated
PINS, CHINS, MINS, JINS); Beyond-Control Child; Ungovernable Child; Incorrigible Child; Unruly Child; Wayward Child; Miscreant Child—the jurisdictional
thrust is essentially the same, allowing coercive judicial intervention in cases of
juvenile misbehavior that would not be criminal if committed by an adult.

Because the laws conferring this jurisdiction are typically couched in terms of
the child's condition rather than in terms of the commission of specific acts—for
example, a child's being "habitually beyond the control of his parents," or being
"an habitual truant"—cases brought under such statutes are frequently (albeit a
bit ineptly) referred to as "status offenses." Though there are many variations

*Substantial portions of this chapter are taken from the introduction and commentary
to *Juvenile Justice Standards: Non-Criminal Misbehavior*, for which the author served as
Reporter.

among the states, the status offense jurisdiction typically and essentially comprehends a wide spectrum of behavior, such as disobedience to a parent or guardian or school authorities, being truant, running away from home, being sexually promiscuous or otherwise "endangering morals," or acting in a manner "injurious to self or others." A majority of states include status offenders within the category of "delinquents." The remainder attempt in various ways to "break out" status offenses by creating a separate category in addition to the traditional classifications of neglect and delinquency. As will be seen, however, the treatment has not followed the label, and status offenders are generally subjected to the same modes of disposition as are juveniles who violate the criminal law. Additionally, they likely bear the same burdens of stigma as do delinquents [3].

The juvenile court's jurisdiction over unruly children is based on assumptions—most often implicit—that parents are reasonable persons seeking proper ends; that youthful independence is malign; that the social good requires judicial power to backstop parental command; that the juvenile justice system can identify non-criminal misbehavior which is predictive of future criminality; and that its coercive intervention will effectively remedy family-based problems and deter further offense [4].

On the available evidence, these haruspical assumptions and pretensions do not prove out; it simply cannot be established that the behavior encompassed by the status offense jurisdiction is accurately "proto-criminal" [5]. Indeed, as the California legislature noted, "Not a single shred of evidence exists to indicate that any significant number of [beyond control children] have benefited [by juvenile court intervention]. In fact, what evidence does exist points to the contrary" [6].

Most parental defiance and other forms of non-criminal misbehavior—troublesome though they are—represent a youthful push for independence and are both endemic and transitory. They are at worst "transitional deviance" which is outgrown [7]. It is widely conceded that unruly child cases are usually the most intractable and difficult matters with which the juvenile court has to deal; perhaps this is in part so precisely because the court is not the place to deal with them. The judicial system is simply an inept instrument for resolving intrafamily conflicts, and dealing with these cases in it results in a vast and disproportionate draining of time and resources, to the detriment of cases of neglect, abuse or delinquency which are properly there and represent threats to safety which the court must address. Erik Erickson has written;

> Youth after youth, bewildered by the incapacity to assume a role forced on him by the inexorable standardization of American adolescence, runs away in one form or another, dropping out of school, leaving jobs, staying out all night, or withdrawing into bizarre and inaccessible moods. Once "delinquent," his greatest need and often his only salvation is the refusal on the part of older friends, advisors and judiciary personnel to type him

further by pat diagnoses and social judgments which ignore the special dynamic conditions of adolescence [8].

A study done of PINS cases in New York City in 1973 revealed not only a wide range of conduct alleged to demonstrate a need for official intervention, but also the fact that the status offense jurisdiction was used in many cases of violation of the criminal law, supporting the conclusion that it masks cases which are properly delinquency or neglect matters and should be dealt with on that basis. "Short runaway" was the allegation in 51 percent of the cases; "refusal to obey" in 47 percent; truancy in 43 percent; late hours in 36 percent; possession of drugs in 23 percent; staying out overnight in 19 percent; undesirable boyfriends in 19 percent; and undesirable companions in 14 percent. Assault was alleged in 9 percent of the cases; larceny in 5 percent; possession of drugs for sale and possession of a dangerous weapon in 2 percent. Twenty-one percent of the cases involved "other" allegations, including refusal to bathe regularly; having an abortion against parental wishes; sleeping all day; refusal to do household chores; being "selfish and self-centered"; banging a door in reaction to a parental command; wanting to get married; suicide attempts, and "being an invertebrate (*sic*) liar" [9]. All studies encountered suggest that the range of family-centered problems is immense and that these allegations are typical of those in status offense cases elsewhere.

To address the operation of the status offense jurisdiction with some particularity, clearly the greatest vice is our treatment of non-criminal but ungovernable children in essentially the same way as we treat youthful violators of the criminal law, with maximum impetus (and opportunity for tutelage) given the former to become the latter. In the great majority of American jurisdictions, status offenders are subject to exactly the same dispositions as minors who commit crimes, including commitment to state training schools. Only a handful of states have followed New York in prohibiting the commitment of PINS to state schools which house delinquent youth, and even in the few states where intermixing is prohibited, status offenders are likely to be treated similarly to delinquents [10]. Furthermore, very few states have prohibited the temporary detention of ungovernable youth with delinquents pending adjudication; in the remainder, they are held in the same secure institutions as serious law violators.

A system which allows the same sanctions for parental defiance as for armed robbery—often with only the barest glance at the reasonableness of parental conduct—can only be seen as inept and unfair. Moreover, secure institutions housing youthful violators of the criminal law are necessarily geared to the custodial demands of the worst of their inmates, and the "treatment" for which the unruly child was committed is very often non-existent. Some such institutions are both illegal and inhumane [11].

Accurate national data are simply not available, but the number of unruly children inducted into the juvenile justice system under ungovernability statutes, and subjected as a consequence of that induction to the same dispositions as youth whose behavior has been criminal, is substantial indeed. The National Council on Crime and Delinquency estimates that more than 66,000 youth are confined in state training schools or their equivalents, and that between 45 and 55 percent of them are status offenders [12]. One study of probation officers' recommendations showed that juveniles referred for law violations had an eight times greater chance of having the probation officer recommend discharge or probation than did children referred for being ungovernable and "offending against parents" [13]. Roughly a dozen states have prohibitions against direct commitment of status offenders to state training schools, but a number of these states appear to allow an unruly child to be so committed on a second status offense, on the rationale that that juvenile has then violated a court order and thus become a delinquent [14].

Though the "labeling theory" of criminal causation—that a young person who has not committed a criminal act but is treated as and stigmatized as a delinquent is likely to become one—has been under recent attack, there is also some recent evidence to the contrary. A study of 222 inmates of the Indiana Boys Training School showed a "significant and linear decrease" in self-concept in the cases of boys not previously incarcerated. Conversely, minors showing an increase in self-concept had become increasingly involved in criminal behavior. The study found a correlation between incarceration and the internalization of delinquent values and self-concept. Put another way, it demonstrated that the minors had become what they were labeled to be [15]. On commonsense grounds *vice* the lack of conclusive empirical data, it seems likely that (1) coercive judicial intervention in unruly child cases produces some degree of labeling and stigmatization; and (2) whatever effect this has on the child's self-perception and future behavior will be adverse.

Even in cases where there is no order of institutional commitment, the juvenile court's status offense jurisdiction is not apt. A fourteen year old's being lazy, failing to do assigned chores, buying a sandwich at a place her mother had told her not to go, and "being a disruptive influence" should not support secure interim custody, judicial intervention, or official probation supervision [16]. These are significant consequences—as indeed, any juvenile court disposition is—and not only are they inept to resolve the problems presented by the unruly child, they are often imposed by a process that denies to the unruly youth before the court procedural rights which must be afforded to juveniles accused of delinquent acts. In some jurisdictions, status offenders may be denied the right to counsel [17].

It is the rule rather than the exception that the status of "being beyond control" is established by a preponderance of the evidence, rather than by the rigorous standard of proof beyond a reasonable doubt required by the U.S. Supreme Court in a delinquency adjudication [18]. Moreover, it is likely that evidence may be admissible at a PINS hearing which would not be admissible in the trial of a delinquency petition, and some statutes expressly authorize this [19]. This, together with the lower standard of proof commonly required, may explain in part why criminal offenses are not infrequently dealt with under the PINS or other unruly child rubric.

They may also be dealt with there because juvenile courts and their personnel believe a PINS adjudication to be less stigmatizing than an adjudication of delinquency. This reasoning seems perverse. It is probable that a greater stigmatizing effect will result from an adjudication of incorrigibility, based on a pattern of behavior, than from an adjudication of a single act. Furthermore, proof of unruliness is, in the words of one judge, "easy to present and usually impossible to controvert successfully" [20]. As a result, and because of the inherently greater power of the complainant parent, contests of PINS cases appear to be rare, at least in many courts. The New York study indicated that in New York County 69 percent of the youths appearing on PINS petitions admitted all the allegations; 24 percent made partial admissions, i.e., to some of the allegations; and only 7 percent denied all allegations and went to trial. In Rockland County, 94 percent of the cases involved a full admission and 7 percent a partial admission; there were no denials in the sample studied [21].

Parenthetically, it would appear that the existence of the status offense jurisdiction may be an important element in perpetuating plea-bargaining in the juvenile court; it has been described as "a kid's way of copping a plea" [22].

A further problem is that almost invariably the ungovernability statutes are impermissibly vague in wording and overbroad in scope. Such language as that extending jurisdiction over a child "who is in danger, from any cause, of leading an idle, dissolute or immoral life" or who is "ungovernable" or who is "growing up in idleness and crime" falls far short of the specificity that would allow a minor to determine what behavior fell within the prohibitions of the statute and what lay without [23]. Given the overbreadth of these statutes, every child in the United States could theoretically be made out to be a status offender. How many children have not disobeyed their parents at least twice?

The last few years have seen sharply-mounting attacks—in the literature, in the legislatures, and in the courts—on the statutes conferring the status offense jurisdiction, for their vagueness and their overbreadth, as well as on the dispositions that attend their use [24].

However, it must be said that attacks on such statutes based on the void-for-vagueness doctrine have thus far largely been turned back by the upper courts, and the Supreme Court of the United States has not closed with the issue, despite its striking down of a classic adult vagrancy (status) statute in *Papachristou v. City of Jacksonville* [25] on vagueness grounds, and its affirmance without opinion of a three-judge federal court's decision invalidating New York's youthful offender statute, which extended court jurisdiction (as a wayward minor) to one who was "morally depraved or . . . in danger of becoming morally depraved" [26]. In *Mercado v. Carey* [27], the Supreme Court summarily dismissed for want of a substantial federal question a challenge on void-for-vagueness grounds to New York's PINS law, N.Y. Family Court Act § 712(b) and in *Mailliard v. Gonzalez* [28], the Court vacated and remanded a decision by a three-judge federal court striking down that portion of the California beyond-control statute which extended the juvenile court's jurisdiction to minors leading or in danger of leading an "idle, dissolute, lewd, or immoral life" [29].

One cannot properly conclude, however, that juvenile status offense statutes have therefore been certified as constitutionally valid. In *Gonzalez*, the high court vacated and remanded for re-consideration of the lower court's grant of injunctive relief; the sparse memorandum decision suggests that the issuance of an injunction was deemed improvident. The Court's directions on remand indicate that the declaratory aspect of the lower court's opinion is still valid. One may surmise that the Court was moved by the factual mootness of the case at bar, the youngest petitioner in the case presumably having reached eighteen years of age and passed beyond the jurisdiction of the juvenile court when the Supreme Court's decision was handed down. Further, it is not unlikely that the Court recoiled from the prospect of facing the innumerable challenges to the status offense laws of the various states, and to commitments made under them, which would result if the lower court were upheld on the merits. One suspects, also, that state courts have been moved by similar considerations [30].

In summary, federal courts at the level of the "firing line" have thus far generally concluded (in the comparatively few cases that have posed the question) that juvenile status offense statutes at issue before them were void because of vagueness, and deprived youth of due process of law. Upper courts seem to have concluded, at least by implication, that reformation of the status offense jurisdiction of the juvenile court must be a legislative rather than a judicial task, perhaps because the sheer volume of cases of children affected would swamp the courts.

The statutes conferring juvenile court jurisdiction over ungovernable youth are arguably infected with constitutional infirmity on yet another basis: infringement of the Equal Protection clause. Virtually without exception, the defined class—children—is underinclusive and hence suspect, because the child is subject to sanction and the parent, who shares responsibility for the child's behavior, is untouched by the law [31].

Finally, the Supreme Court of the United States has ruled that it is constitutionally impermissible to impose sanctions on a status in the case of an adult [32]. Yet, as was discussed above, that is what the juvenile court's status offense jurisdiction does with respect to unruly children.

The jurisdiction over unruly children is thus a kind of moral thumbscrew by which we seek to demand of our communities' children a greater and more exacting adherence to desired norms than we are willing to impose upon ourselves. And infirmities of constitutional law aside, the jurisdiction in operation is otherwise maladroit in several major respects.

First, far more than in matters involving allegations of child abuse or delinquency, ungovernability cases present for resolution issues which are peculiarly ill-suited for, and unbenefited by, legal analysis and judicial fact-finding. The judicial system can decide quite well whether or not a person committed a given act; it is "incapable, however, of effectively managing, except in a very gross sense, so delicate and complex a relationship as that between parent and child" [33]. The law is simply inept as a corrective of the kinds of family dysfunction these cases most frequently involve, which are "of vastly greater duration, intimacy, complexity and (frequently) emotional intensity" than other cases in the justice system [34]. Using legal compulsion to restore (or provide) parent-child understanding and tolerance, and to build up mechanisms for conflict resolution within the family unit, is akin to doing surgery with a trowel.

Further, allowing formalized coercive intervention (which is coercive only on one side—the child's) in unruly child cases undermines family autonomy, isolates the child, polarizes parents and children, encourages parents to abdicate their functions and roles to the court, may blunt the effectiveness of any ameliorative services that are provided, and cuts against the development of controls and means within the family for the resolution of conflicts. It thus may impede the child's maturation into an adult who possesses effective ways of handling and adjusting problems of interpersonal relationships because it misplaces the focus of service onto the child as a person with problems, rather than upon the family complex [35]. Relinquishment by a parent of his or her child to court control is probably the ultimate rejection. As the President's Commission on Law Enforcement and Administration of Justice observed, "It is within the family that the child must learn to curb his desires and to accept rules that define the time, place and circumstances under which highly personal needs may be satisfied in socially acceptable ways" [36].

The juvenile court's status offense jurisdiction may actually retard the range of services available to the unruly child and the family, and their chances of getting effective help, in two different ways. First, many community agencies of service may be leary of "court-associated" youth and be reticent to take a youth who has been processed by the juvenile justice system. Second, the existence of the ungovernability jurisdiction in the juvenile court may have provided an unfortunate incentive to schools and other community resources to avoid developing mechanisms for handling family problems, which are basically not susceptible of forced solution. So long as the juvenile court must take and deal with the problems, they need not; no matter that the judicial system is not the place for solution.

Finally, and at least as importantly, it is likely that the existence of the juvenile status offender jurisdiction furthers racial, sexual, and economic discrimination, particularly in urban centers [37]. Because very little national information is available and one must extrapolate from the few studies that have been done, it is difficult to estimate the degree to which this occurs; the literature is very thin. The Juvenile Justice Standards Project's study of PINS cases in the New York City courts showed that a majority of the youth involved were non-white (assuming a definition, as the study did, of "white" as including Hispanic ethnicity): Black youths comprised 40 percent of the cases, white youths 31 percent, and Hispanic youths 28 percent. Sixty-eight percent of the youths were over fourteen years of age, 44 percent over fifteen, and the cases predominantly involved girls (62 percent) [38].

A study done for the New York Judicial Conference indicated a predominance of boys among PINS cases (57 percent); black youths constituted 48 percent of the sample; Puerto Rican youths, 25 percent; and white youths, 24 percent. It also disclosed a sharp disparity between the levels of service afforded the three groups. Placement in a residential treatment center was recommended for 116 children in the sample; it was actually secured for 28. Black children for whom residential treatment was recommended were so placed in 10 percent of the cases, Puerto Rican children in 9 percent, and white children in 62.5 percent [39].

A number of states have had different age levels for the assertion of ungovernability (and sometimes delinquent and neglect) jurisdiction as between boys and girls. Where challenged, these definitions of the susceptible class based on the gender of the child have quite uniformly been struck down as denying equal protection of the laws [40]. It is probable, however, that the status offense jurisdiction is in fact more often invoked for girls than for boys, as the New York study found [41]. As American society has traditionally been more concerned over the preservation of the sexual virtue of girls than of boys, so this concern is reflected in the invocation of the ungovernability jurisdiction. The Juvenile Justice Standard Project's New York City study found that although girls only accounted for 62 percent of the total PINS sample, they accounted for 100 percent of the cases involving allegations of prostitution, promiscuity, "cohabiting," and "general sex innuendo" (whatever in God's world that may mean, if anything) [42].

For these reasons, the juvenile court's status offense jurisdiction has been under increasing scrutiny for some time, with consequent and mounting pressure for its abridgement. In 1967, the President's Commission on Law Enforcement and Administration of Justice recommended that "serious consideration" should be given to completely eliminating from the juvenile court's jurisdiction conduct illegal only for children [43]. The National Council on Crime and Delinquency adopted a policy in 1974 that all status offenses—those acts of youthful misbehavior which would not be crimes if committed by adults—should be removed from court jurisdiction [44]. This position conforms to its proposed Model Juvenile Court Statute, the commentary to which states "This is the arch-instance by which courts confirm that children are not people; that they are the property of their parents and other custodians such as schools" [45]. A similar position was taken by the California Assembly Committee on Criminal Procedure in 1971 [46], and a Select Committee of the same body later observed that

> The court functions in a world of definite alternatives; not situations that are ambivalent, changing and little understood. . . . Not only is the court not able to cope with the real, underlying problems of youth brought before it on [a status offense petition], it is hardly able to cope with the symptoms [47].

Similar conclusions have been reached by legislative committees in other states [48].

On the federal level, there have been two recent developments of considerable significance. In 1974, the Department of Health, Education and Welfare recommended the elimination of juvenile court jurisdiction over status offenses [49], and in the same year, the Juvenile Justice and Delinquency Prevention Act of 1974 was enacted by the Congress and signed into law, providing in pertinent part that a state must, within two years from the date of submission of a plan for funding, treat "juveniles who are charged with or who have committed offenses that would not be criminal if committed by an adult" in shelter facilities and cease placing them in juvenile correctional or detention facilities [50]. The Act expresses the "clear legislative intent that states be offered the incentive to move toward minimizing contact between law enforcement personnel and non-criminal juvenile 'offenders', especially runaways" [51].

Juvenile Justice Standards Project. The *Standards* promulgated by the Juvenile Justice Standards Project eliminate the general juvenile court jurisdiction over status offenses and non-criminal juvenile misbehavior [52]. They recognize, however, that the problems presented by such youth are very real and very complex, and that there will have to be established varieties of innovative services, both crisis-oriented and longer term, to offer help in resolving them. The *Standards* adopt the general principle that, although there must be tightly-drawn possibilities of limited coercive intervention—"coercive exposure," if you will—in situations where the youth is in immediate jeopardy, services to youth and their families for the amelioration and resolution of family problems should be community-based, voluntarily sought, and readily accessible. They permit limited coercive intervention in their provisions for limited custody; for dealing with runaway youth; for court approval of substitute residential placement; and for emergency medical services to minors in crisis. Even in these limited instances, the least-detrimental alternative consonant with the youth's needs is stressed.

It is the position of the *Standards* that the de-judicialization of status offenses and reliance on voluntarily-based services will make those services more appropriate to the needs of the youth and his or her family; it is both true and a truism that help which a person selects to receive and in which he or she willingly participates has a better likelihood of success than services imposed at the end of a writ. Removal of the status offense jurisdiction will, it is submitted, encourage more people to get more effective help; stimulate the creation and extension of a wider range of voluntary services than is presently available; end the corrosive effects of treating non-criminal youth as though they had committed crimes; and free up a substantial part of the resources of the juvenile justice system to deal with the cases of delinquency and of abused and neglected children which belong in it.

The critical question is, of course, will it work? And the short answer is, we will not know until we have tried it, but it is quite plain that what we are doing now with status offenders does not work. Two pilot programs underway in California offer both interest and some hope. Both are aimed at the diversion of the juvenile status offender from the judicial process, but each adopts a different model.

In the first program, that of Sacramento County, beyond-control youth are referred by law enforcement agencies or parents to the probation department in the usual way, and are then deflected from the usual procedures of intake and petition by referral to a team of probation officers specially-trained in crisis-intervention techniques and family counseling. A two-year study demonstrated that beyond-control youths handled by diversion recidivated noticeably less frequently than did a control group of such children handled by the usual processes of intake and petition [53]. It also reflected impressive savings in terms of cost and resources freed up for other purposes: The average beyond-control case handled in the usual way consumed 23.7 work-hours from initial booking to informal settlement or adjudication (not counting any after-care or informal supervision) and cost $561.63 to handle, while the average diversion case required 14.2 work-hours for conclusion and cost $274.01.

In the second pilot program, in Santa Clara County, a different process of diverting status offenders was adopted: Rather than involving the probation staff in the mechanics of diversion, on the belief that diversion before a youth got into the juvenile court system was preferable to induction into and deflection out of it, that responsibility was placed on the local law enforcement agencies. Each police department in the county (which has a population of roughly 1,400,000 and twelve local law enforcement agencies) cooperated with the program and received a share of grant monies, based on population and volume of cases, for additional personnel and the development of local resources. Under this program, the police attempted to resolve the problem at the local level without referral to the probation department or the juvenile court. Youth and families were assisted by officers specially assigned to the program who arranged referrals to community agencies, developed alternative voluntary placements where necessary, and rendered other assistance as required. The program's goal in the first two years of operation was to reduce by two-thirds the number of youth referred to the juvenile court and probation department for beyond-control behavior; in fact, a reduction of 67.2 percent in the number of beyond-control referrals was achieved [54].

Both in terms of the frequency of reinvolvement with the juvenile justice system and in terms of the severity of that reinvolvement, youth handled by this program showed a distinctly better track record than a one-year sample of pre-project youth. A total of 21 percent of all diverted youth became reinvolved on a new offense, while 48.5 percent of the pre-project sample of status offenders handled by the usual processes, tracked for a one-year period, committed a new offense. Of that sample, 22 percent had reentered the juvenile justice system for a *third* time within one year [55].

It was found that 70.8 percent of the youths in a sample of cases handled by the diversion project made contact with the agencies recommended to them by the police, and 62.9 percent actually received services. A sample of parents, on the other hand, followed police recommendations in 51.2 percent of the cases and received help in 44 percent. Roughly 49 percent of the youths and parents indicated that the services were helpful; one-third of the parents, however, felt the services were of little help. Service agency and resource records indicated that the police initiated the contact in more than half the cases, while clients were the initiating party in 35.5 percent of the cases [56]. Twenty percent of a sample of parents felt the handling was too lenient and stated they thought the youth should have been booked into the juvenile hall; 73 percent of those parents said booking "would have impressed upon the child the seriousness of the pre-delinquent behavior" [57].

Perhaps most impressive, a countywide pre-program survey revealed that prior to the diversion project, the county's law enforcement agencies used a total of 15 community resources of various kinds, public and private, in attempts to obtain services for unruly children. During the first two years of the program, the number of community resources utilized by police in handling beyond-control cases had grown to 110, about equally divided between public and private resource agencies in frequency of use [58]. It is not known how many of these were in existence before the project began; it seems safe, however, to assume that some of the resources were created or developed because of the demand created by diversion and referral for help on a voluntary basis.

Without the diversion program, to handle the beyond-control referrals in the first two years of the project would have cost the probation department and the juvenile court not less than $1,785,319 and 51,645 work-hours in delivering services. With the program in operation, servicing beyond-control cases during this period cost approximately $744,756 and consumed 23,930 work-hours, a savings of approximately $1,040,563 and 27,715 work-hours. The cost of providing police services during the two year period was $346,401, with such project expenses as consultation by probation personnel, supplies, transportation, and research and evaluation making up the balance [59].

These studies certainly provide no final answers. They do suggest, however, that abridgement of the status offense jurisdiction and reliance on services outside the juvenile justice system, for the most part voluntarily utilized, may be a feasible and realistic approach to the handling of non-criminal misbehavior. It appears not unlikely that as the juvenile court's possiblity of intervention is removed, the responsiveness and efficacy of the resources in handling unruly youth and their families will increase, as will the satisfaction of the clients. It also seems reasonable to suppose that some resources, at least, hitherto have not brought to bear the full measure of effort they might have given had the court not always been there as a last resort.

In particular, the studies appear to support the following points which underscore the feasibility of curtailing the juvenile court's status offense jurisdiction:

1. Runaway, beyond-parental-control, and other forms of non-criminal misbehavior can be successfully dealt with outside the juvenile justice system.
2. Formalized detention in such cases can be avoided through counseling services and alternative residential placements that are non-secure, temporary and voluntary.
3. Youths involved in non-criminal misbehavior who are handled in this way, rather than by induction into the intake and adjudication processes, are likely to have fewer subsequent brushes with the law and to have a better general adjustment to life and its problems than those drawn into the juvenile justice system.
4. Though many resources which do not now exist will have to be created, and many of those extant will have to be strengthened and re-directed, a start on handling non-criminal misbehavior cases outside the juvenile justice system can feasibly be made, in most cases, with resources now available. And at least to some notable extent, the services now lacking may be created when the demand is created.

One of the principal reasons for the present retention of the status offense jurisdiction is, one assumes, that it provides something of a base from which the court can respond to a youth's presented needs by directing appropriate orders to school authorities and other social agencies. It should be noted that elimination of that jurisdiction should not hinder the ability of courts to so respond. Enabling statutes and orders issued pursuant to the court's inherent powers can provide the basis of judicial leverage and assistance without the need to sweep in the youth under the status-offense jurisdiction [60]. It is a perversion of basic fairness and the system of justice when coercive jurisdiction over a child is the only way to reach a recalcitrant official in breach of his or her duty to the child.

The *Standards* posit the elimination of the status offense jurisdiction of the juvenile court and the substitution of services outside the formal justice system, largely voluntarily based, on the assumptions that (1) non-criminal misbehavior cases will benefit from the immediate intensive handling which this will allow, rather than the piecemeal investigation, adjudication, and referral which is now more the rule than the exception; (2) the majority of service and helping time should be at the onset of the problem, when the family confronts a crisis, rather than weeks or months later after attitudes and positions have hardened with the passage of time; and (3) such services will be of greater help if they are not coerced. Our experience with the divorce law has demonstrated that the legal system is too blunt an instrument to resolve the complexities of family dysfunction, and that the legal system cannot by compulsion order personal relationships [61]. When, as an example, a sixteen-year-old girl must petition the juvenile court to declare her incorrigible as the only way out of a home she finds intolerable, the ineptitude of the present mechanisms for resolving the intrafamily conflicts which status offenses represent is apparent [62]. The old saw is perfectly true and hard cases do indeed make bad law; in respect of status offense cases, it is not beyond the mark to conclude that they are all hard.

As has been noted, virtually all existing status offense laws comprehend an extremely wide range of behavior, typically including disobedience to the orders of a parent or custodian; truancy; disobedience to the orders of school authorities; sexual misconduct; behaving in a manner allegedly injurious to the minor or other absence from home without parental or custodial permission; the presence of circumstances constituting immediate jeopardy to the minor; and so forth. It may be useful to consider the status offense jurisdiction with respect to some of these specific behaviors.

Disobedience to Parent or Custodian. State intervention has proven a poor buttress of parental authority and family harmony in handling the problems of rebellious children. As American society moves toward granting young persons greater rights at an earlier age, it is increasingly less adroit to give the weight of legal authority to what is frequently rigid and arbitrary parentage [63]. Furthermore, there appears to be no evidence that "the viability of the family will be jeopardized by more freedom for the children," or that the present possibilities of judicial intervention as a parent surrogate, under the status offense jurisdiction, help to restore harmony to the dysfunctional family or benefit the child [64].

Again, to apply to behavior that is not criminal, no matter how vexing, the same sanctions that obtain in cases of behavior that is criminal is fundamentally perverse. There is evidence that children develop the capacity and perception for intricate moral judgments much earlier than is commonly supposed [65]. A young person who is incarcerated for parental defiance in the same place and program as a youth who has committed five armed robberies is not likely to perceive as fair the legal process that put him or her there, nor internalize its values, nor through normal developmental processes come to see delinquent behavior as inconsistent with, and adverse to, his or her self-concept. In short, justice will not be seen to be done.

Judicial intervention in beyond-parental-control cases would appear to encourage parents to resign their parental roles to the court. The studies discussed above suggest that parents of ungovernable children regard the juvenile court and detention facilities as there to provide the "control" they cannot; they also demonstrate that the court has been visibly unsuccessful as a substitute parent in such cases.

Moreover, the family problems encountered in the exercise of the status offense jurisdiction range from seemingly trivial matters to complicated and many-faceted dilemmas which virtually defy solution. All represent, to a greater or lesser degree, failures of communication within the family unit which are likely to be worsened by judicial intervention, and which in most cases will be better served by non-coerced assistance. Many status offense cases are in reality cases of neglect, abuse or delinquency and should be dealt with on that ground. The line is often exceedingly thin, and decisions to invoke the status offense jurisdiction in a particular case may be based on such fragile considerations as having no evidence to proceed on another ground (but thinking that the youth's situation requires that *something* be done, however unlikely of success), or for convenience (e.g., that the youth in question presents an age and level of independence with which the dependent shelter is unsuited to deal).

The *Standards* take the position that conduct which infringes the criminal law should be dealt with under the procedures for handling youth crime. Cases of parental or custodial defiance which evince neither culpable parental neglect or abuse (which should of course also be dealt with under that jurisdictional rubric) nor criminal conduct on the part of the youth should not have the possibility of resulting in coercive judicial intervention, but should be channeled to services outside the justice system.

Truancy. School attendance is properly the business of the schools, not the courts. Judicial coercion can at best (and that very seldom, short of twenty-four-hour confinement) dragoon the physical presence of the youth's body, with strong indications that the "heart and mind" will not only not follow, but will be strongly repelled. Truancy represents a highly complex set of problems. The failure of a child to attend school may stem from parental disinterest or other neglect; from disability; from a fear of violence, at or enroute to school; from a defeat of motivation for learning by wooden and insensitive school programs which utterly fail to respond to the child's needs; and from a host of other factors.

The typical American response to failure to attend school has long been for the school to suspend the child for non-attendance and to refer the problem to the juvenile court in order that the latter may compel attendance. It could hardly be more disserving. The ultimate sanction for failing to obey the court's order, in most jurisdictions, is commitment to the same system of state facilities charged with the maintenance and treatment of the most violent and depredatory youthful offenders [66].

Whatever the causes of truancy, in the aggregate or in the particular case, the existence of the truancy jurisdiction in the juvenile court cuts against the school's assumption of its own responsibilities and the improvement of its programs. As long as that jurisdiction remains, the schools have a ready dumping-ground for their problem children. As with the other areas of non-criminal misbehavior, the problems of school attendance are best met by non-coercive services based outside the juvenile justice system. The court's forcing a child back into school is likely to have malignant consequences for all. As one court observed, "Forcing [the student] into classical schoolrooms introduces a disruptive element which is not good for the school, the teachers, the other students and likewise is not good for [him]" [67].

Providing for the excision of juvenile court intervention in truancy cases in no sense denigrates the importance of a decent education, nor the devastating impact of a child's not having one. It reflects, rather, the conviction that coercive judicial intervention has not proven demonstrably effective in securing that education, and in many cases has worked positive mischief by treating truant youth in the same way as if they had committed criminal acts.

Finally, withdrawal of the court's truancy jurisdiction is not antagonistic (though at first glance it may seem logically impure) to maintaining a requirement of compulsory education. A variety of other means and sanctions may be invoked to promote attendance, such as proper educational counseling suited to the child's circumstances and needs; realistic alternative curricula and special programs of education; "escort" services to school provided by the school or by community groups or agencies; even curtailment of the youth's franchise to attend when all other avenues of promoting attendance have been tried; and various programs involving the parents.

Disobedience to School Authorities. As in the case of the truancy jurisdiction in the juvenile court, the existence of the "school insubordination" jurisdiction encourages the off-loading of problems which ought to be handled by the schools, and dampens the school's responsibility and ability to develop means of doing so.

In the case of violent or threatening behavior or other conduct which significantly disrupts the school and endangers or disturbs others, the responsible youths can and should be handled under the appropriate laws relating to juvenile crimes. If the behavior does not rise to that level of gravity, it should not be susceptible of being dealt with by the juvenile court.

Sexual Misconduct. In virtually every case, the status offense statutes of the several states extend the jurisdiction of the juvenile court on the basis of ungovernability to youthful sexual promiscuity, which is essentially to say whenever any sexual activity is shown. The available evidence indicates that the "morals jurisdiction" is much more frequently invoked with respect to girls than boys [68].

Constitutional issues of due process and equal protection aside, in cases of sexual misconduct as in cases of other non-criminal misbehavior, judicial intervention rarely reaches root causes and too often exacerbates problems rather than having its intended effect. Adolescent sexual activity is certainly of grave concern to parents, and it is perfectly true that in many cases the youth will need help. It is submitted, however, that the juvenile justice system is neither the place to get it nor to be referred from for it. While the aphorism is that morality cannot be legislated, the equal reality is that it cannot be worked even upon the young by adjudication and judicial decree—even if there were general agreement as to what it was. One person's deviance is another person's pluralism [69].

If the sexual behavior is such as to threaten harm to another, it should be dealt with as a violation of the applicable criminal law. If it is not, and is not proscribed by the criminal code, it should not be the subject of juvenile court handling unless it evidences child abuse or neglect, in which case it should be dealt with under the abuse and neglect jurisdiction.

Acting in a Manner Allegedly Injurious to Self or Others. It is recognized that some children will be found to be in need of immediate help and treatment. Most of these problems are essentially medical—drug or alcohol intoxication or overdose and severe mental disturbance are perhaps the most obvious. The status offense jurisdiction is frequently used at present to cover such cases because the law provides no firmer ground for court intervention and possible mental health commitment [70]. The *Standards* envision procedures for the provision of help in crises of this sort which do not entail the assertion of the juvenile court's ungovernability jurisdiction over the affected youth. Establishing a form of emergency short-term civil commitment, they define crisis intervention services and impose requirements of informed consent, when the youth's medical condition permits, and limits on invasive therapy [71].

Runaways. Nationally, juvenile court control over runaway youth—excepting those who have fled from court-ordered placements—is almost invariably imposed by reliance upon the ungovernability and status offense statutes. The problem is an increasing one: In 1968, FBI statistics reported more than 100,000 arrests of youth for running away; in 1972, more than 260,000 [72]. It is widely agreed that such figures in no way reflect the true dimensions of the problem; informal estimates for 1973 and 1974 run to better than one million runaways each year.

The status offense laws of the several states commonly do not define runaways in terms of a specific period of time away from home, though specific law enforcement departments, youth corrections agencies and juvenile courts may have particular rules-of-thumb. However, it appears that short runaways are quite common and frequently result in parents seeking judicial intervention. It will be recalled that "short runaway" was the single most frequently alleged ground of non-criminal misbehavior in the Juvenile Justice Standards Project's study of New York PINS cases comprising 51 percent of PINS cases [73]. A study made of 1664 cases received in the first three and a half months of the DHEW-funded National Runaway Switchboard (now located in Chicago at 800—621—4000, from Illinois 800—972—6004, originally in Houston, Texas) indicated that 35 percent had been away from home less than five days, and 52.8 percent had been away less than ten days [74]. Better than 73 percent of the youth had run away one, two, or three times before, suggesting that although a majority of runaway youth do not stay away for extended periods of time, they are likely to leave again if the family situation has not significantly changed. Nearly 64 percent of the youth were reported as being in their home state when they called. Seventeen and one-half percent of the calls were from potential or pre-runaways. Three and one-half percent were from "kick-outs," youth who had left home because they were forced to [75]. Sixty-four percent of the young people calling were girls; the callers' average age was 16.5 years.

The available evidence—though it must be said that the surface of the runaway problem is only just beginning to be scratched by research—indicates that runaway youth are no more likely to violate the criminal law than youth who remain at home [76]. Like other forms of non-criminal misbehavior, running away from home should not be treated as, nor subjected to the same sanctions as, behavior which violates the criminal law. The family may be in greater disharmony in the cases of runaways than in perhaps any other single class of status offense behavior, and juvenile court intervention is perhaps least likely to be helpful. This is at least partly because the juvenile justice system affords precious few resources short of secure confinement for children with histories of flight. Yet, there is some evidence that these cases are especially susceptible to family and communication therapy [77].

From whatever perspective the act of running away is viewed, it "cannot be seen solely as a negative, unbalanced and impulsive response" [78]. Indeed, in some cases it may be the most rational, mature and adaptive response to an intolerable situation, "a sign of health seeking surface" [79].

On the federal level, the Juvenile Justice and Delinquency Prevention Act of 1974 [80], which contains as Title III the Runaway Youth Act of 1974 [81], makes clear the congressional intent that runaway youth should not be subjected to juvenile court jurisdiction and treated within the juvenile justice system. The Act states it to be the finding of the Congress that "the problem of locating, detaining and returning runaway children should not be the responsibility of already overburdened police departments and juvenile justice authorities . . ." [82]. It posits instead locally-controlled runaway houses to provide temporary shelter and counseling. To receive federal funding, the runaway house must be located in an area which is "demonstrably frequented by or easily reachable by" runaway youth; must have a maximum capacity of no more than twenty youth, with an appropriate children-to-staff ratio to assure adequate supervision and treatment; and "shall develop adequate plans for contacting the child's parents or relatives [if required by state law] and assuring the safe return of the child according to the best interests of the child . . ." [83].

To comport with the requirements of the Act, the *Standards* provide that runaway houses should not be secure facilities, should be state-licensed, but not necessarily state-run (indeed, local management is desirable), and place responsibility for parental notification, child and parent counseling and arrangements for return or alternative living arrangements upon the house's staff [84]. As nearly as may be determined, the evidence available suggests that runaway youths do seek out non-coercive runaway shelters, and that the great majority of runaways may be expected to avail themselves of such facilities. The DHEW-sponsored Switchboard study discussed above indicated that many runaways had as a principal fear the possibility that they might be forced home against their will. It also found that 68.2 percent of all its runaway calls were made to have a message delivered to the youth's parents, which may suggest that runaways are not, in most cases, so implacably hostile or headstrong as to wish to cut all ties with their families [85].

It is inevitable that there will be some hard cases where the juvenile refuses to go home, and refuses to agree to any acceptable alternative living arrangements, or refuses to stay in the temporary facility. The *Standards* do not provide coercive sanctions to keep the juvenile there, on the conviction that the existence of such sanctions will inevitably lead back to a status offense jurisdiction. It is the stated intent of Congress that the immediate needs of runaway youth who have violated no criminal law should be dealt with "in a manner which is outside the law enforcement structure and juvenile justice system" [86]. While it seems reasonable to expect that the vast majority of runaway youth will be amenable to acceptable alternative living arrangements if they are not ordered to accept them and are not ordered to return home, some will not. Some juveniles will simply flee, and keep fleeing, and some will commit crimes while in flight. If they do, they will be subject to and should be dealt with under the delinquency jurisdiction. As with the rest of the status offense jurisdiction, it is submitted that the social costs of retaining it to provide for secure detention or other sanctions in what is expected to be a relatively small number of cases, are too great.

If the juvenile and the family are in intractable conflict and cannot agree upon mutually-acceptable living arrangements, the *Standards* provide an additional instance of restricted official intervention, in the form of the juvenile court's approval or disapproval of alternative residential placement [87]. This is to be done upon motion, without the possibility of wardship or other jurisdiction over the child. The court should approve the placement of the juvenile's choice unless it finds, upon a preponderance of the evidence, that the placement imperils the juvenile and that it is probable that the juvenile's living conditions will be improved by available alternatives. When practicable, the court should provide an opportunity for the chosen placement to correct defects before final disapproval. The court may remove the child from a placement that imperils him or her, but may not compel a return to the parents' residence. A placement is considered to imperil a juvenile if it fails to provide physical protection, adequate shelter or nutrition; seriously and unconscionably obstructs the juvenile's medical care, education or development; or exposes the juvenile to unconscionable exploitation. The *Standards* provide that no placement should be made in a secure facility, and that services should be provided to juveniles and their families during such placements to facilitate their reunion.

Presence of Circumstances Constituting Immediate Jeopardy. Realistically, there must be some means of dealing with youth who have committed no crime but are in circumstances of immediate jeopardy, such as the twelve year old who is prowling the subways at midnight. At present, that is frequently accomplished by invoking the ungovernable child jurisdiction. While the *Standards* abridge that jurisdiction, they provide for limited coercive intervention by law enforcement officers when a juvenile is in circumstances amounting to a substantial and immediate danger to his or her physical safety, by empowering the officer to take the minor into "Limited Custody." Such custody should not include holding in a secure detention facility; should be terminated as soon as practicable; and cannot in any event extend beyond six hours from the time of initial contact by the law enforcement officer [88]. In so providing, the *Standards* attempt to strike the difficult balance of preserving a means of necessary official action, while at the same time sufficiently circumscribing that intervention and its consequences to prevent the court's status offense jurisdiction from regenerating itself.

In all instances, the *Standards* call for the least-restrictive course of action consistent with the minor's immediate safety, and caution the avoidance of ethnic stereotypes in determining whether or not danger exists. It is to be recognized that the particular focus of societal concern about juvenile behavior will vary, depending upon the particular local community. However, all of the component behaviors that constitute the present status offense jurisdiction are prevalent, and concern over them all transcends minority community, urban-rural and affluence lines.

Summary

Thus, the *Standards* posit a structure of services to juveniles in conflict with their families, who are not victims of abuse or neglect and have not violated the criminal law, which would for the most part be voluntarily based and which would not lead to juvenile court wardship. The court is given limited and special jurisdiction to approve or disapprove alternative residential placements for minors who cannot come to agreement with their parents or custodians as to where, how and with whom they will live. Additionally, restricted powers of official intervention are given where the minor is at substantial risk from his or her condition or circumstances.

The sources of assistive services should be convenient, well-publicized, decentralized in most cases, aligned to the needs of the people they serve, and so set up and run that their function does not become submerged in their form.

This scheme is grounded upon the conviction that assistance which lets the youth have a say in what happens to him or her will far more likely result in the youth's developing mature and socially-acceptable means of resolving conflicts than will help-by-court-order, which in these sorts of cases is too often no help at all [89]. It is also more likely to promote family harmony, if that can be achieved, and it follows the concept that the court should properly be concerned only with securing the least-invasive alternative that will afford help. Many resources now exist to help families and children, some effective and some feeble indeed. Many more need to be developed, and many of those extant must be greatly strengthened or radically and imaginatively changed. However, in many instances services exist which could provide at least the starting point for appropriate voluntarily-based help to the child and family, if properly used on that basis without judicial compulsion.

I am under no illusion that the proposals provide firm solutions, and I am aware that in some individual courts, the status offense jurisdiction is wisely and humanely used, at least most of the time, which is perhaps all we can reasonably demand of our juridical systems. Viewed nationally, however, the picture is catastrophic and the juvenile justice system is clotted with cases that do not belong there. The *Standards* seek to provide a starting point to correct that, from which to proceed to a rigorous evaluation of how they work, and the scrutiny of regular review once the proposals are tried.

Inevitably, if the status offense jurisdiction is removed, some cases will be lost to help and some youth will go unassisted who might have been aided if the formal scheme of coercive intervention in cases of non-criminal misbehavior were kept. It is believed, however, that their numbers will be relatively few, and that the social costs of retaining the status offense jurisdiction as it now exists far outweigh the relatively small benefits. In the great majority of cases, it is to be expected that voluntarily-based services will be accepted, and will prove far more effective than wardship and court-ordered commitment. And the removal of beyond-control cases from the juvenile court's jurisdiction should allow the vigorous application of its now-taxed resources to cases of abuse and criminal conduct, to the benefit of all.

Many years ago, the British legal historian Sir Henry Maine wrote that the progress of civilized society was marked by the transition from status to contract [90]. It is time we took that transitional step in our response to family-rooted problems centered on the non-criminal misbehavior of children, and the *Standards* attempt to provide the basis for it.

NOTES TO CHAPTER 9

1. Note, "Ungovernability: The Unjustifiable Jurisdiction," 83 *Yale L.J.* 1383 at note 5 (1974); *cf. Mass. Provincial Stats.* 1699–1700, c.8 §§2–6, in *Mass. Colonial Laws* 27 (1887 ed.), in which the court was invested with criminal jurisdiction over "stubborn servants or children"; Commonwealth v. Brasher, 359 Mass. 550, 270 N.E.2d 389 (1970); Katz and Schroeder, "Disobeying A Father's Voice: A commentary on *Commonwealth v. Brasher*," 57 *Mass. L.Q.* 43 (1972); Kleinfeld, "The Balance of Power Among Infants, Their Parents and the State," 4 *Fam. L.Q.* 319 (1970), 4 *Fam. L.Q.* 410 (1970), 5 *Fam. L.Q.* 63 (1971).

2. In one California county of better than 500,000 population, a thorough study done in preparation for a diversion program revealed than non-criminal misbehavior cases accounted for 40 percent of all minors detained in juvenile hall and 72 percent of court-ordered out-of-home placements and commitments. *R. Baron* and *F. Feeney, The Sacramento Diversion Project: A Preliminary Report* (Sacramento Co. Probation Dept./Center for Admin. of Criminal Justice, Univ. of California at Davis, 1971).

3. Stiller and Elder, "PINS: A Concept in Need of Supervision," 12 *Am. Crim. L. Rev.* 33 (1974).

4. *Cf.* Bazelon, "Beyond Control of the Juvenile Court," 21 *Juv. Ct. Judges J.* 42 (1970); Glen, "Juvenile Court Reform: Procedural Process and Substantive Stasis," [1970] *Wis. L. Rev.* 431, 444 (1970); Fox, "Juvenile Justice Reform: An Historical Perspective," 22 *Stanford L. Rev.* 1187, 1192, 1233; Lemert, "The Juvenile Court—Quest and Realities," in President's Commission on Law Enforcement and Administration of Justice, *Report of the Task Force on Juvenile Delinquency: Delinquency and Youth Crime* at 91, 93 (1967) [hereinafter cited as *Task Force Report*].

5. *See generally* E. Schur, *Radical Non-Intervention: Rethinking the Delinquency Problem* 46–51 (1973); Bureau of Social Science Research Legal Action Support Project, *Research Memorandum on Status Offenders* 3, 22 (1973); *Task Force Report.*

6. *Report of the California Assembly Interim Committee on Criminal Procedure: Juvenile Court Processes* 7 (1971).

7. Rosenheim, "Notes on 'Helping': Normalizing Juvenile Nuisances," 50 *Soc. Serv. Rev.* 177 (1976); Rosenheim, "Youth Service Bureau: A Concept in Search of a Definition," 20 *Juv. Ct. Judges' J.* 69 (1969).

8. *E. Erickson, Identity: Youth and Crisis* 132 (1968).

9. Note, "Ungovernability: The Unjustifiable Jurisdiction," 83 *Yale L.J.* 1383, 1387–8 at note 33, 1408 (1974).

10. See Appendix; Lavette M. v. City of N.Y., 35 N.Y.2d 136, 316 N.E.2d 314, 359 N.Y.S.2d 20 (1974); *In the Matter of Ellery C.*, 32 N.Y.2d 588, 300 N.E.2d 424, 347 N.Y.S.2d 51 (1973); Blondheim v. State, 84 Wash.2d 874, 529 P.2d 1096 (1975) ("incorrigible dependents" not to be committed for treatment or confinement in same area of institution where they may associate with delinquent youth); *cf. The Ellery C. Decision: A Case Study of Judicial Regulation of Juvenile Status Offenders* (I.J.A. 1975).

11. *See, e.g.*, Nelson v. Heyne, 355 F. Supp. 451 (N.D. Ind. 1972), supp. opin. 355 F. Supp. 458, *aff'd.* 491 F.2d 352 (7th Cir. 1974); Morales v. Turman, 364 F. Supp. 166 (E.D. Tex. 1973); Martarella v. Kelley, 349 F. Supp. 575 (S.D.N.Y. 1972); *In the* Matter of Ilone I., 64 Misc. 2d 878, 316 N.Y.S.2d 356 (Fam. Ct., 1970); Note, "Persons in Need of Supervision: Is There a Constitutional Right to Treatment?", 39 *Brooklyn L. Rev.* 624 (1973); Gough, "The Beyond-Control Child and The Right to Treatment: An Exercise in the Synthesis of Paradox," 16 *St. Louis U.L.J.* 182 (1971).

12. *M. Rector, PINS: An American Scandal* (Nat'l Council on Crime and Delinquency, 1974). In Nelson v. Heyne, *supra* note 11, the court observed that nearly one-third of the inmates of the Indiana Boys Training School—which it described as a medium-security prison for boys twelve to eighteen years of age—had committed no criminal offense whatever, but were incarcerated for being truants or beyond parental control.

13. Cohn, "Criteria for the Probation Officer's Recommendations to the Juvenile Court Judge," 9 *Crime and Del.* 262 (1963).

14. *See* Appendix; L.A.M. v. State, 547 P.2d 827 (Alaska 1976); *J. Dineen, Juvenile Court Organization and Status Offenses: A Statutory Profile* 43 Nat'l. Center for Juvenile Justice (monograph, 1974).

15. Culbertson, "The Effect of Institutionalization on the Delinquent Inmate's Self-Concept," 66 *J. Crim. L. and C.* 88 (1975); for a contrary view, *see* Mahoney, "The Effect of Labelling on Youths in the Juvenile Justice System: A Review of the Evidence," 8 *Law and Soc. Rev.* 583 (1974).

16. *See In re* Walker, 14 N.C. App. 356, 188 S.E.2d 731 (1972), *aff'd.* 282 N.C.28, 191 S.E.2d 702 (1972).

17. *See, e.g.*, *In re* Spaulding, *273* Md. *690*, 332 A.2d 246 (1975); *In re* Walker, *supra* note 16.

18. *In re* Winship, 397 U.S. 358 (1970). It appears that only one-fourth of the states require adjudication of a need for supervision to be based upon proof beyond a reasonable doubt. *Compare In re* E., 327 N.Y.S. 2d 84 (1971) *with In Interest of Potter*, 237 N.W.2d 461 (Iowa 1976); *In re* Henderson, 199 N.W.2d 111 (Iowa 1972), and *In re* Waters, 13 Md. App.95, 281 A.2d 560 (1971).

19. *See, e.g.*, *Calif. Welf. and Instn's. Code* §701 (West Supp. 1976), providing that the admissibility of evidence at the trial of beyond-control cases is governed by the rules of evidence applicable to civil causes, rather than by the stricter rules applicable in cases of criminal law violation.

20. *M. Midonick* and *D. Besharov, Children, Parents and the Courts; Juvenile Delinquency, Ungovernability and Neglect* 92 (1972).

21. Note, "Ungovernability: The Unjustifiable Jurisdiction," 83 *Yale L.J.* 1383, 1389 at note 50 (1974)

22. Office of Children's Services, Judicial Conference of the State of New York, *The PINS Child: A Plethora of Problems* 17 (1973).

23. *See, e.g., Del. Code Ann.* title 10 §901 (1974); *D.C. Code Ann.,* §16–2301, (Supp. 1975); *Hawaii Rev. Stat.* §571–11(B) (Supp. 1975); *Mich. Comp. Law Ann.* §712 A.2 (Supp. 1976); *Wash. Rev. Code Ann.* §13.04.010 (1962); *Wyo. Stats. Ann.* §14–41 (Supp. 1975).

24. *See generally* Wald, "The Rights of Youth," 4 *Human Rights* 13, 21 (1974); Note, "Parens Patriae and Statutory Vagueness in the Juvenile Court," 82 *Yale L.J.* 745 (1972); McNulty, "The Right to Be Left Alone," 11 *Am. Crim. L. Rev.* 141 (1972); Comment, "Juvenile Statutes and Non-Criminal Delinquents: Applying the Void-for-Vagueness Doctrine," 4 *Seton Hall L. Rev.* 184 (1972); Comment, "Delinquent Child: A Legal Term Without Meaning," 21 *Baylor L. Rev.* 352 (1969).

25. 405 U.S. 156 (1972).

26. Gesicki v. Oswald, 336 F. Supp. 371 (S.D.N.Y. 1971), *aff'd.* Oswald v. Gesicki, 406 U.S. 913 (1972).

27. 420 U.S. 925 (1974).

28. 416 U.S. 918 (1974).

29. *Cal. Welf. and Instn's Code* §601 (West Supp. 1975); that portion of the statute was stricken by A.B. 432, 1975 Cal. Legis. Reg. Sess., effective 1/1/76.

30. *See, e.g., In re* Napier, 532 P.2d 423 (Okla. 1975); *In re* L.N., 109 N.J. Super. 278, 263 A.2d 150 (App. Div.), *aff'd.* 57 N.J. 165, 270 A.2d 409 (1970), *cert. den. sub. nom.* Norman v. New Jersey, 402 U.S. 1009 (1971); E.S.G. v. State, 447 S.W.2d 225 (Tex. Civ. App., 1969), *cert. den.* 398 U.S. 956 (1970); *cf.* District of Columbia v. B.J.R., 332 A.2d 58 (D.C. App. 1975).

31. Sidman, "The Massachusetts Stubborn Child Law: Law and Order in the Home," 6 *Fam. L.Q.* 33, 49–56 (1972); *see also* State v. In Interest of S.M.G., 313 So.2d 761 (Fla. S.Ct., 1975) (juvenile court lacks jurisdiction to order the parent of a delinquent child to participate in the child's rehabilitative program).

32. Robinson v. California, 370 U.S. 660 (1972).

33. J. Goldstein, A. Freud, and A. Solnit, *Beyond the Best Interests of the Child* 8 (1973).

34. Note, "Ungovernability: The Unjustifiable Jurisdiction," 83 *Yale L.J.* 1383, 1402 at note 119 (1974).

35. *Cf. V. Satir, Conjoint Family Therapy* 2 (1967).

36. *Task Force Report, supra* note 4, at 45 (1967).

37. *See* Paulsen, "Juvenile Courts, Family Courts and the Poor Man," 54 *Calif. L. Rev.* 694 (1966).

38. *Supra* note 34 at 1387, notes 26 and 27.

39. Office of Children's Services, Judicial Conference of the State of New York, *The PINS Child: A Plethora of Problems* 21–22 (1973).

40. *See, e.g.,* People v. Ellis, 57 Ill.2d 127, 311 N.E.2d 98 (1974); *In the Matter of* Patricia A., 31 N.Y.2d 83, 286 N.E.2d 432, 31 N.Y.S.2d 83 (1972); *cf.* Stanton v. Stanton, 421 U.S.F. (1975).

41. *Accord, R. Baron* and *F. Feeney, Preventing Delinquency Through Diversion, A Second Year Report* at Appendix A (Sacramento Co. Probation Dept./ Center for Admin. of Criminal Justice, Univ. of California at Davis, 1973);

American Justice Institute, *Research and Evaluation Study of the Santa Clara County, Calif., Pre-Delinquent Diversion Program* 61 (1974).

42. *Supra* note 34 at 1388–1389; note 41; *see generally* Green and Esselstyn, "The Beyond-Control Girl," 23 *Juv. Justice* 13 (Nov. 1972).

43. *Task Force Report*, *supra* note 4 at 27.

44. Nat'l. Council on Crime and Delinquency, "Jurisdiction Over Status Offenses Should Be Removed from the Juvenile Court," 21 *Crime and Del.* 97 (1975).

45. Nat'l. Council on Crime and Delinquency, *A Model Juvenile Court Statute* 7 (draft submitted to the N.C.D. Council of Judges, Oct. 1973).

46. *Report of the California Assembly Interim Committee on Criminal Procedure: Juvenile Court Processes* (1971).

47. *Report of the California Assembly Select Committee on Juvenile Violence: Juvenile Violence* 56–7 (1974).

48. *See, e.g., Report of the Virginia Advisory Legislative Council*, 1 *Fam. L. Reporter* 2515–6 (1975). It may be noted that the director of Youth Services in the Virginia Department of Corrections, speaking in support of the proposal to remove the status offense jurisdiction, stated that the removal of such minors from state institutions would reduce the number of girls in state care by 80 percent and the number of boys in state care by 50 percent.

49. Office of Youth Development, DHEW, *Model Acts for Family Courts and State-Local Children's Programs* 14–15 (1974).

50. Juv. Justice and Delinquency Prevention Act of 1974, 88 Stat. 1109–43 (codified in widely scattered sections of Titles 18 and 42 U.S.C.A.), at §223(a) (12) *et seq.*

51. Note, "California Runaways," 26 *Hastings L.J.* 1013, 1043 (1975).

52. Juvenile Justice Standards Project (I.J.A.–A.B.A.), *Juvenile Justice Standards: Non-Criminal Misbehavior* (1976).

53. The study and its results are discussed in Feeney, "The PINS Problem— A No Fault Approach," *supra* pp. 249–269, and hence are not detailed here. See also *R. Baron* and *F. Feeney*, *Preventing Delinquency Through Diversion, A Second-Year Report* (Sacramento County Probation Department/Center for Administration of Justice, Univ. of California at Davis, 1973).

54. American Justice Institute, *Research and Evaluation Study of the Santa Clara County, California Pre-Delinquent Diversion Program* v (1974).

55. *Id.* at v, 20,26.

56. *Id.* at vii, 46–52.

57. *Id.* at 50.

58. *Id.* at 37.

59. *Id.* at v, 57.

60. *See, e.g., N.Y. Fam. Ct. Act* §255; Janet D. v. Carros, Ct. Common Pleas, (Allegheny Co.) No. 1079–73 (unreptd.), 6 *Juv. Ct. Dig.* 139 (Pa. 1974; director of county child welfare services cited for contempt for failure to obtain care as directed for runaway girl); Carrigan, "Inherent Powers of the Courts," 24 *Juv. Justice* 38 (May 1973); State ex rel. Weinstein v. St. Louis Co., 451 S.W.2d 99 (Mo. 1970); State on inf. of Anderson v. St. Louis Co., 421 S.W.2d 249 (Mo. 1967).

61. *Cf.* Uniform Marriage and Divorce Act; *Report of the California Governor's Commission on the Family* (1966).

62. *See In re* Snyder, 85 Wash.2d, 182, 532 P.2d 278 (1975); *cf.* Wald, "The Rights of Youth," 4 *Human Rights* 13, 21 (1974).

63. *See* Wald, *supra* note 62 at 13; *M. Paulsen* and *C. Whitebread, Juvenile Law and Procedure* 44 (1974); *J. Holt, Escape from Childhood* 45–53 (1974).

64. Wald, *supra* note 62 at 24.

65. *See, e.g.*, Juvenile Justice Standards Project, *Summary of Symposium on Moral Development and Juvenile Justice* (Oct. 13–15, 1974); Konopka, "Formation of Values in the Developing Person," 43 *Am. J. Orthopsychiatry* 86 (1973); Kleinfeld, "The Balance of Power Among Infants, Their Parents and the State," 5 *Fam. L.Q.* 64, 69 at note 29 (1971); *J. Piaget, The Moral Judgment of the Child* (Gabain transl. 1965).

66. *See, e.g.*, Nelson v. Heyne, 355 F. Supp. 451 (N.D. Ind. 1972), *Supp. opin.* 355 F. Supp. 458, *aff'd.* 491 F.2d 352 (7th Cir. 1974); *In The Matter of* Mario, 317 N.Y.S.2d 659 (Fam. Ct. 1971); *but cf. In re* Shinn, 195 C.A.2d 683, 16 Cal. Reptr. 165 (1961); State ex rel. Pulakis v. Superior Ct., 128 P.2d 649 (Wash. 1942).

67. *In re* Peters, 14 N.C. App. 426, 430–31, 188 S.E.2d 619, 621–22, *aff'd.* 288 N.C. 28, 191 S.E.2d 702 (1972).

68. *Supra* note 42; *cf.* E.S.G. v. State, 447 S.W.2d 225 (Tex. Civ. App. 1970), *cert. den.* 398 U.S. 956 (1970).

69. *See H. Packer, The Limits of the Criminal Sanction* (1968).

70. *See, e.g.*, Office of Children's Services, Judicial Conference of the State of New York, *The PINS Child: A Plethora of Problems* 48–50 (1973). (Eighteen children of a sample of 254 PINS cases or 7 percent, were diagnosed as schizophrenic; fifty-five, or 22 percent were diagnosed as having a "personality disorder.")

71. *Juvenile Justice Standards: Non-Criminal Misbehavior*, Part VI, Emergency Services to Juveniles in Crisis (1976).

72. Federal Bureau of Investigation, *Uniform Crime Reports 1968* and *1972*; *cf. Hearing on the Runaway Child Before the California Senate Select Committee on Children and Youth*, 1973–74, *Reg. Sess.* 10, 111. In 1970, the last year for which figures were separately reported, there were 25,012 youths admitted to California juvenile halls for running away. *State of California, Dept. of the Youth Authority, Annual Report: 1970* at 100.

73. Note, "Ungovernability: The Unjustifiable Jurisdiction," 83 *Yale L.J.* 1383, 1408 (App. A) (1974).

74. Palmer, "A Profile of Runaway Youth," *D.H.E.W. Youth Reporter* (March 1975) at 5,6.

75. *Cf.* Cornfield, "Emancipation by Eviction: The Problem of the Domestic Push-Out," 1 *Fam. L. Reptr.* 4021 (1975).

76. *See Hearings on Runaway Youth Before the Subcommittee to Investigate Juvenile Delinquency of the U.S. Senate Committee on Judiciary*, 92d Cong., 1st Sess. (1972) [hereinafter cited as *U.S. Senate Hearings*]; Shellow et al., "Suburban Runaways of the 1960's," 32 *Monographs of the Society of Re-*

search in Child Development (1967), reprinted in U.S. Senate Hearings, *supra*, at 201.

77. *See generally* Suddick, "Runaways: A Review of the Literature," 24 *Juv. Justice* 47 (1973).

78. Note, "California Runaways," 26 *Hastings L.J.* 1013, 1016 (1975).

79. L. *Ambrosino, Runaways* (1971), quoted in *U.S. Senate Hearings, supra* note 76, at 238.

80. 88 Stat. 1109–43 (1974).

81. 42 U.S.C.A. §5701–5751, (Supp. 1976).

82. 42 U.S.C.A. §5701(4) (Supp. 1976).

83. 42 U.S.C.A. §5712 (Supp. 1976).

84. *Juvenile Justice Standards: Non-Criminal Misbehavior*, Part III (Runaway Youth).

85. Palmer, *supra* note 74 at 5–7.

86. 42 U.S.C.A. §5711 (Supp. 1976).

87. *Juvenile Justice Standards: Non-Criminal Misbehavior*, Part V (Alternative Residential Placement for Juveniles in Family Conflict).

88. *Id.*, Part II (Juveniles in Circumstances Endangering Safety: Limited Custody).

89. Youth should be the time, Ambrose Bierce reminds us, when "Justice never is heard to snore." A. *Bierce, The Devil's Dictionary* 144 (Dover ed. 1958).

90. *H. Maine, Ancient Law* 182 (Pollock ed. 1906).

Appendix

**Statutory Breakdown of Unruly
Child Jurisdiction in the United
States (July 1976)**

Legend: Statutory cites to sections covering jurisdiction; prohibitions against temporary detention or long-term commitment with delinquents; and standard of proof are given in that order for each state. Prohibitions against temporary detention with delinquents is indicated by T, against any commitment with delinquents by C, and against commitment to state facilities with delinquents by S.

Jurisdiction	Delinquent Child	Incorrigible Child	CINS	PINS	Unruly Child	Wayward Child	Other	No Title	Beyond Control	Ungovernable	Incorrigible	Runaway	Wayward	Truant	Habitually Disobedient	Children's Offense	Idle, Dissolute Life	Danger to Self/Others	Other	Prohib. Against Placement/Commitment	Std. of Proof B.R.D.
ALABAMA CODE TIT. 13, §350 (1959)	X								X		X						X		X		
ALASKA STAT. §47.10.010 §47.10.080 (Supp. 1974)			X						X					X	X			X	X	C	
ARIZ. REV. STAT. ANN. §8–201 (1974)	X	X							X		X		X	X	X			X			

ARK. STAT. ANN. §45–403 (3)(a) (Supp. 1976)	X	X*		X	X		
CAL. WELF. & INST'NS. CODE §601 (West Supp. 1976)		X		X	X		
COLO. REV. STAT. ANN. §19–1–103 (5) §19–3–112 (1973)	X		X	X	X	T** C**	X
CONN. GEN. STAT. ANN. §17–53 (Supp. 1974)	X		X	X	X X		
DEL. CODE ANN. TIT. 10 §901 (1974)	X	X		X			
D.C. CODE ANN. §16–2301 §16–2313 §16–2320 (Supp. 1970)	X		X	X X X	X	T	

*Juvenile in Need of Supervision.
**Without court approval, by judicial construction.

Appendix A. continued

Jurisdiction	Delinquent Child	Incorrigible Child	CINS	PINS	Unruly Child	Wayward Child	Other	No Title	Beyond Control	Ungovernable	Incorrigible	Runaway	Wayward	Truant	Habitually Disobedient	Children's Offense	Idle, Dissolute Life	Danger to Self/Others	Other	Prohib. Against Placement/Commitment	Std. of Proof B.R.D.
FLA. STAT. ANN. §39.01* §39.09 §39.11 (Supp. 1976)					X				X	X		X		X	X					S (first offenders)	X
GA. CODE ANN., JUV. Ct. CODE §24A–401 §24A–1403 §24A–2201 (Supp. 1974)								X	X			X		X	X	X			X	T	X
HAWAII REV. STAT. §671–11 (Supp. 1974)								X	X									X			

Statute							
IDAHO CODE ANN. §16–1803 (Supp. 1975)	X			X		X	X
ILL. ANN. STAT. CH. 37 §702–3 Smith-Hurd (Supp. 1976)		X**		X		X	X
IND. ANN. STAT. §31–5–7–4.1 (Supp. 1975)		X	X	X X X X		X	X
IOWA CODE ANN. §232.2 (Supp. 1976)		X†		X X	X		
KAN. STAT. ANN §38–802 (d) §38–802 (f)†† (Supp. 1975)		X		X X	X		
KY. REV. STAT. §208.020 §208.060 (Supp. 1974)	X		X X	X X X			

*"Dependent child" includes runaways, truants and youths alleged to be beyond control for the first time.
**Minor Otherwise in Need of Supervision.
†Child in Need of Assistance.
††Truant is separate classification.

Appendix A. continued

Jurisdiction	Characterization								Behavior Encompassed											Prohib. Against Placement/ Commitment	Std. of Proof B.R.D.
	Delinquent Child	Incorrigible Child	CINS	PINS	Unruly Child	Wayward Child	Other	No Title	Beyond Control	Ungovernable	Incorrigible	Runaway	Wayward	Truant	Habitually Disobedient	Children's Offense	Idle, Dissolute Life	Danger to Self/Others	Other		
LA. REV. STAT. ANN. §13–1569 §13–1578.1 §13–1580 (Supp. 1976)			X						X	X		X		X	X	X				T S	
ME. REV. STAT. ANN. TIT. 15, §2502, 2552 (Supp. 1974)								X			X			X					X		
MD. ANN. CODE, CTS. & JUDIC. PROCEEDINGS, §3–801 §3–815 (Supp. 1975)			X						X	X				X	X	X		X		T	

			C	X
			S (first offenders)	
MASS. ANN. LAWS,	X*	X X X		X
Ch. 119				
§21				
Ch. 119 §39G (c)				
Ch. 119 §39G				
(1975)				
MICH. COMP. LAW. ANN.	X	X X X X		
§712.A.2				
(Supp. 1976)				
MINN. STAT. ANN.	X	X X X X	S (first offenders)	
§260.015				
§260.185				
(Supp. 1976)				
MISS. CODE ANN.	**X	X X X X X X X X		
§43–21–5				
(Supp. 1975)				
MO. ANN. STAT.	X	X		
§211.031				
§211.041				
(1962)				

*Child in Need of Services.
**Includes Youth Who Violate School Rules.

Appendix A. continued

Jurisdiction	Delinquent Child	Incorrigible Child	CINS	PINS	Unruly Child	Wayward Child	Other	No Title	Beyond Control	Ungovernable	Incorrigible	Runaway	Wayward	Truant	Habitually Disobedient	Children's Offense	Idle, Dissolute Life	Danger to Self/Others	Other	Prohib. Against Placement/Commitment	Std. of Proof B.R.D.
							Characterization					Behavior Encompassed									
MONT. REV. CODE. ANN §10–1203 (Supp. 1974)	X						X*		X	X				X	X	X			X		
NEB. REV. STAT. §43–202 §43–206.03 (1974)								X		X		X	X	X	X			X			X
NEV. REV. STAT. §62.040 (1973)	X	X								X		X	X	X					X		

N.H. REV. STAT. ANN §169.2 §169.7 §169:13–a (Supp. 1975)	X		X X	X X X			X	T
N.J. STAT. ANN §2A:4–45 §2A:4–61 (Supp. 1976)	X	X**	X X	X X X X X X			X	C
N.M. STAT. ANN. §13–14–3 §13–14–31 (Supp. 1976)		X	X X	X X X	X			C
N.Y. FAMILY CT. ACT §712 (1975)	X		X X X	X X			X†	C†
N.C. GEN. STAT. §7A–278 (Supp. 1975)		X	X	X X	X X X		X	X**
N.D. CENT. CODE §27–20–02 §27–20–29 (Supp. 1975)	X		X	X X X	X X		X	

*Youth in Need of Supervision.
**Juvenile in Need of Supervision.
†By Judicial Decision.

Appendix A. continued

Jurisdiction	Delinquent Child	Incorrigible Child	CINS	PINS	Unruly Child	Wayward Child	Other	No Title	Beyond Control	Ungovernable	Incorrigible	Runaway	Wayward	Truant	Habitually Disobedient	Children's Offense	Idle, Dissolute Life	Danger to Self/Others	Other	Prohib. Against Placement/Commitment	Std. of Proof B.R.D.
			Characterization									Behavior Encompassed									
OHIO REV. CODE ANN. §2151.022 (Supp. 1975)					X				X			X	X	X	X	X		X	X		
OKLA. STAT. ANN. TIT. 10 §1101 (Supp. 1975)			X						X					X	X			X			
ORE. REV. STAT. §419.476 §419.500 (1975)							X	X	X			X						X			
PA. STAT. TIT. 11, §50–102 (Supp. 1976)	X									X					X						X

R.I. GEN. LAWS ANN. §14–1–3 (1970)			X			
S.C. CODE ANN. §15–1095.9 (Supp. 1975)			X X			X X
S.D. CODE §26–8–7.1 §26–8–40.1 §26–8–22.9 (Supp. 1976)	X	S	X	X		X
TENN. CODE ANN. §37–202 §37–232 (Supp. 1975)		S	X	X X X		X
VERNON'S TEX. CODE ANN., FAM. CODE §51.03 §54.04 §54.03 (1975)	X	S	X	X		X
UTAH CODE ANN. §55–10–77 (1974)			X X	X		X X

Appendix A. continued

Jurisdiction	Characterization								Behavior Encompassed											Prohib. Against Placement/ Commitment	Std. of Proof B.R.D.
	Delinquent Child	Incorrigible Child	CINS	PINS	Unruly Child	Wayward Child	Other	No Title	Beyond Control	Ungovernable	Incorrigible	Runaway	Wayward	Truant	Habitually Disobedient	Children's Offense	Idle, Dissolute Life	Danger to Self/Others	Other		
VT. STAT. ANN. TIT. 33 §632 (Supp. 1975)		X					X		X												
VA. CODE ANN. §16.1–158 §16.1–178 (1975)								X	X	X	X	X		X	X			X		S (truants only)	
VIRGIN ISLANDS CODE, TIT. 4 §172 (1967)								X	X					X				X	X		

WASH. REV. CODE ANN.
§13.04.010
(1962)

W. VA. CODE ANN.
§49–1–4
(1976)

WISC. STAT.
§48–12
(Supp. 1975)

WYO. STAT. ANN.
§14–41
§14–115.2
§14–115.26
(Supp. 1975)

Prepared for Juvenile Justice Standards Project: Aidan R. Gough, Professor of Law, Reporter
Coeta J. Chambers, Research Assistant
Patricia P. White, Research Assistant
Susan C. Hultberg, Research Assistant

University of Santa Clara School of Law

Selected Bibliography

BOOKS, MONOGRAPHS, REPORTS

J. Addams, ed., *The Child, The Clinic, and The Court* (1925).

P. Aries, *Centuries of Childhood: A Social History of Family Life* (R. Baldick, tr., 1962).

B. Bailyn, *Education in the Forming of American Society* (1960).

R. Baron and F. Feeney, *Juvenile Diversion Through Family Counseling* (1976).

R. Baron and F. Feeney, *The Sacramento Diversion Projects: A Preliminary Report* (Sacramento County Probation Department/Center on Administration of Criminal Justice, University of California at Davis, 1971).

S. Barrows, ed., *Children's Courts in the United States: Their Origin, Development, and Results* (1904).

M. Bloch, *Feudal Society* (L.A. Manyon, tr., 1961).

S. Breckenridge & E. Abbot, *The Delinquent Child and the Home* (1912, 1970).

R. Bremner, ed., *Children and Youth in America: A Documentary History* (3 vols., 1970–1972).

K. Burkhart, *Women In Prison* (1973).

A. Calhoun, *A Social History of the American Family from Colonial Times to the Present* (4 vols., 1917).

M. Carpenter, *Reformatory Schools* (1851) (Reprinted 1969).

H. Clark, *The Law of Domestic Relations in the United States* (1968).

Committee on Mental Health Services Inside and Outside the Family Court in the City of New York, *Juvenile Justice Confounded: Pretensions and Realities of Treatment Services* (1972).

R. Coser, ed., *The Family: Its Structure and Functions* (1964).

J. Dineen, *Juvenile Court Organization and Status Offenses: A Statutory Profile* (1974).

D. Easton and J. Dennis, *Children in the Political Systems: Origins of Political Legitimacy* (1969).

Family in America (1972) (Repr. of papers and proceedings of the American Sociological Society, 1908).

D. Flaherty, *Privacy in Colonial New England* (1972).

H. Folks, *The Care of Destitute, Neglected, and Delinquent Children* (repr. 1970).

L. Fuller, *The Morality of Law* (1964).

J. Goebel, Jr., *Cases and Materials on the Development of Legal Institutions* (3d ed. 1946).

P. Goodman, ed., *Essays on American Colonial History* (2d ed. 1972).

P. J. Greven, ed., *Child-Rearing Concepts, 1628−1861* (1973).

O. & M. Handlin, *Facing Life: Youth and Family in American History* (1971).

Hearings on Runaway Child Before The California Senate Select Committee on Children and Youth, 1973−74, *Reg. Sess.*

Hearings on Runaway Youth Before The Subcommittee to Investigate Juvenile Delinquency of the U.S. Senate Committee on Judiciary, 92d Cong. 1st *Sess.* (1972).

C. Hill, *Society and Puritanism in pre-Revolutionary England* (1964).

R. Hofstadter, *Anti-Intellectualism in American Life* (1963).

Institute of Judicial Administration, *The Ellery C. Decision: A Case Study of Judicial Regulation of Juvenile Status Offenders* (1975).

IJA−ABA, Juvenile Justice Standards Project, *Standards Relating to Non-Criminal Behavior* (Tentative draft, 1976).

G. Konopka, *The Adolescent Girl in Conflict* (1966).

M. Levin and R. Sarri, *Juvenile Delinquency: A Study of Juvenile Codes in the U.S.* (1974).

B. Lindsey and W. Evans, *The Revolt of Modern Youth* (1925).

H. Maine, *Ancient Law* (1864).

E. Morgan, *The Puritan Family* (1966).

N. Morris and G. Hawkins, *The Honest Politician's Guide to Crime Control* (1970).

F.I. Nye, *Family Relationships and Delinquent Behavior* (1958).

Office of Children's Services of the Judicial Conference of the State of New York, *The PINS Child − A Plethora of Problems* (1973).

W. O'Neill, *Divorce in the Progressive Era* (1967).

M. Paulsen and C. Whitebread, *Juvenile Law and Procedure* (1974).

J. Piaget, *The Moral Judgment of the Child* (M. Gabain, tr., 1965).

A. Platt, *The Child Savers: The Invention of Delinquency* (1969).

President's Commission on Law Enforcement and the Administration of Justice, *Task Force Report: Juvenile Delinquency and Youth Crime* (1967).

T.K. Rabb and R.I. Rotberg, eds., *The Family in History: Interdisciplinary Essays* (1973).

M. Rector, "PINS: An American Scandal," (National Council on Crime and Delinquency 1974).

D.J. Rothman, *The Discovery of the Asylum: Social Order and Disorder in the New Republic* (1971).

E. Ryerson, *Between Justice and Compassion: The Rise and Fall of the Juvenile Court* (Ph.D. dissertation, Yale University, 1973).

W. Sanders, ed., *Juvenile Offenders for a Thousand Years: Selected Readings from Anglo-Saxon Times to 1900* (1970).

R. Sarri, *Under Lock and Key: Juveniles in Jails and Detention* (1974).

E. Schur, *Radical NonIntervention: Rethinking the Delinquency Problem* (1973).

E. Shorter, *The Making of the Modern Family* (1975).

W. Thomas, *The Unadjusted Girl* (1967).

W. Trattner, *From Poor Law to Welfare State: A History of Social Welfare in America* (1974).

R. Unger, *Knowledge and Politics* (1975).

ARTICLES

Andrews and Cohn, "Ungovernability: The Unjustifiable Jurisdiction," 83 *Yale Law Journal* 1383 (1974).

Bazelon, "Beyond Control of the Juvenile Court," 21 *Juvenile Court Judges Journal* 42 (Summer, 1970).

Cabot, "The Detention of Children as a Part of Treatment" in *The Child, The Clinic and The Court* 246 (J. Addams, ed., 1925).

Comment, " 'Delinquent Child': A Legal Term Without Meaning," 21 *Baylor Law Review* 352 (1969).

Comment, "The Juvenile Court and the Runaway: Part of the Solution or Part of the Problem?," 24 *Emory Law Journal* 1075 (1975).

Davis and Chaires, "Equal Protection for Juveniles: The Present Status of Sex-Based Discrimination in Juvenile Court Laws," 7 *Georgia Law Review* 494 (1973).

John Demos, "Notes on Life in Plymouth Colony," 22 *William and Mary Quarterly* 264 (3d series 1965).

Demos and Demos, "Adolescence in Historical Prospective," 31 *Journal of Marriage and the Family* 632 (1969).

Fox, "Juvenile Justice Reform: An Historical Perspective," 22 *Stanford Law Review* 1187 (1970).

Friedman, "Delinquency and the Family System," in *Family Dynamics and Female Sexual Delinquency* 34 (O. Polak and A. Friedman, eds., 1969).

Gonion, "Section 601 California Welfare and Institutions Code: A Need for a Change" 9 *San Diego Law Review* 294 (1972).

Glen, "Juvenile Court Reform: Procedural Process and Substantive Stasis," [1970] *1970 Wisconsin Law Review* 431.

Gold, "Equal Protection for Juvenile Girls In Need of Supervision in New York State," 17 *New York Law Forum* 570 (1971).

Gough, "The Beyond-Control Child and the Right to Treatment: An Exercise in the Synthesis of Paradox," 16 *St. Louis University Law Journal* 182 (1971).

Gough and Grilli, "The Unruly Child and the Law: Toward a Focus on the Family," 23 *Juvenile Justice* 9 (No. 3, 1972).

Greene and Esselstyn, "The Beyond Control Girl," 23 *Juvenile Justice* 13 (No. 3, 1972).

Greven, "Family Structure in 17th-Century Andover, Massachusetts," 23 *William and Mary Quarterly* 234 (3d series 1966).

Henderson, "Are Modern Industry and City Life Unfavorable to the Family?" in *Family in America* 93 (1972).

Katz, "Dangerousness: A Theoretical Reconstruction of the Criminal Law: I," 19 *Buffalo Law Review* 1 (1969).

Katz and Schroeder, "Disobeying a Father's Voice: A Comment on *Commonwealth v. Brasher*," 57 *Massachusetts Law Quarterly* 43 (1972).

Katz, Schroeder & Sidman, "Emancipating Our Children — Coming of Legal Age in America," 7 *Family Law Quarterly* 211 (1973).

Kett, "Adolescence and Youth in 19th-Century America," in *The Family in History: Interdisciplinary Essays* 95 (T.K. Rabb and R.I. Rotberg, eds., 1973).

Klapmuts, "Children's Rights: The Legal Rights of Minors in Conflict with Law or Social Custom," 4 *Crime and Delinquency Literature* 449 (1972).

Kleinfeld, "The Balance of Power Among Infants, Their Parents and The State," 4 *Family Law Quarterly* 320 (1970), 4 *Family Law Quarterly* 410 (1970), 5 *Family Law Quarterly* 64 (1971).

McNulty, "The Right to be Left Alone," 11 *American Criminal Law Review* 141 (1972).

Mack, "The Chancery Procedure in the Juvenile Court," in *The Child, The Clinic and The Court* 310 (J. Addams, ed., 1925).

Mack, "The Juvenile Court," 23 *Harvard Law Review* 104 (1909).

Mahoney, "The Effect of Labeling Upon Youths in the Juvenile Justice System: A Review of the Evidence," 8 *Law and Society Review* 583 (1974).

Matza, "Position and Behavior Patterns of Youth," in *Handbook of Modern Sociology* 191 (R. Farris, ed., 1964).

National Council on Crime and Delinquency, "Jurisdiction Over Status Offenses Should Be Removed from the Juvenile Court," 21 *Crime and Delinquency* 97 (1975).

Note, "California Runaways," 26 *Hastings Law Journal* 1013 (1975).

Note, "Juvenile Court Jurisdiction over 'Immoral' Youth in California," 24 *Stanford Law Review* 568 (1972).

Note, "Juvenile Statutes and Noncriminal Delinquents: Applying the Void-for-Vagueness Doctrine," 4 *Seton Hall Law Review* 184 (1972).

Note, "Nondelinquent Children in New York: The Need for Alternatives to Institutional Treatment," 8 *Columbia Journal of Law and Social Problems* 251 (1972).

Note, "*Parens Patriae* and Statutory Vagueness in the Juvenile Court," 82 *Yale Law Journal* 745 (1973).

Note, "Persons in Need of Supervision: Is There A Constitutional Right to Treatment?", 39 *Brooklyn Law Review* 624 (1973).

Note, "Rights and Rehabilitation in the Juvenile Courts," 67 *Columbia Law Review* 281 (1967).

Note, "The 'Void-for-Vagueness' Doctrine in the Supreme Court," 109 *University of Pennsylvania Law Review* 67 (1960).

Reiss, "Sex Offenses: The Marginal Status of the Adolescent," 25 *Law and Contemporary Problems* 309 (1960).

Riback, "Juvenile Delinquency Laws: Juvenile Women and the Double Standard of Morality," 19 *U.C.L.A. Law Review* 313 (1971).

Riesenfeld, "The Formative Era of American Public Assistance Law," 43 *Calif. Law Review* 175 (1955).

Rosenheim, "Notes on 'Helping': Normalizing Juvenile Nuisances," 50 *Social Services Review* 177 (1976).

Rosenheim, "Youth Service Bureau: A Concept in Search of Definition," 20 *Juvenile Court Judges' Journal* 69 (Summer 1969).

Rubin, "Legal Definition of Offenses by Children and Youths," 1960 *University of Illinois Law Forum* 512.

Sheridan, "Juveniles Who Commit Noncriminal Acts: Why Treat in a Correctional System," 31 *Federal Probation* 26 (March 1967).

Sidman, "The Massachusetts Stubborn Child Law: Law and Order in the Home," 6 *Family Law Quarterly* 33 (1972).

Slater, "Social Change and the Democratic Family," in W. Bennis and P. Slater, *The Temporary Society* 20 (1968).

Snyder, "The Impact of the Juvenile Court Hearing on the Child," 17 *Crime and Delinquency* 180 (1971).

Stiller and Elder, "PINS: A Concept in Need of Supervision," 12 *American Criminal Law Review* 33 (1974).

Stone, "Marriage Among the English Nobility," in *The Family: Its Structure and Functions* 153 (R. Coser, ed., 1964).

U.S. Bureau of Education, "Legal Rights of Children" (1880), repr. in the *Legal Rights of Children* (1974).

Van Waters, "The Juvenile Court from the Child's Viewpoint," in *The Child, The Clinic and The Court* 217 (J. Addams, ed., 1925).

Wald, "Making Sense Out of the Rights of Youth," 4 *Human Rights* 13 (1974).

Walters and Stinnett, "Parent-Child Relationships: A Decade Review of Research," 33 *Journal of Marriage and the Family* 70 (1971).

Walzer, "Puritanism as a Revolutionary Ideology," in *Essays on American Colonial History* 25 (P. Goodman, ed.) (2d ed., 1972).

Index

and judges, 182—84
and PINS statute, 180—82, 187—91, 278
racial, 278
sex-based, 187—90, 278
Disobedience, of children
and PINS cases, 210—12, 215—21,
224—25
and state intervention, 283—85
Disposition
of child protection measures, 128—29
and delinquency allegations, 83—84
and informal supervision, 63, 65n
length of time for, 52n
and neglected children, 76
and PINS cases, 50, 82
and probation, 62
types of, 73
Due process
and federal courts, 276
and intervention, 238—39
and PINS statutes, 202
Dutch Civil Code, 117—19, 128, 136

Economic goals
and dependency of children, 11, 256
and the family, 4—5, 17—18, 33—34
and women, 26—28
Edgar A. Levy Leasing Co. v. Siegel, 210
Education (19th-century). *See also*
Compulsory education; Progressive
education
and children, 15, 18—19, 24—25, 33—34
Elizabethan statute, 8, 12
England
and child protection measures, 134
and legal institutions, 133
and PINS cases, 115—16, 123, 147—49
and rights, 134—35
and state agencies, 124
Enlightenment, the, 14—16, 18—20, 24
Environmentalism, 15—16, 18—23, 26, 29
Erikson, Erik, 272
Ethnic groups
and adjudication, 72n
and court referral, 71
and discrimination, 278
and neglected children, 74—75
Europe, and juveniles, 135—36
vs. U.S., 116—22, 124, 132—34
Extended family, 3, 165

Family. *See also* Parent-child relationship;
Parental authority
and authority, 7, 1—13, 18—20, 163—64,
213—14, 217—21, 224—26
and counseling, 258—59, 261—62
and delinquency, 169—72

in 18th-19th century, 14—20, 25—26,
31—34
extended vs. nuclear, 3, 165
in feudal society, 3—5
income, 26—28, 84n, 166
and judges, 59—60
and law guardians, 57—58
and new statutes, 258—60
and PINS cases, 162—65, 169—72,
251—52, 255—62
and probation officers, 56
and Puritan society, 7—14
and socialization, 15—16, 20, 217—21
as status relationship, 206—208
Family conflicts (problems)
and community agencies, 239—40, 250,
277—83
and counseling, 258—59, 261—62,
280, 283
and the courts, 162—63, 167—68, 173,
241—42, 251—52, 272—73
and Juvenile Justice Standards Project,
279—80, 289—91
and state intervention, 239—40,
283—84, 290—91
Family Court
and decision-making process, 85
and judges, 59—60
and law guardians, 57—58
in New York County, 47—53, 85
and PINS cases, 50
and probation officers, 56
in Rockland County, 47—53, 85
Family Court Act, 80
Family crisis counseling, 162—63,
167—69, 174
and new statute, 261—62, 264
Family guardians, 117, 128, 137—38
Family in Need of Service (FINS), 242
Fault
and counseling, 255—62, 264
and Dutch Civil Codes, 118—19, 128
of parents, 118—22, 128
and new statute, 258—59, 263—64
Federal Juvenile Justice and Delinquency
Prevention Act, 262
Females, 3—4, 12, 17—18, 72n, 74—75,
81n, 287
and court treatment, 71, 179—80
and discrimination, 186—87, 189—91
and institutionalization, 131, 184—86
and PINS study, 162, 179—81, 187—91,
252, 278
and sexual misconduct, 79, 80n,
179—80, 183—84, 251, 278, 286
Feminists, 27—28
Feudal society, and the family, 2—5

About the Contributors

R. Hale Andrews, Jr.
Member of the Massachusetts Bar. B.A., Harvard, 1971; J.D., Yale, 1975.

Lindsay A. Arthur
Judge of the District Court, Juvenile Division, Hennepin County, Minneapolis, Minnesota. Judge Arthur is past president of the National Council of Juvenile Court Judges.

Andrew H. Cohn
Member of the Massachusetts Bar. B.A., University of Pennsylvania, 1966; M.A., Harvard, 1970; Ph.D., Harvard, 1972; J.D., Yale, 1975.

Floyd Feeney
Professor and Executive Director, Center for the Administration of Criminal Justice, University of California at Davis.

Aidan R. Gough
Professor of Law, University of Santa Clara. A.B., Stanford University, 1956; A.M., Stanford University, 1957; J.D., University of Santa Clara, 1962; LL.M. Harvard University, 1966. Professor Gough served as Reporter for the IJA—ABA Juvenile Justice Standards Project, *Standards Relating to Non-Criminal Misbehavior.*

Leslie Harris
Staff Attorney, Public Defender Service for the District of Columbia. B.A., New Mexico State University, 1973; J.D., University of New Mexico School of Law, 1976.

Al Katz
Professor of Law, State University of New York, Buffalo. B.S., Temple University, 1963; J.D., University of California, Berkeley, 1966; L.L.M., 1967.

Fré LePoole
Magister Juris, University of Amsterdam, 1964; LL.B., Yale, 1969. Currently in private practice in New York City.

Anne R. Mahoney
Assistant Professor, Department of Sociology, University of Denver. B.A., Kent State University, 1959; M.A., Northwestern University, 1961; Ph.D., Columbia University, 1970.

Alan Sussman
Member of the New York Bar. B.A., University of Chicago, 1966; M.A., 1967; J.D., New York University Law School, 1970. Mr. Sussman is adjunct Assistant Professor of Law at New York University Law School and editor of the Children's rights report, published by the American Civil Liberties Union.

Lee E. Teitelbaum
Professor of Law, University of New Mexico School of Law. B.A., Harvard College, 1963; LL.B., Harvard Law School, 1966; LL.M, Northwestern University School of Law.